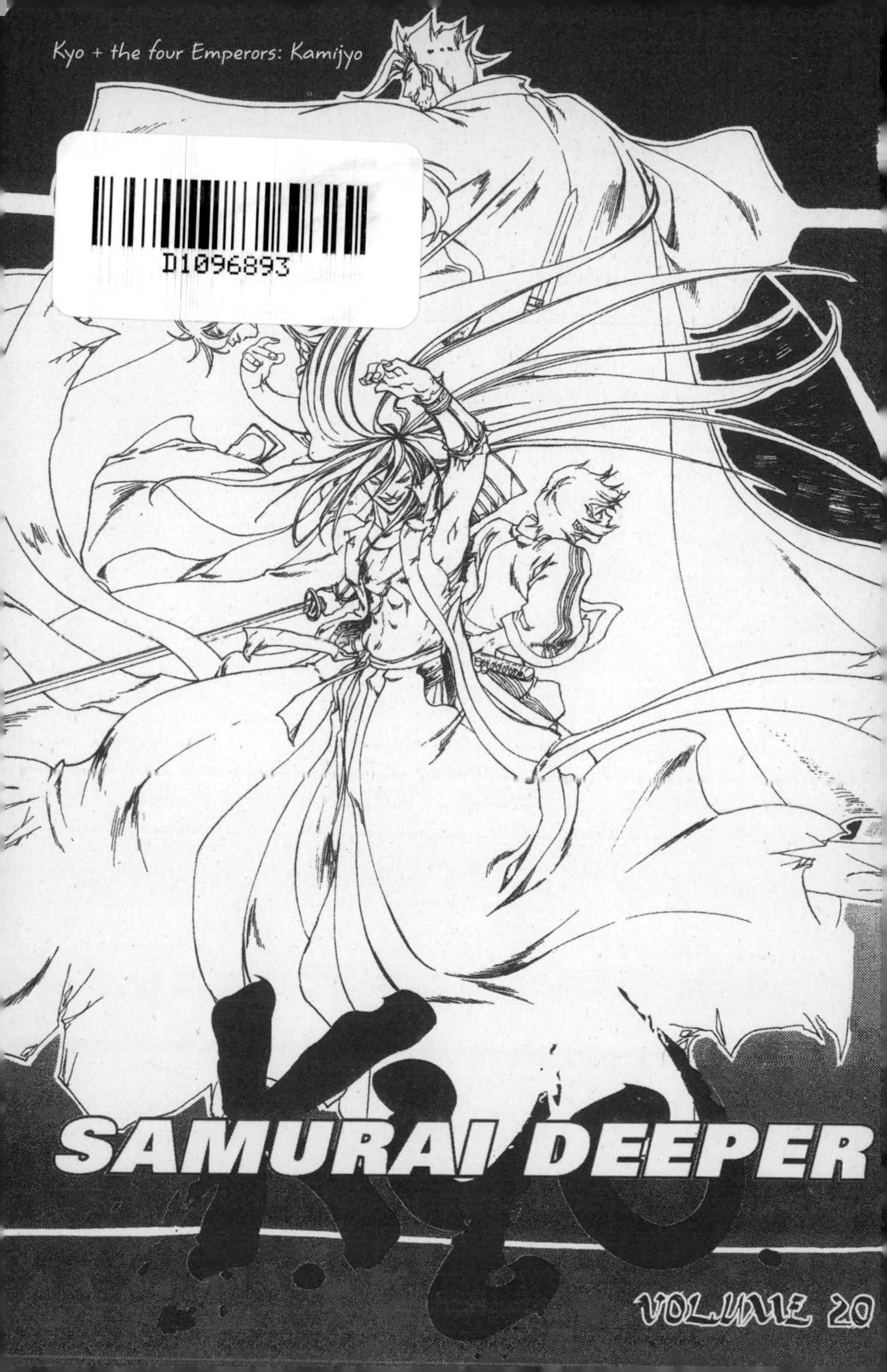
Kyo + the four Emperors: Kamijyo
SAMURAI DEEPER
KYO
VOLUME 20

Samurai Deeper Kyo Vol. 20
Created by Akimine Kamijyo

Translation - Alexander O. Smith
English Adaptation - Rich Amtower
Retouch and Lettering - Cybermedia
Cover Design - Louis Csontos

Editor - Katherine Schilling
Digital Imaging Manager - Chris Buford
Production Manager - Elisabeth Brizzi
Managing Editor - Vy Nguyen
Editor-in-Chief - Rob Tokar
VP of Production - Ron Klamert
Publisher - Mike Kiley
President and C.O.O. - John Parker
C.E.O. and Chief Creative Officer - Stuart Levy

A  Manga

TOKYOPOP Inc.
5900 Wilshire Blvd. Suite 2000
Los Angeles, CA 90036

E-mail: info@TOKYOPOP.com
Come visit us online at www.TOKYOPOP.com

ISBN: 1-59532-460-7

First TOKYOPOP printing: November 2006
10 9 8 7 6 5 4 3 2 1
Printed in the USA

SAMURAI DEEPER KYO

Vol. 20
by Akimine Kamijyo

HAMBURG // LONDON // LOS ANGELES // TOKYO

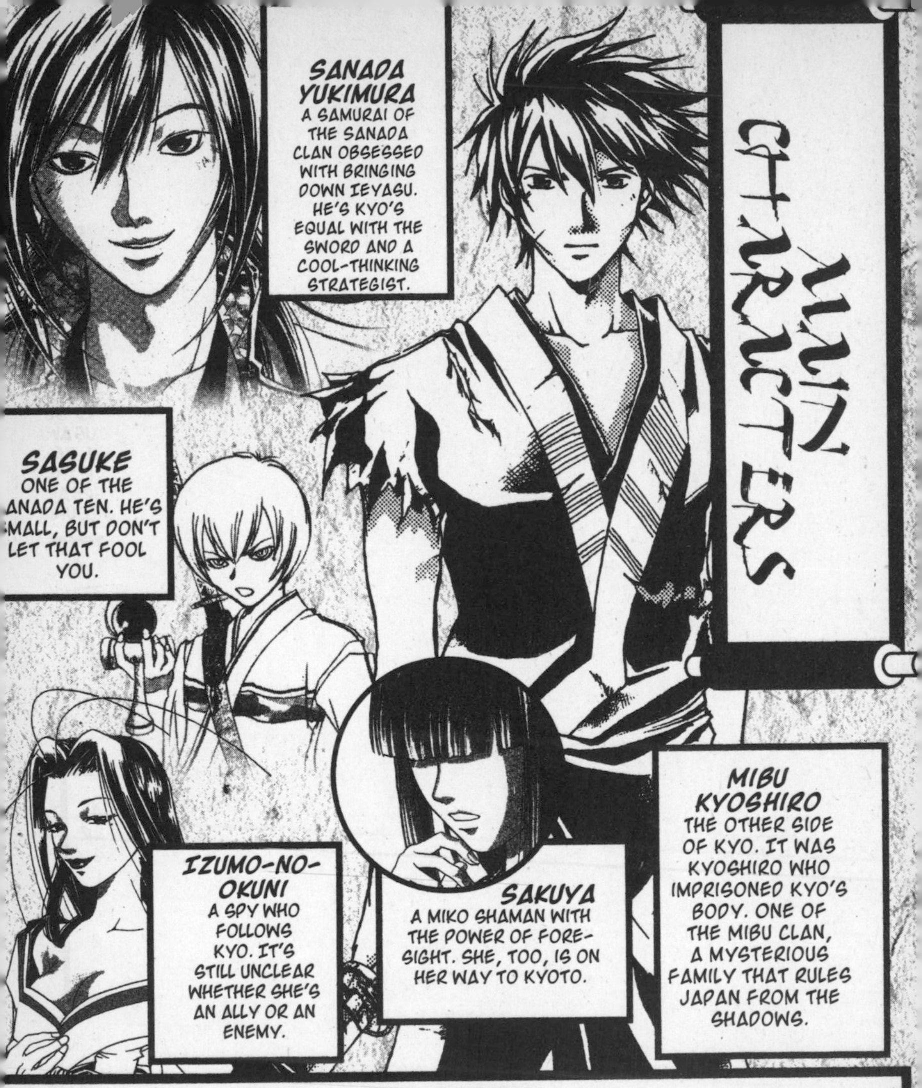
MAIN CHARACTERS
SANADA YUKIMURA
A SAMURAI OF THE SANADA CLAN OBSESSED WITH BRINGING DOWN IEYASU. HE'S KYO'S EQUAL WITH THE SWORD AND A COOL-THINKING STRATEGIST.
SASUKE
ONE OF THE ANADA TEN. HE'S MALL, BUT DON'T LET THAT FOOL YOU.
MIBU KYOSHIRO
THE OTHER SIDE OF KYO. IT WAS KYOSHIRO WHO IMPRISONED KYO'S BODY. ONE OF THE MIBU CLAN, A MYSTERIOUS FAMILY THAT RULES JAPAN FROM THE SHADOWS.
SAKUYA
A MIKO SHAMAN WITH THE POWER OF FORE-SIGHT. SHE, TOO, IS ON HER WAY TO KYOTO.
IZUMO-NO-OKUNI
A SPY WHO FOLLOWS KYO. IT'S STILL UNCLEAR WHETHER SHE'S AN ALLY OR AN ENEMY.

THE STORY

THANKS TO SHINREI OF THE FIVE'S WATERWYRMS, YUYA HAS ONLY EIGHT HOURS LEFT TO LIVE. KYO AND THE REST CONTINUE TOWARD THE FORMER CRIMSON KING, BOTH TO SAVE YUYA AND TO UNCOVER THE SECRET OF KYO'S BIRTH.

AFTER FIGHTING THROUGH THE FIRST GATE OF THE MIBU LAND, PROTECTED BY HOTARU, THEY REACH SAISHI AND SAISEI'S SECOND GATE ONLY TO FIND THE TRAITOR YUKIMURA WAITING FOR THEM.

MORTAL COMBAT ENSUES AT THE SECOND GATE. STEPPING IN FOR THE WOUNDED KYO, AKIRA FACES OFF AGAINST SAISEI. THE FIGHT IS BITTER, AND SAISHI LAUGHS AT HER SISTER'S RESOLVE...ANGERING AKIRA WHO TAKES HER DOWN NEXT.

AT THE THIRD GATE STANDS CHINMEI, THE MAN RESPONSIBLE FOR THE TRAGIC DEATH OF MAHIRO'S SISTER AT MURAMASA'S HOME FOUR YEARS BEFORE. MAHIRO ATTACKS TO AVENGE HER SISTER, BUT CHINMEI WIELDS THE POWER OF EARTH, MANIPULATING GRAVITY TO HOLD MAHIRO AT BAY. CHINMEI LAUNCHES HIS COUNTERATTACK. HOWEVER, KYO DEFEATS CHINMEI'S "CHINSEI KOKUTENKYU" WITH "SUZAKU."

NOW TAIHAKU, THE LEADER OF THE FIVE, APPEARS AT THE FOURTH GATE. HE IS A TRUE GOD OF WAR WHO VOWS TO PROTECT THE FUTURE OF MIBU AND THOSE CREATED BY THE MIBU CLAN, BUT CAN BENITORA DEFEAT HIM?

SAMURAI DEEPER KYO

KYO
THE STRONGEST SAMURAI, SAID TO HAVE KILLED 1,000 MEN. HIS EYES BURN WITH A DEEP CRIMSON LIGHT THAT HAS EARNED HIM THE NAME "DEMON EYES KYO." IN THE PAST, HE LED THE FOUR EMPERORS, FORMING A KILLING TEAM SECOND TO NONE. HE SEARCHES NOW FOR HIS TRUE BODY.

BENITORA
ALSO KNOWN AS BENITORA THE SHADOW-MAN. HIS REAL NAME IS HIDETADA, THE THIRD SON OF TOKUGAWA IEYASU. HE'S ONE OF THE BEST SPEAR-MEN AROUND.

SHIINA YUYA
A BOUNTY HUNTER WHO SEARCHES FOR THE "MAN WITH A SCAR ON HIS BACK," WHO KILLED HER BROTHER.

THE FIVE STARS
THE CORE OF THE MIBU CLAN, EACH MASTER OF HIS OWN SPECIAL TECHNIQUE.

FUBUKI
ONE OF THE FOUR ELDERS, THE MIBU CLAN'S RULING CLASS. HE'S A HIGH NECROMANCER.

BONTENMARU
A POWERFUL ONE-EYED WARRIOR INTENT ON RULING THE WORLD. HIS REAL NAME IS DATE MASAMUNE--CONQUEROR OF THE NORTH.

AKIRA
ONE OF THE FOUR EMPERORS. HE'S CURRENTLY HIDING IN KYOTO WITH KYO'S REAL BODY.

...OF KYO!

WHERE DID KYO MEET ALL HIS FRIENDS? WHO DID THEY FIGHT? SWIFTER THAN KYO CAN SWING HIS SWORD, HERE'S A RECAP OF ALL THAT'S HAPPENED IN SDK SO FAR!

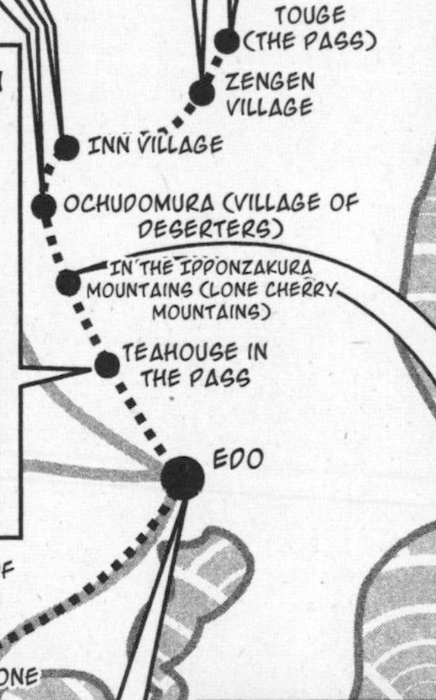

一 (1) THE JOURNEY OF KYOSHIRO AND YUYA BEGINS! (SDK VOL. 1)

▲ SHIINA YUYA

▲ MIBU KYOSHIRO

THE BEAUTIFUL BOUNTY HUNTER YUYA MEETS MIBU KYOSHIRO BY CHANCE (OR WAS IT FATE?!). WHEN THEY FIGHT THE BANTOUJI BROTHERS, KYOSHIRO'S OTHER SIDE IS REVEALED: THAT OF DEMON EYES KYO!

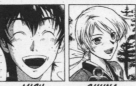

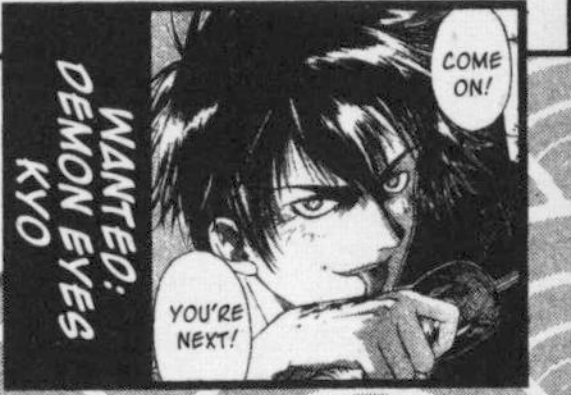

COME ON!
YOU'RE NEXT!

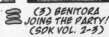

WANTED: DEMON EYES KYO

二 (2) THE WOMAN IZUMO-NO-OKUNI (SDK VOL. 1-2)

THEY MEET THE WOMAN IZUMO-NO-OKUNI IN AN INN TOWN--AND SHE SEEMS TO KNOW A LOT ABOUT KYO AND KYOSHIRO'S PAST. THEN, IN THE VILLAGE OF DESERTERS, KYO AWAKENS AND SHOWS HIS FULL STRENGTH!

TOUGE (THE PASS)
ZENGEN VILLAGE
INN VILLAGE
OCHUDOMURA (VILLAGE OF DESERTERS)
IN THE IPPONZAKURA MOUNTAINS (LONE CHERRY MOUNTAINS)
TEAHOUSE IN THE PASS
EDO
THE FOREST OF AOKIGAHARA
HAKONE
MT. FUJI

三 (3) BENITORA JOINS THE PARTY! (SDK VOL. 2-3)

THE PARTY GETS INTO A FIGHT WITH A GROUP OF TREASURE-SEEKING ASSASSINS KNOWN AS THE KITOU FAMILY SANSAISHU. ONE OF THEIR NUMBER, BENITORA, ENDS UP JOINING SIDES WITH KYO. KYO FIGHTS THE SHIROKARASU (WHITE CROW) AND FULLY AWAKENS! KYOSHIRO, HOWEVER, IS NOWHERE TO BE SEEN.

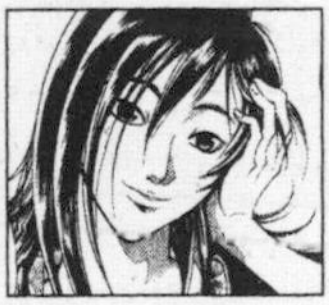

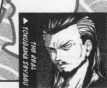

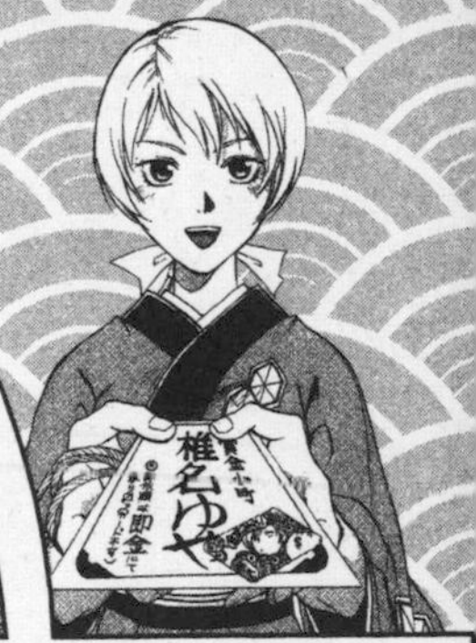

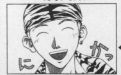

にかっ

▲ BENITORA

四 (4) KYO AND YUKIMURA MEET! (SDK VOL. 3)

A DRUNK CALLS OUT TO THEM AT A TEAHOUSE--AND TURNS OUT TO BE A SWORDSMAN OF SUCH SKILL HE CAN SLIP PAST EVEN KYO'S DEFENSES!

▶ SANADA YUKIMURA

▲ THE REAL TOKUGAWA IEYASU

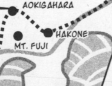

五 (5) FIGHT BEFORE THE SHOGUN! (SDK VOL. 3-5)

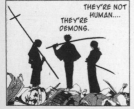

THEY'RE NOT HUMAN....
THEY'RE DEMONS.

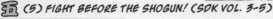

KYO, YUKIMURA, AND BENITORA ENTER A TOURNEY HELD BY THE RULER OF THE LAND, TOKUGAWA IEYASU. BUT THE TOURNEY WAS A TRAP! SET UPON BY TOKUGAWA'S ELITES, THE THREE MANAGE TO DESTROY THEM ALL WITHOUT BREAKING A SWEAT! THEN YUKIMURA TELLS KYO A SECRET: THE LOCATION OF HIS BODY!

IN JUST 3 MINUTES!

LEARN THE LEGEN

(6) MORTAL COMBAT VERSUS ODA NOBUNAGA AND THE TWELVE GOD SHOGUNS! (SDK VOL. 5-10)

KYO'S BODY LIES HIDDEN IN THE DEEPEST REACHES OF THE AOKIGAHARA FOREST AT THE FOOT OF MT. FUJI. BUT BETWEEN KYO AND HIS BODY STAND THE TWELVE--GUARDIANS OF THE MASTER, ODA NOBUNAGA. AFTER A STRING OF BLOODY BATTLES, KYO'S DEMONBLADE, MURAMASA, RELIEVES NOBUNAGA'S BODY OF ITS HEAD, BUT AKIRA MAKES HIS ESCAPE WITH KYO'S BODY!

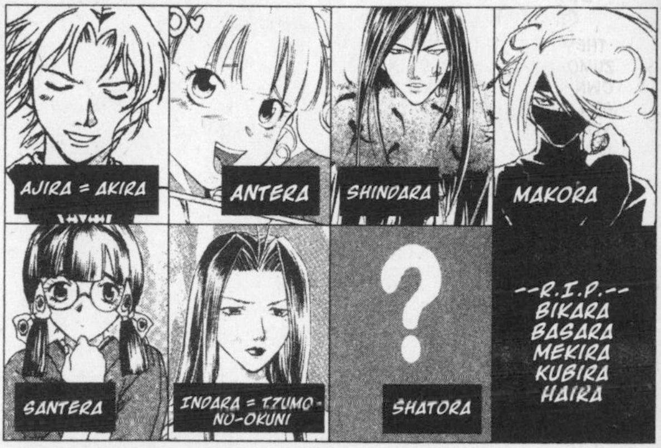
AJIRA = AKIRA
ANTERA
SHINDARA
MAKORA
SANTERA
INDARA = IZUMO-NO-OKUNI
?
SHATORA
--R.I.P.--
BIKARA
BASARA
MEKIRA
KUBIRA
HAIRA

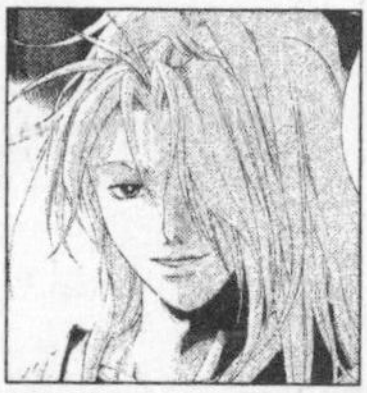

NOBUNAGA AWAITS THE TIME OF HIS RESURRECTION IN THE VILLAGE OF THE MIBU, DEEP WITHIN THE LAND OF THE FIRE LOTUS.

▲ ODA NOBUNAGA

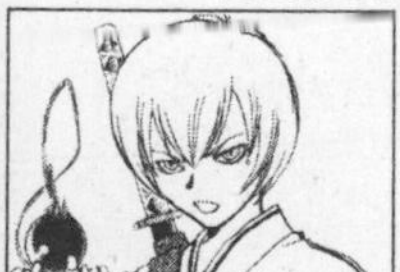

◀ SASUKE

ONE OF THE SANADA TEN, HE RETURNED TO THE FOREST WHERE HE WAS BORN ON YUKIMURA'S ORDERS.

(8) NOW, THE BATTLE BEGINS WITH THE MIBU CLAN. IT'S THEIR SECRETS AGAINST KYO'S BLADE!! (SDK VOL. 11-)

THE ENIGMATIC MIBU FAMILY HOLDS THE KEY TO THE MYSTERY BEHIND KYO'S BIRTH. AFTER HOLDING THE POWER TO CONTROL JAPAN'S HISTORY FROM THE DARK SIDE, SUDDENLY THE FACE-TO-FACE SHOWDOWN HAS BEGUN! AT THE SAME TIME, THE POWER TO SAVE YUYA'S LIFE LIES WITH THE ENEMY. KYO HAS CONFRONTED THE FIVE STARS, THE FOUR EMPERORS AND, MOST RECENTLY, THE CRIMSON KING (AKA NO OU), HIS LATEST ULTIMATELY STRONG FOE. ON THE OTHER HAND, KYO IS MARCHING INTO ENEMY TERRITORY ARMED WITH THE MUMYO JINPU TECHNIQUE THAT MURAMASA TRADED HIS LIFE TO OBTAIN.

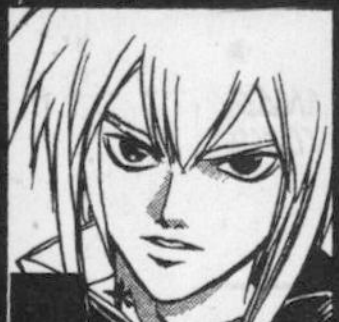

SHINREI

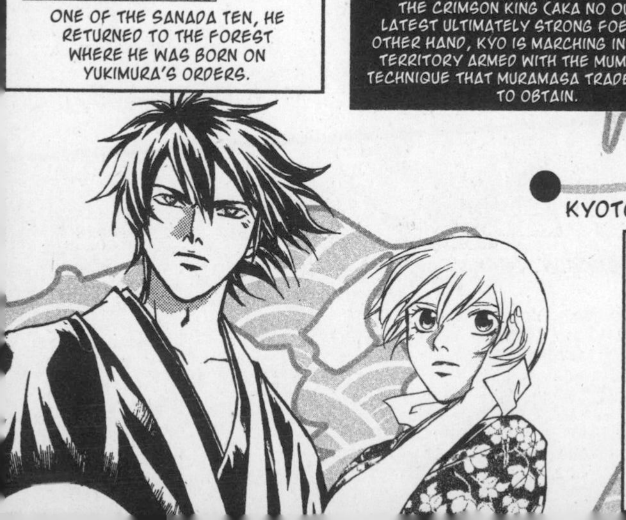
NAKASENDO ROAD
TOKAIDO ROAD
OWARI
KYOTO

(7) ENTER BONTENMARU! (SDK VOL. 10)

THE ONE-EYED DATE MASAMUNE APPEARS BEFORE KYO AND LEADS THE PARTY TO KYO'S MASTER, MURAMASA.

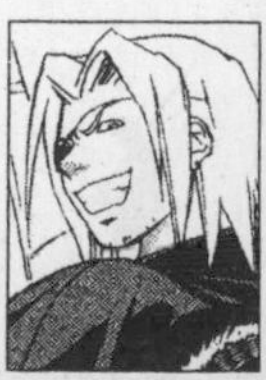

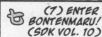

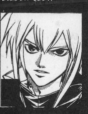

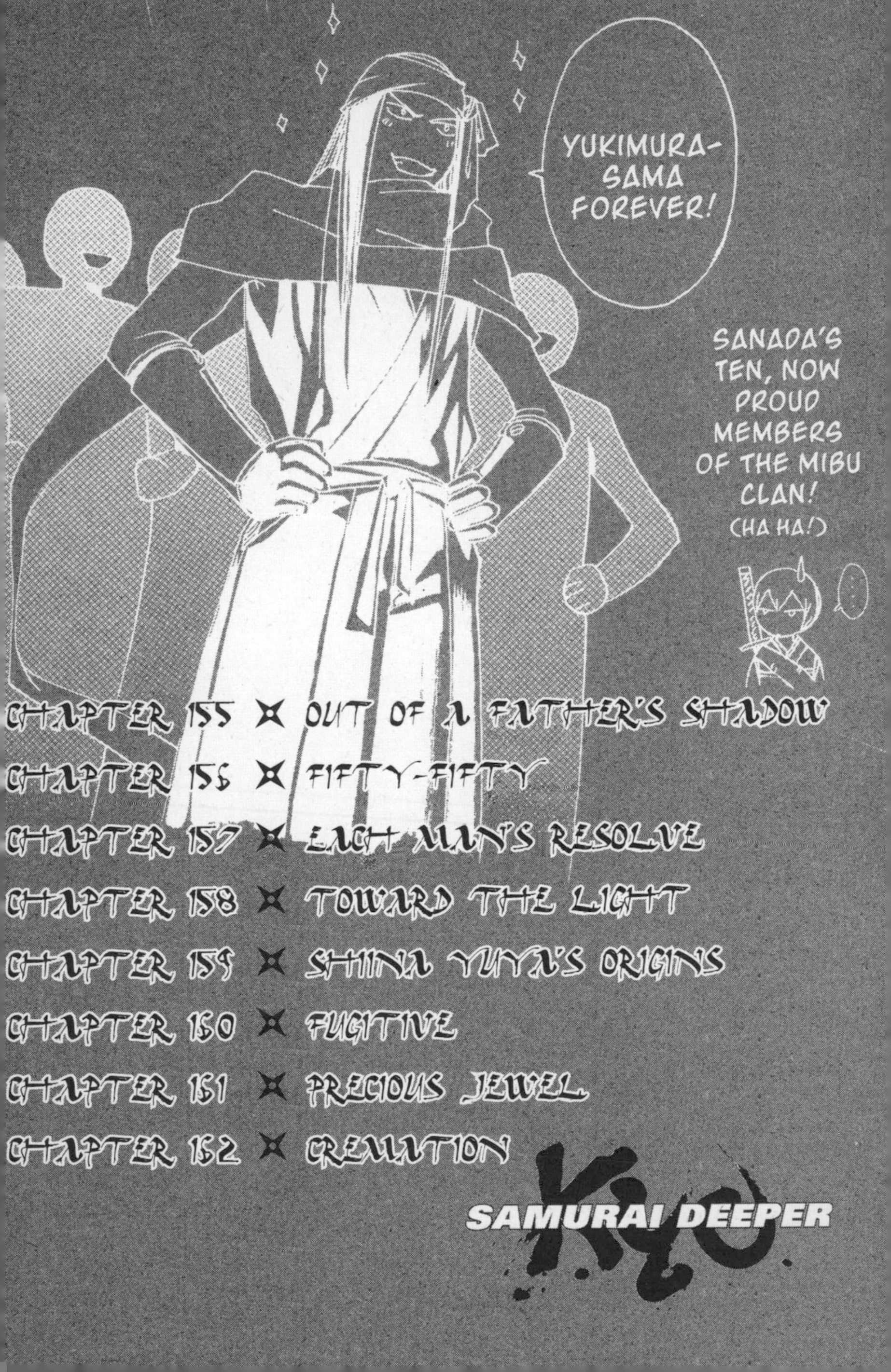
YUKIMURA-SAMA FOREVER!
SANADA'S TEN, NOW PROUD MEMBERS OF THE MIBU CLAN! (HA HA!)
...

SAMURAI DEEPER KYO

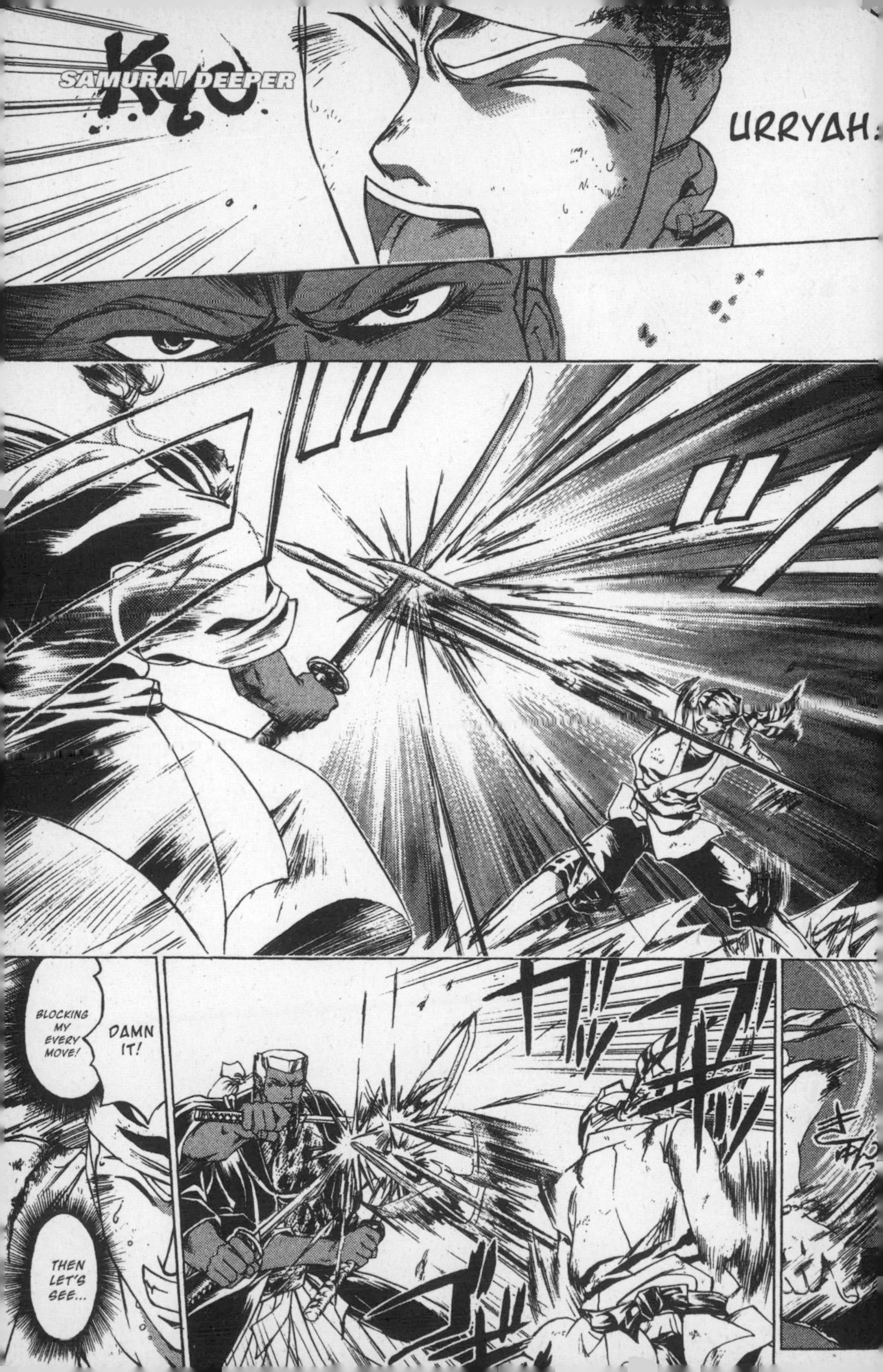
SAMURAI DEEPER KYO
URRYAH!
DAMN IT!
BLOCKING MY EVERY MOVE!
THEN LET'S SEE...

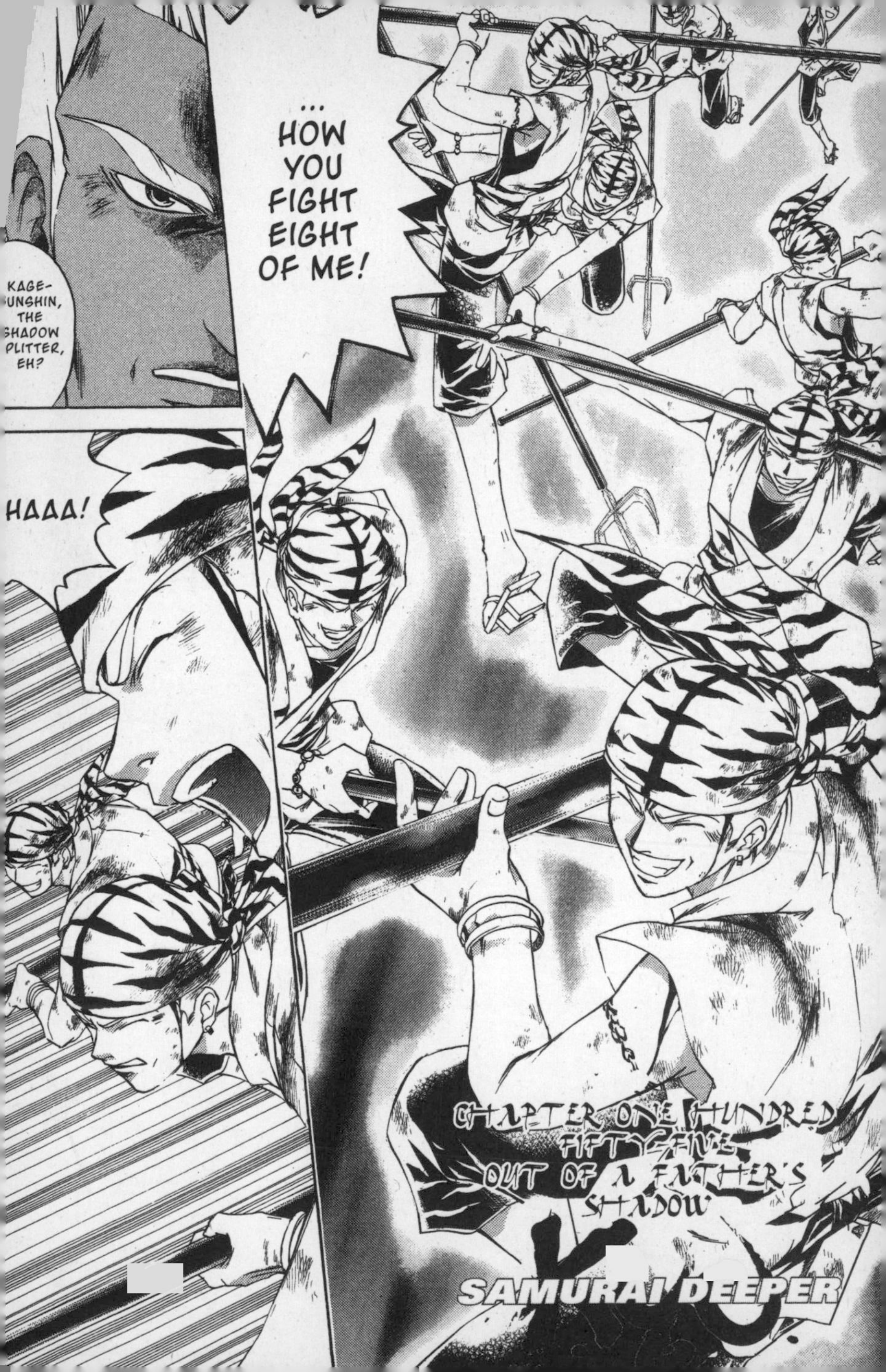
... HOW YOU FIGHT EIGHT OF ME!
CHAPTER ONE HUNDRED FIFTY-FIVE:
OUT OF A FATHER'S SHADOW
SAMURAI DEEPER
KAGE-BUNSHIN, THE SHADOW SPLITTER, EH?
HAAA!

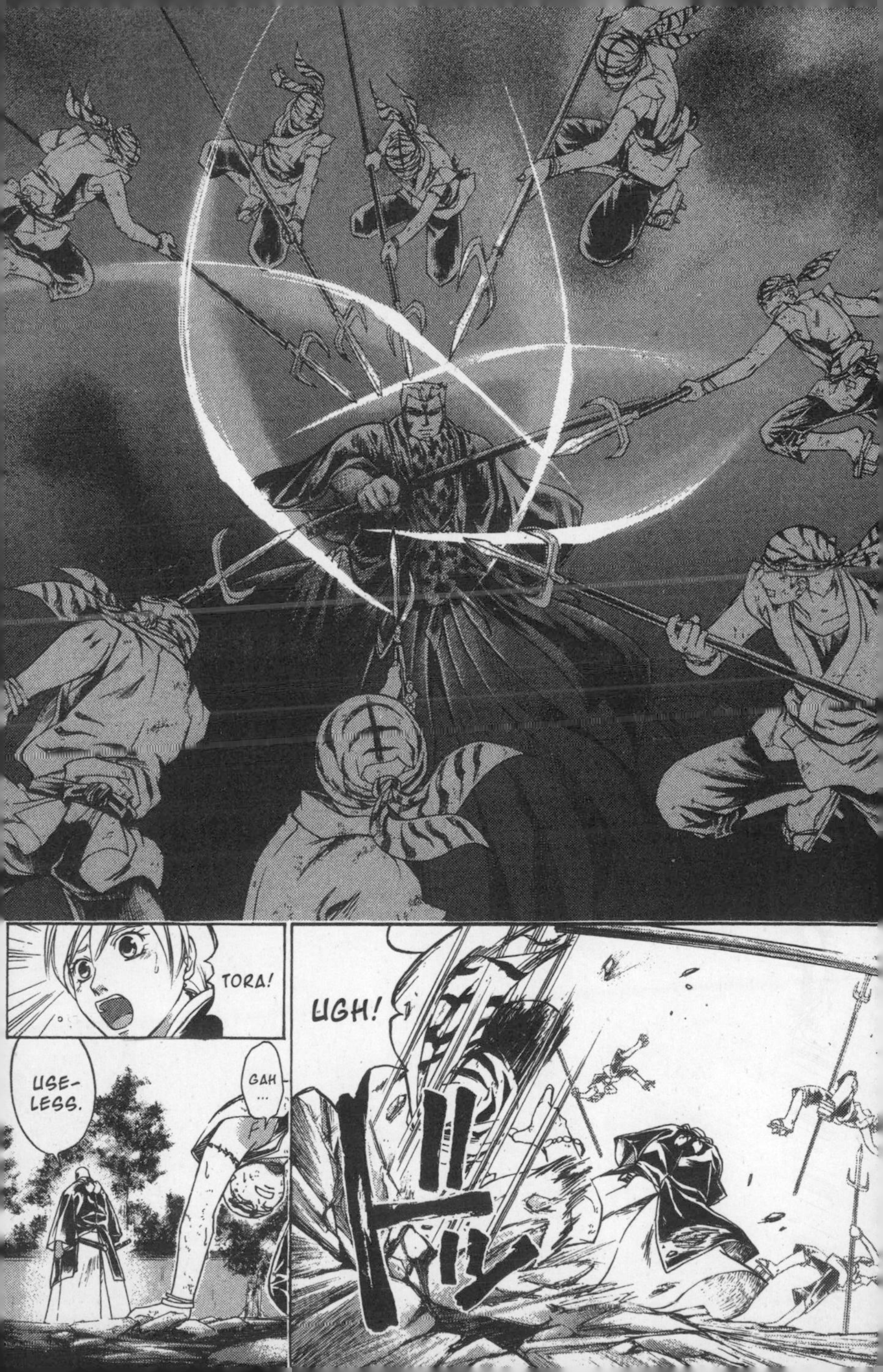
UGH!
TORA!
GAH ...
USE-LESS.

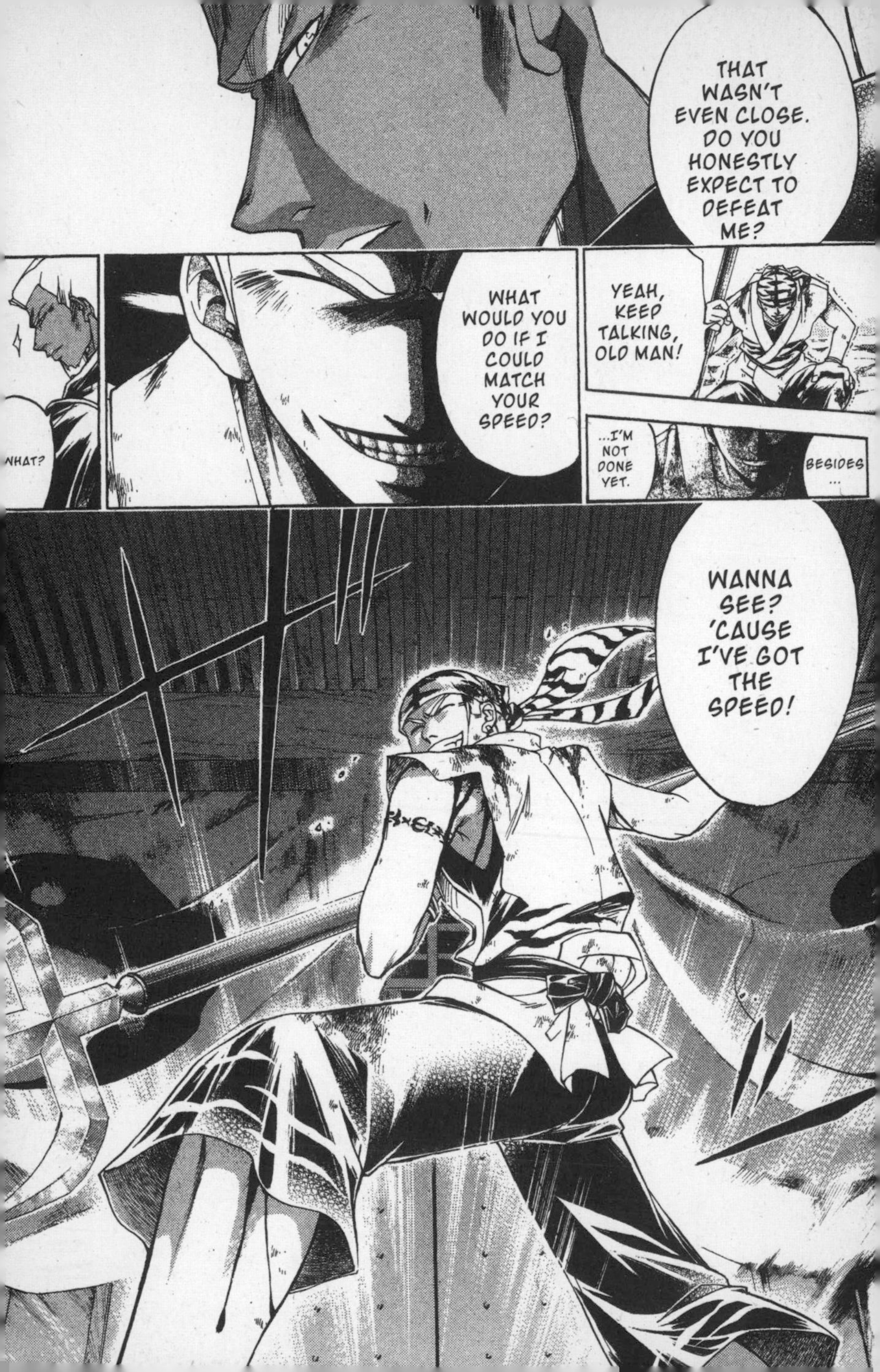
THAT WASN'T EVEN CLOSE. DO YOU HONESTLY EXPECT TO DEFEAT ME?
YEAH, KEEP TALKING, OLD MAN!
BESIDES...
...I'M NOT DONE YET.
WHAT WOULD YOU DO IF I COULD MATCH YOUR SPEED?
WHAT?
WANNA SEE? 'CAUSE I'VE GOT THE SPEED!

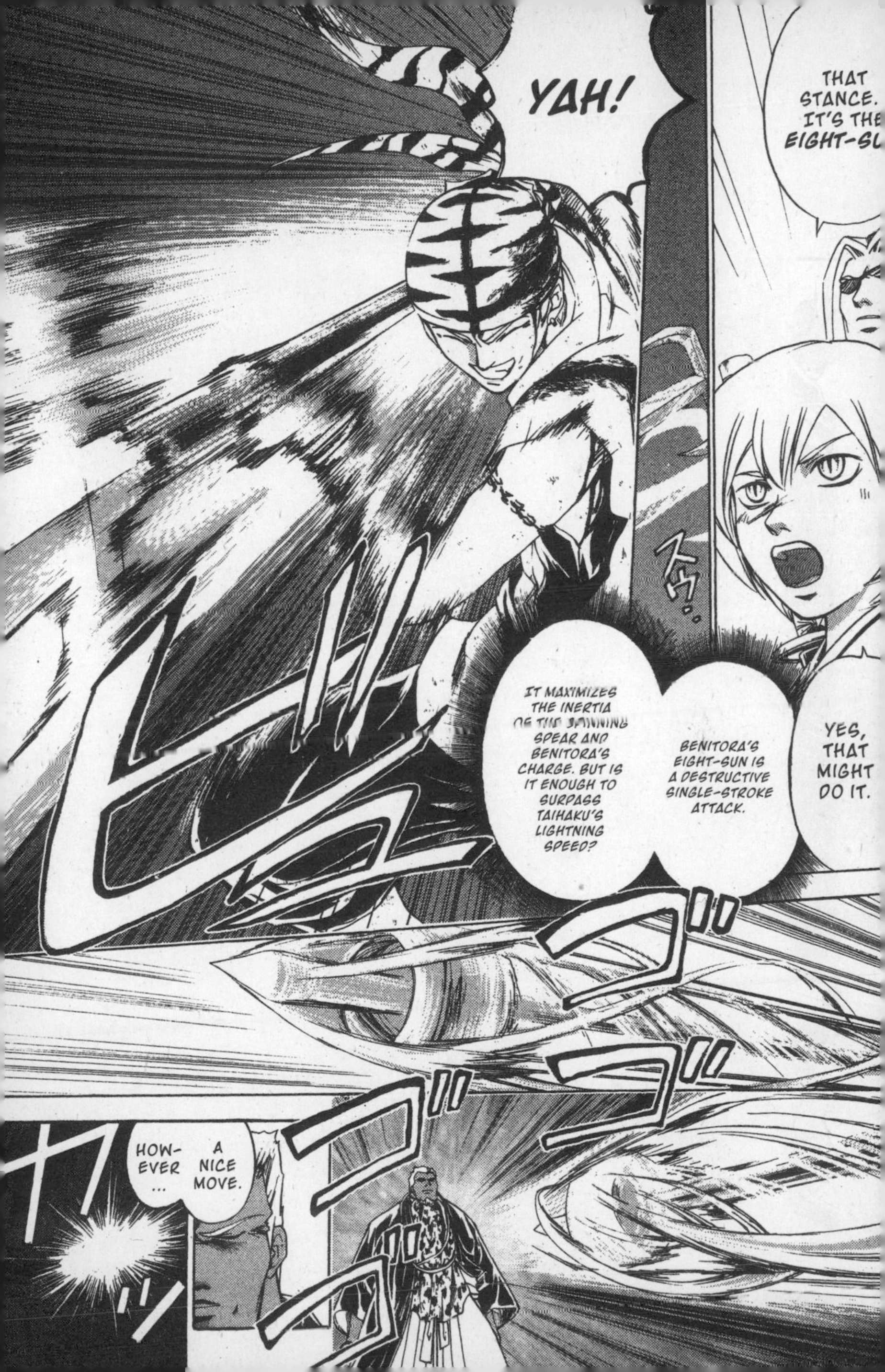
THAT STANCE. IT'S THE EIGHT-SU
YAH!
YES, THAT MIGHT DO IT.
BENITORA'S EIGHT-SUN IS A DESTRUCTIVE SINGLE-STROKE ATTACK.
IT MAXIMIZES THE INERTIA OF THE SPINNING SPEAR AND BENITORA'S CHARGE. BUT IS IT ENOUGH TO SURPASS TAIHAKU'S LIGHTNING SPEED?
A NICE MOVE.
HOW-EVER ...

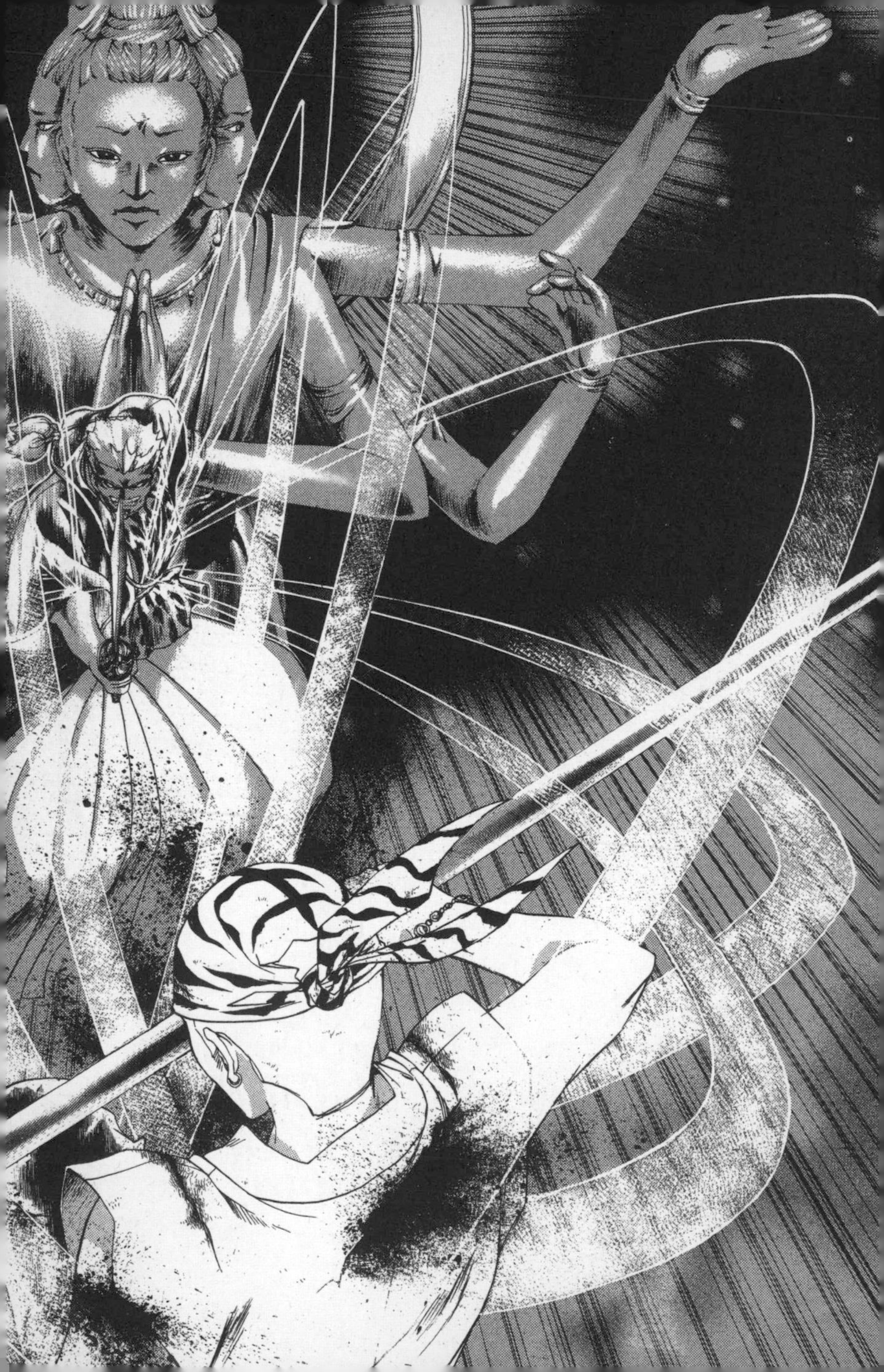

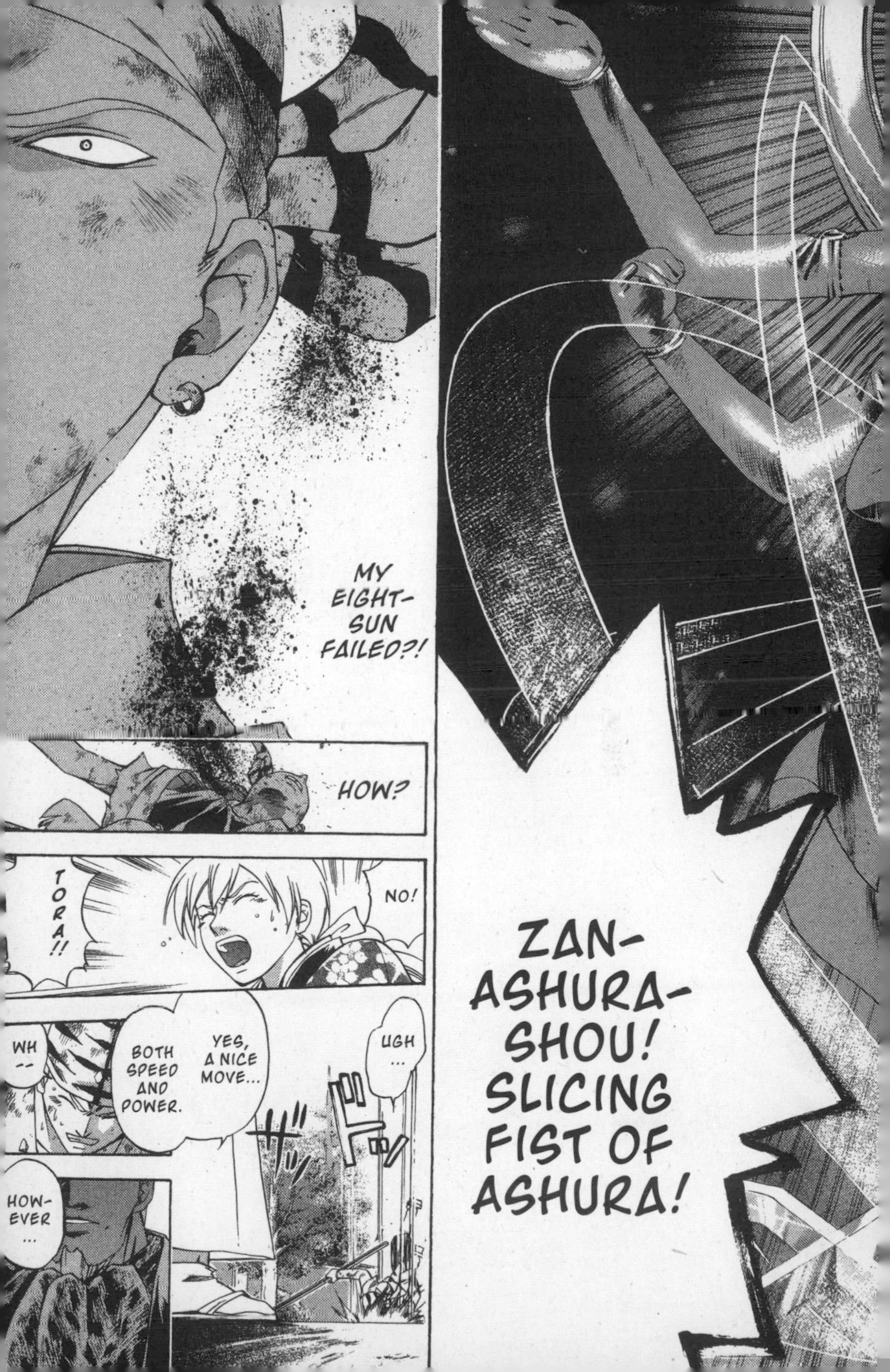
ZAN-ASHURA-SHOU! SLICING FIST OF ASHURA!
MY EIGHT-SUN FAILED?!
HOW?
NO!
TORA!!
UGH ...
YES, A NICE MOVE...
BOTH SPEED AND POWER.
WH --
HOW-EVER ...

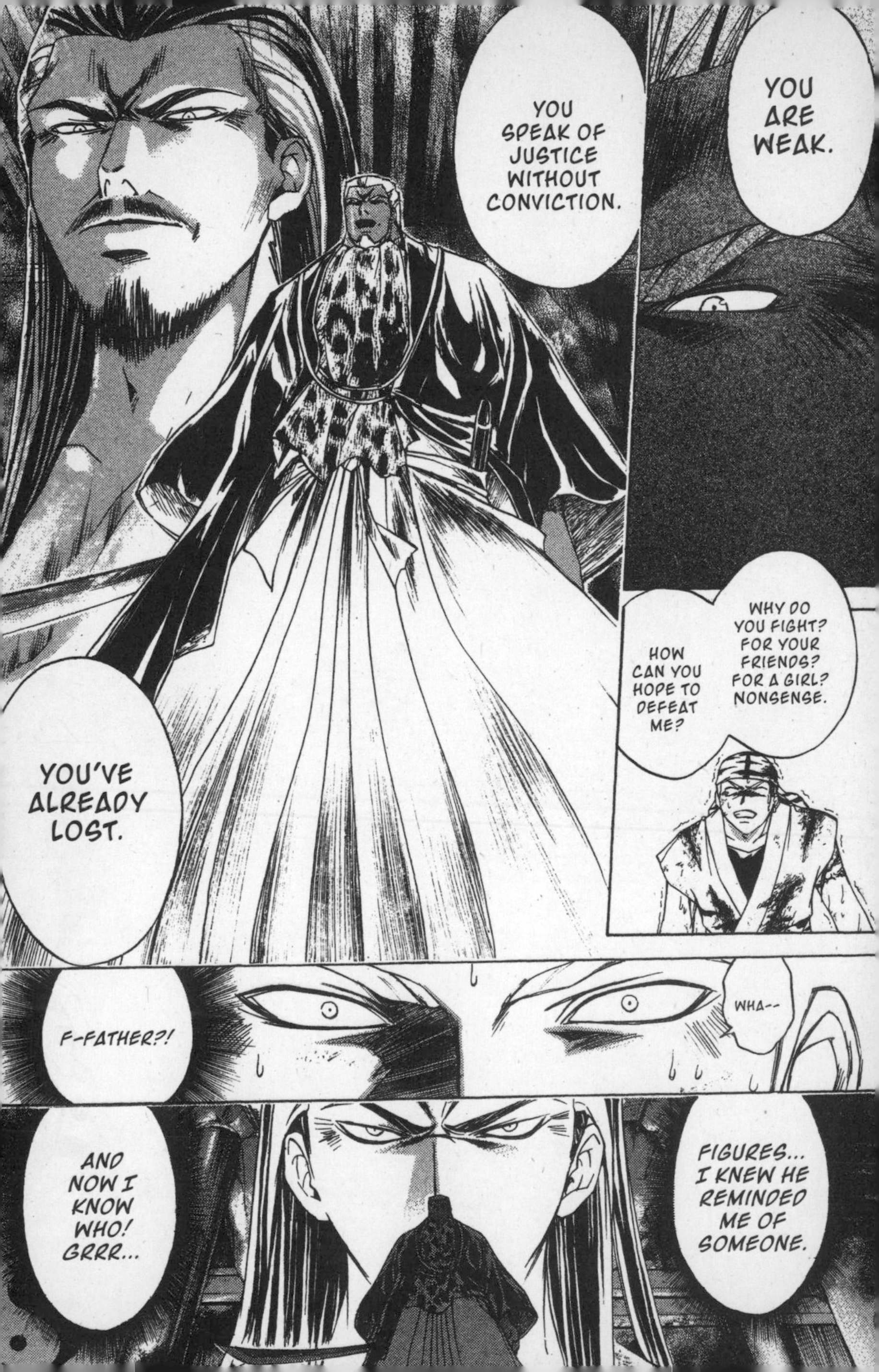
YOU ARE WEAK.
WHY DO YOU FIGHT? FOR YOUR FRIENDS? FOR A GIRL? NONSENSE.
HOW CAN YOU HOPE TO DEFEAT ME?
YOU SPEAK OF JUSTICE WITHOUT CONVICTION.
YOU'VE ALREADY LOST.
WHA--
F-FATHER?!
FIGURES... I KNEW HE REMINDED ME OF SOMEONE.
AND NOW I KNOW WHO! GRRR...

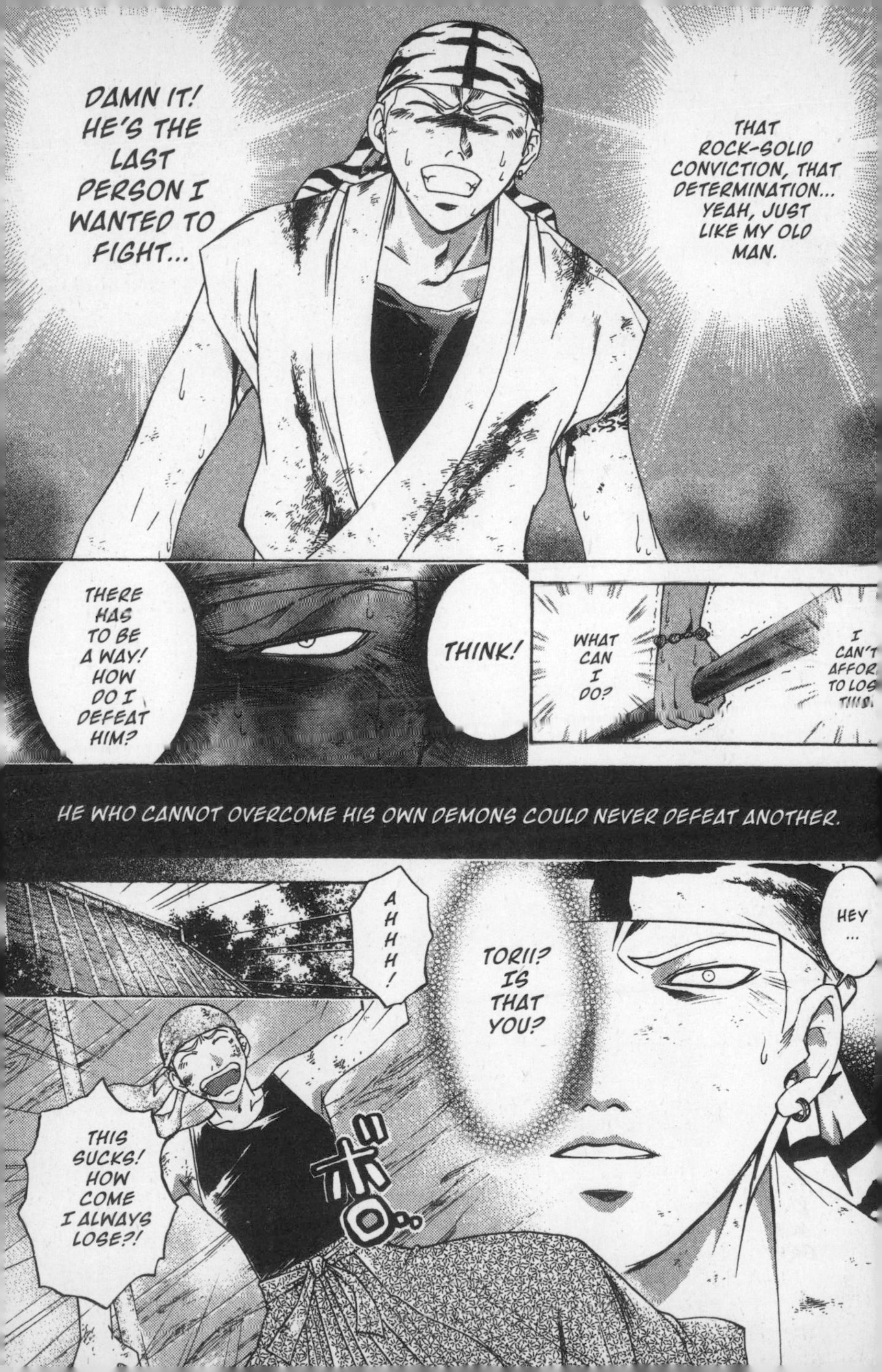
THAT ROCK-SOLID CONVICTION, THAT DETERMINATION... YEAH, JUST LIKE MY OLD MAN.
DAMN IT! HE'S THE LAST PERSON I WANTED TO FIGHT...
I CAN'T AFFOR TO LOS THIS.
WHAT CAN I DO?
THINK!
THERE HAS TO BE A WAY! HOW DO I DEFEAT HIM?
HE WHO CANNOT OVERCOME HIS OWN DEMONS COULD NEVER DEFEAT ANOTHER.
HEY...
TORII? IS THAT YOU?
AHHH!
THIS SUCKS! HOW COME I ALWAYS LOSE?!

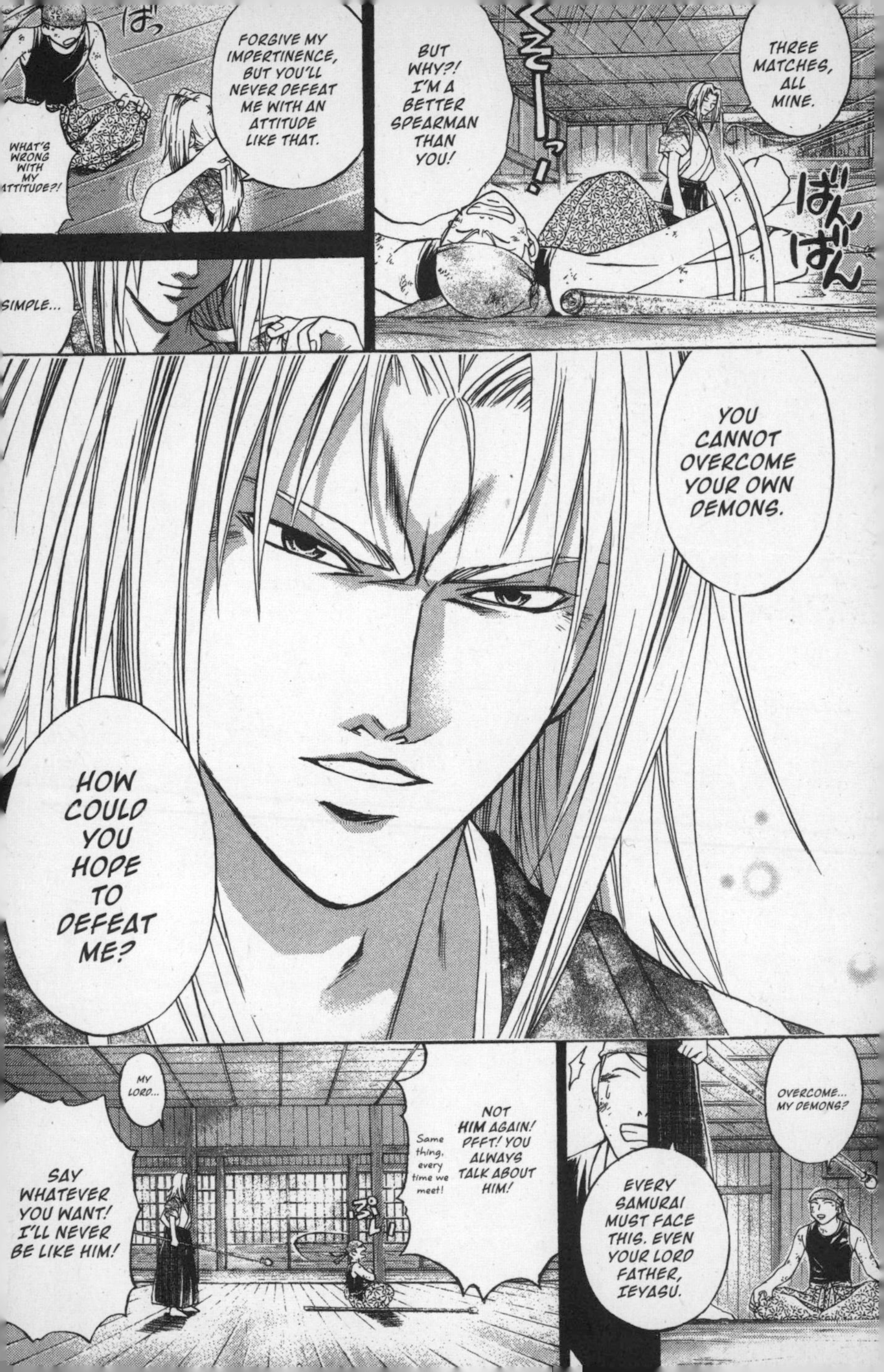
THREE MATCHES, ALL MINE.
ばんばん
くそーっ!
BUT WHY?! I'M A BETTER SPEARMAN THAN YOU!
ばっ
FORGIVE MY IMPERTINENCE, BUT YOU'LL NEVER DEFEAT ME WITH AN ATTITUDE LIKE THAT.
WHAT'S WRONG WITH MY ATTITUDE?!
SIMPLE...
YOU CANNOT OVERCOME YOUR OWN DEMONS.
HOW COULD YOU HOPE TO DEFEAT ME?
OVERCOME... MY DEMONS?
EVERY SAMURAI MUST FACE THIS. EVEN YOUR LORD FATHER, IEYASU.
NOT HIM AGAIN! PFFT! YOU ALWAYS TALK ABOUT HIM!
Same thing, every time we meet!
MY LORD...
SAY WHATEVER YOU WANT! I'LL NEVER BE LIKE HIM!

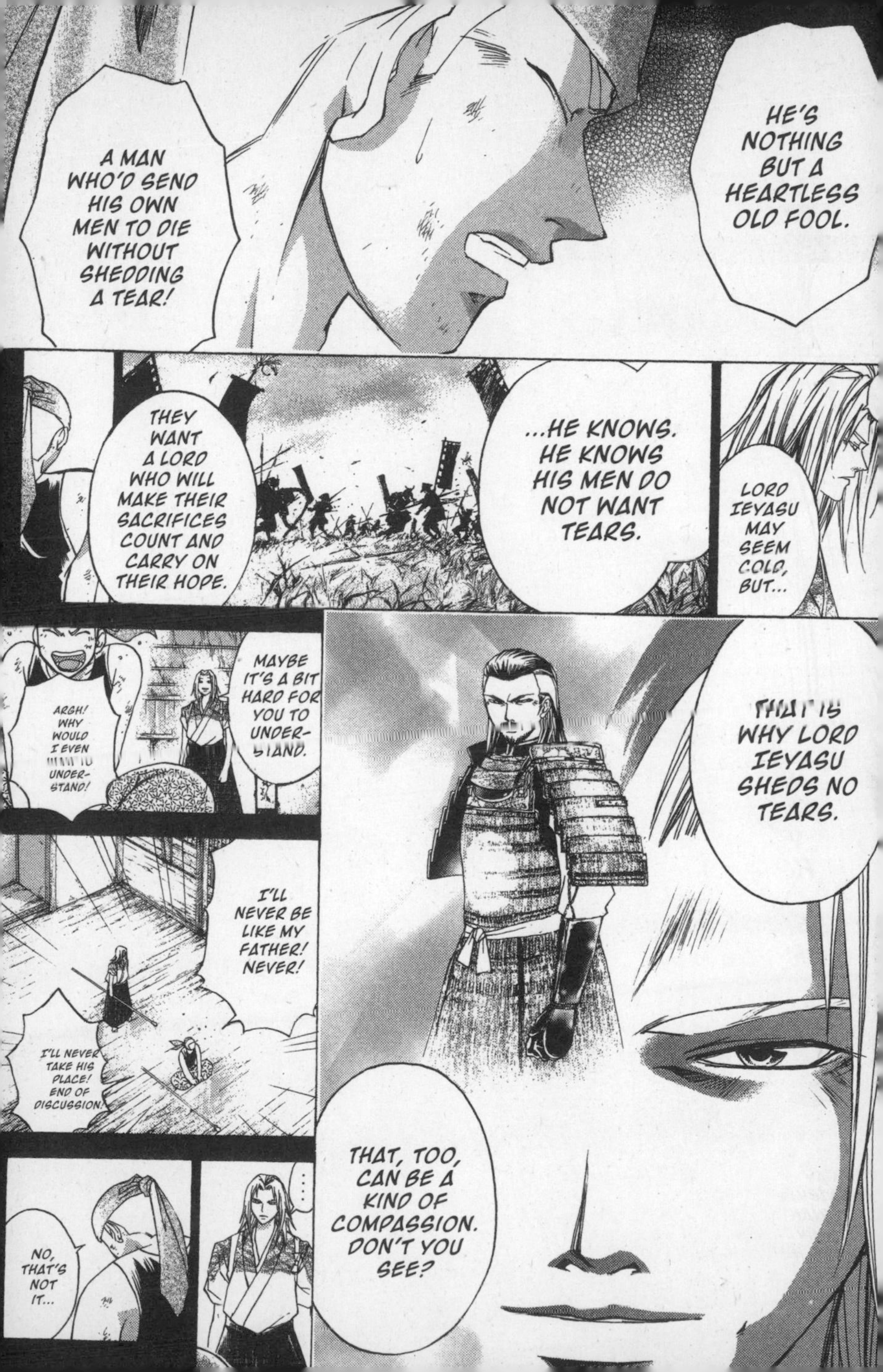
HE'S NOTHING BUT A HEARTLESS OLD FOOL.
A MAN WHO'D SEND HIS OWN MEN TO DIE WITHOUT SHEDDING A TEAR!
LORD IEYASU MAY SEEM COLD, BUT...
...HE KNOWS. HE KNOWS HIS MEN DO NOT WANT TEARS.
THEY WANT A LORD WHO WILL MAKE THEIR SACRIFICES COUNT AND CARRY ON THEIR HOPE.
THAT IS WHY LORD IEYASU SHEDS NO TEARS.
THAT, TOO, CAN BE A KIND OF COMPASSION. DON'T YOU SEE?
MAYBE IT'S A BIT HARD FOR YOU TO UNDER-STAND.
ARGH! WHY WOULD I EVEN UNDER-STAND!
I'LL NEVER BE LIKE MY FATHER! NEVER!
I'LL NEVER TAKE HIS PLACE! END OF DISCUSSION!
....
NO, THAT'S NOT IT...

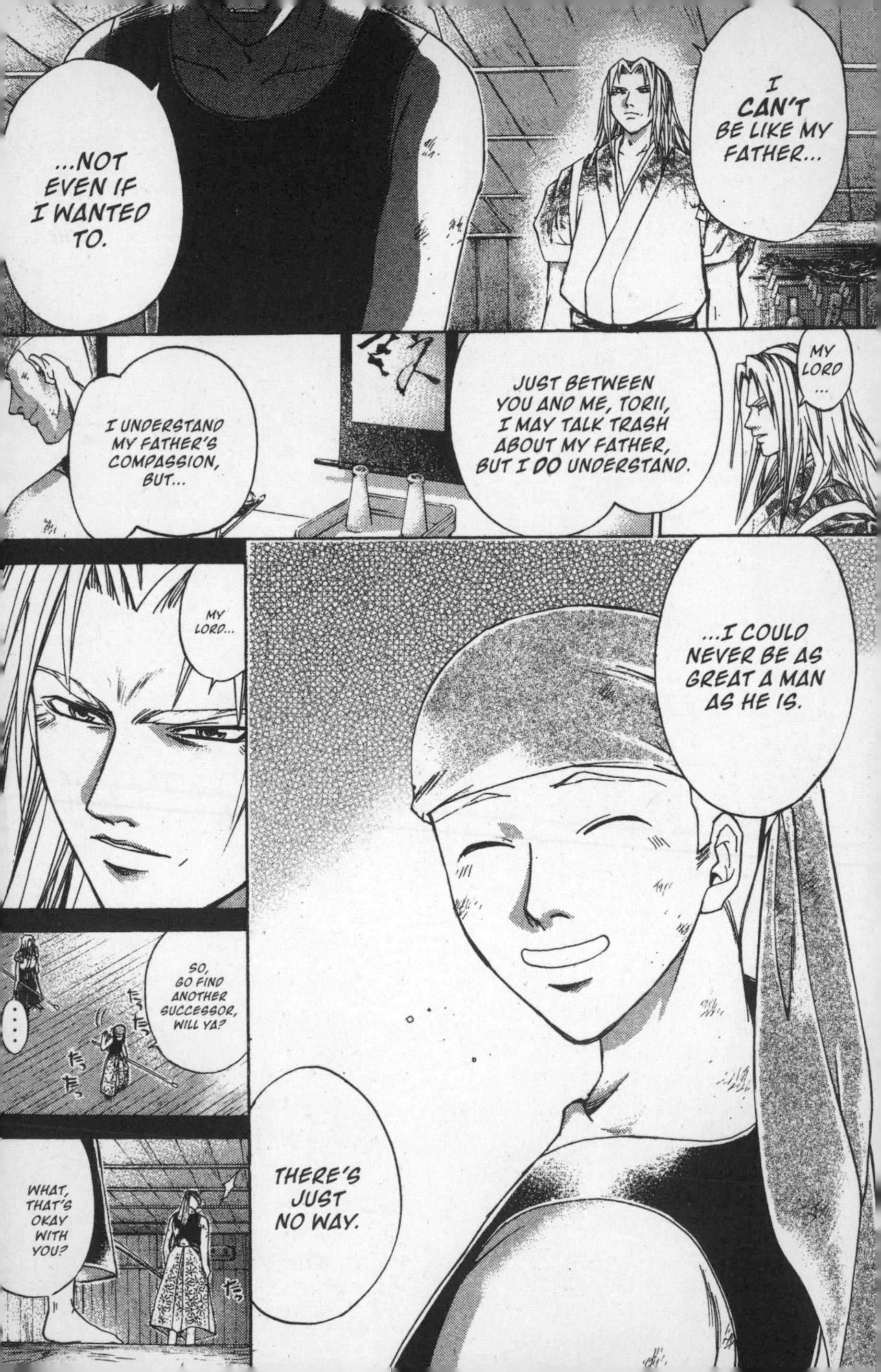
I CAN'T BE LIKE MY FATHER...
...NOT EVEN IF I WANTED TO.
MY LORD...
JUST BETWEEN YOU AND ME, TORII, I MAY TALK TRASH ABOUT MY FATHER, BUT I DO UNDERSTAND.
I UNDERSTAND MY FATHER'S COMPASSION, BUT...
...I COULD NEVER BE AS GREAT A MAN AS HE IS.
THERE'S JUST NO WAY.
MY LORD...
SO, GO FIND ANOTHER SUCCESSOR, WILL YA?
....
WHAT, THAT'S OKAY WITH YOU?

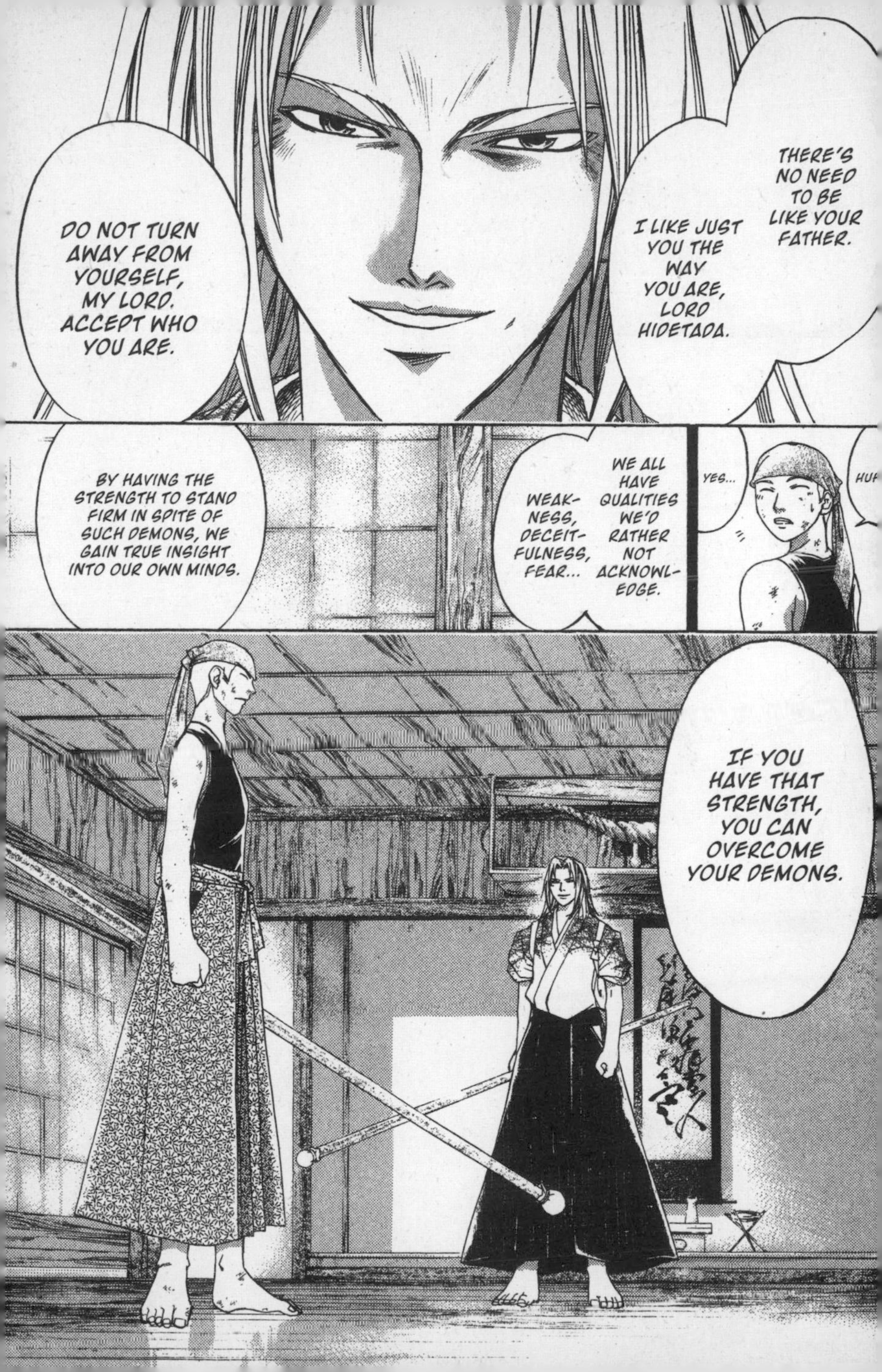
THERE'S NO NEED TO BE LIKE YOUR FATHER.
I LIKE JUST YOU THE WAY YOU ARE, LORD HIDETADA.
DO NOT TURN AWAY FROM YOURSELF, MY LORD. ACCEPT WHO YOU ARE.
YES...
WE ALL HAVE QUALITIES WE'D RATHER NOT ACKNOWLEDGE.
WEAKNESS, DECEITFULNESS, FEAR...
BY HAVING THE STRENGTH TO STAND FIRM IN SPITE OF SUCH DEMONS, WE GAIN TRUE INSIGHT INTO OUR OWN MINDS.
IF YOU HAVE THAT STRENGTH, YOU CAN OVERCOME YOUR DEMONS.

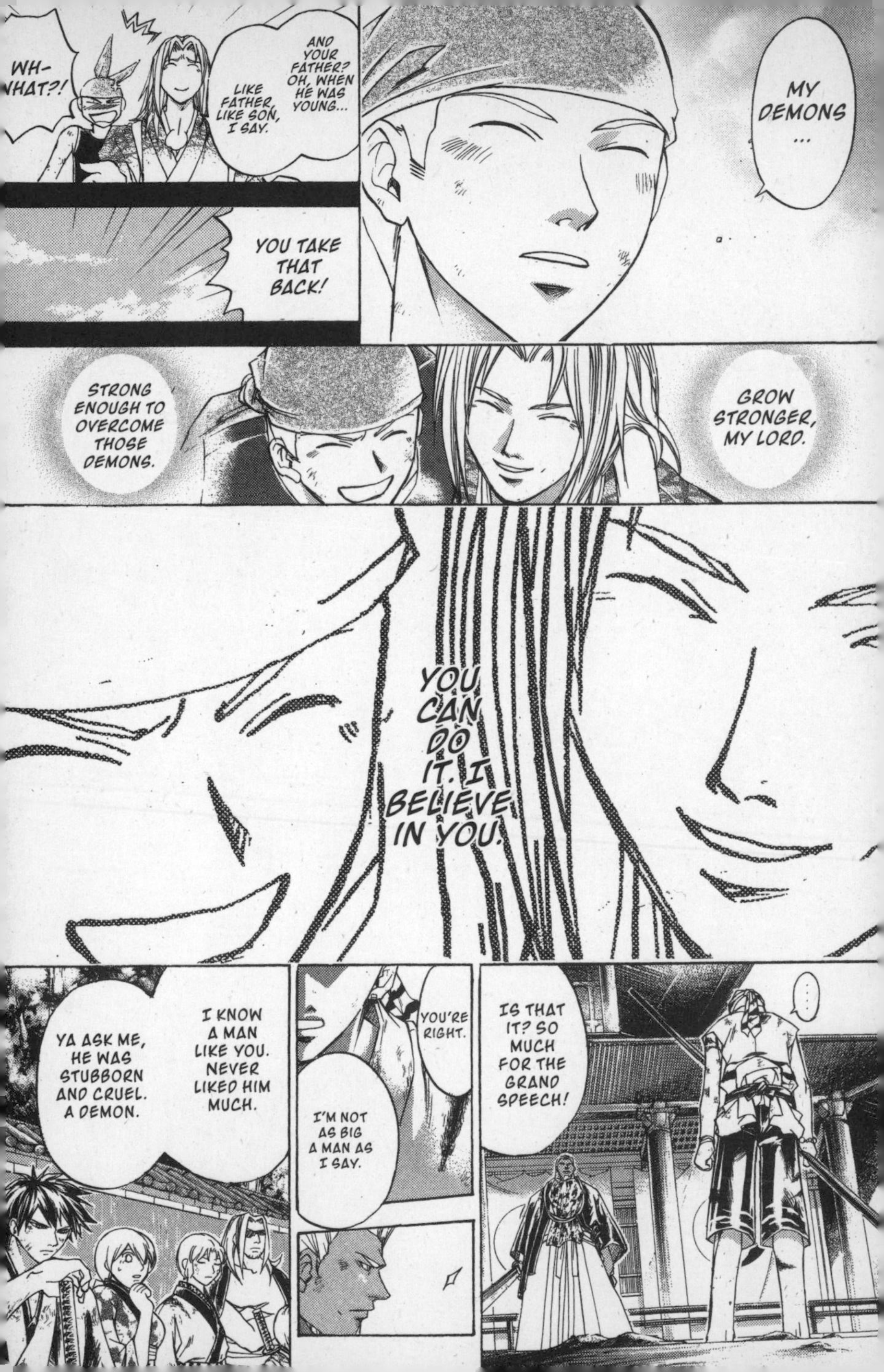
MY DEMONS ...
AND YOUR FATHER? OH, WHEN HE WAS YOUNG...
LIKE FATHER, LIKE SON, I SAY.
WH-WHAT?!
YOU TAKE THAT BACK!
GROW STRONGER, MY LORD.
STRONG ENOUGH TO OVERCOME THOSE DEMONS.
YOU CAN DO IT. I BELIEVE IN YOU.
...
IS THAT IT? SO MUCH FOR THE GRAND SPEECH!
YOU'RE RIGHT.
I'M NOT AS BIG A MAN AS I SAY.
I KNOW A MAN LIKE YOU. NEVER LIKED HIM MUCH.
YA ASK ME, HE WAS STUBBORN AND CRUEL. A DEMON.

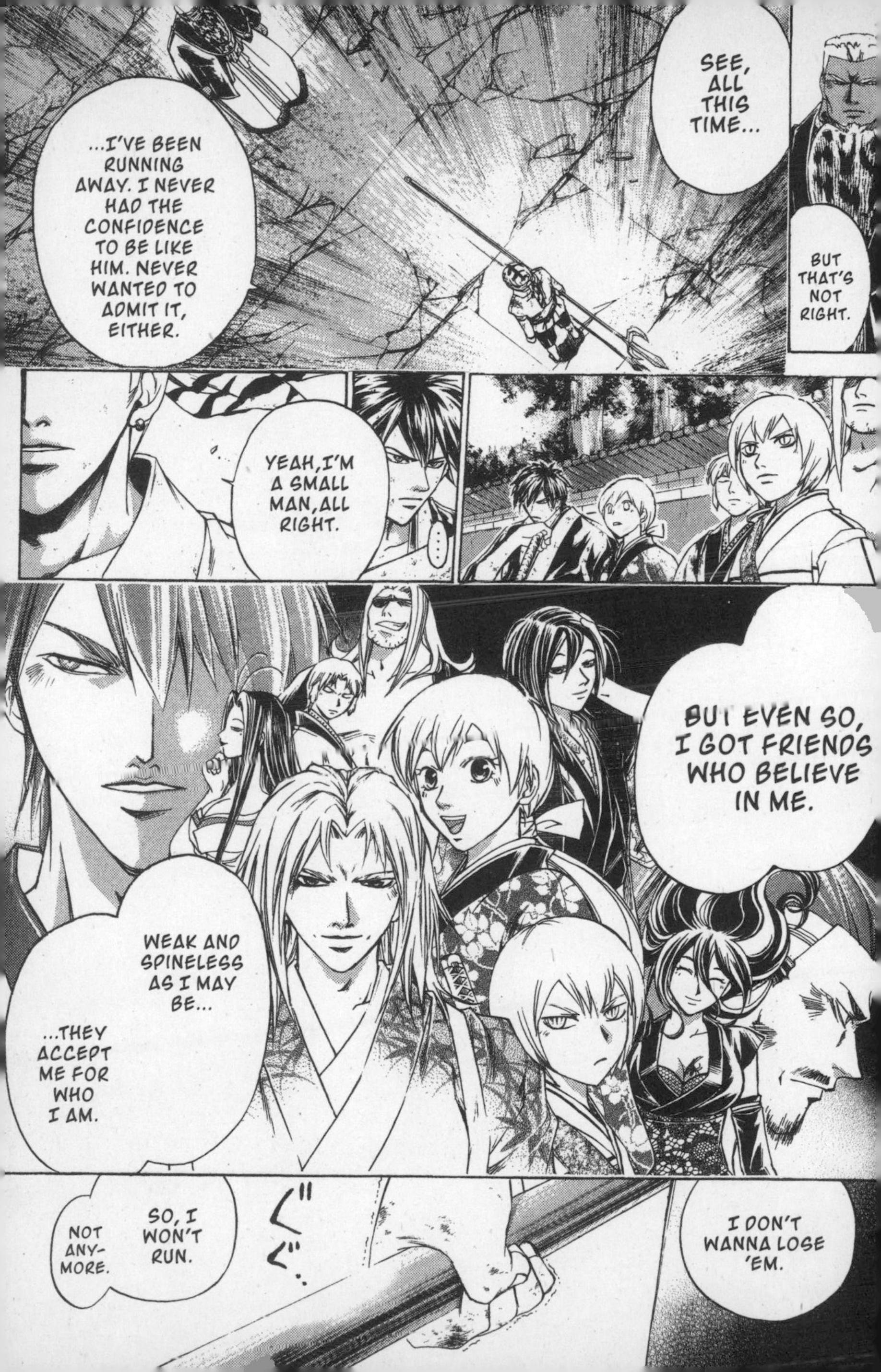
SEE, ALL THIS TIME...
BUT THAT'S NOT RIGHT.
...I'VE BEEN RUNNING AWAY. I NEVER HAD THE CONFIDENCE TO BE LIKE HIM. NEVER WANTED TO ADMIT IT, EITHER.
YEAH, I'M A SMALL MAN, ALL RIGHT.
BUT EVEN SO, I GOT FRIENDS WHO BELIEVE IN ME.
WEAK AND SPINELESS AS I MAY BE...
...THEY ACCEPT ME FOR WHO I AM.
I DON'T WANNA LOSE 'EM.
ぐぐ…
SO, I WON'T RUN.
NOT ANYMORE.

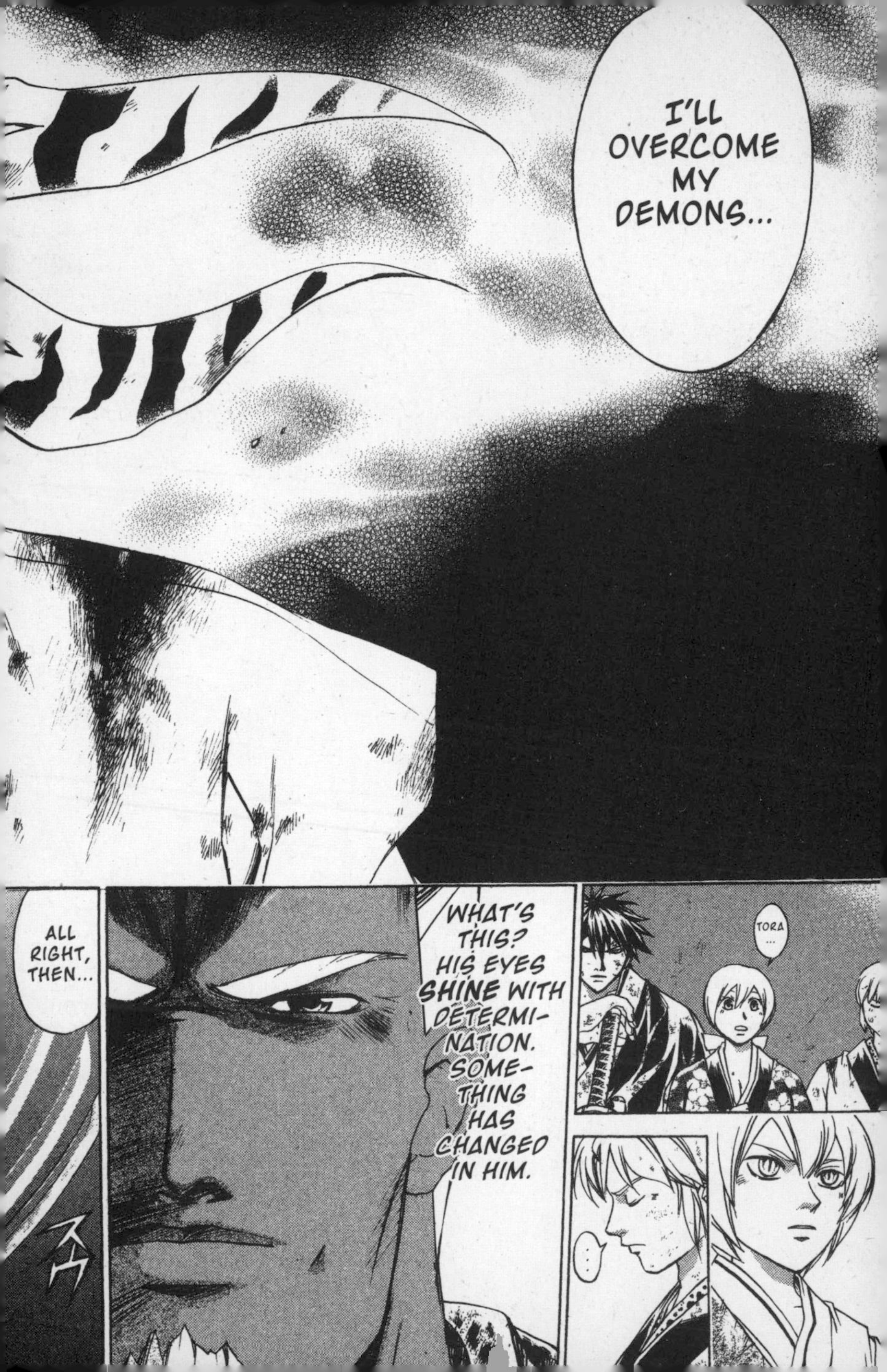
I'LL OVERCOME MY DEMONS...
TORA ...
...
WHAT'S THIS? HIS EYES SHINE WITH DETERMINATION. SOMETHING HAS CHANGED IN HIM.
ALL RIGHT, THEN...

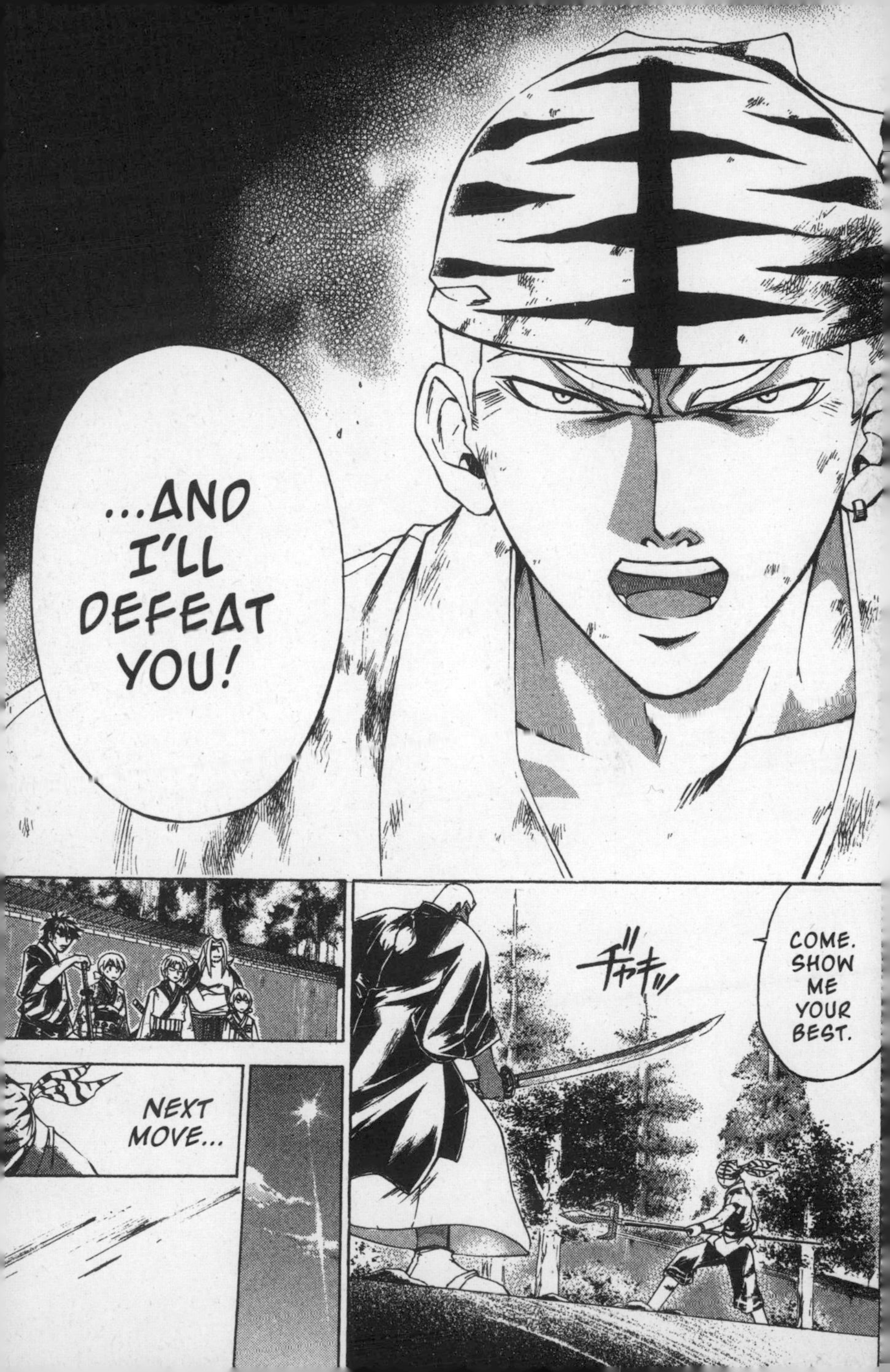
...AND I'LL DEFEAT YOU!
チャキッ
COME. SHOW ME YOUR BEST.
NEXT MOVE...

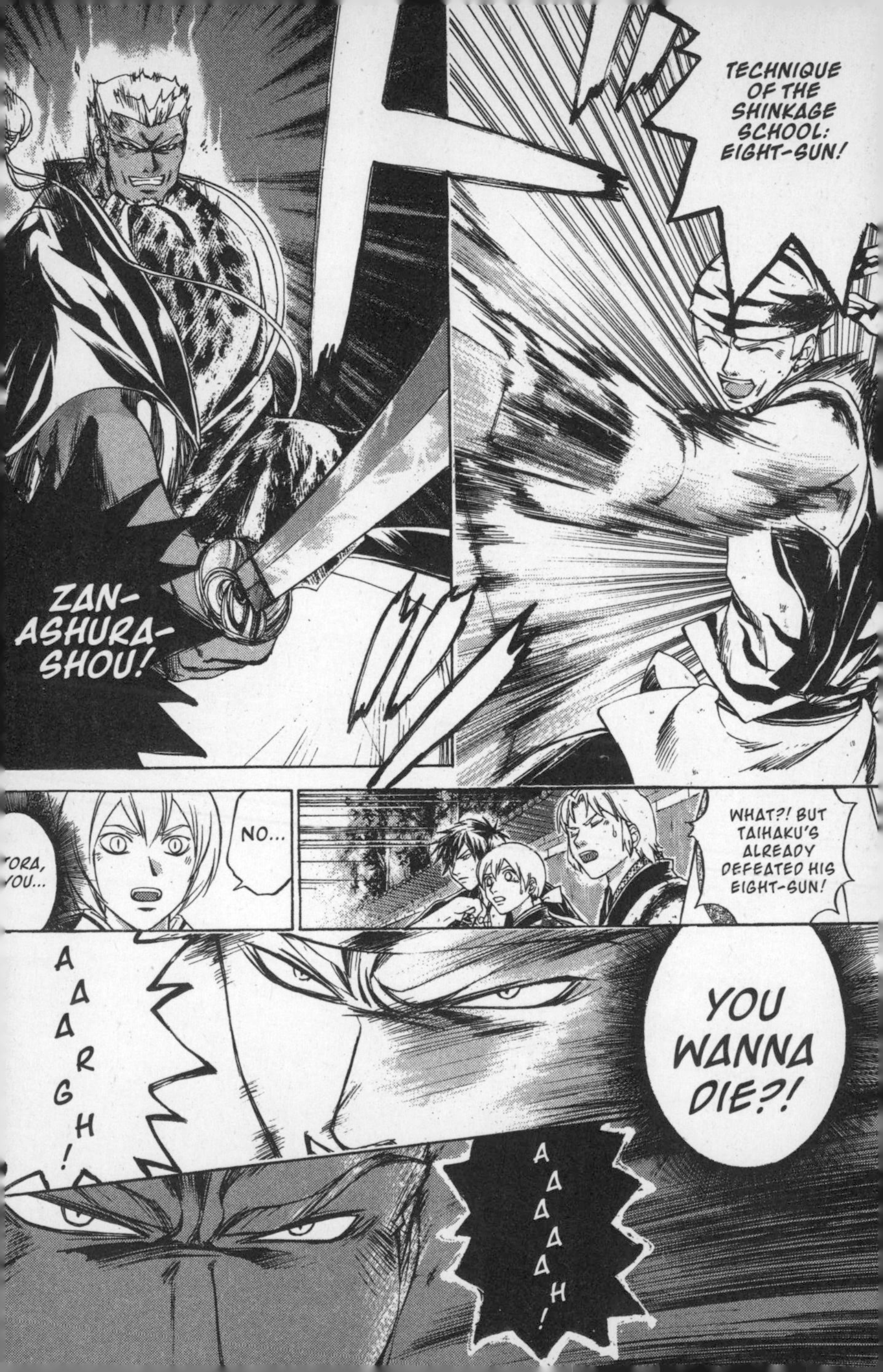
TECHNIQUE OF THE SHINKAGE SCHOOL: EIGHT-SUN!
ZAN-ASHURA-SHOU!
WHAT?! BUT TAIHAKU'S ALREADY DEFEATED HIS EIGHT-SUN!
NO...
TORA, YOU...
YOU WANNA DIE?!
AAAAAAH!
AAARGH!

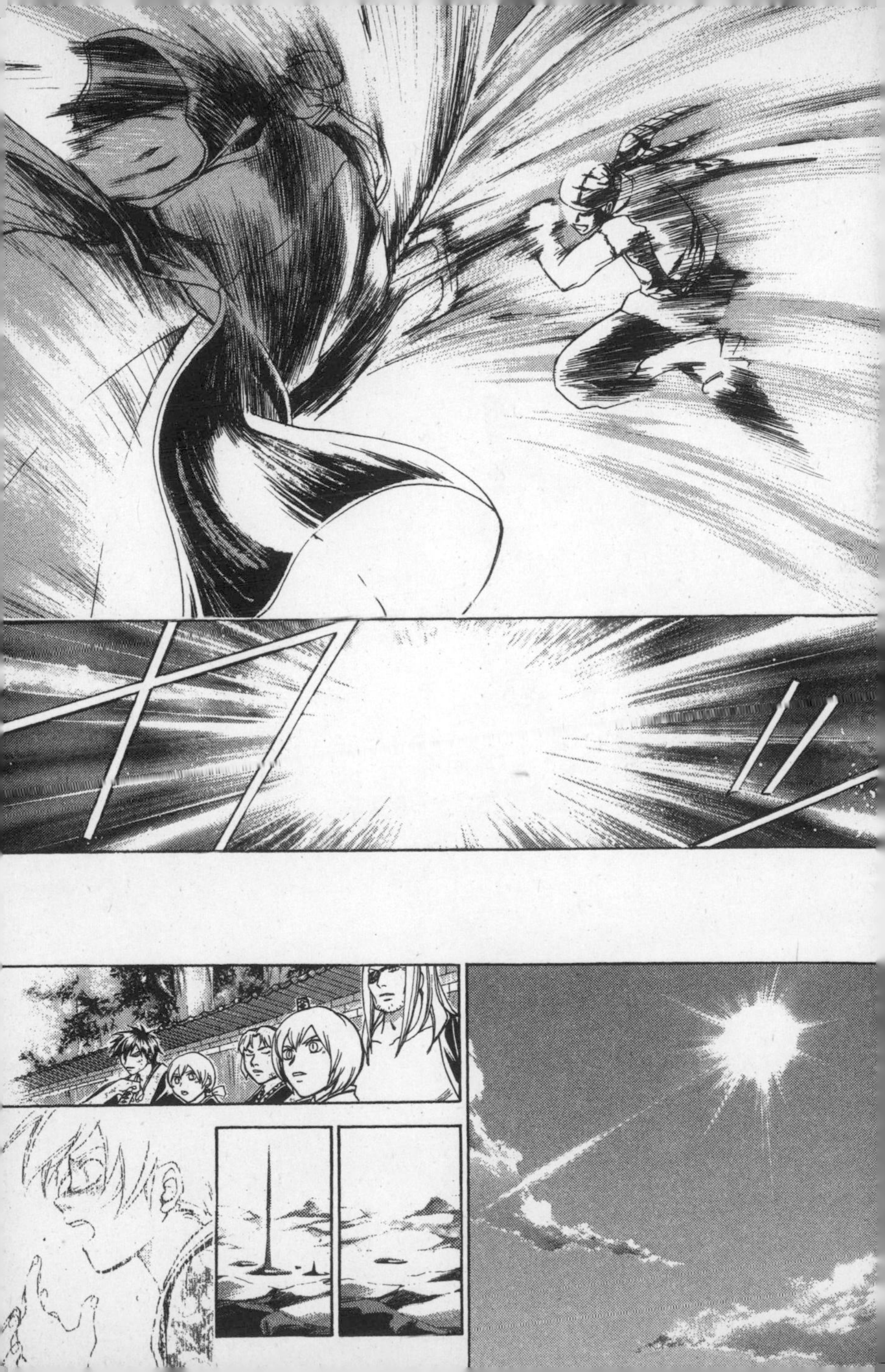

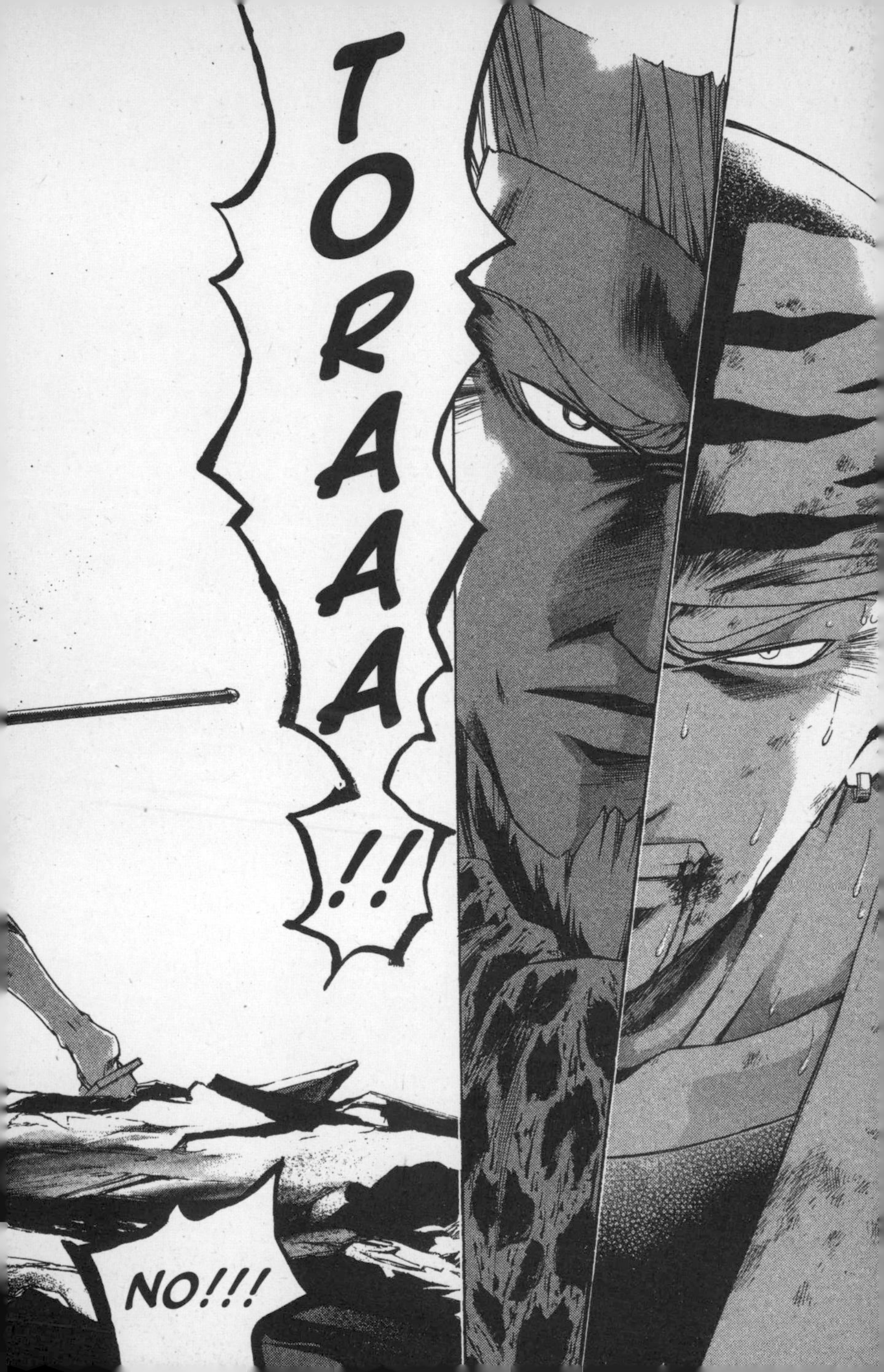
TORAAAA!!
NO!!!

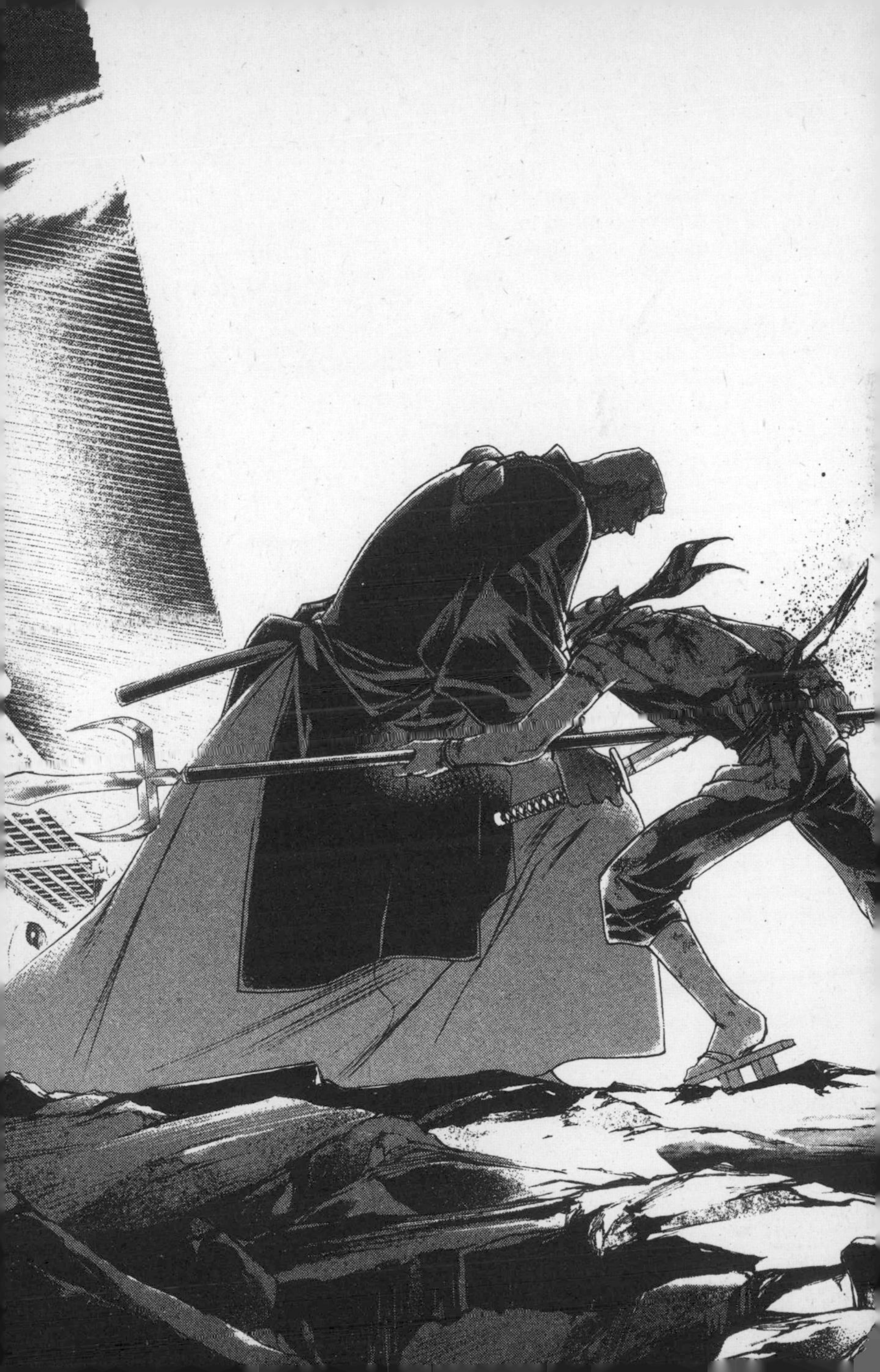

Hi! This is Kamijyo. Here we are at volume 20 of *SDK*. I couldn't have done it without you. I'll continue to work hard, so keep the love coming!

Thanks to everyone who sent me a holiday card. It was nice to see so many color illustrations, instead of the usual B&W (which I also like). By the time I received your cards, though, I could barely keep my head above water with work, so I couldn't send anything back. Sorry! I promise to show my thanks through my comic.

I often write about what's going on at the moment, which can be embarrassing when I read it back afterwards. (Especially when I write strange things.) But I don't care! I'll keep on writing about what's going on and how I feel at the moment.

So here's what's going on right now: Thanks for sending in your postcards for the fan book! I'm happy to see that so many more came in than I expected. Both the editor and I are committed to making a fun book. Keep your eyes peeled!

Looking forward to seeing you again in the next issue. Bye!

SASUKE AND AKIRA'S FEELINGS

ABOUT HOW AKIRA USED TO BE AN ENEMY:
NONE OF MY BUSINESS.
IT'S NONE OF HIS BUSINESS.
ABOUT HOW YUKIMURA BECAME A MEMBER OF MIBU:
I BELIEVE IN HIM.
HE BETRAYED US.
ABOUT HOW YOU'RE BOTH TRAVELING TOGETHER:
WHAT-EVER.
...
OH, NO! THEY'RE BOTH SO TERSE! NO PUNCH LINE!
KYO!
I WOULDN'T MIND FIGHTING HIM AT LEAST ONCE.
Sorry.

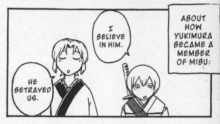

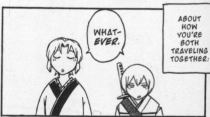

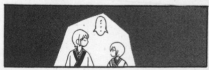

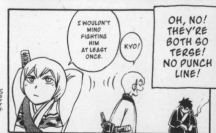

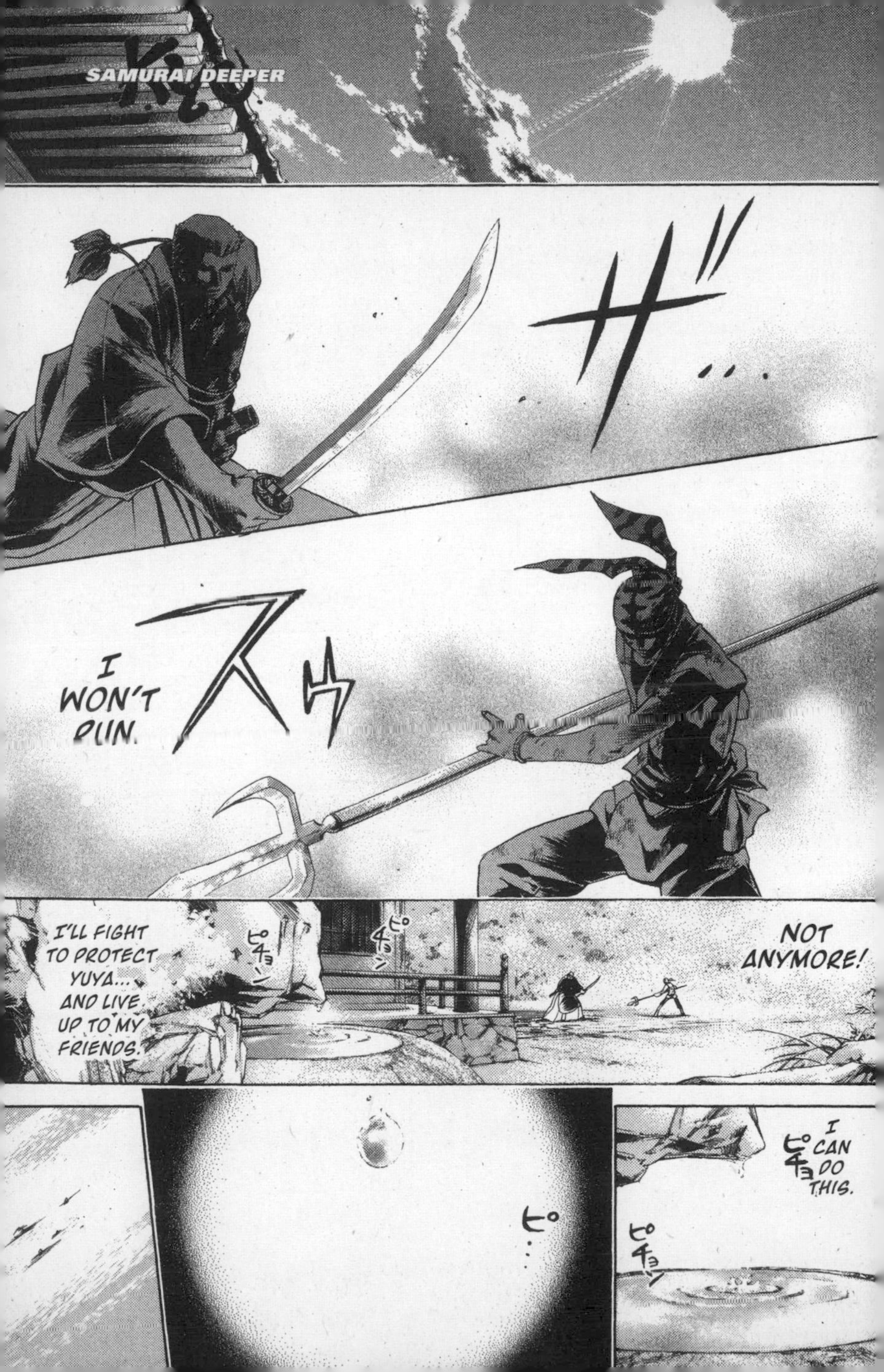
SAMURAI DEEPER
ザ…
I WON'T RUN.
スッ
NOT ANYMORE!
ピチョン
ピチョン
I'LL FIGHT TO PROTECT YUYA... AND LIVE UP TO MY FRIENDS.
I CAN DO THIS.
ピチョ
ピチョン
ピ…

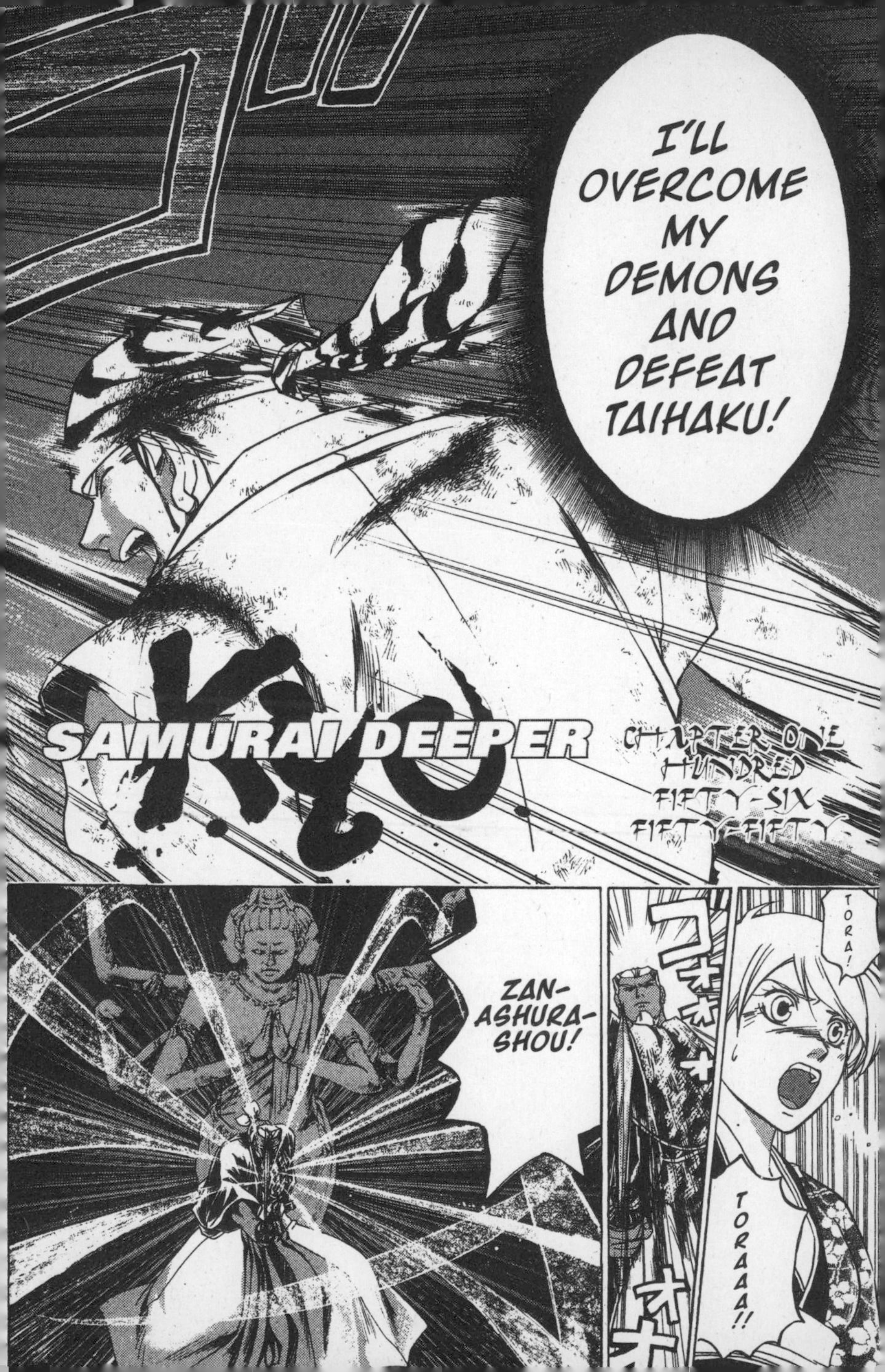
I'LL OVERCOME MY DEMONS AND DEFEAT TAIHAKU!
SAMURAI DEEPER KYO
CHAPTER ONE HUNDRED FIFTY-SIX
FIFTY-FIFTY
TORA!
TORAAAA!!
ZAN-ASHURA-SHOU!

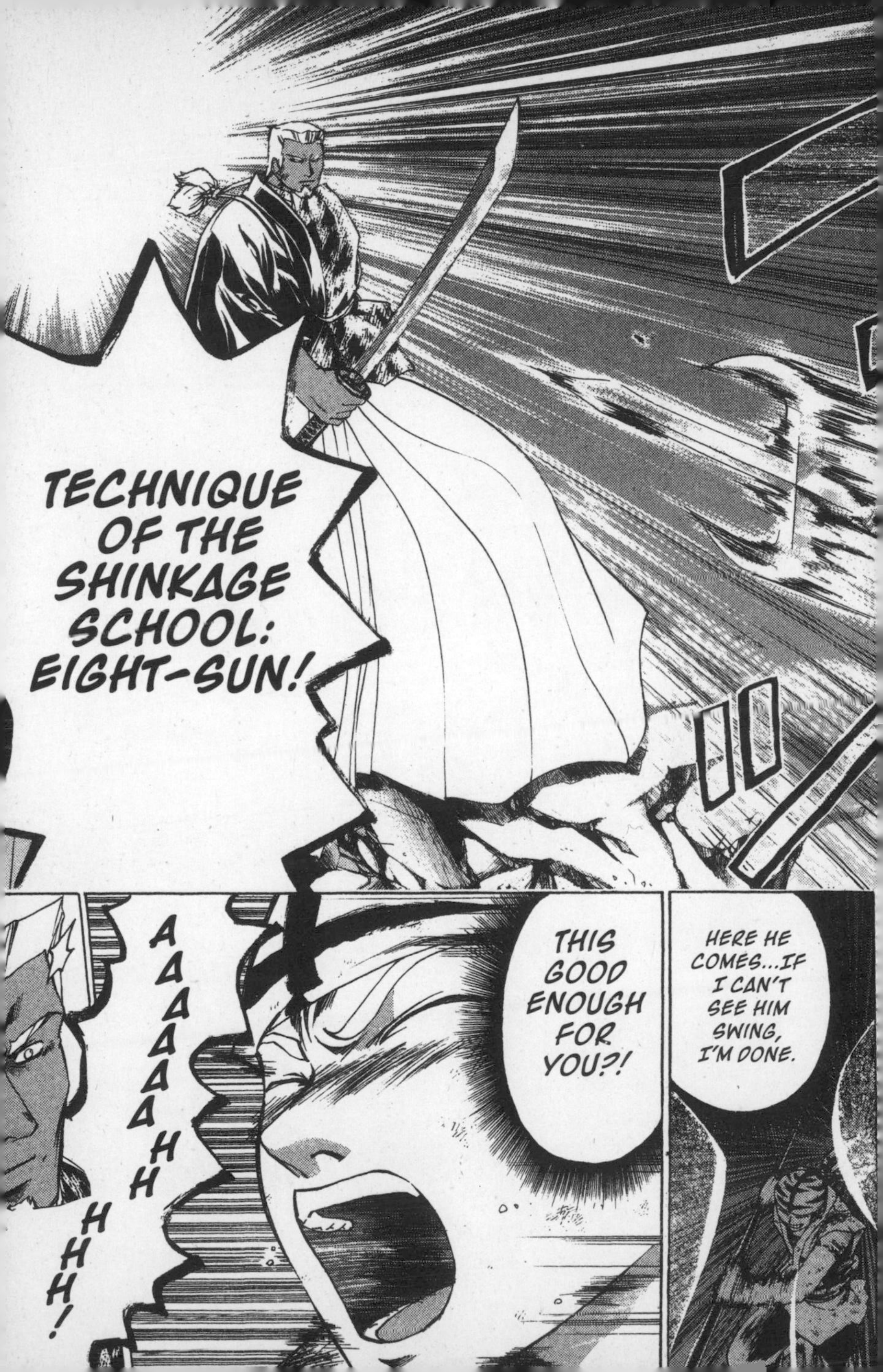
TECHNIQUE OF THE SHINKAGE SCHOOL: EIGHT-SUN!
HERE HE COMES...IF I CAN'T SEE HIM SWING, I'M DONE.
THIS GOOD ENOUGH FOR YOU?!
AAAAAAHHHHH!

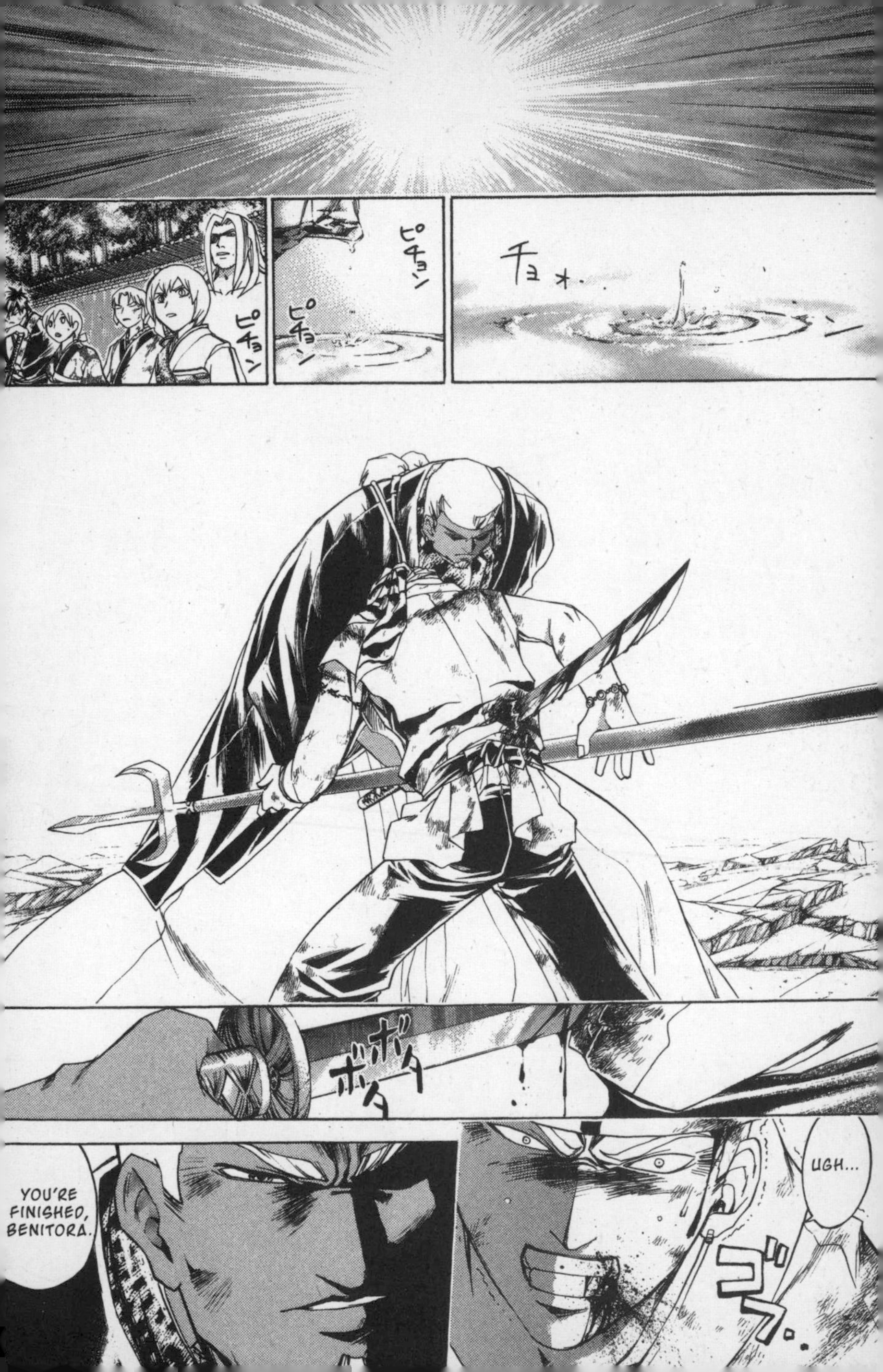
チョォ・・・ン
ピチョン
ピチョン
ピチョン
ボタ
ボタ
UGH...
ゴフ。
YOU'RE FINISHED, BENITORA.

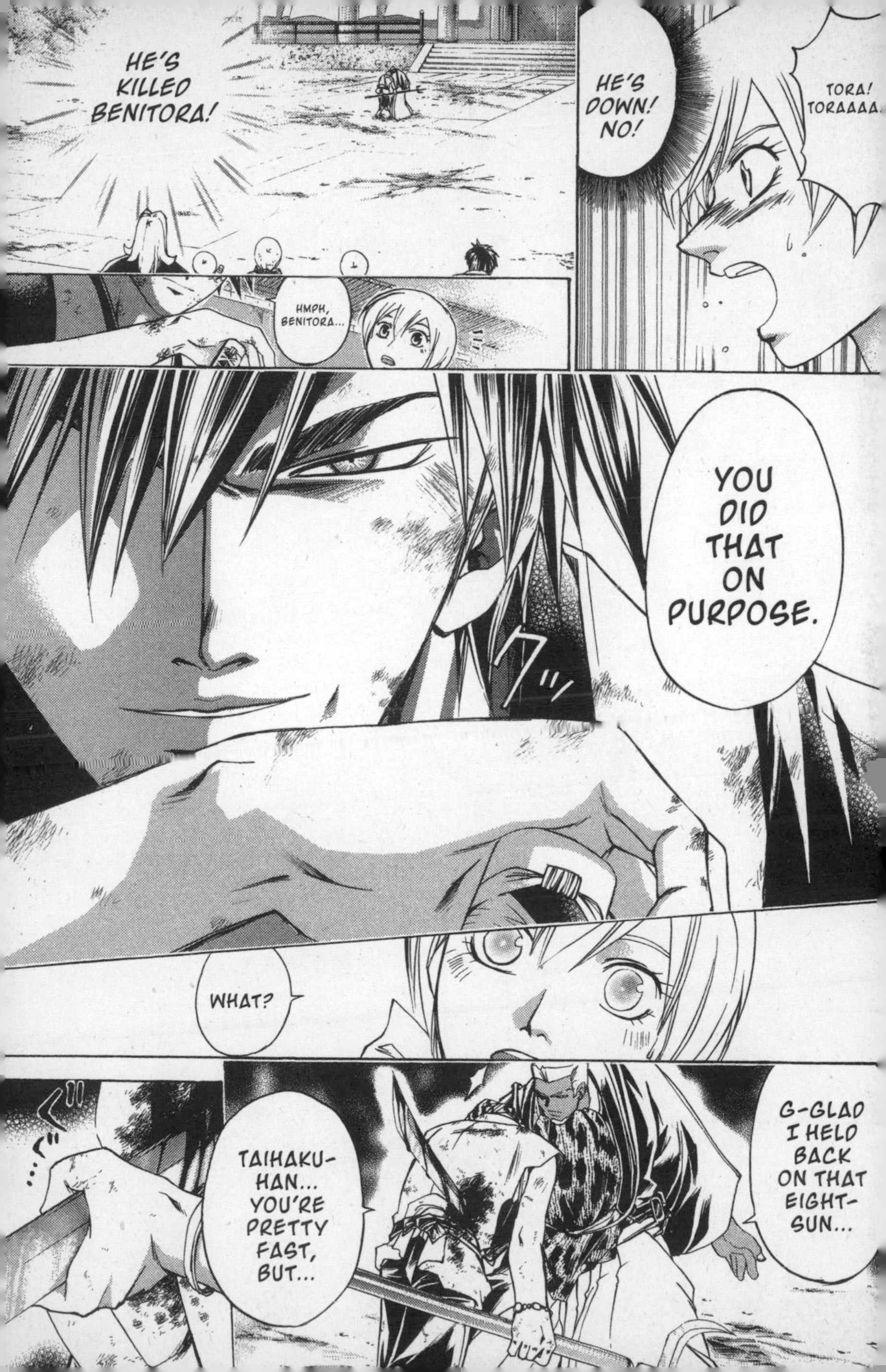
TORA! TORAAAA.
HE'S DOWN! NO!
HE'S KILLED BENITORA!
HMPH, BENITORA...
YOU DID THAT ON PURPOSE.
WHAT?
G-GLAD I HELD BACK ON THAT EIGHT-SUN...
TAIHAKU-HAN... YOU'RE PRETTY FAST, BUT...

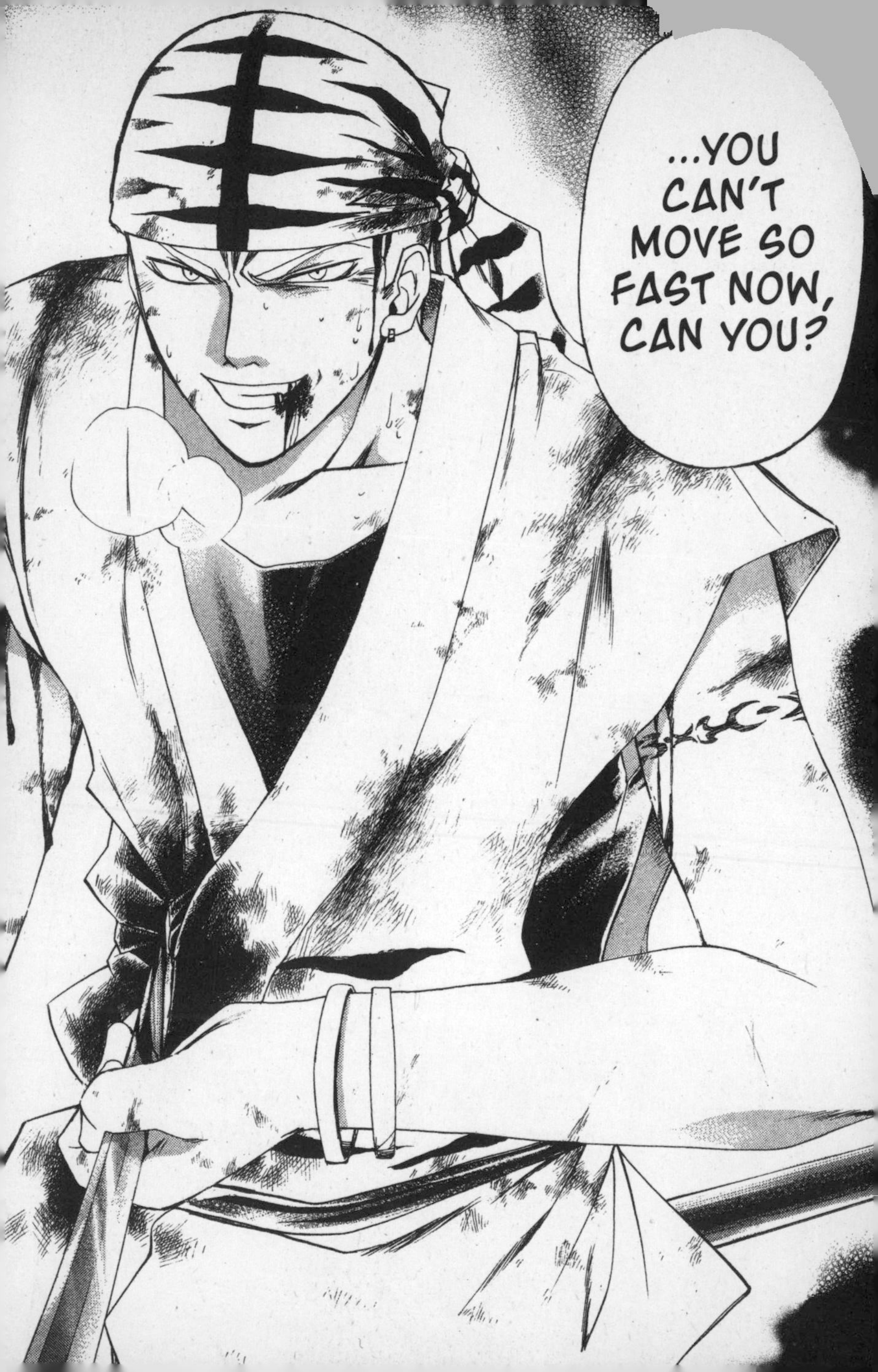
...YOU CAN'T MOVE SO FAST NOW, CAN YOU?

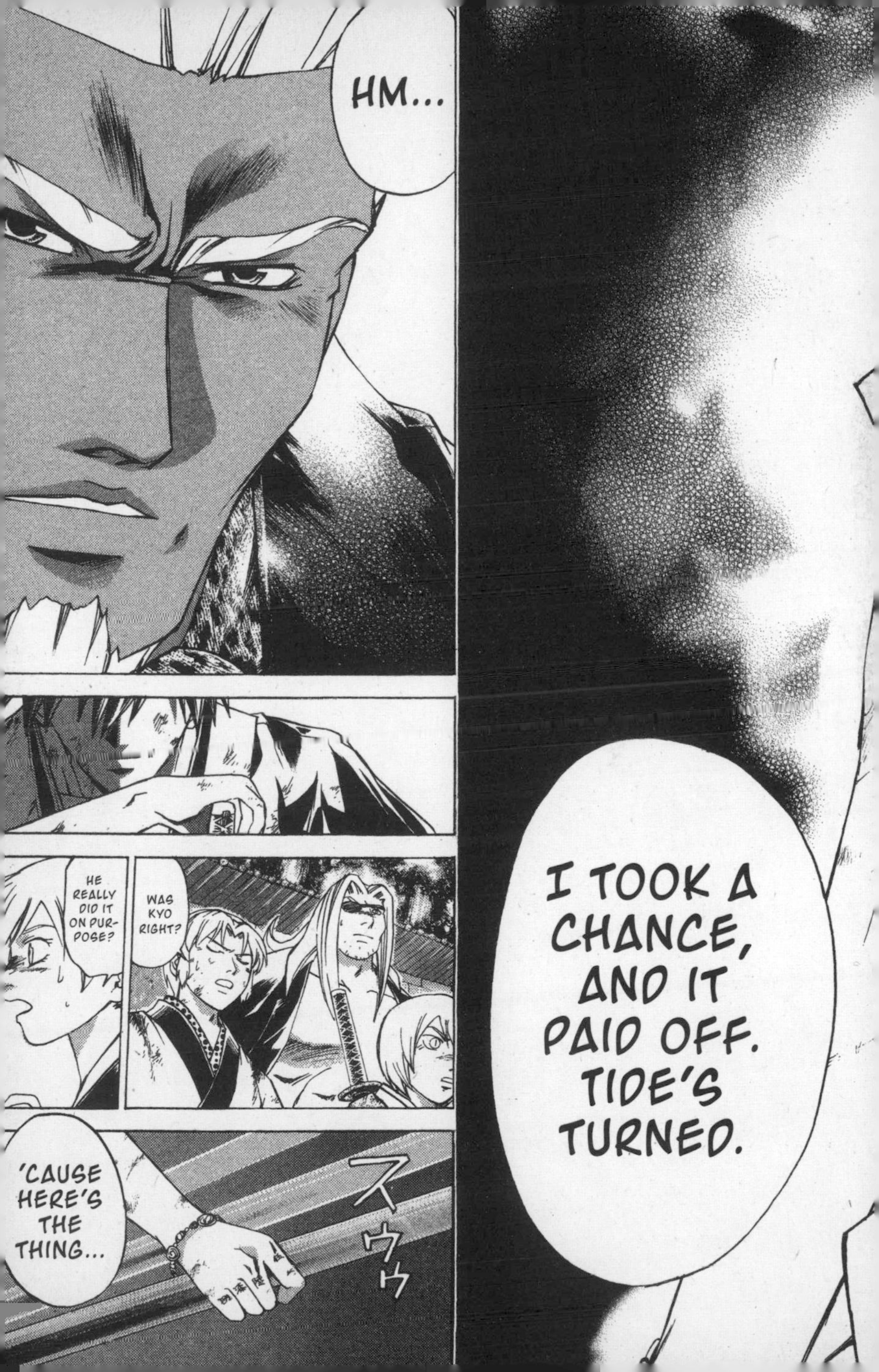
I TOOK A CHANCE, AND IT PAID OFF. TIDE'S TURNED.
HM...
WAS KYO RIGHT?
HE REALLY DID IT ON PURPOSE?
'CAUSE HERE'S THE THING...
スゥ

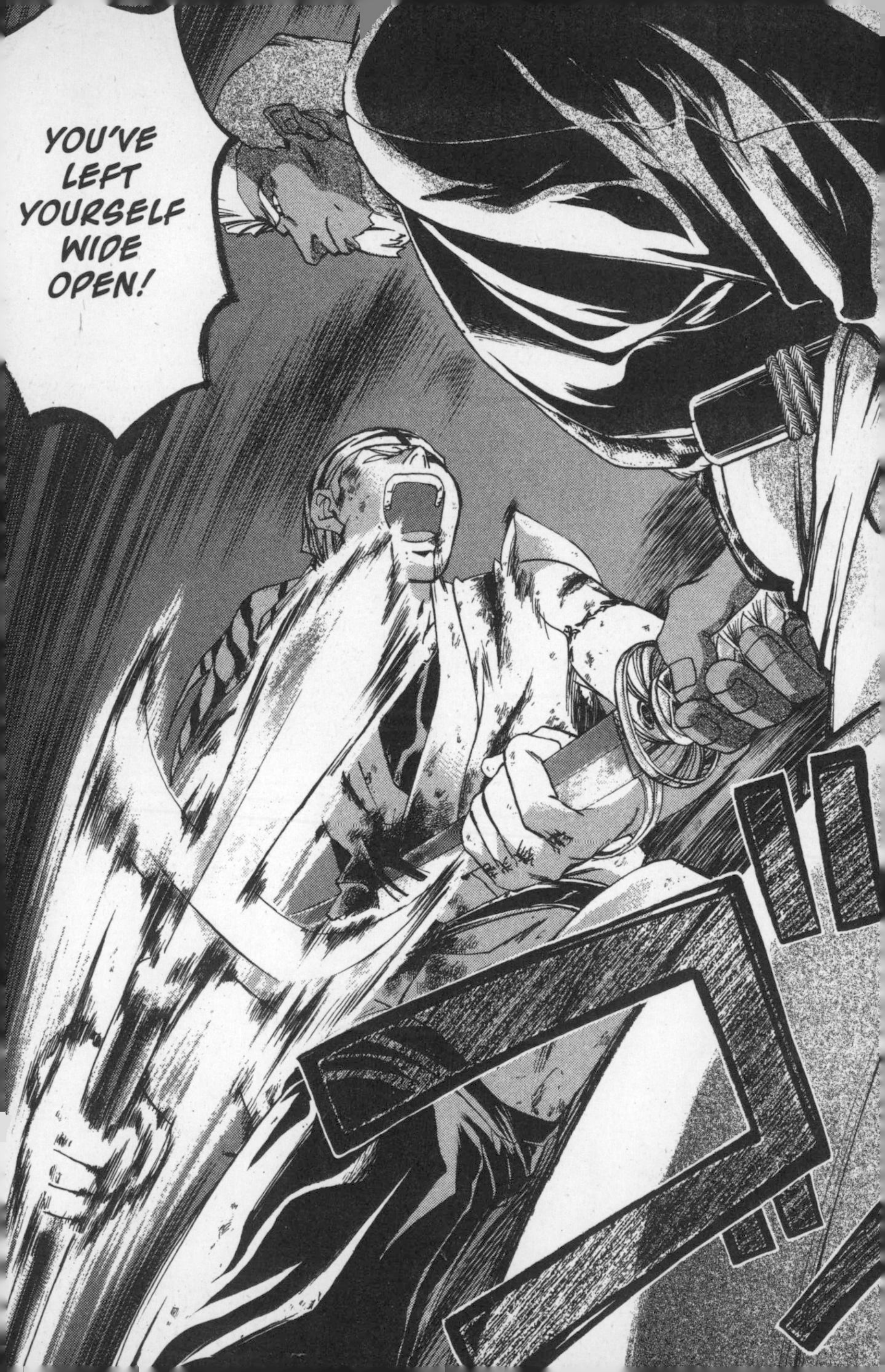
YOU'VE LEFT YOURSELF WIDE OPEN!

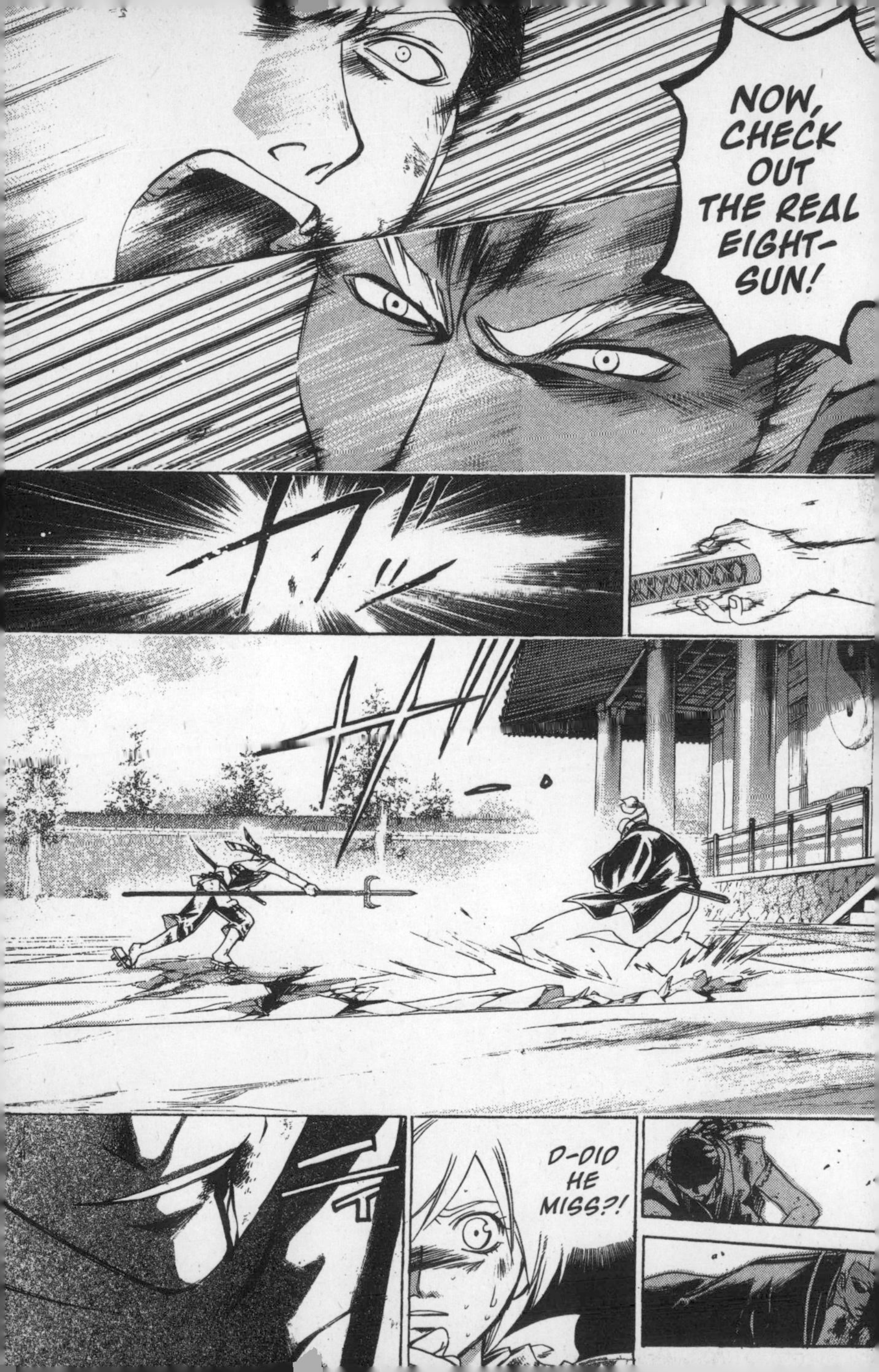
NOW, CHECK OUT THE REAL EIGHT-SUN!
D-DID HE MISS?!

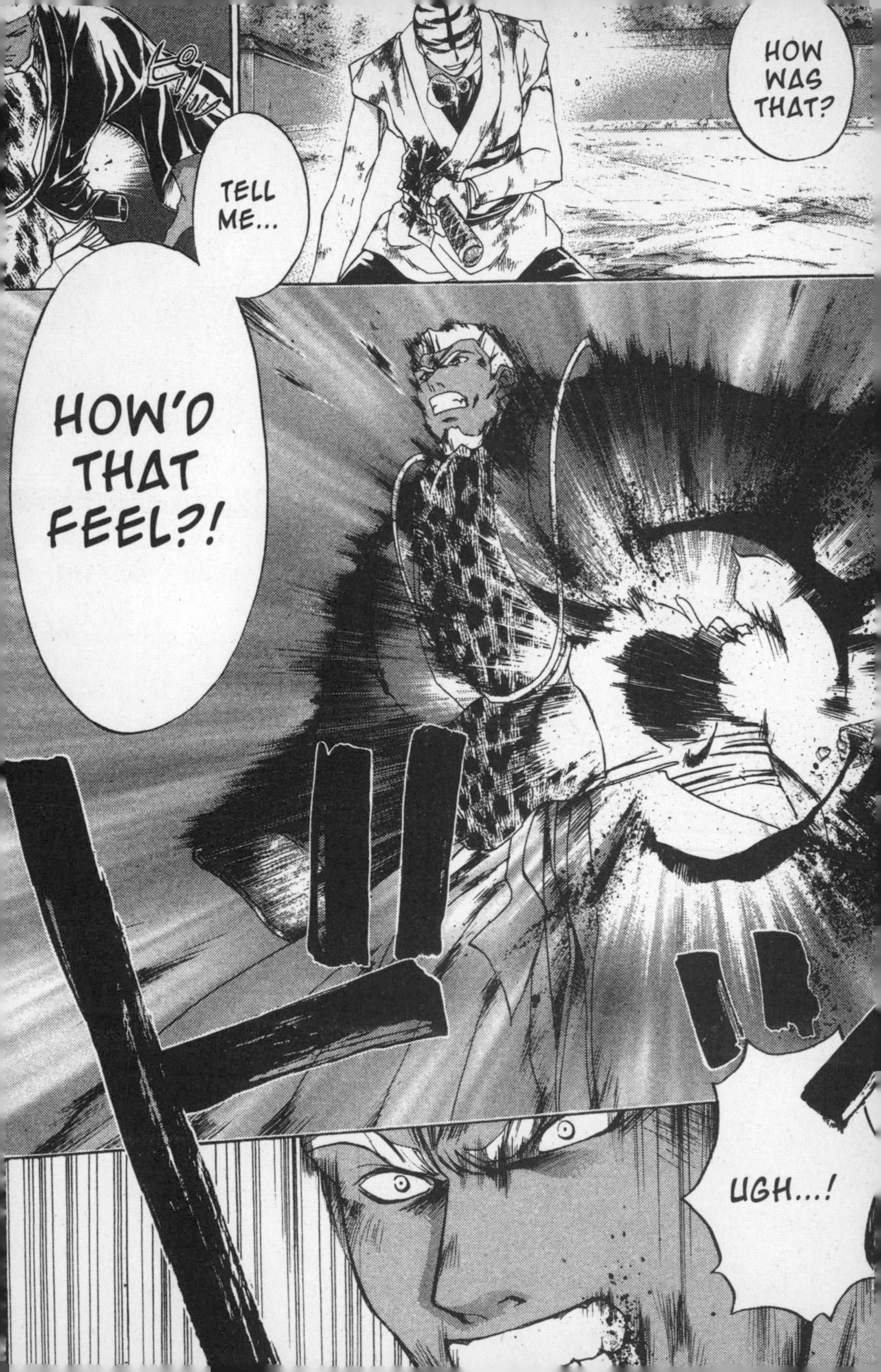
HOW WAS THAT?
TELL ME...
HOW'D THAT FEEL?!
UGH...!

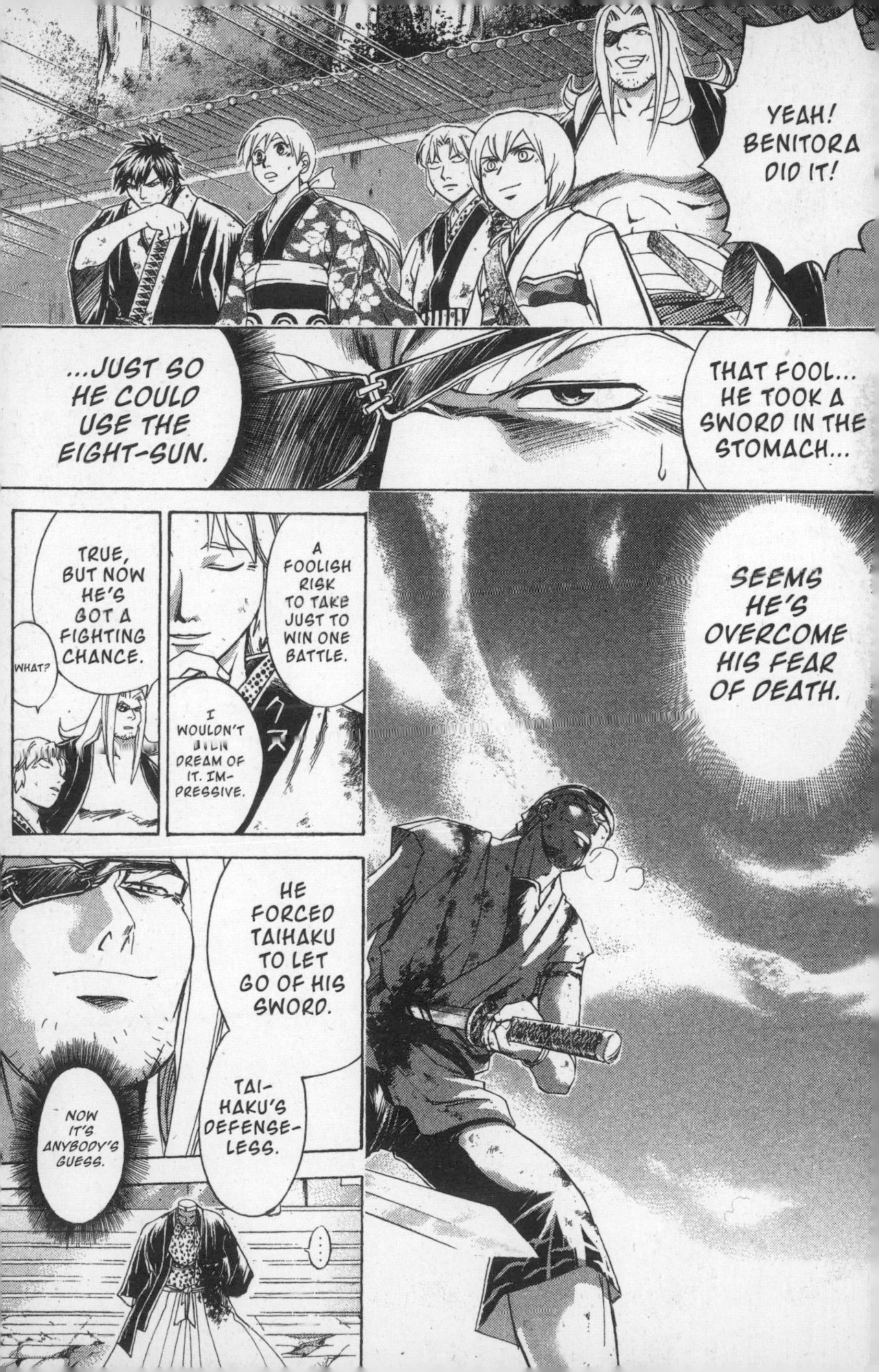
YEAH! BENITORA DID IT!
THAT FOOL... HE TOOK A SWORD IN THE STOMACH...
...JUST SO HE COULD USE THE EIGHT-SUN.
SEEMS HE'S OVERCOME HIS FEAR OF DEATH.
A FOOLISH RISK TO TAKE JUST TO WIN ONE BATTLE.
クス
I WOULDN'T DREAM OF IT. IM-PRESSIVE.
TRUE, BUT NOW HE'S GOT A FIGHTING CHANCE.
WHAT?
HE FORCED TAIHAKU TO LET GO OF HIS SWORD.
TAI-HAKU'S DEFENSE-LESS.
NOW IT'S ANYBODY'S GUESS.
...

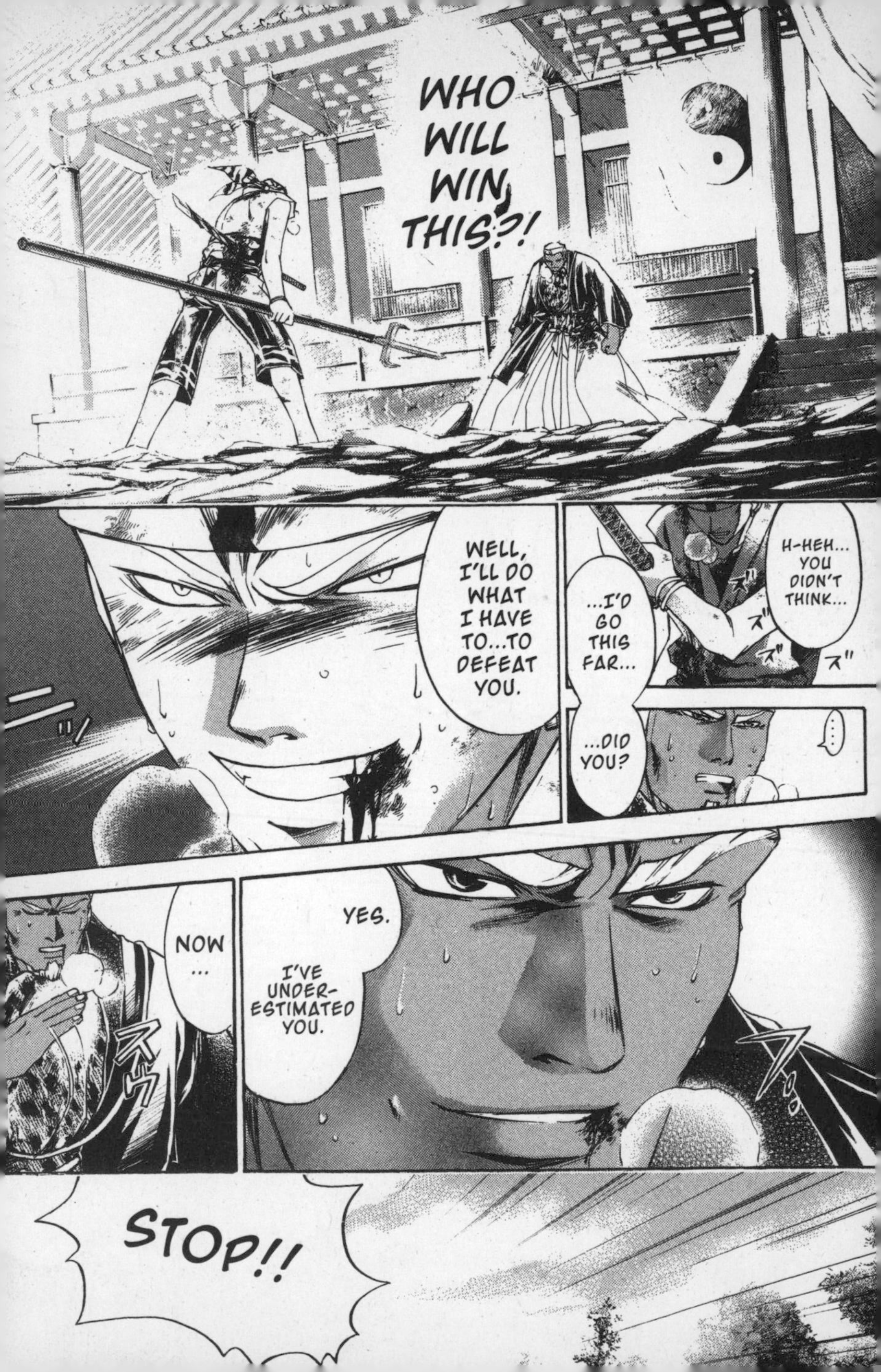
WHO WILL WIN THIS?!
H-HEH... YOU DIDN'T THINK...
...I'D GO THIS FAR...
...DID YOU?
...
WELL, I'LL DO WHAT I HAVE TO...TO DEFEAT YOU.
YES.
I'VE UNDER-ESTIMATED YOU.
NOW ...
STOP!!

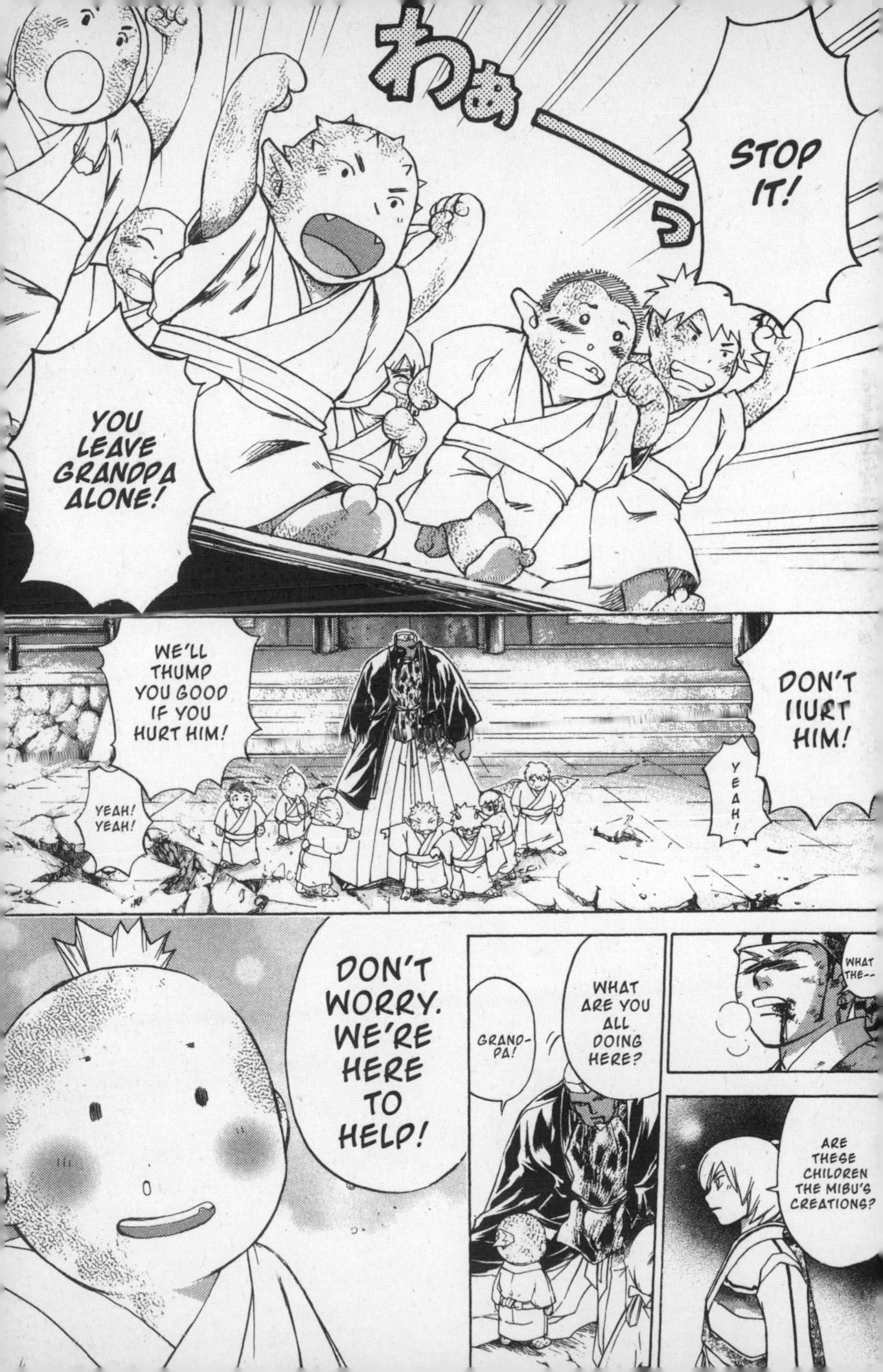

わぁーっ
STOP IT!
YOU LEAVE GRANDPA ALONE!
DON'T HURT HIM!
YEAH!
WE'LL THUMP YOU GOOD IF YOU HURT HIM!
YEAH! YEAH!
WHAT THE--
ARE THESE CHILDREN THE MIBU'S CREATIONS?
WHAT ARE YOU ALL DOING HERE?
GRAND-PA!
DON'T WORRY. WE'RE HERE TO HELP!

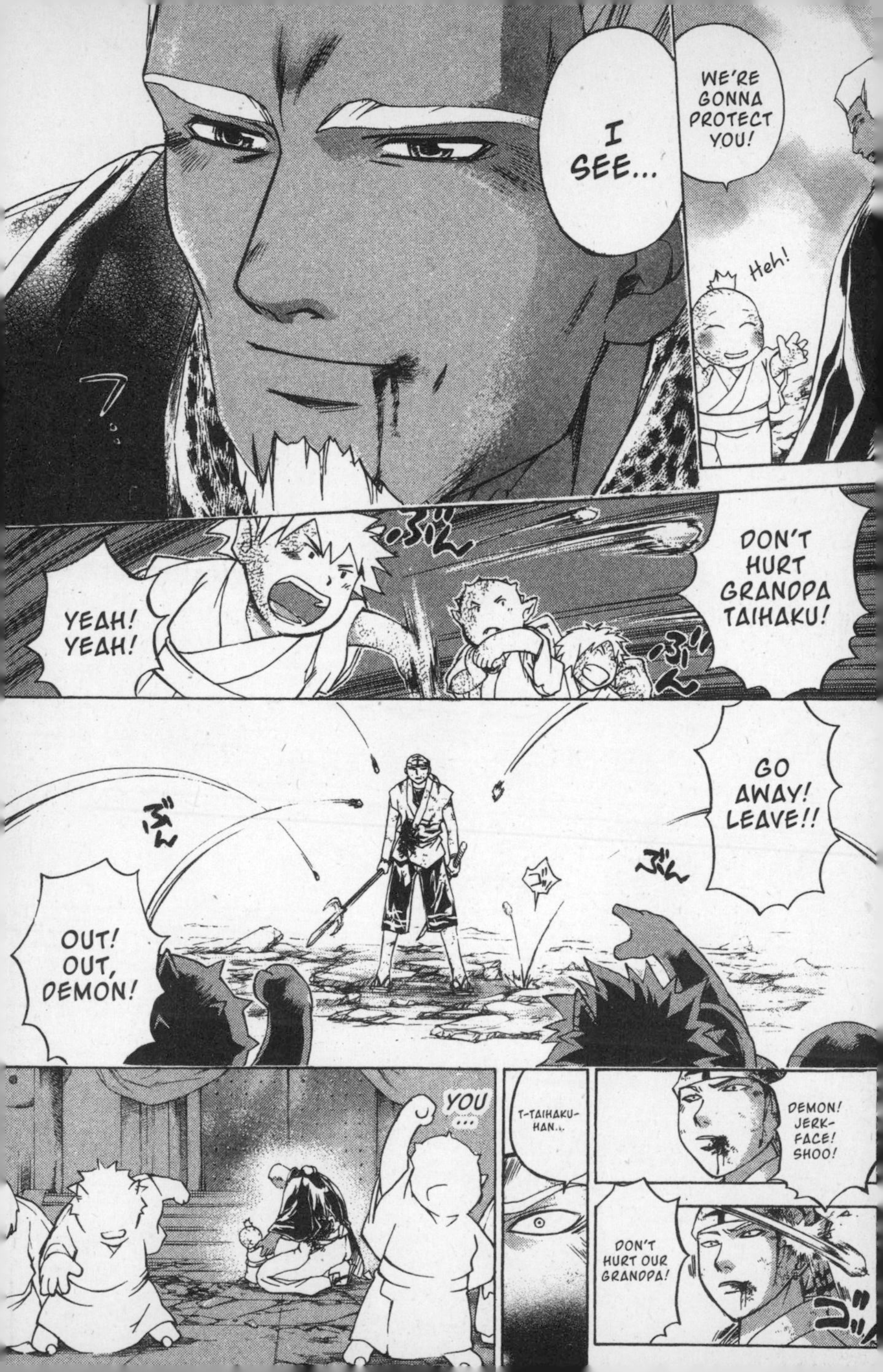
WE'RE GONNA PROTECT YOU!
Heh!
I SEE...
DON'T HURT GRANDPA TAIHAKU!
ぶん
ぶん
YEAH! YEAH!
GO AWAY! LEAVE!!
ぶん
ぶん
OUT! OUT, DEMON!
DEMON! JERK-FACE! SHOO!
DON'T HURT OUR GRANDPA!
T-TAIHAKU-HAN...
YOU ...

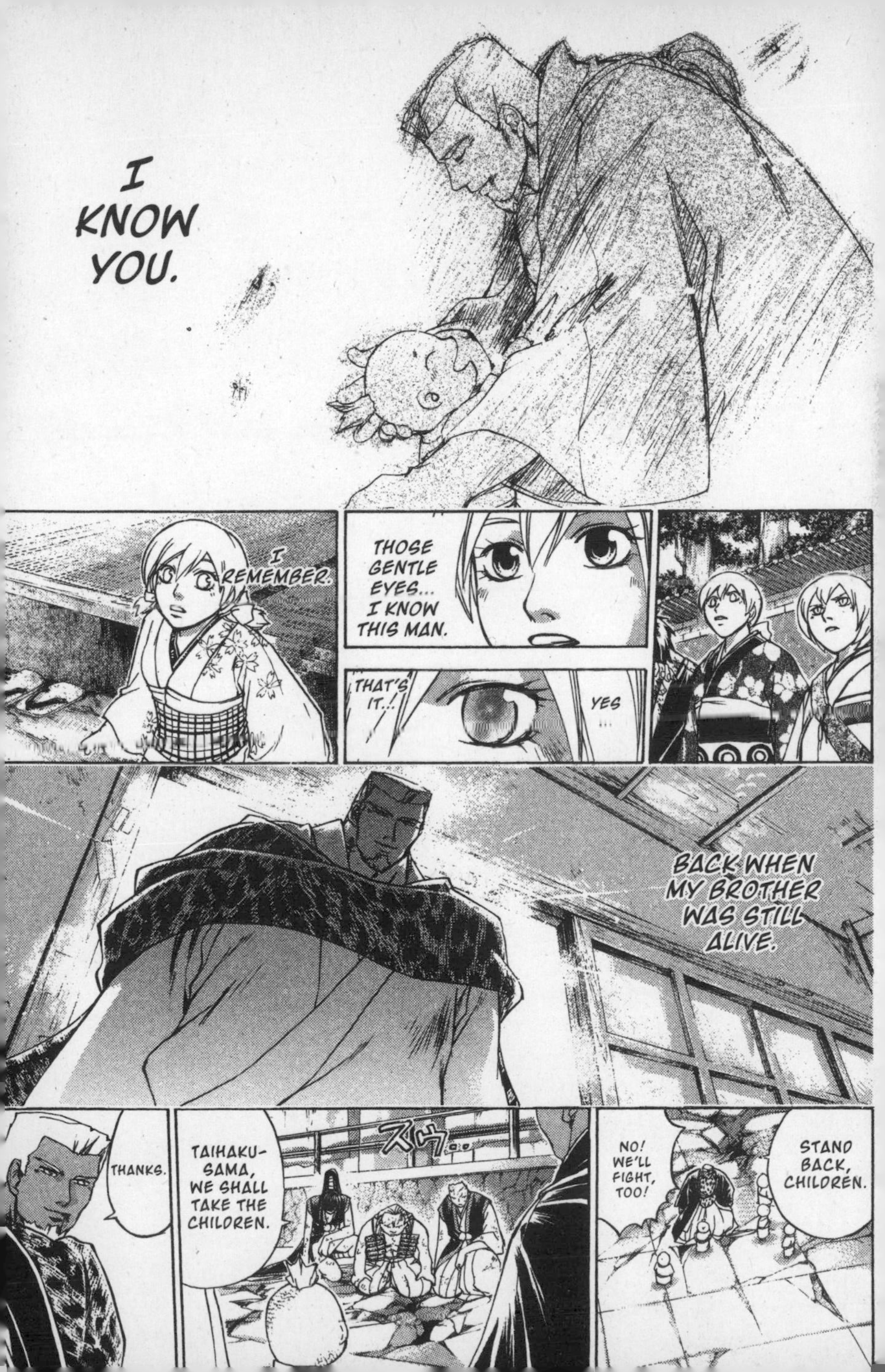
I KNOW YOU.
THOSE GENTLE EYES... I KNOW THIS MAN.
YES ...
THAT'S IT...
I REMEMBER.
BACK WHEN MY BROTHER WAS STILL ALIVE.
STAND BACK, CHILDREN.
NO! WE'LL FIGHT, TOO!
スゥ..
TAIHAKU-SAMA, WE SHALL TAKE THE CHILDREN.
THANKS.

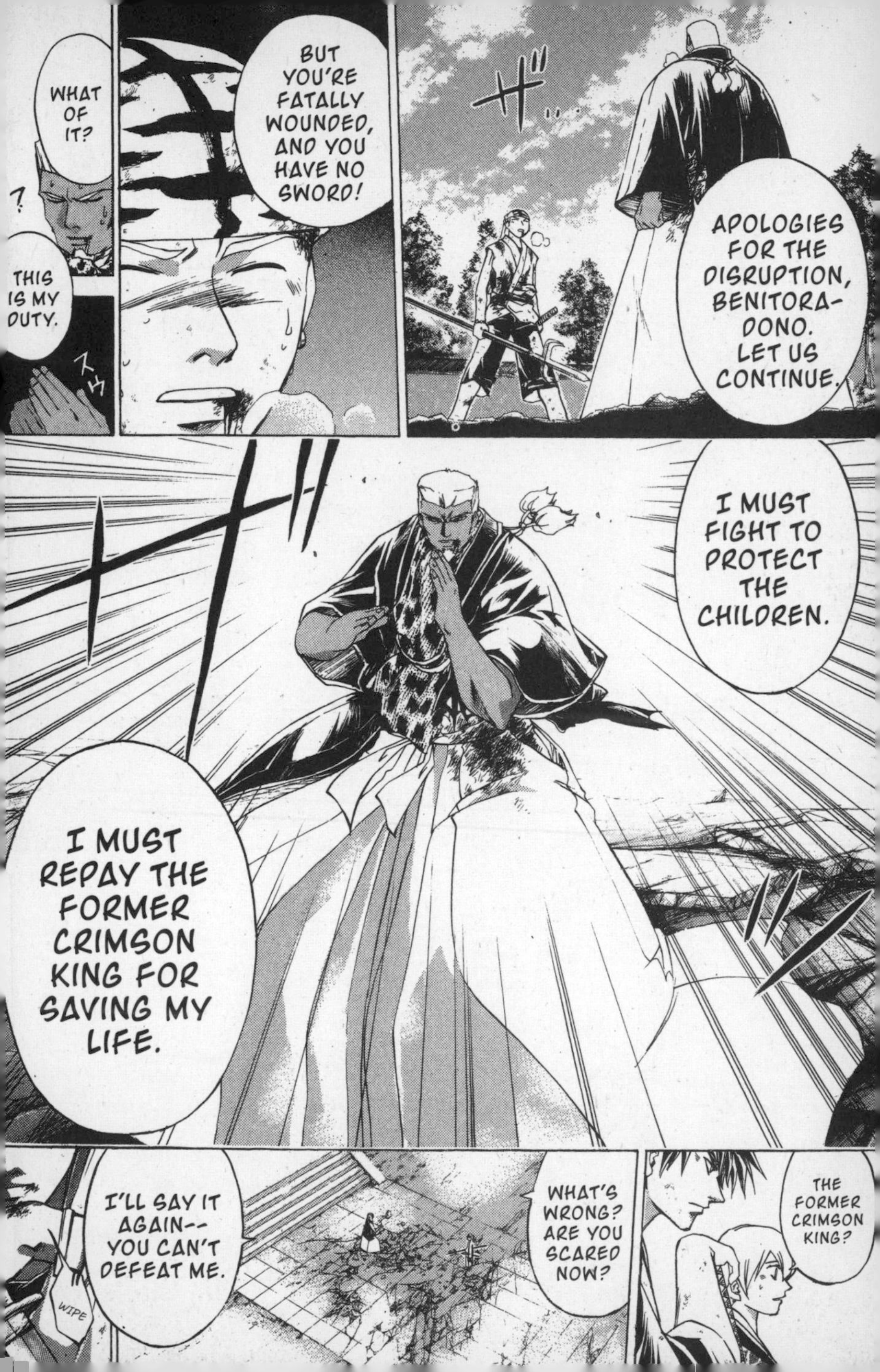
ザ…
APOLOGIES FOR THE DISRUPTION, BENITORA-DONO. LET US CONTINUE.
BUT YOU'RE FATALLY WOUNDED, AND YOU HAVE NO SWORD!
WHAT OF IT?
?
THIS IS MY DUTY.
スッ
I MUST FIGHT TO PROTECT THE CHILDREN.
I MUST REPAY THE FORMER CRIMSON KING FOR SAVING MY LIFE.
THE FORMER CRIMSON KING?
WHAT'S WRONG? ARE YOU SCARED NOW?
I'LL SAY IT AGAIN-- YOU CAN'T DEFEAT ME.
WIPE

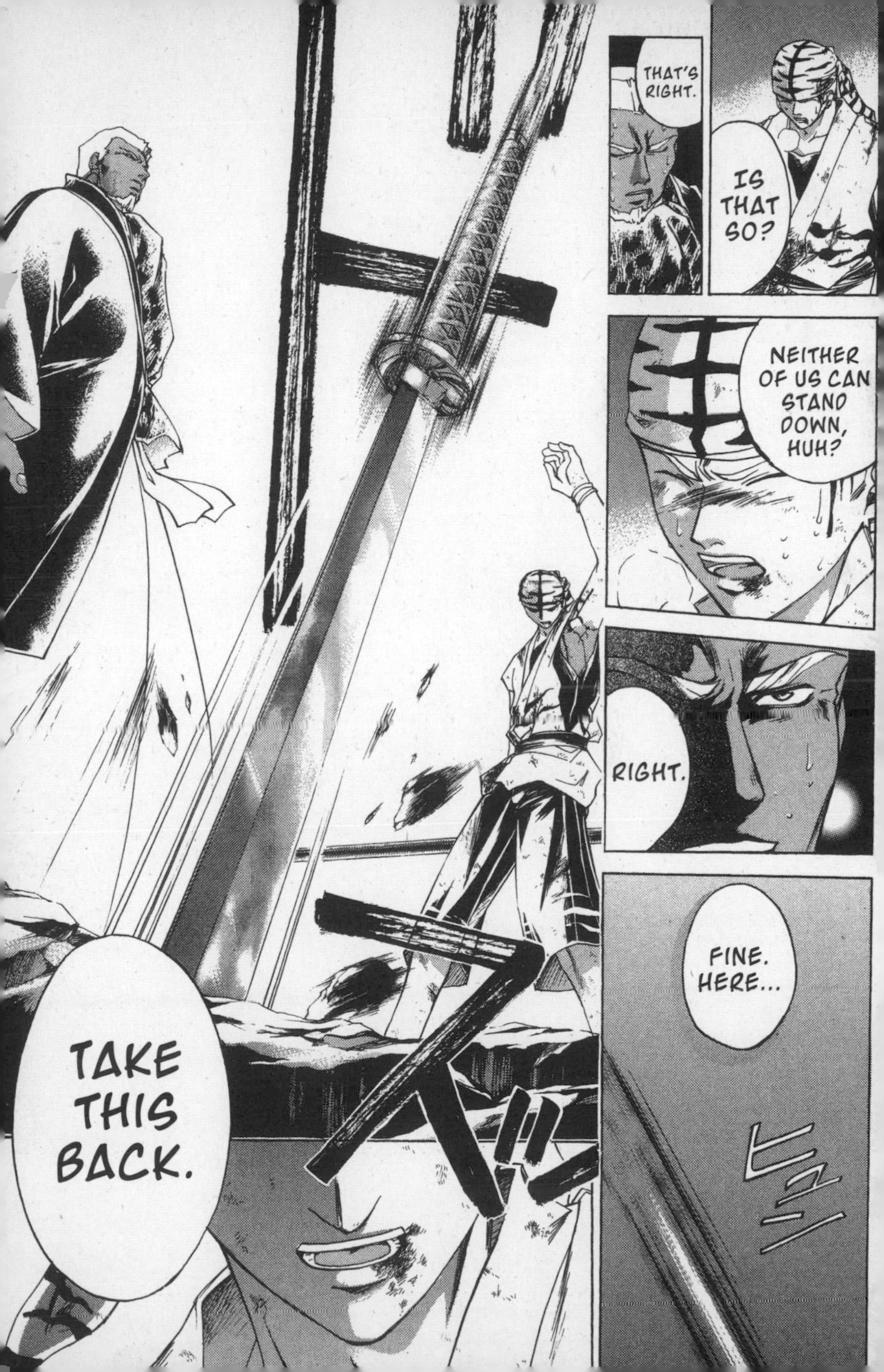
IS THAT SO?
THAT'S RIGHT.
NEITHER OF US CAN STAND DOWN, HUH?
RIGHT.
FINE. HERE...
ヒュン
TAKE THIS BACK.

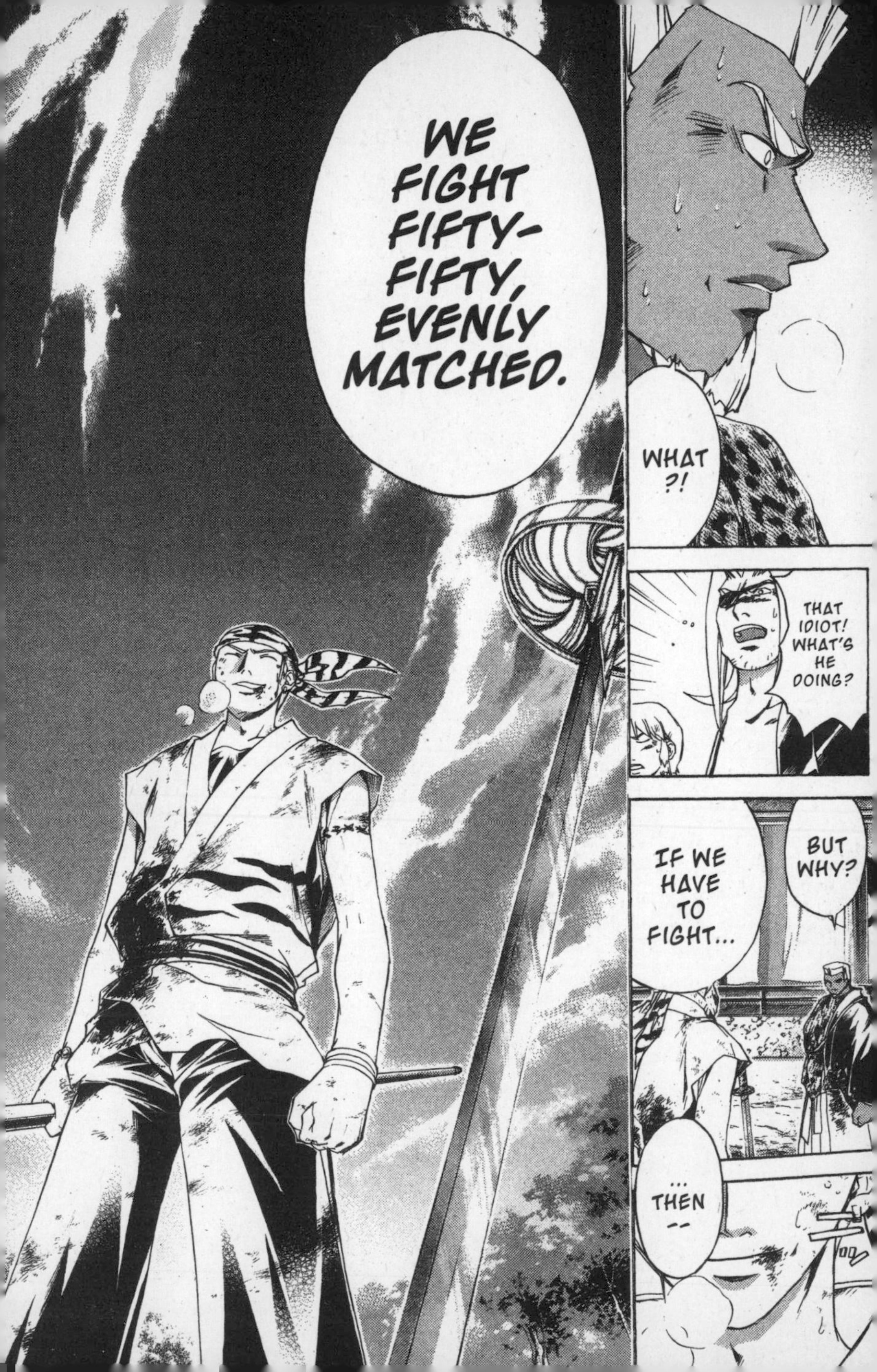
WHAT?!
THAT IDIOT! WHAT'S HE DOING?
BUT WHY?
IF WE HAVE TO FIGHT...
...THEN --
WE FIGHT FIFTY-FIFTY, EVENLY MATCHED.

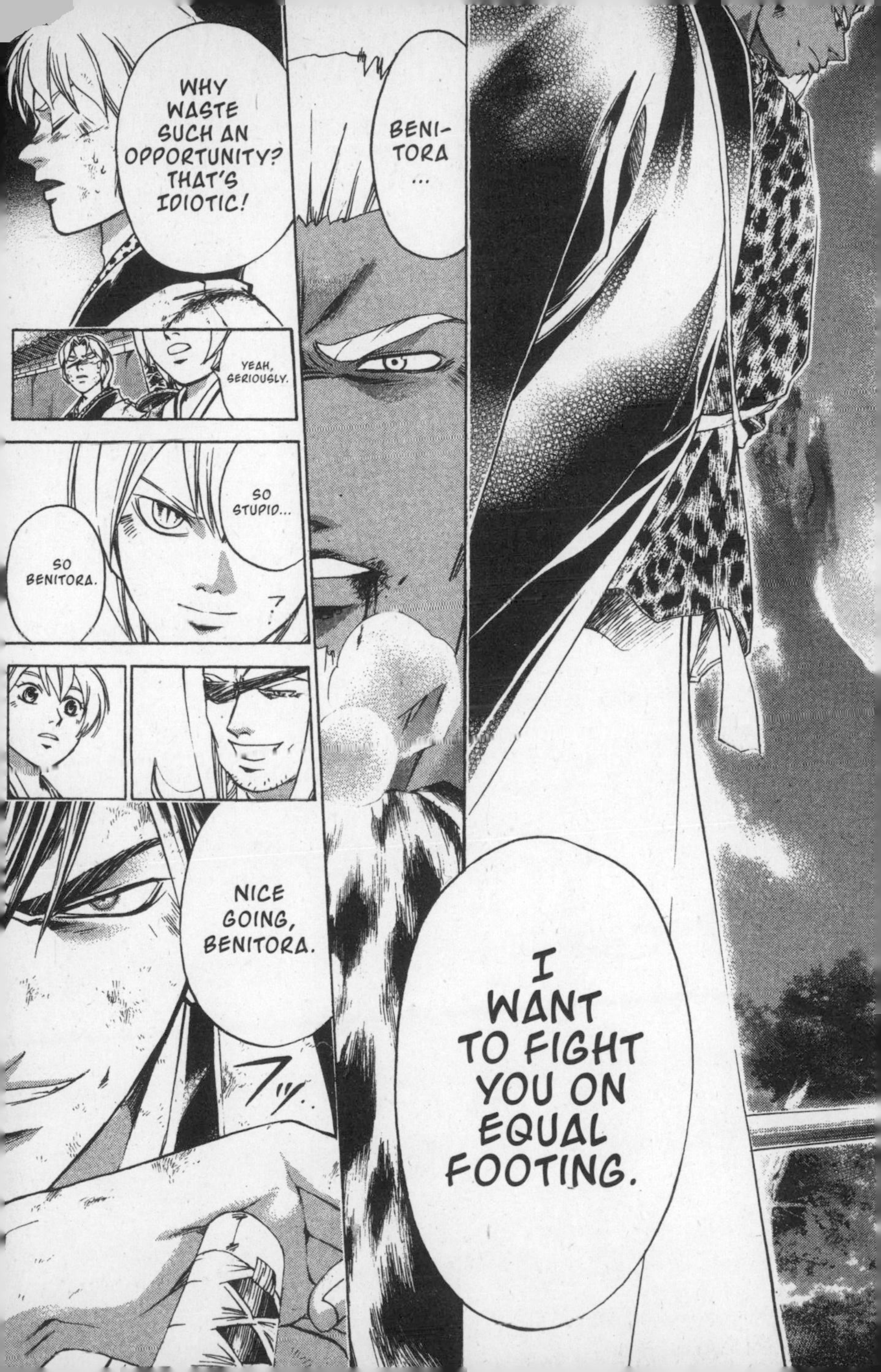
I WANT TO FIGHT YOU ON EQUAL FOOTING.
BENITORA...
WHY WASTE SUCH AN OPPORTUNITY? THAT'S IDIOTIC!
YEAH, SERIOUSLY.
SO STUPID...
SO BENITORA.
NICE GOING, BENITORA.
フッ..

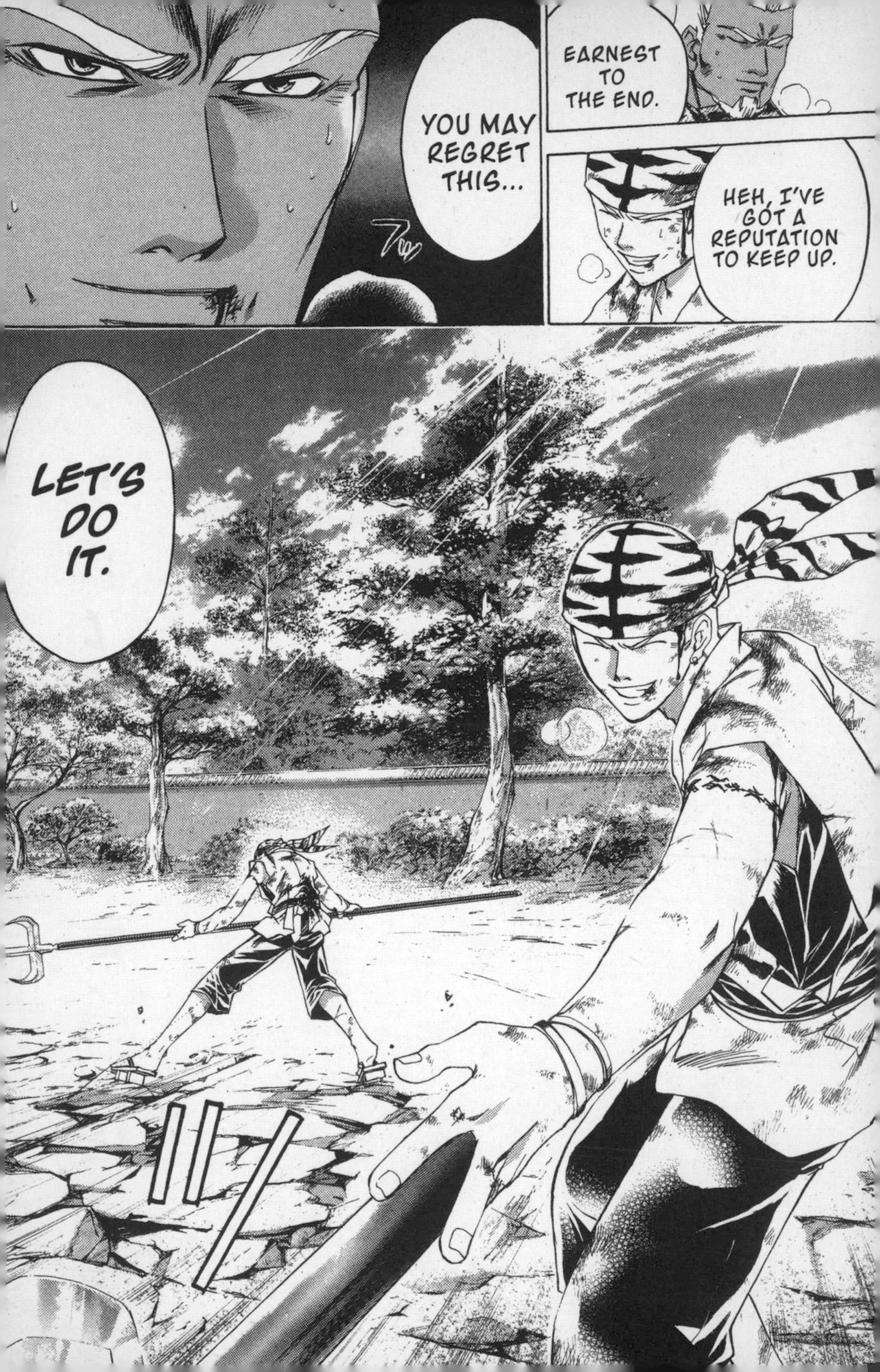
EARNEST TO THE END.
HEH, I'VE GOT A REPUTATION TO KEEP UP.
YOU MAY REGRET THIS...
LET'S DO IT.

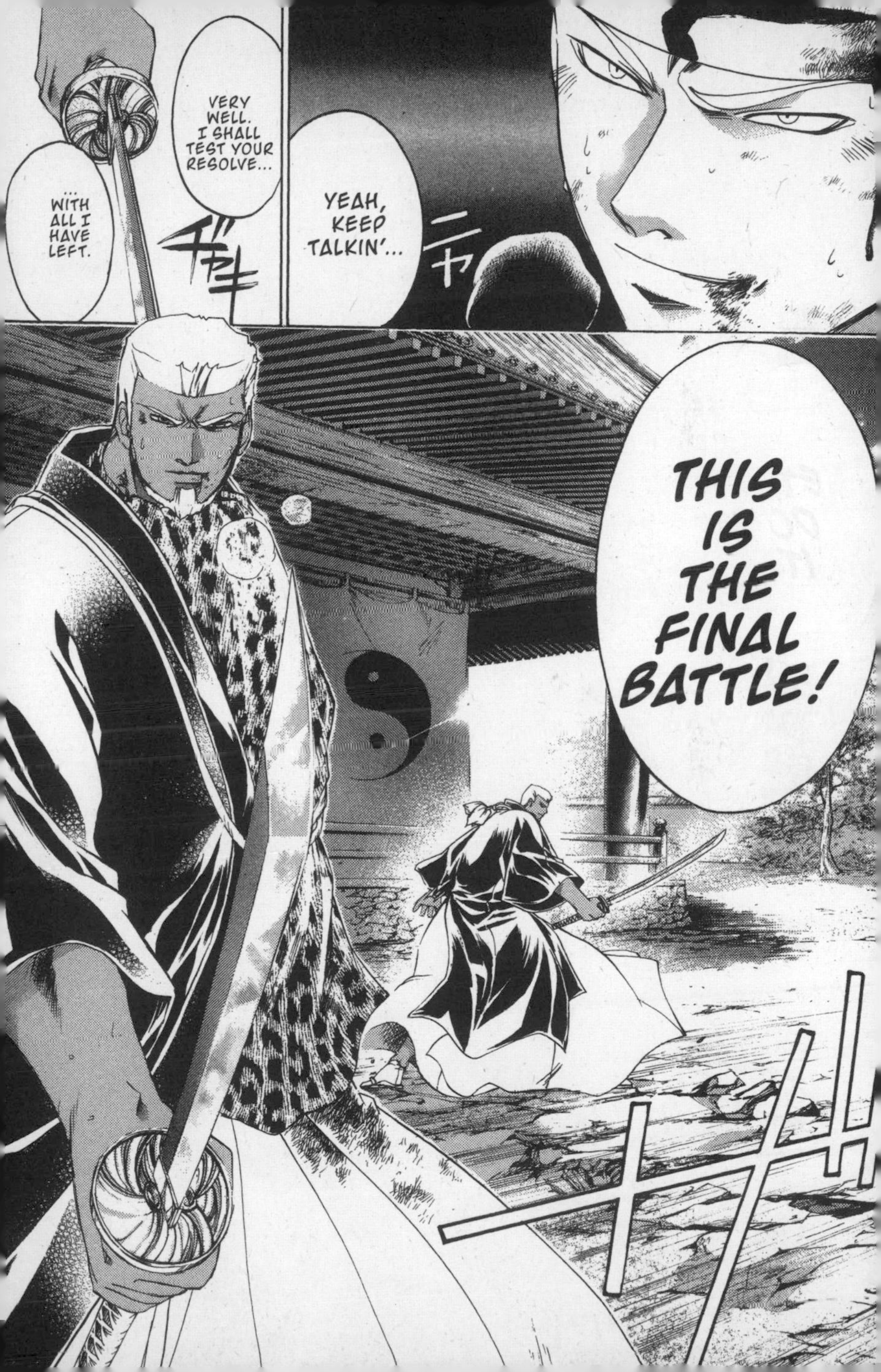
YEAH, KEEP TALKIN'...
ニヤ
VERY WELL. I SHALL TEST YOUR RESOLVE...
...WITH ALL I HAVE LEFT.
THIS IS THE FINAL BATTLE!

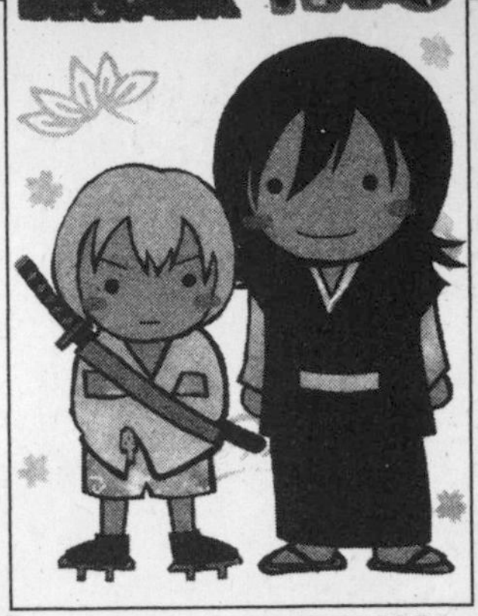

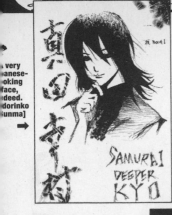

A colored illustration! Truly a masterpiece! [Akane / Kyoto]

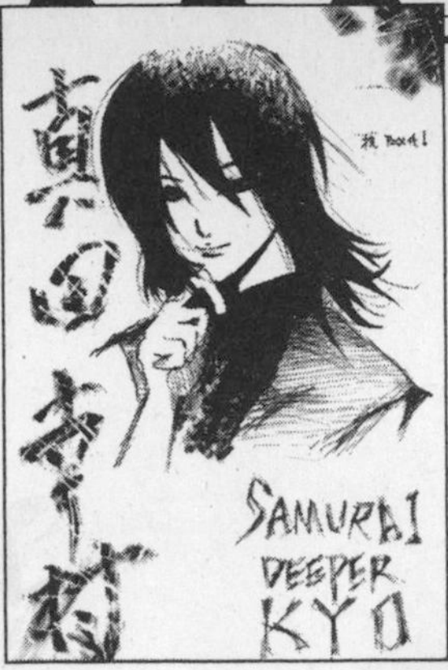

SAMURAI
DEEPER
KYO

very
anese-
oking
face,
deed.
dorinko
unma]

THANKS FOR YOUR INPUT REGARDING THE POSTCARD CORNER! I'M STILL COLLECTING THEM, SO HERE THEY ARE PRESENTED AS IN PREVIOUS ISSUES!

Manly-man! [Imanishi Kazura / Kyoto]

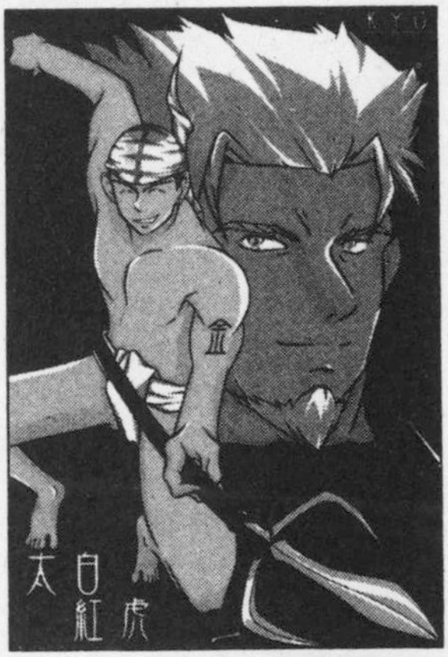

KYO

A steaming hot Tora... [Hakumai / Niigata]

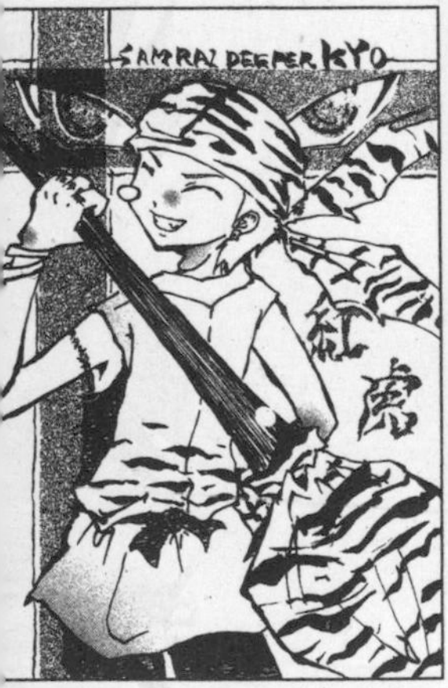

SAMRAI DEEPER KYO

DRAW LIKE KAMIJYO
上条(かみじょう)に挑戦(ちょうせん)!

Bloody makeup! [Watanabe Chihiro / Fukushima]

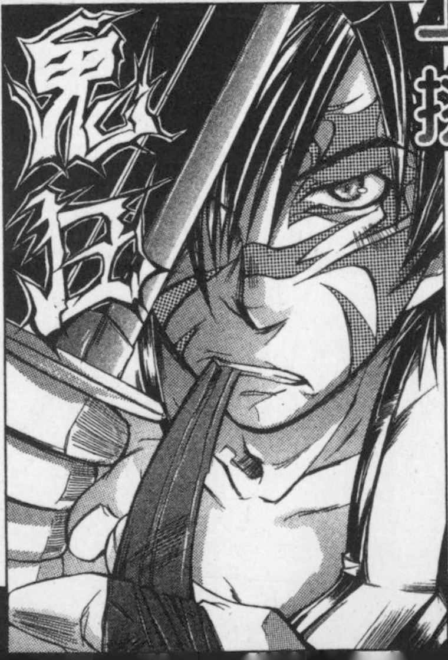

Those were the good old days. [Kayuta / Hiroshima]

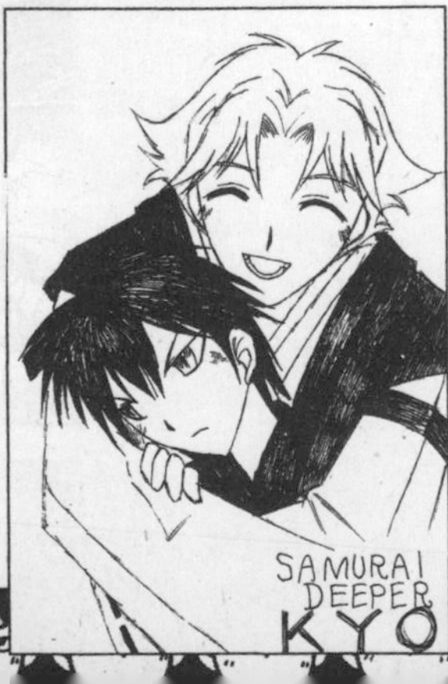

SAMURAI
DEEPER
KYO

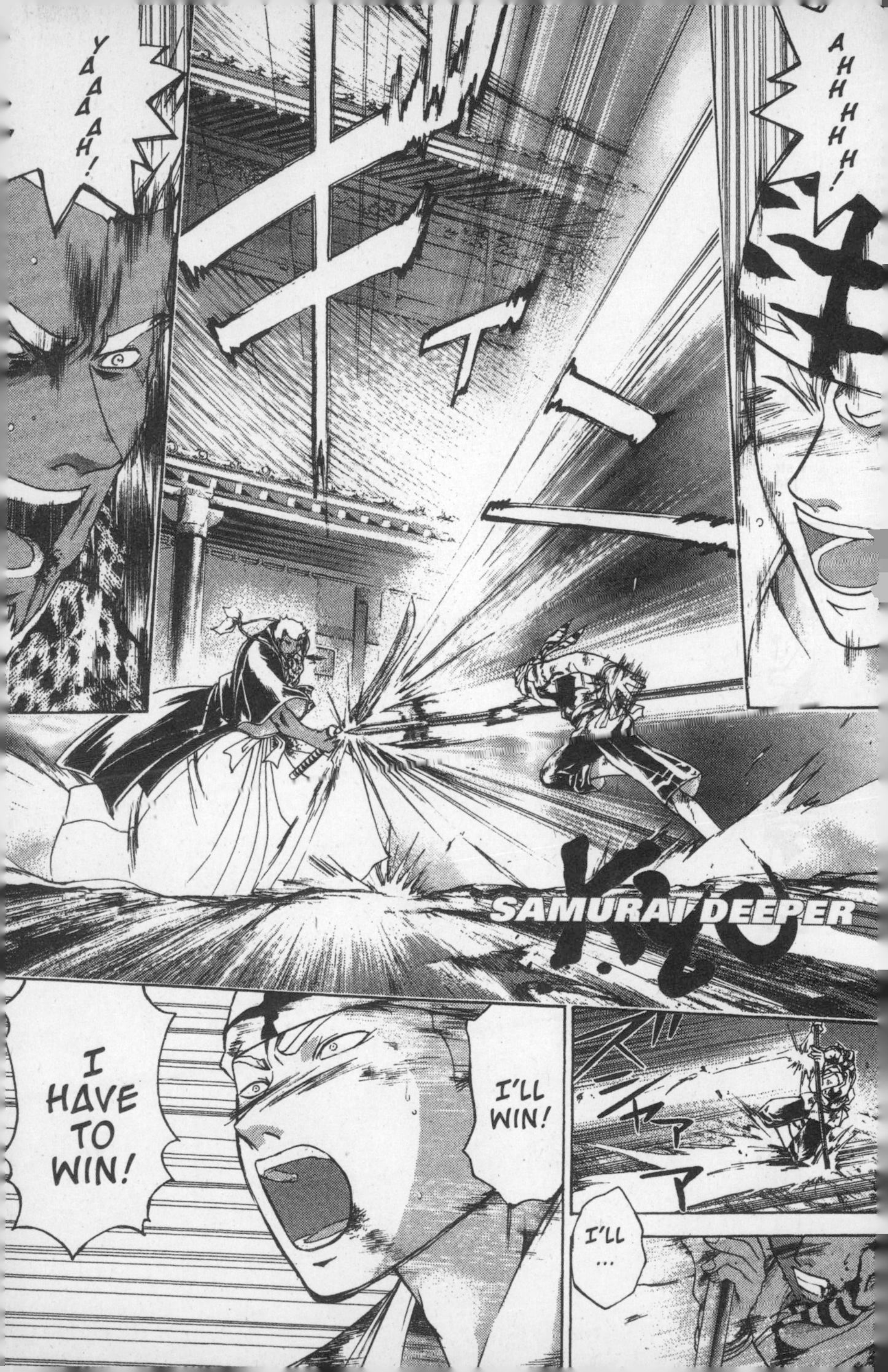
AHHHHH!
YAAAAH!
SAMURAI DEEPER KYO
I'LL ...
I'LL WIN!
I HAVE TO WIN!

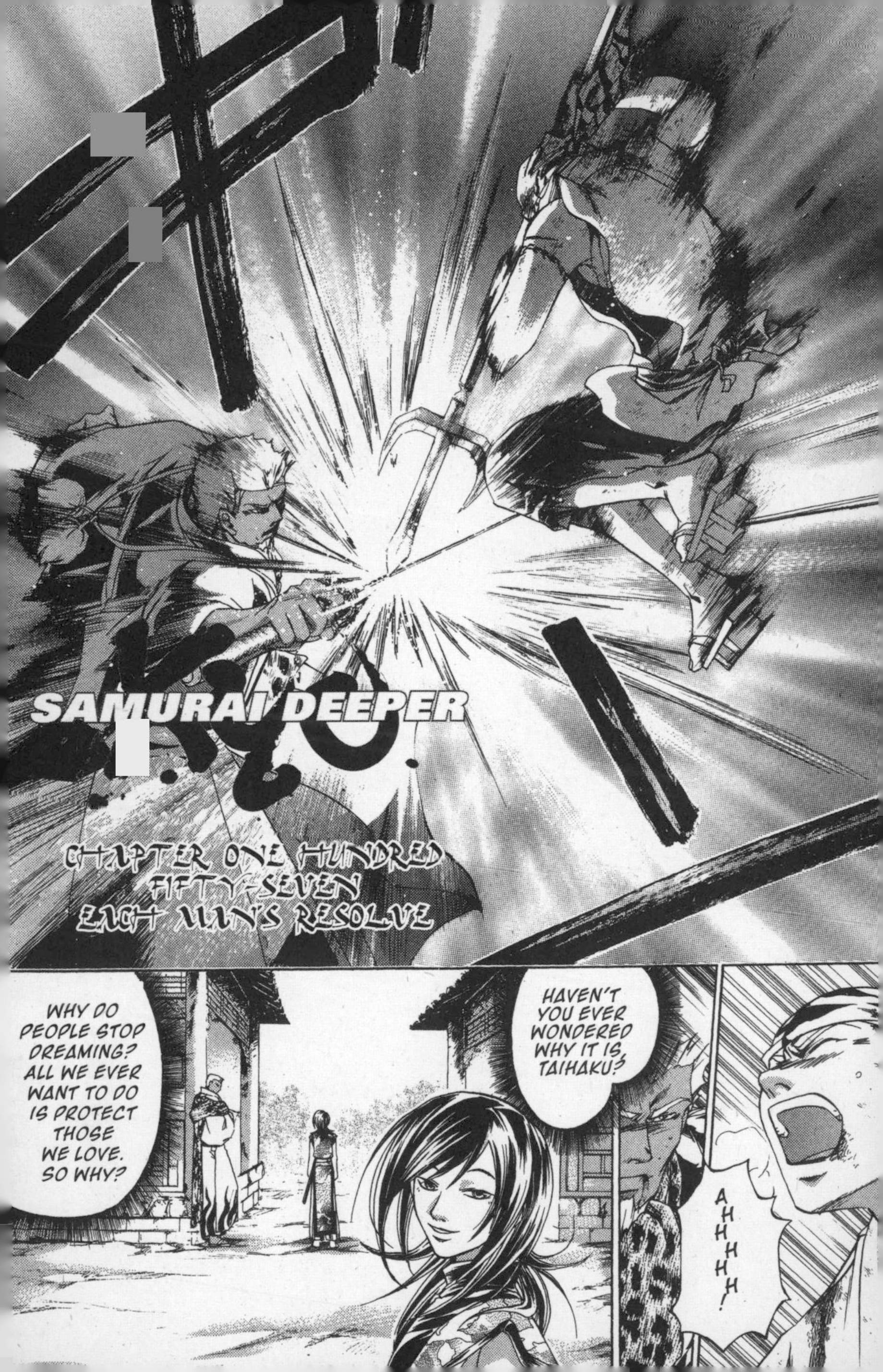
SAMURAI DEEPER
CHAPTER ONE HUNDRED FIFTY-SEVEN
EACH MAN'S RESOLVE
AHHHHH!
HAVEN'T YOU EVER WONDERED WHY IT IS TAIHAKU?
WHY DO PEOPLE STOP DREAMING? ALL WE EVER WANT TO DO IS PROTECT THOSE WE LOVE. SO WHY?

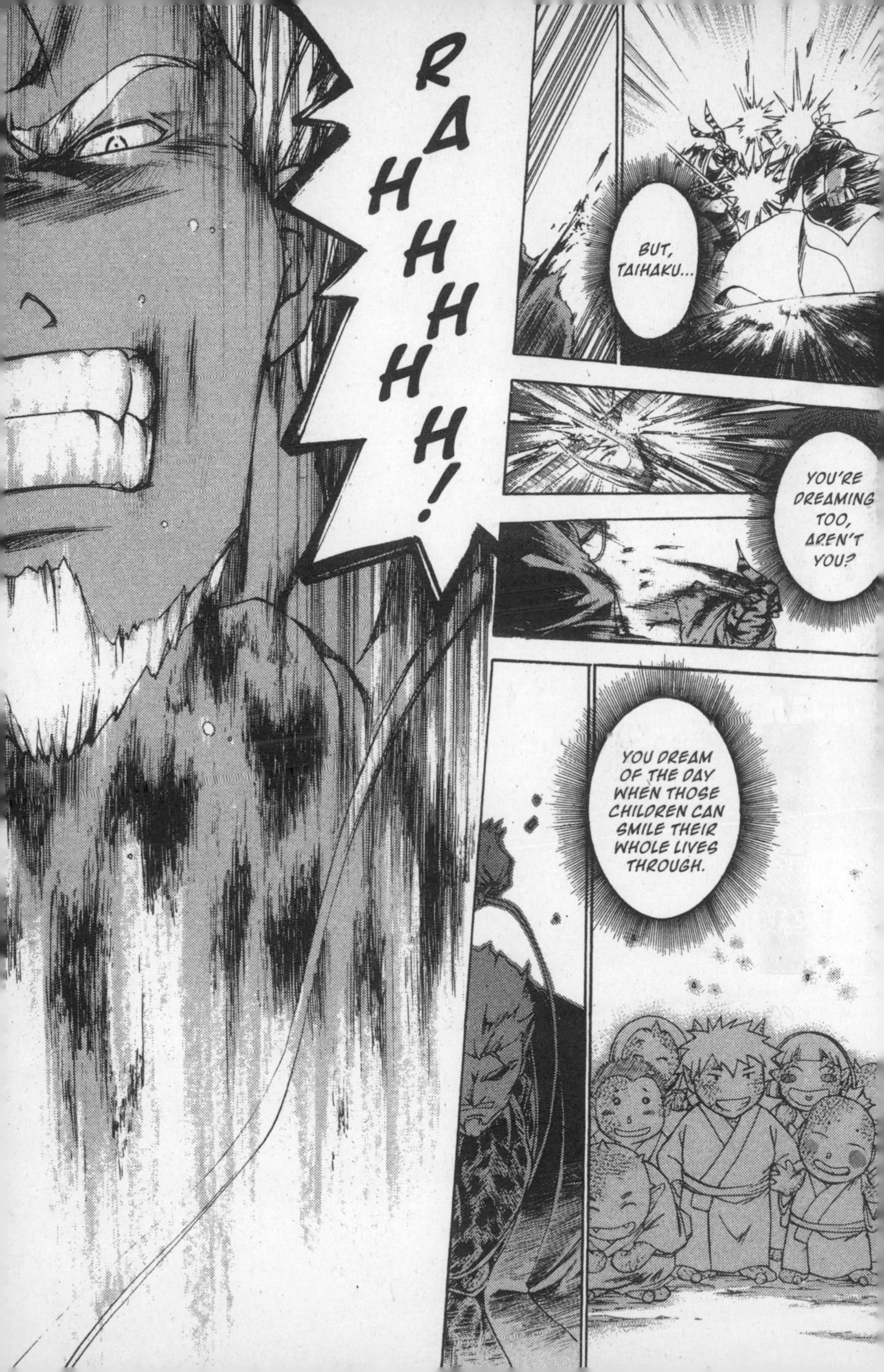
BUT, TAIHAKU...
YOU'RE DREAMING TOO, AREN'T YOU?
YOU DREAM OF THE DAY WHEN THOSE CHILDREN CAN SMILE THEIR WHOLE LIVES THROUGH.
RAHHHHH!

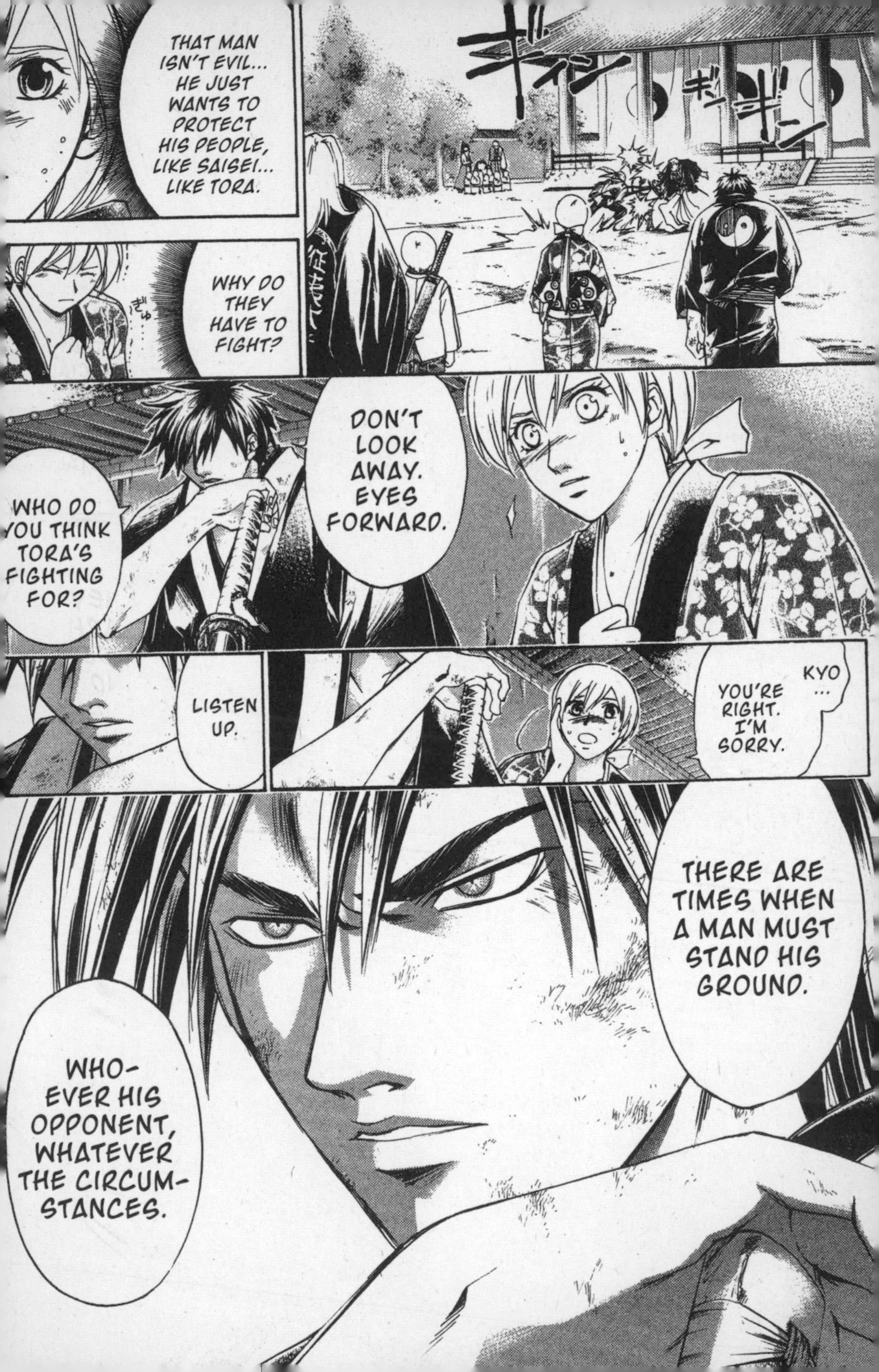
ギィン
ギン ギン
THAT MAN ISN'T EVIL... HE JUST WANTS TO PROTECT HIS PEOPLE, LIKE SAISEI... LIKE TORA.
ぎゅ
WHY DO THEY HAVE TO FIGHT?
DON'T LOOK AWAY. EYES FORWARD.
WHO DO YOU THINK TORA'S FIGHTING FOR?
KYO...
YOU'RE RIGHT. I'M SORRY.
LISTEN UP.
THERE ARE TIMES WHEN A MAN MUST STAND HIS GROUND.
WHO-EVER HIS OPPONENT, WHATEVER THE CIRCUM-STANCES.

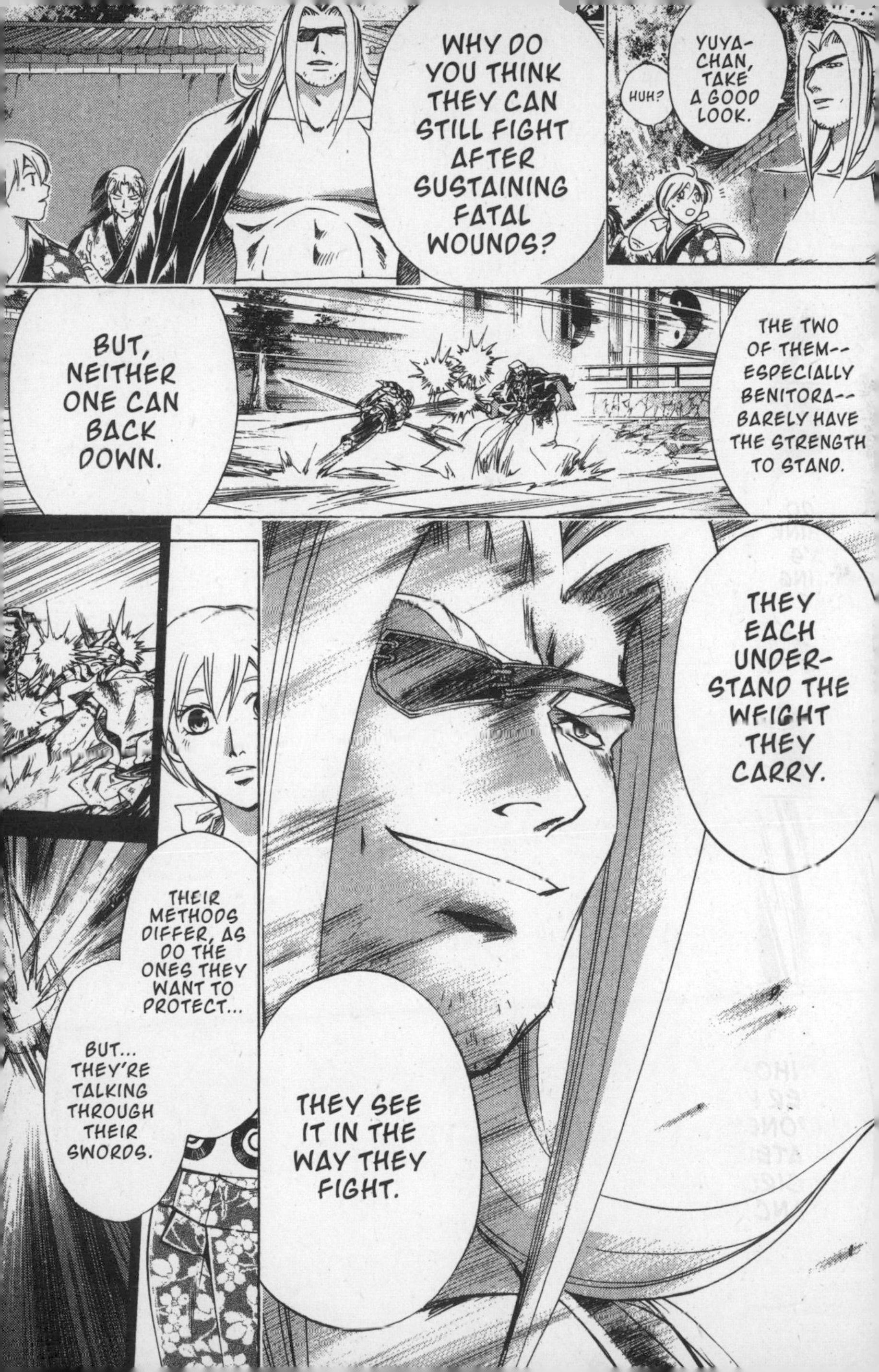
YUYA-CHAN, TAKE A GOOD LOOK.
HUH?
WHY DO YOU THINK THEY CAN STILL FIGHT AFTER SUSTAINING FATAL WOUNDS?
THE TWO OF THEM--ESPECIALLY BENITORA--BARELY HAVE THE STRENGTH TO STAND.
BUT, NEITHER ONE CAN BACK DOWN.
THEY EACH UNDER-STAND THE WFIGHT THEY CARRY.
THEY SEE IT IN THE WAY THEY FIGHT.
THEIR METHODS DIFFER, AS DO THE ONES THEY WANT TO PROTECT...
BUT... THEY'RE TALKING THROUGH THEIR SWORDS.

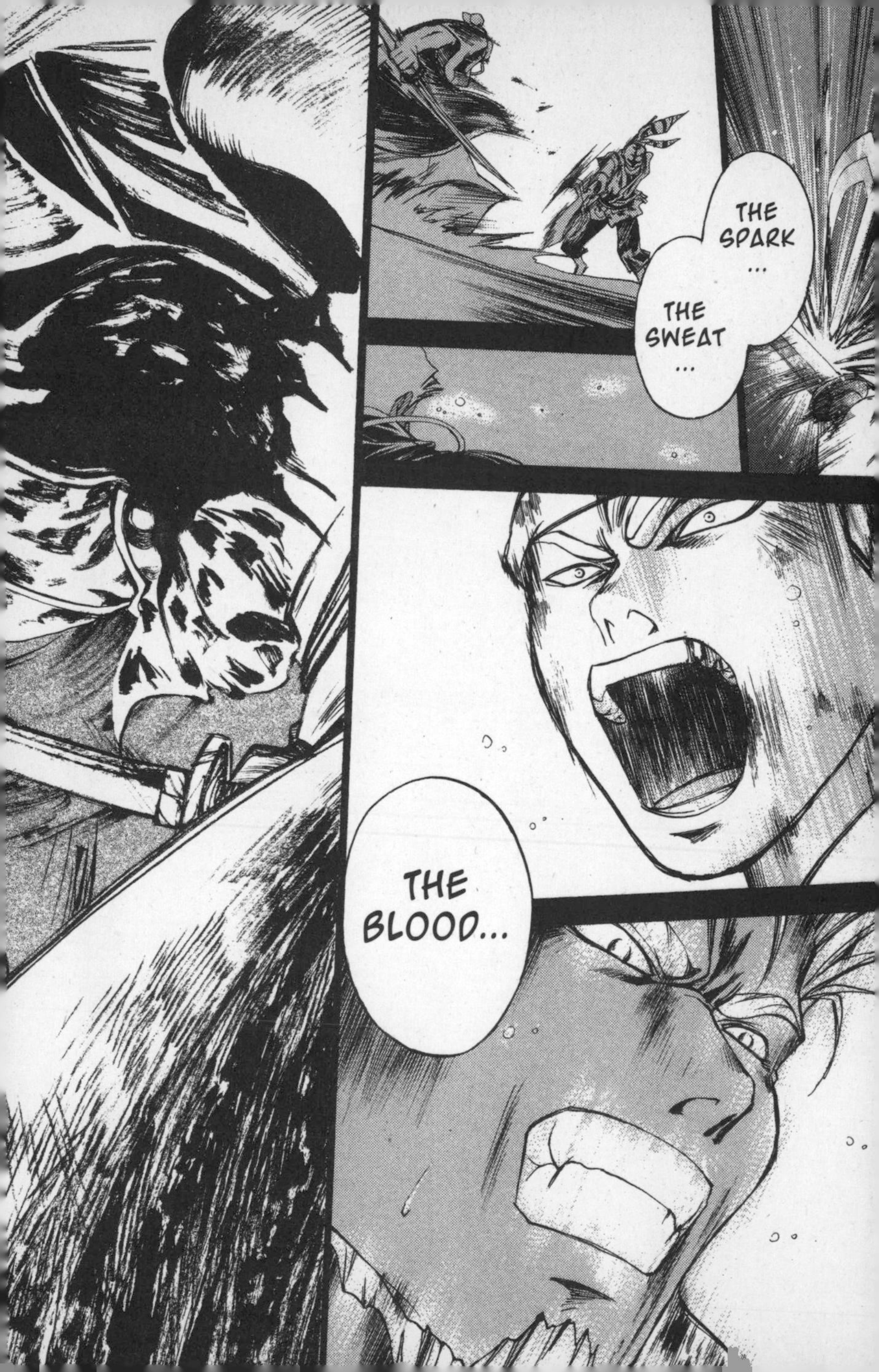
THE SPARK ...
THE SWEAT ...
THE BLOOD...

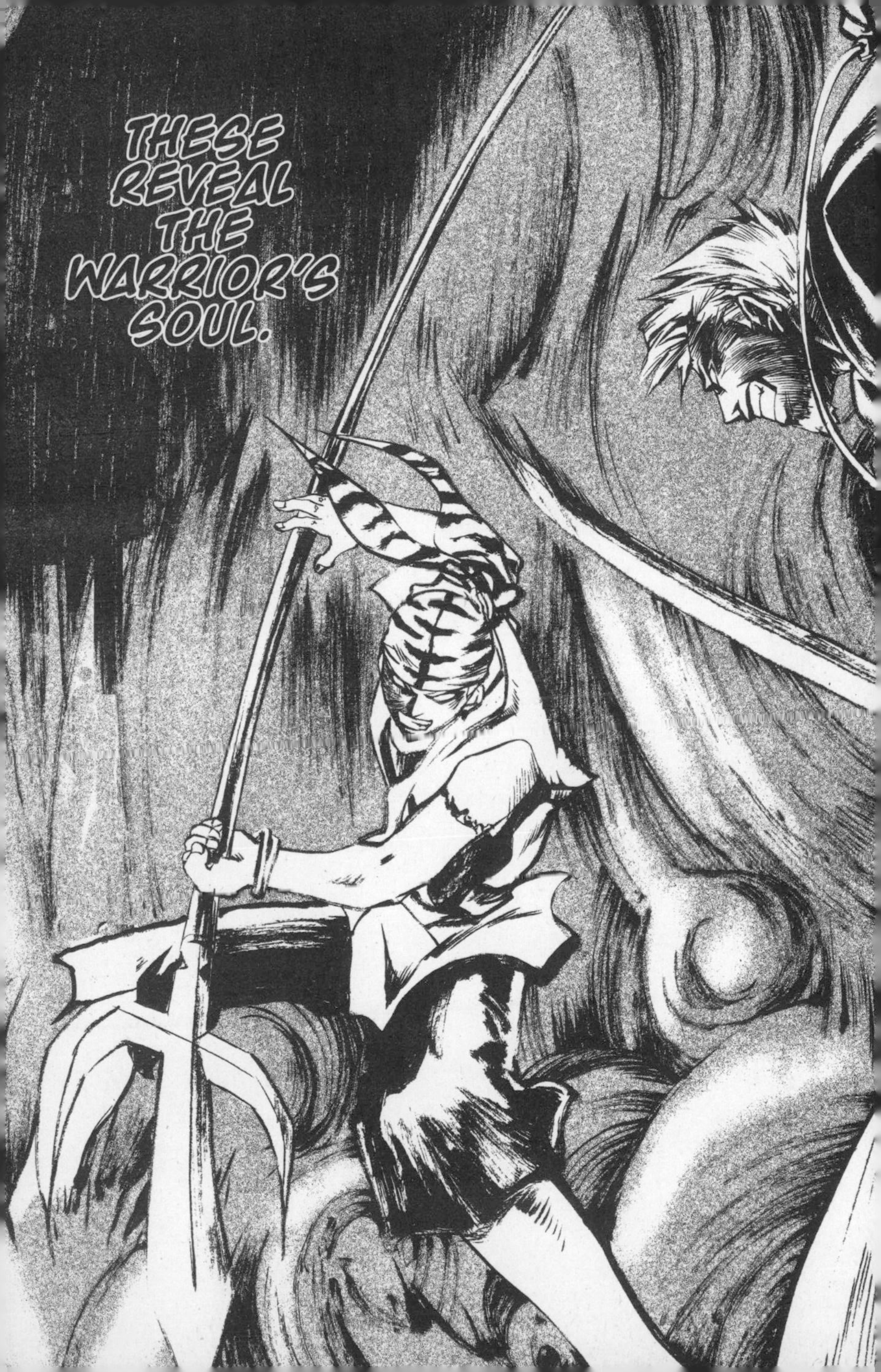
THESE REVEAL THE WARRIOR'S SOUL.

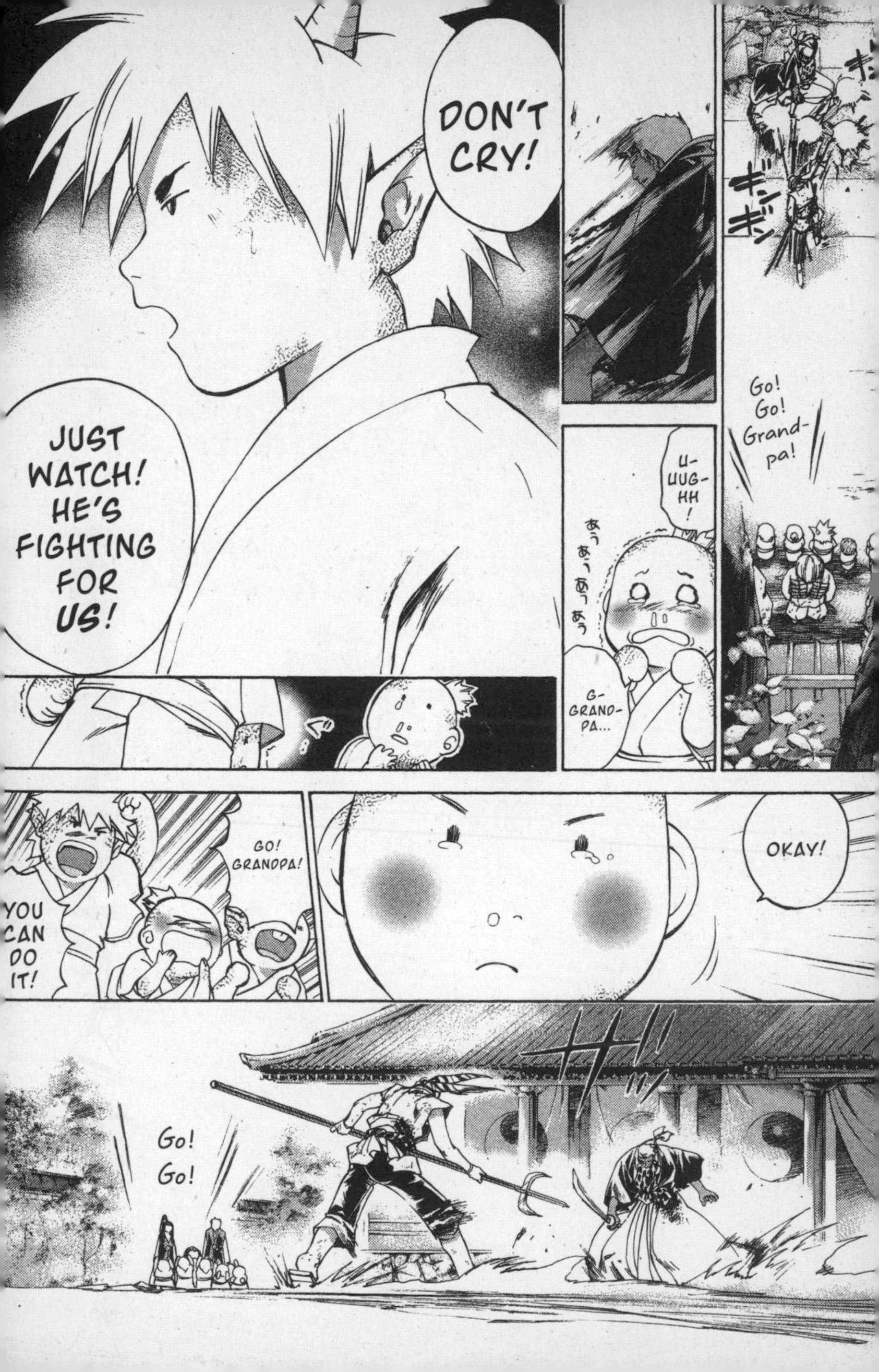

ギン
ギン
Go! Go! Grand-pa!
U-UUG-HH!
あうあうあうあう
G-GRANDPA...
DON'T CRY!
JUST WATCH! HE'S FIGHTING FOR US!
OKAY!
GO! GRANDPA!
YOU CAN DO IT!
Go! Go!

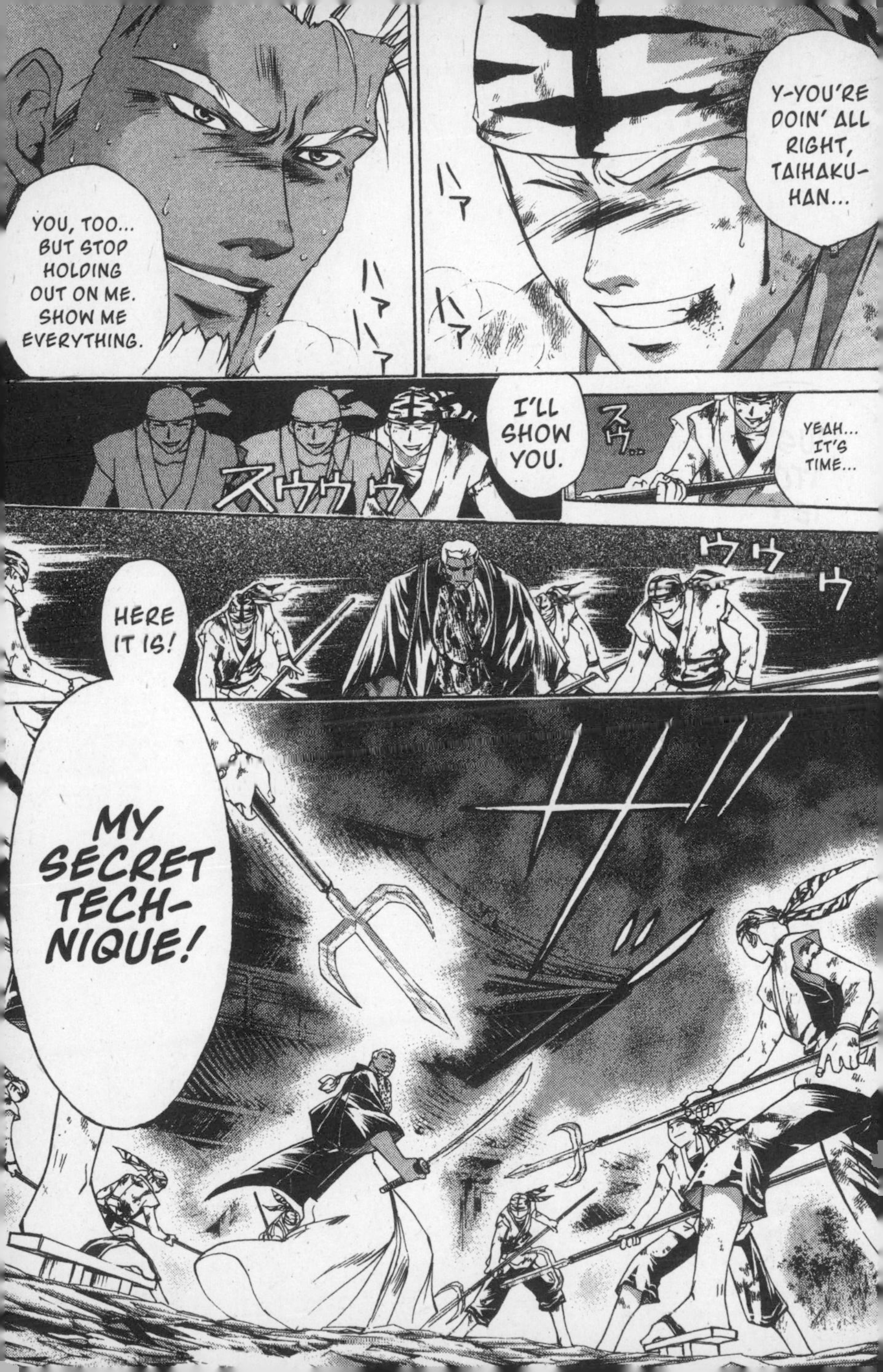
Y-YOU'RE DOIN' ALL RIGHT, TAIHAKU-HAN...
ハァ ハァ
YOU, TOO... BUT STOP HOLDING OUT ON ME. SHOW ME EVERYTHING.
ハァハァ
YEAH... IT'S TIME...
スゥ..
I'LL SHOW YOU.
スウウウ
ウウウ
HERE IT IS!
MY SECRET TECH-NIQUE!

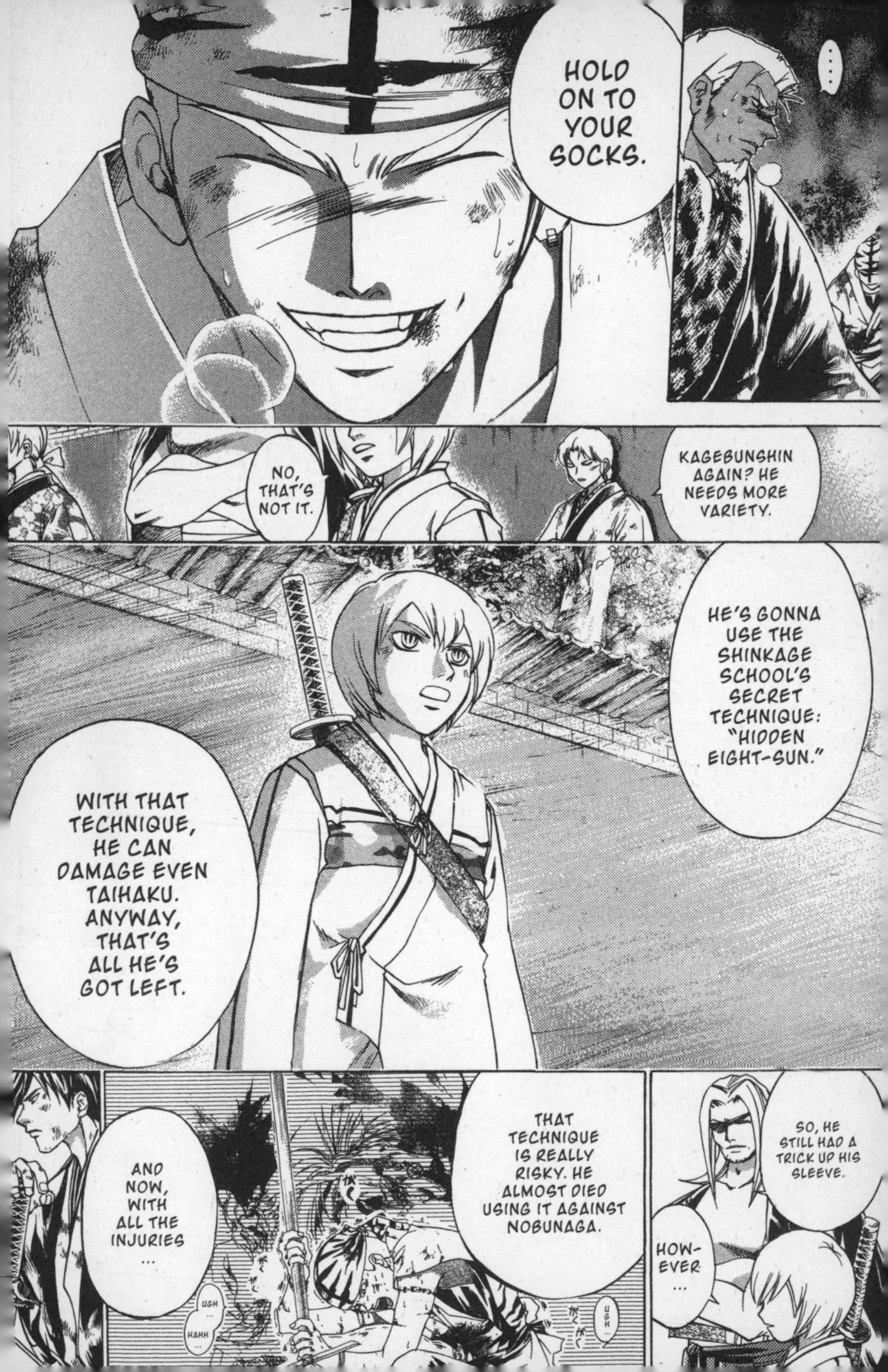
...
HOLD ON TO YOUR SOCKS.
KAGEBUNSHIN AGAIN? HE NEEDS MORE VARIETY.
NO, THAT'S NOT IT.
HE'S GONNA USE THE SHINKAGE SCHOOL'S SECRET TECHNIQUE: "HIDDEN EIGHT-SUN."
WITH THAT TECHNIQUE, HE CAN DAMAGE EVEN TAIHAKU. ANYWAY, THAT'S ALL HE'S GOT LEFT.
SO, HE STILL HAD A TRICK UP HIS SLEEVE.
HOW-EVER ...
THAT TECHNIQUE IS REALLY RISKY. HE ALMOST DIED USING IT AGAINST NOBUNAGA.
UGH ...
UGH ...
HAHH ...
AND NOW, WITH ALL THE INJURIES ...

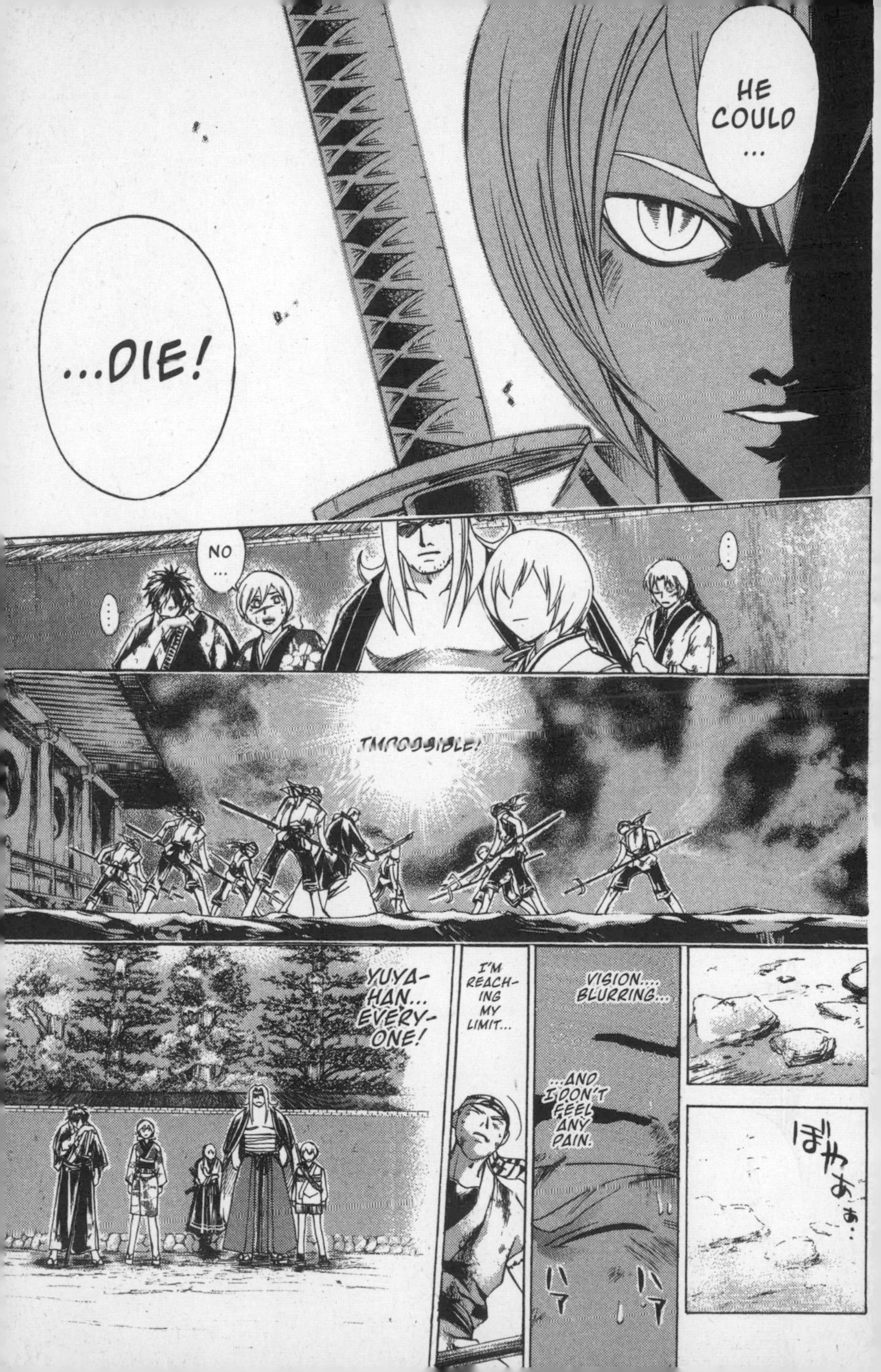
HE COULD ...
...DIE!
...
NO ...
...
IMPOSSIBLE!
ぼやぁぁ・・
VISION... BLURRING...
...AND I DON'T FEEL ANY PAIN.
ハァ
ハァ
I'M REACHING MY LIMIT...
YUYA-HAN... EVERY-ONE!

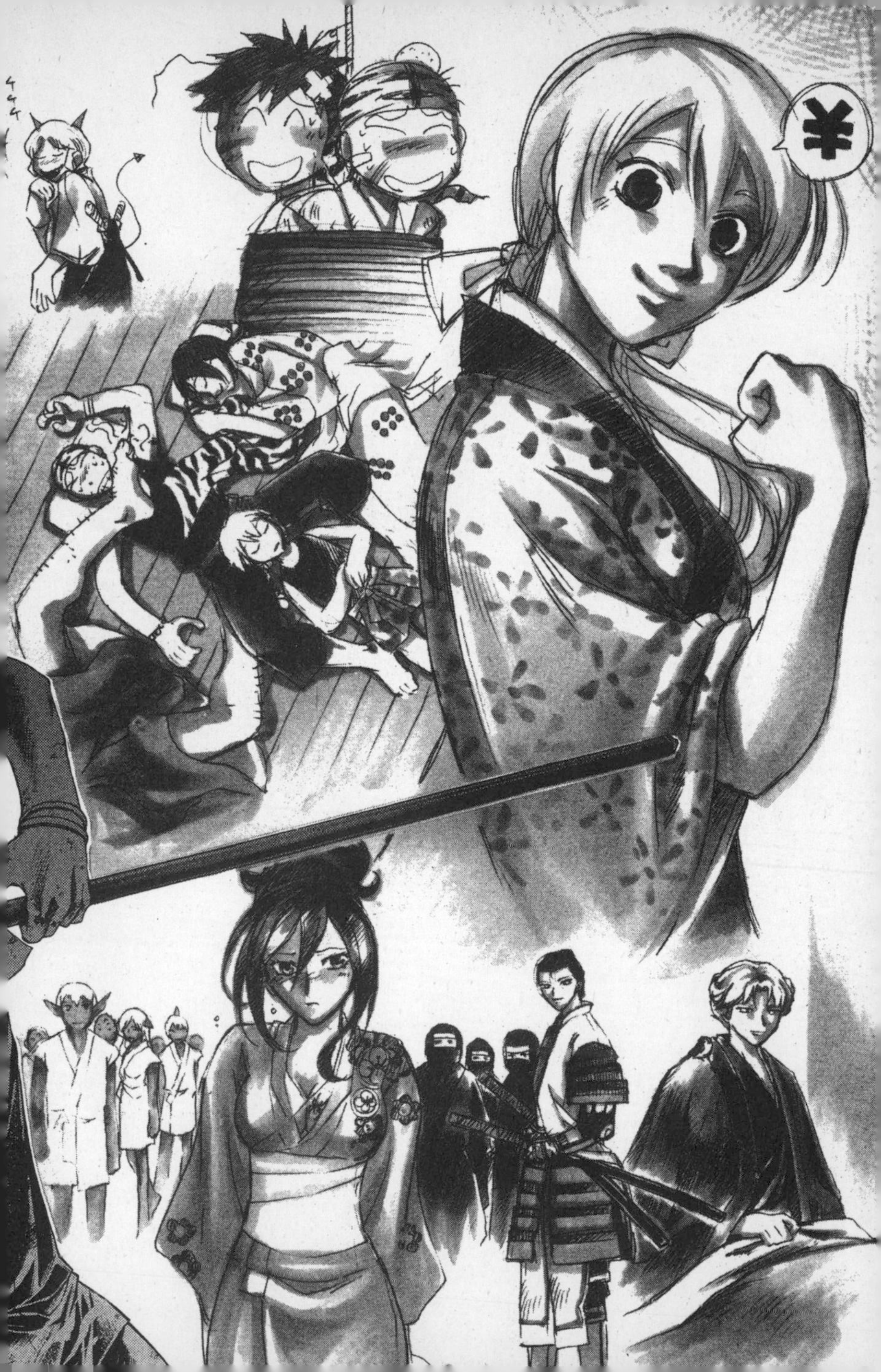
¥

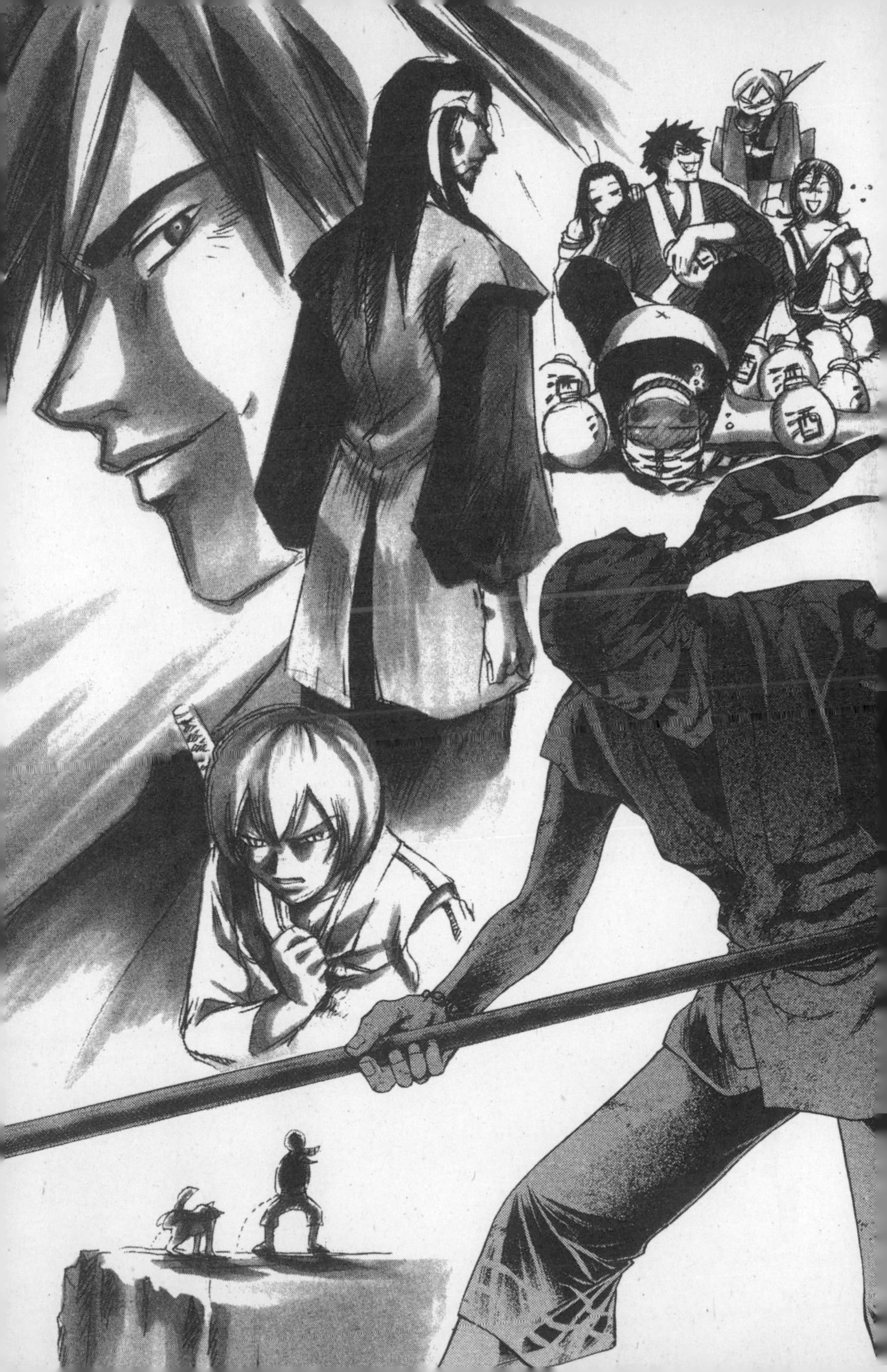
酒
酒
酒

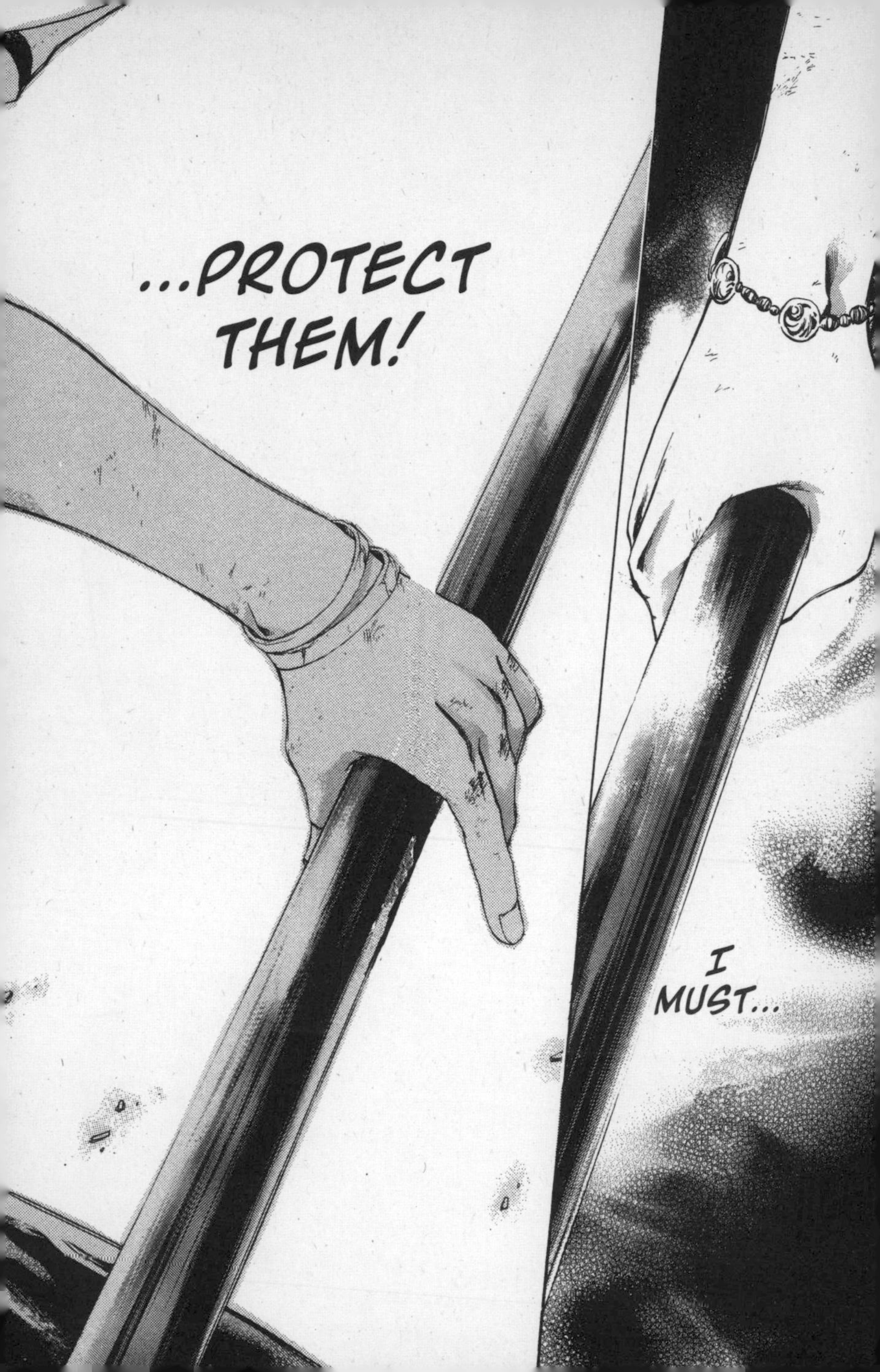
I MUST...
...PROTECT THEM!

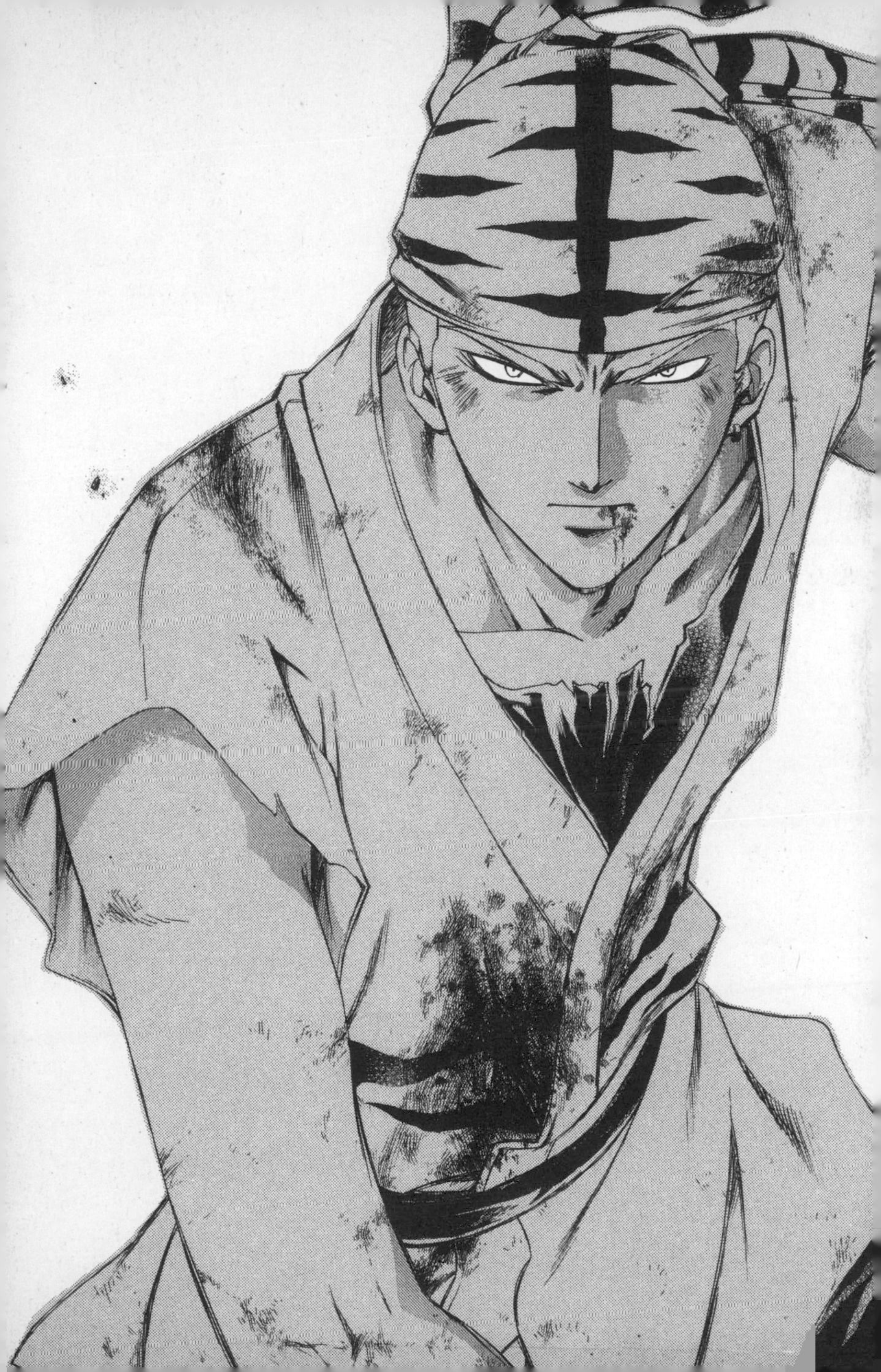

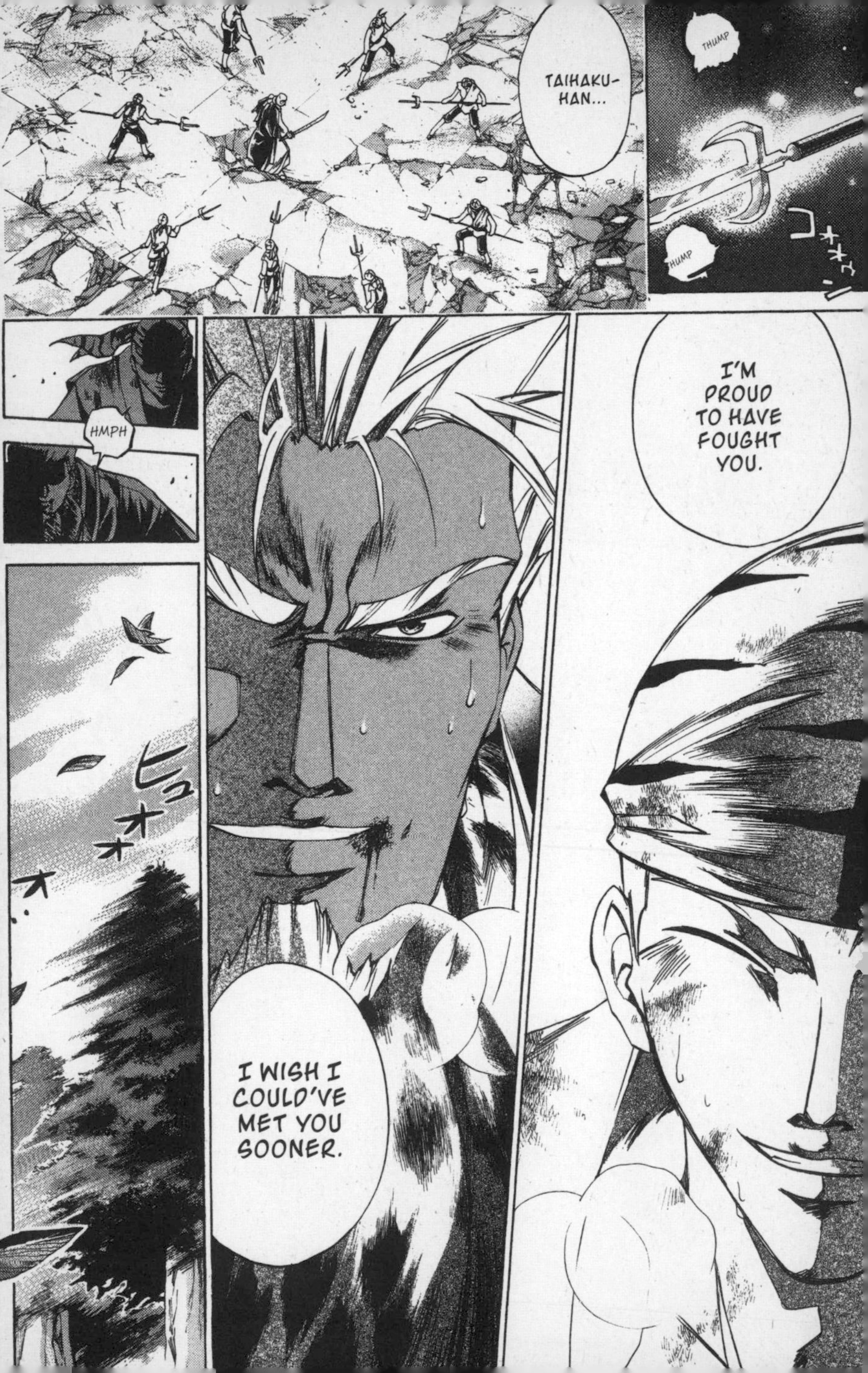
THUMP
HUMP
TAIHAKU-HAN...
I'M PROUD TO HAVE FOUGHT YOU.
I WISH I COULD'VE MET YOU SOONER.
HMPH

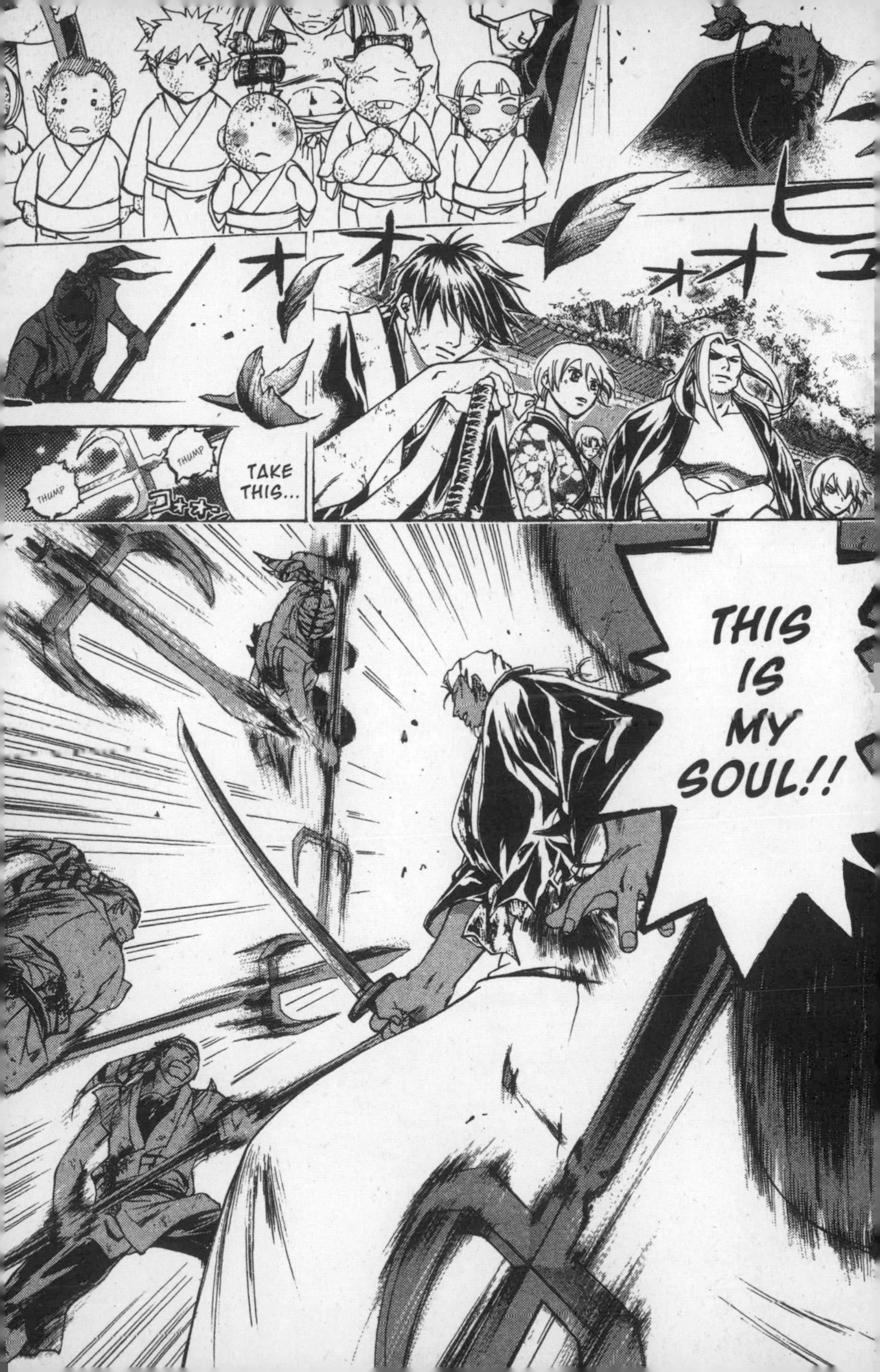
TAKE THIS...
THUMP
THUMP
THIS IS MY SOUL!!

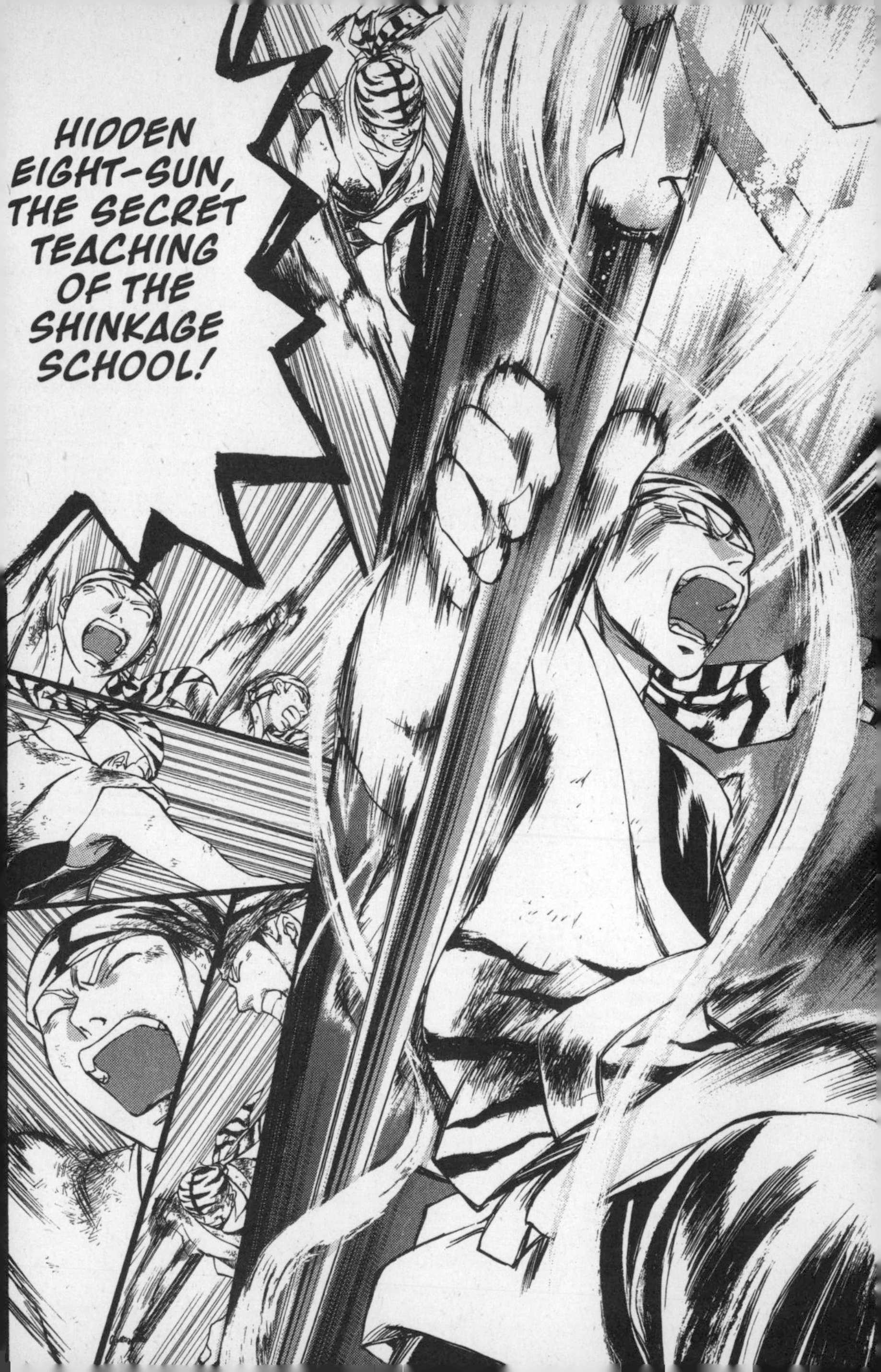
HIDDEN EIGHT-SUN, THE SECRET TEACHING OF THE SHINKAGE SCHOOL!

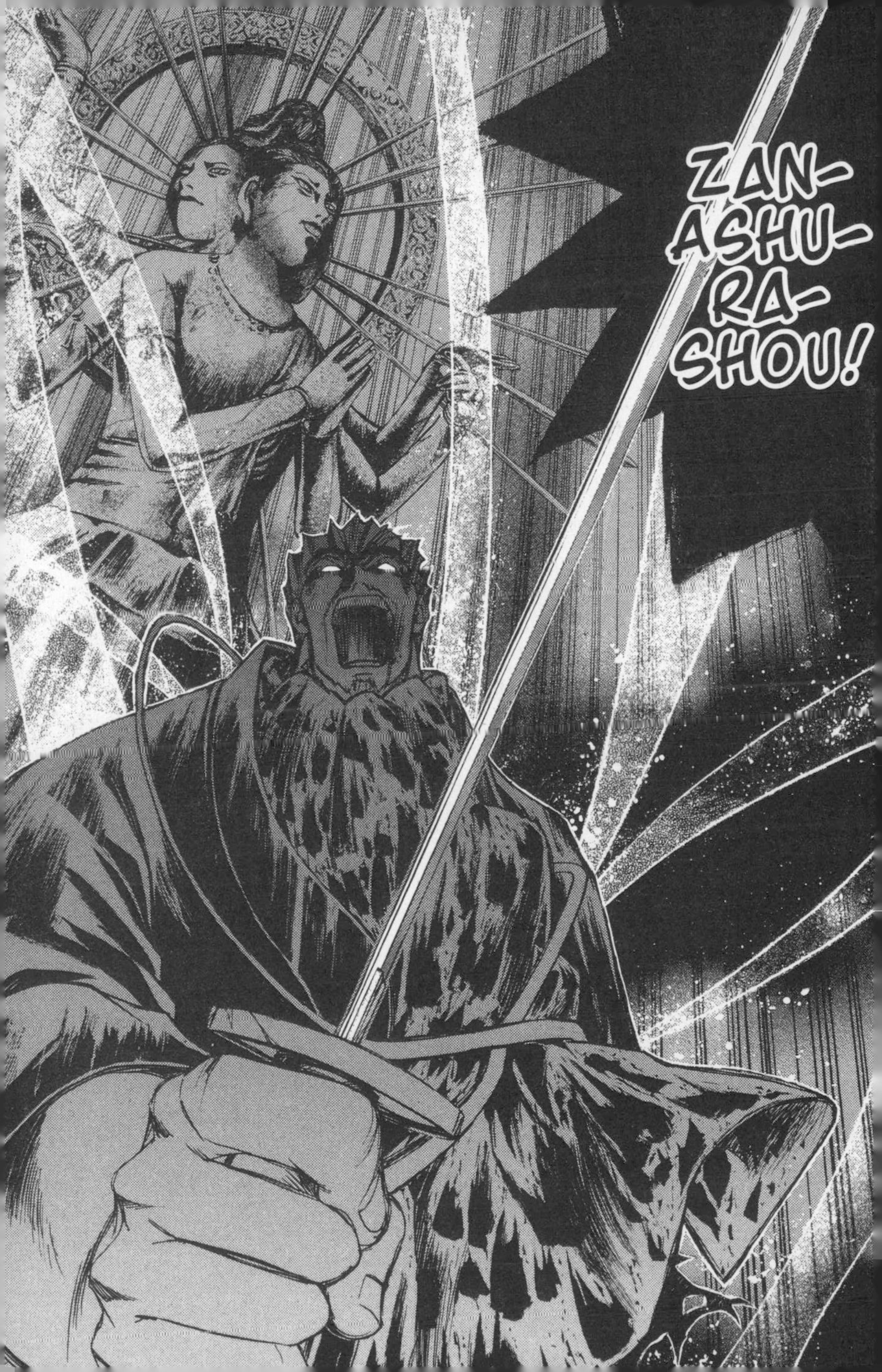
ZAN-
ASHU-
RA-
SHOU!

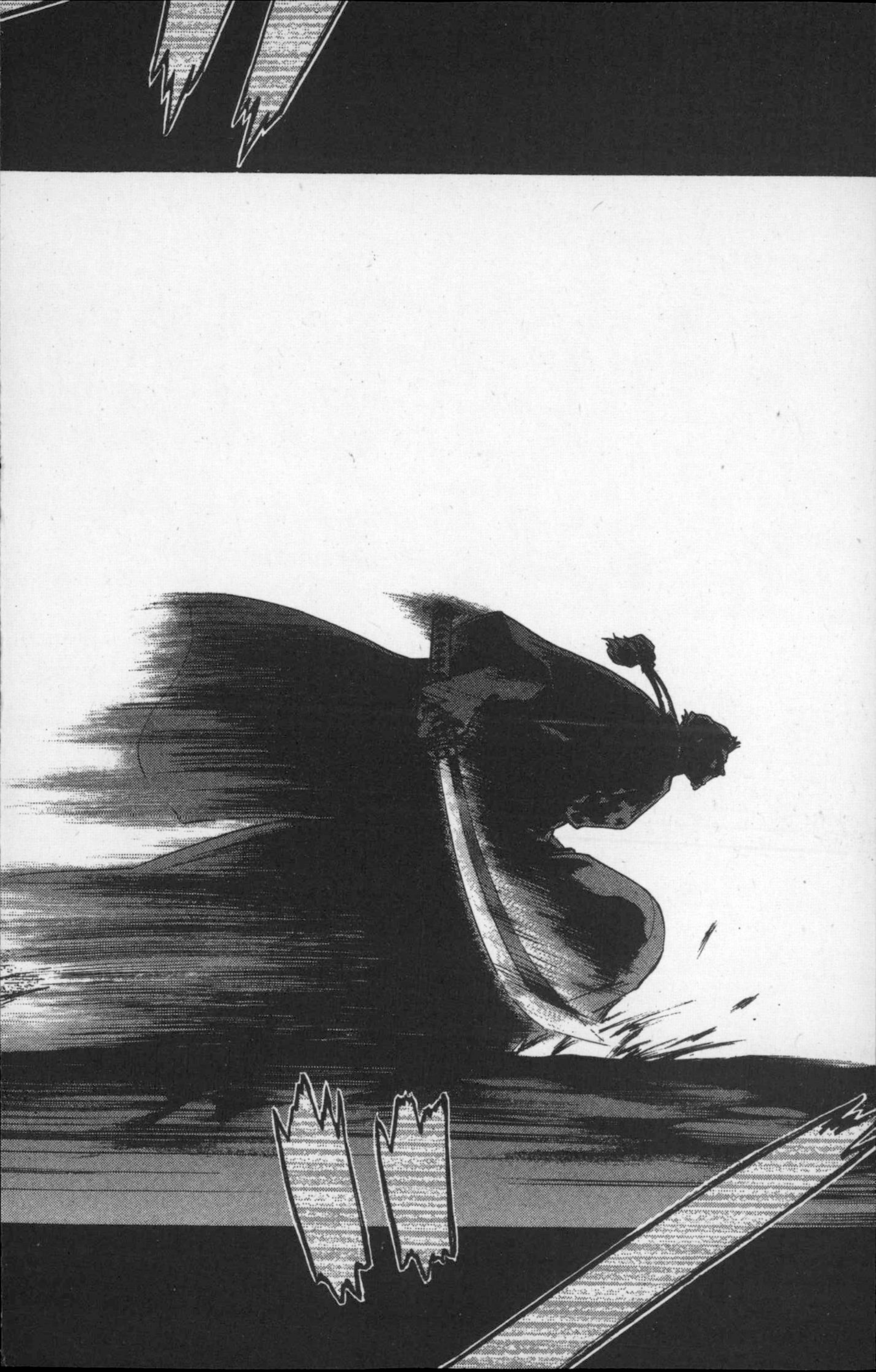

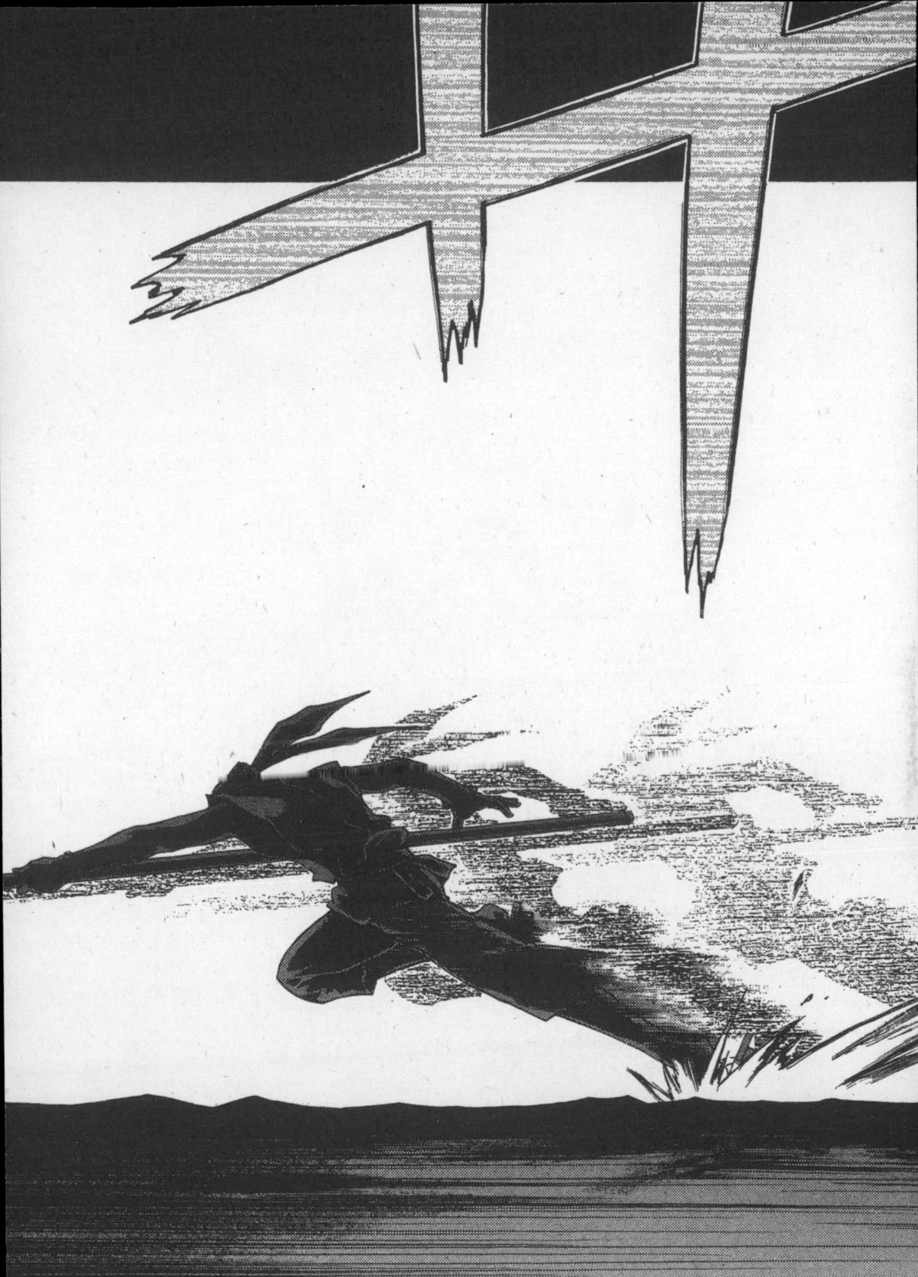

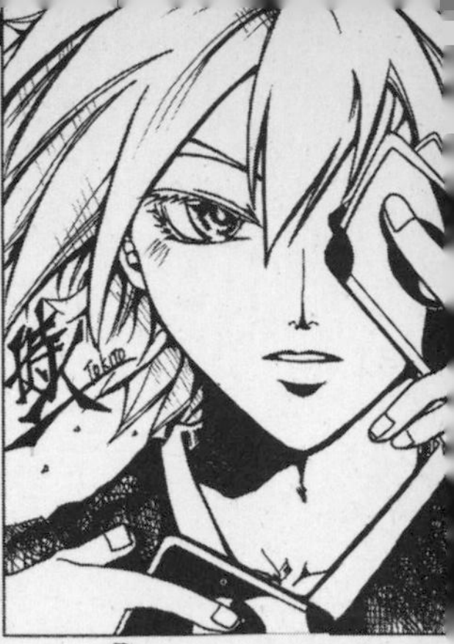

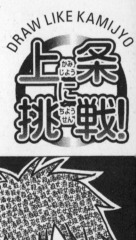

A lovely fortuneteller! ⬆
[Nakamura Kaori / Fukushima]

...but he sure is a lucky rascal. (Ha ha!) ⬇
[Full Monty / Yamaguchi]

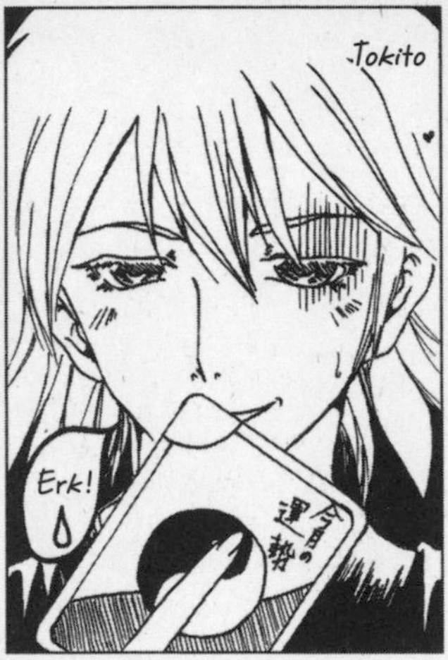
Tokito
Erk!
今月の運勢

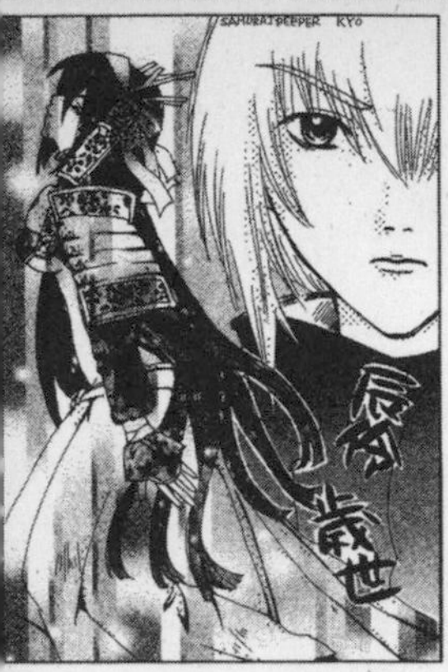
SAMURAIDEEPER KYO

I can really feel the emotion through the paper. ⬆
[Piyoko / Hiyougo]

DRAW LIKE KAMIJYO
上条(かみじょう)に挑戦(ちょうせん)!

Y-y-y-yes, sir! (eep!) ➡
[You / Kumamoto]

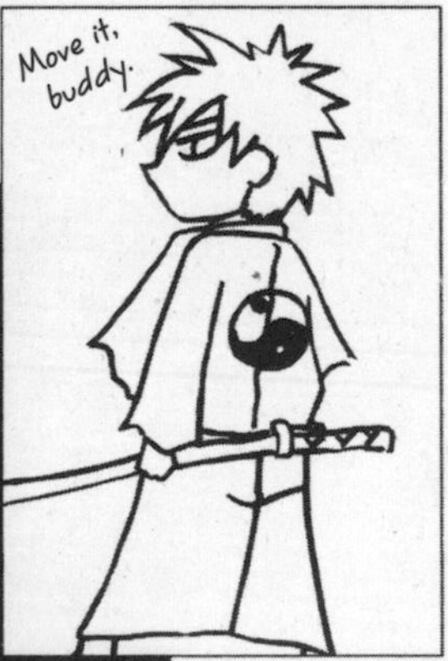
Move it, buddy.

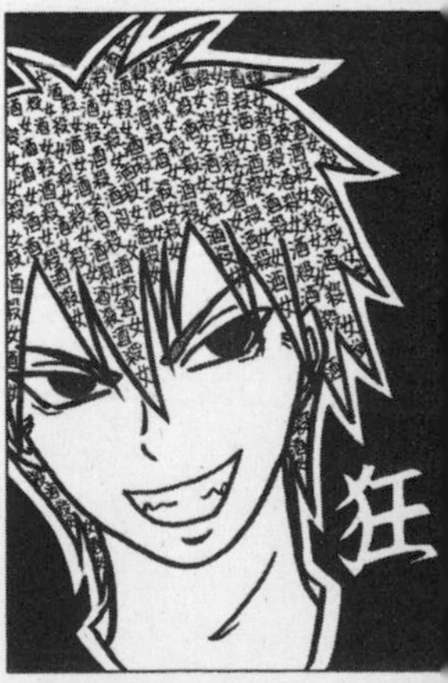
狂

The symbols prove it: Men really do only have beer, women, and murder on the brain! (Ha ha!) ⬆
[Kazu / Saitama]

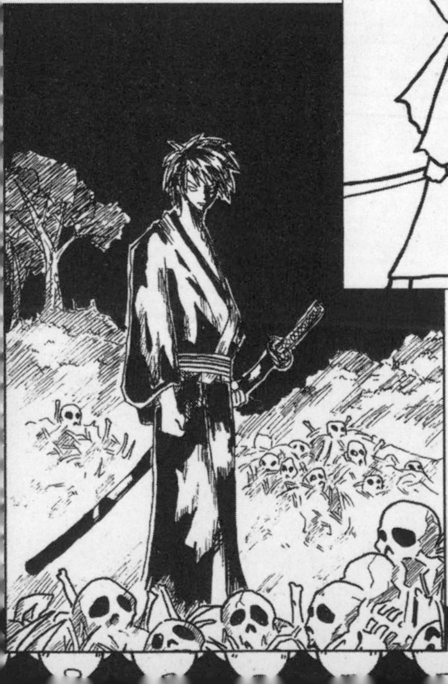

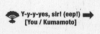

The 1,000 man killer...
[Chisaka Shizuka / Miyagi] ⬅

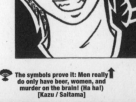

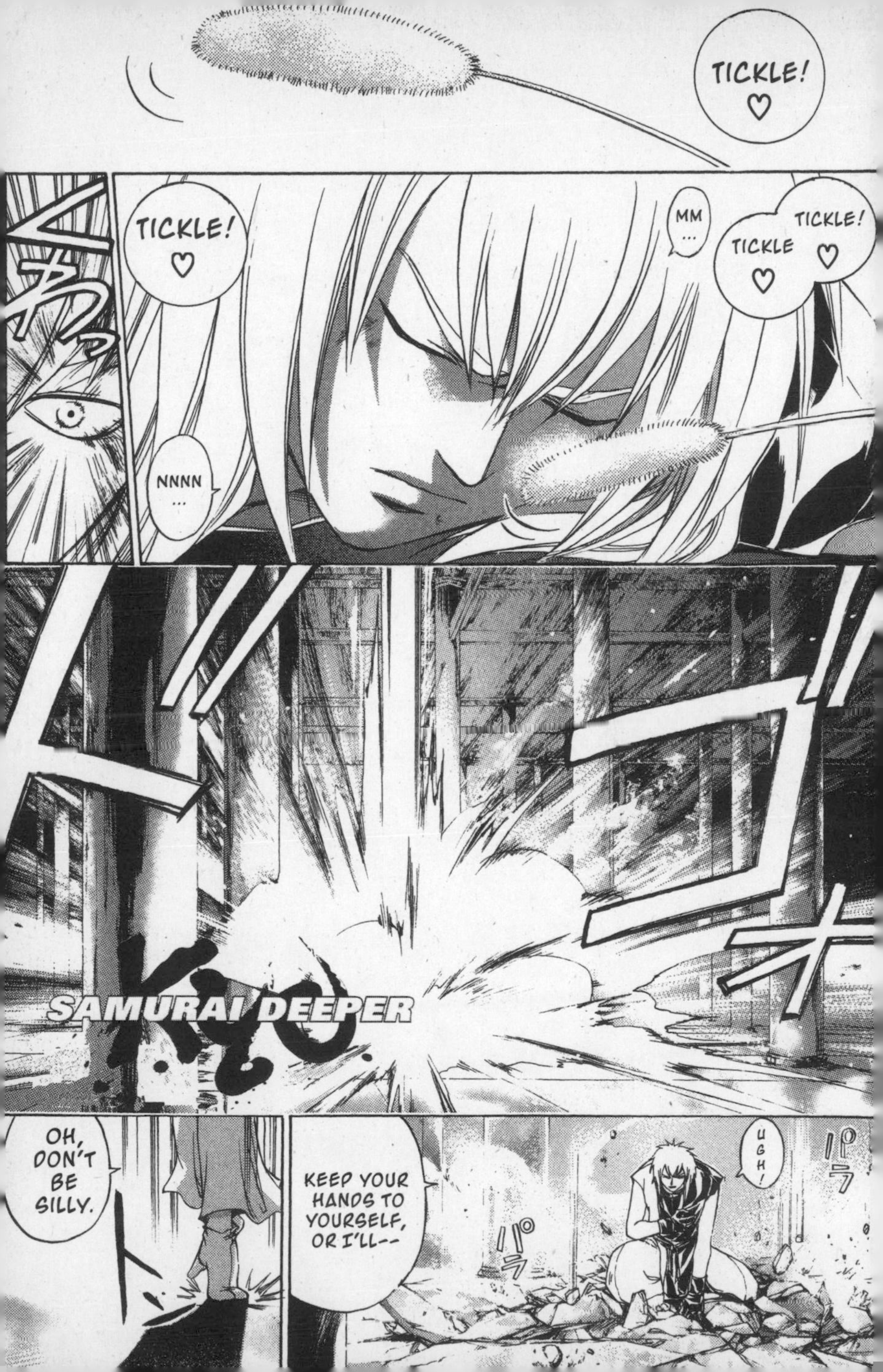
TICKLE! ♡
TICKLE! ♡
TICKLE ♡
MM ...
TICKLE! ♡
NNNN ...
SAMURAI DEEPER KYO
パラ
UGH!
パラ
KEEP YOUR HANDS TO YOURSELF, OR I'LL--
OH, DON'T BE SILLY.

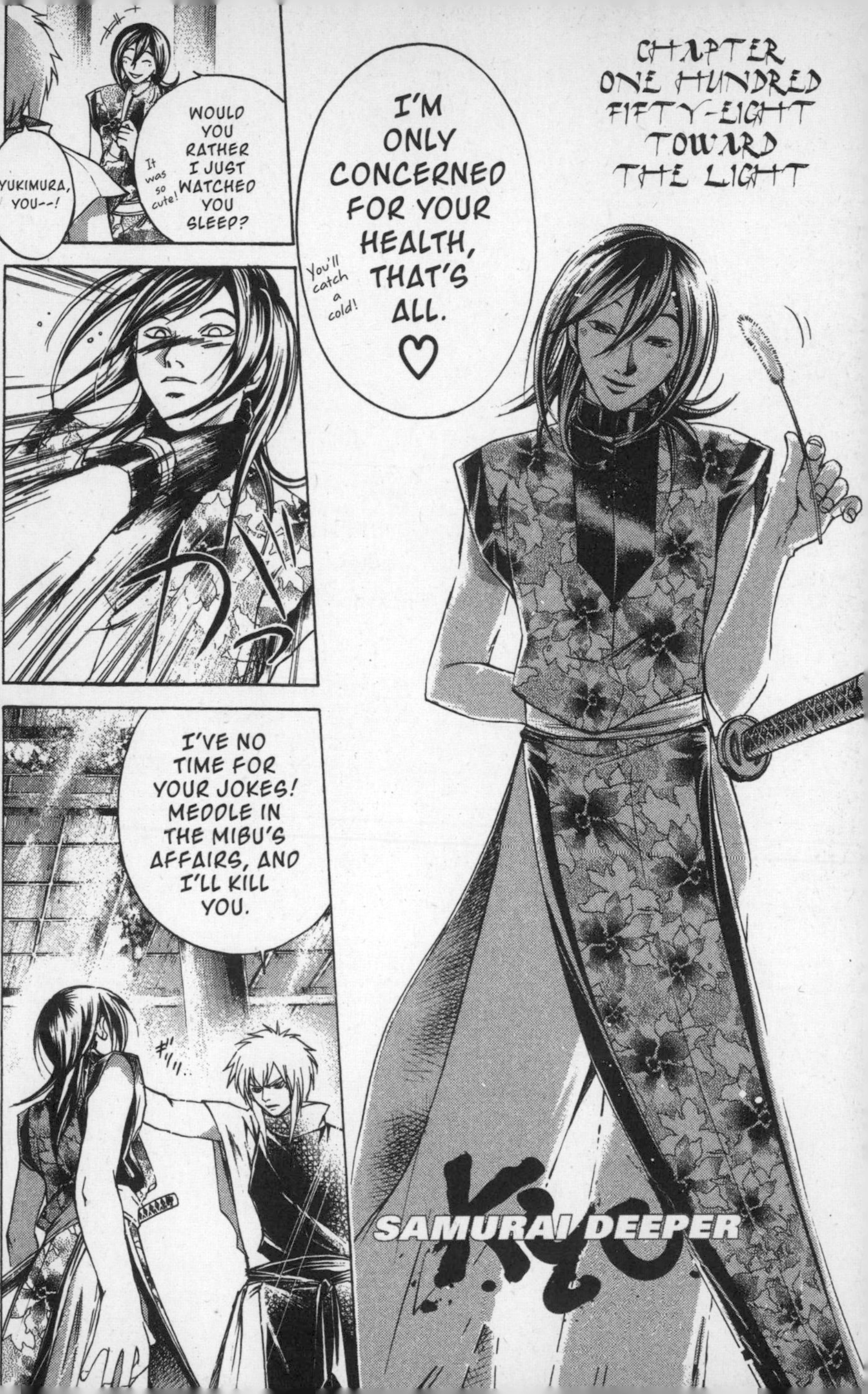
CHAPTER ONE HUNDRED FIFTY-EIGHT
TOWARD THE LIGHT
I'M ONLY CONCERNED FOR YOUR HEALTH, THAT'S ALL. ♡
You'll catch a cold!
SAMURAI DEEPER KYO
WOULD YOU RATHER I JUST WATCHED YOU SLEEP?
It was so cute!
YUKIMURA, YOU--!
I'VE NO TIME FOR YOUR JOKES! MEDDLE IN THE MIBU'S AFFAIRS, AND I'LL KILL YOU.

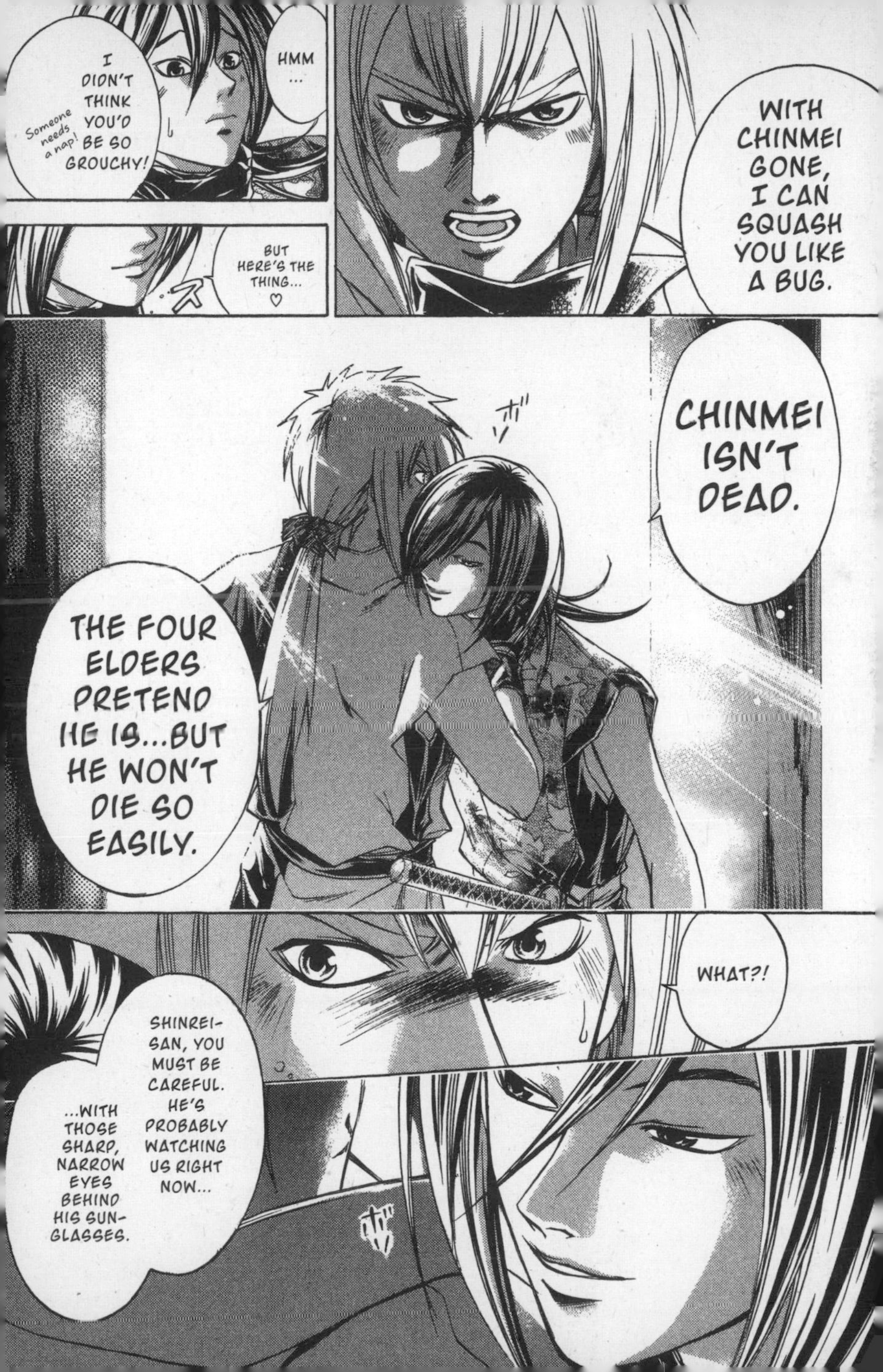
WITH CHINMEI GONE, I CAN SQUASH YOU LIKE A BUG.
HMM...
I DIDN'T THINK YOU'D BE SO GROUCHY!
Someone needs a nap!
BUT HERE'S THE THING... ♡
CHINMEI ISN'T DEAD.
THE FOUR ELDERS PRETEND HE IS...BUT HE WON'T DIE SO EASILY.
WHAT?!
SHINREI-SAN, YOU MUST BE CAREFUL. HE'S PROBABLY WATCHING US RIGHT NOW...
...WITH THOSE SHARP, NARROW EYES BEHIND HIS SUN-GLASSES.

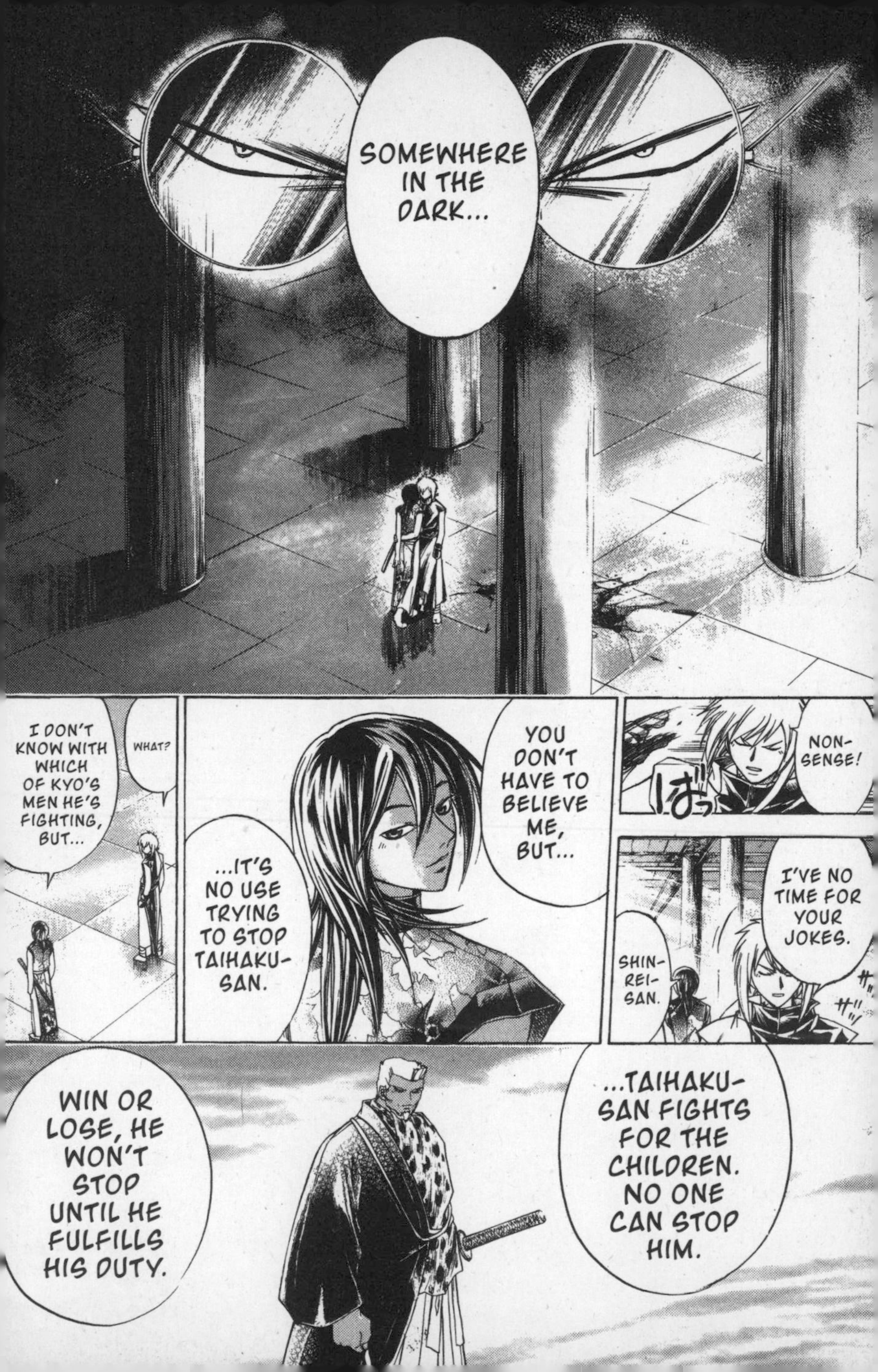
SOMEWHERE IN THE DARK...
NON-SENSE!
ばっ
I'VE NO TIME FOR YOUR JOKES.
SHIN-REI-SAN.
YOU DON'T HAVE TO BELIEVE ME, BUT...
...IT'S NO USE TRYING TO STOP TAIHAKU-SAN.
WHAT?
I DON'T KNOW WITH WHICH OF KYO'S MEN HE'S FIGHTING, BUT...
...TAIHAKU-SAN FIGHTS FOR THE CHILDREN. NO ONE CAN STOP HIM.
WIN OR LOSE, HE WON'T STOP UNTIL HE FULFILLS HIS DUTY.

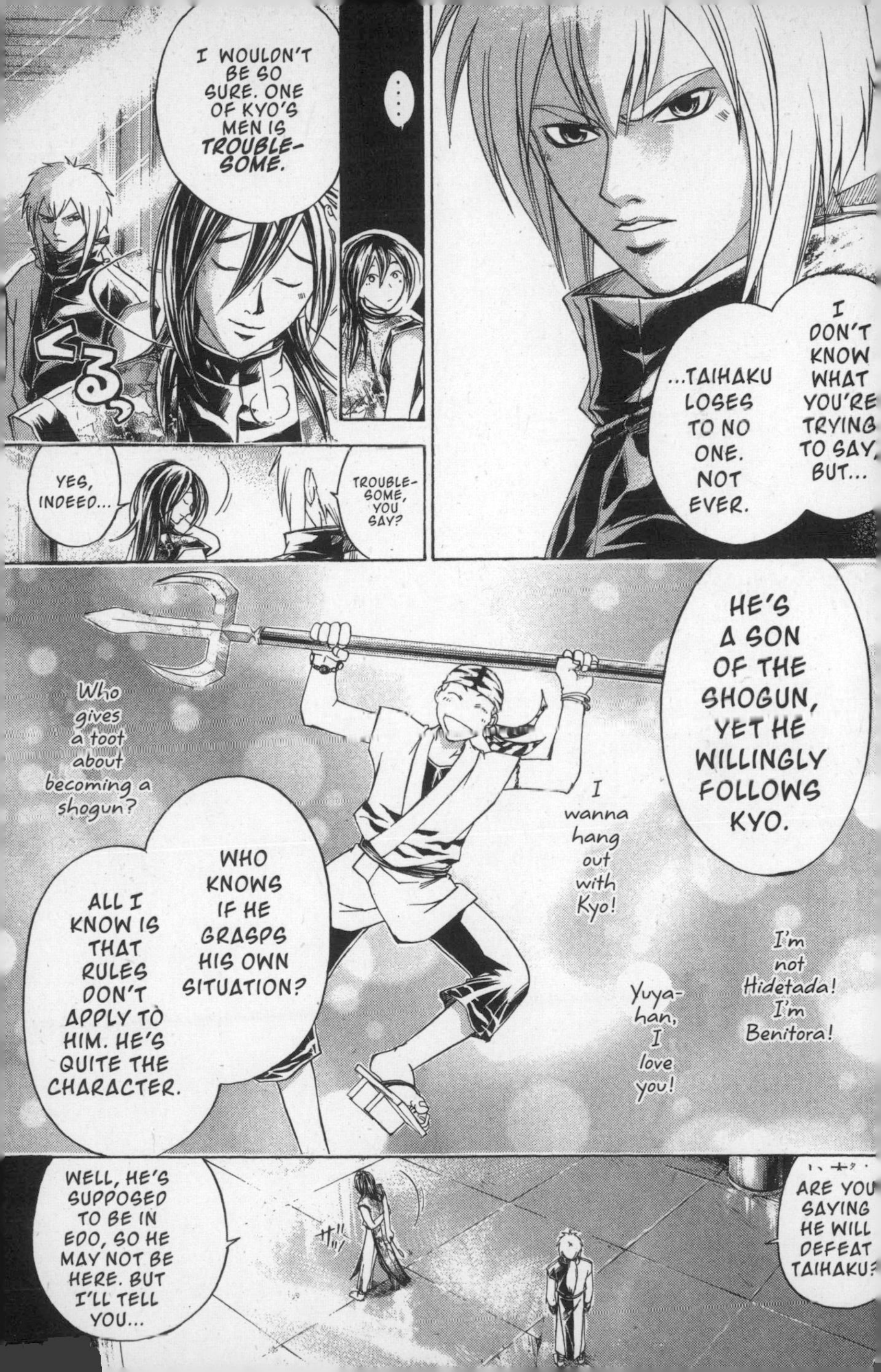

I DON'T KNOW WHAT YOU'RE TRYING TO SAY, BUT...
...TAIHAKU LOSES TO NO ONE. NOT EVER.
...
I WOULDN'T BE SO SURE. ONE OF KYO'S MEN IS TROUBLE-SOME.
くる
TROUBLE-SOME, YOU SAY?
YES, INDEED...
HE'S A SON OF THE SHOGUN, YET HE WILLINGLY FOLLOWS KYO.
I'm not Hidetada! I'm Benitora!
Yuya-han, I love you!
I wanna hang out with Kyo!
Who gives a toot about becoming a shogun?
WHO KNOWS IF HE GRASPS HIS OWN SITUATION?
ALL I KNOW IS THAT RULES DON'T APPLY TO HIM. HE'S QUITE THE CHARACTER.
ARE YOU SAYING HE WILL DEFEAT TAIHAKU?
WELL, HE'S SUPPOSED TO BE IN EDO, SO HE MAY NOT BE HERE. BUT I'LL TELL YOU...

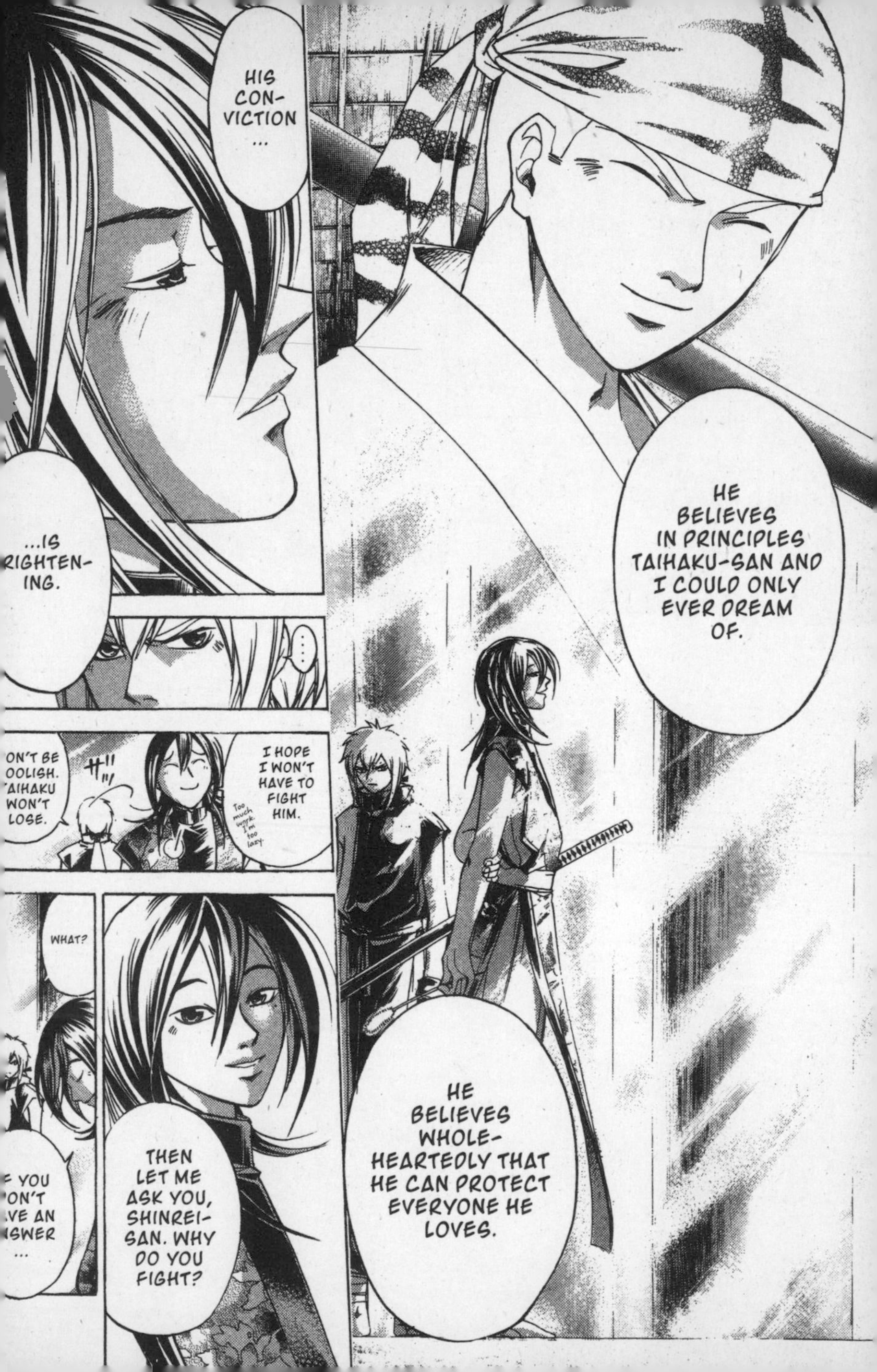
HE BELIEVES IN PRINCIPLES TAIHAKU-SAN AND I COULD ONLY EVER DREAM OF.
HE BELIEVES WHOLE-HEARTEDLY THAT HE CAN PROTECT EVERYONE HE LOVES.
HIS CON-VICTION ...
...IS RIGHTEN-ING.
....
I HOPE I WON'T HAVE TO FIGHT HIM.
Too much work. I'm too lazy.
ON'T BE OOLISH. AIHAKU WON'T LOSE.
WHAT?
THEN LET ME ASK YOU, SHINREI-SAN. WHY DO YOU FIGHT?
F YOU ON'T VE AN SWER ...

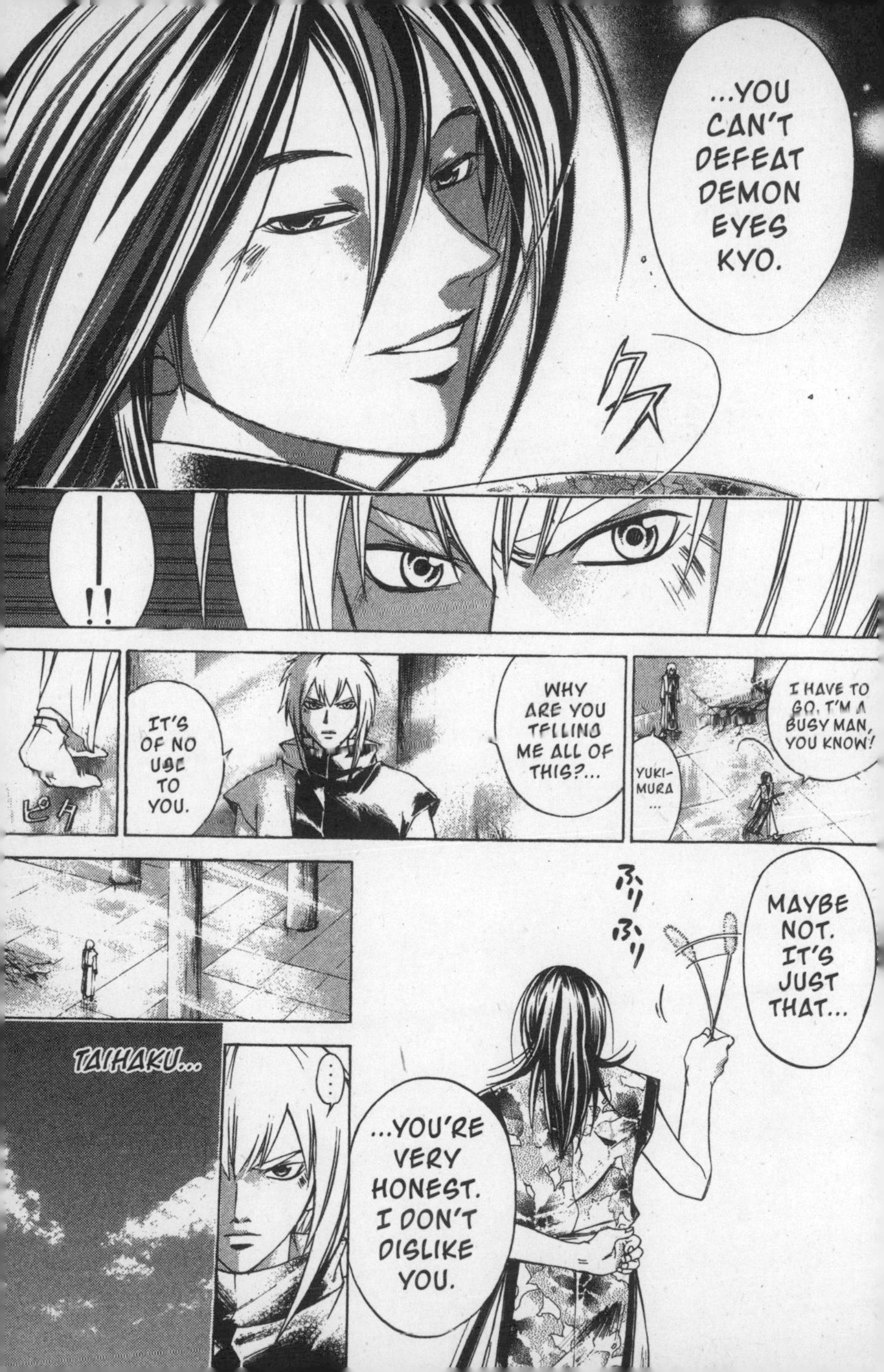
...YOU CAN'T DEFEAT DEMON EYES KYO.
クス
!!
I HAVE TO GO. I'M A BUSY MAN, YOU KNOW!
YUKI-MURA...
WHY ARE YOU TELLING ME ALL OF THIS?...
IT'S OF NO USE TO YOU.
ピク
ふりふり
MAYBE NOT. IT'S JUST THAT...
...YOU'RE VERY HONEST. I DON'T DISLIKE YOU.
....
TAIHAKU...

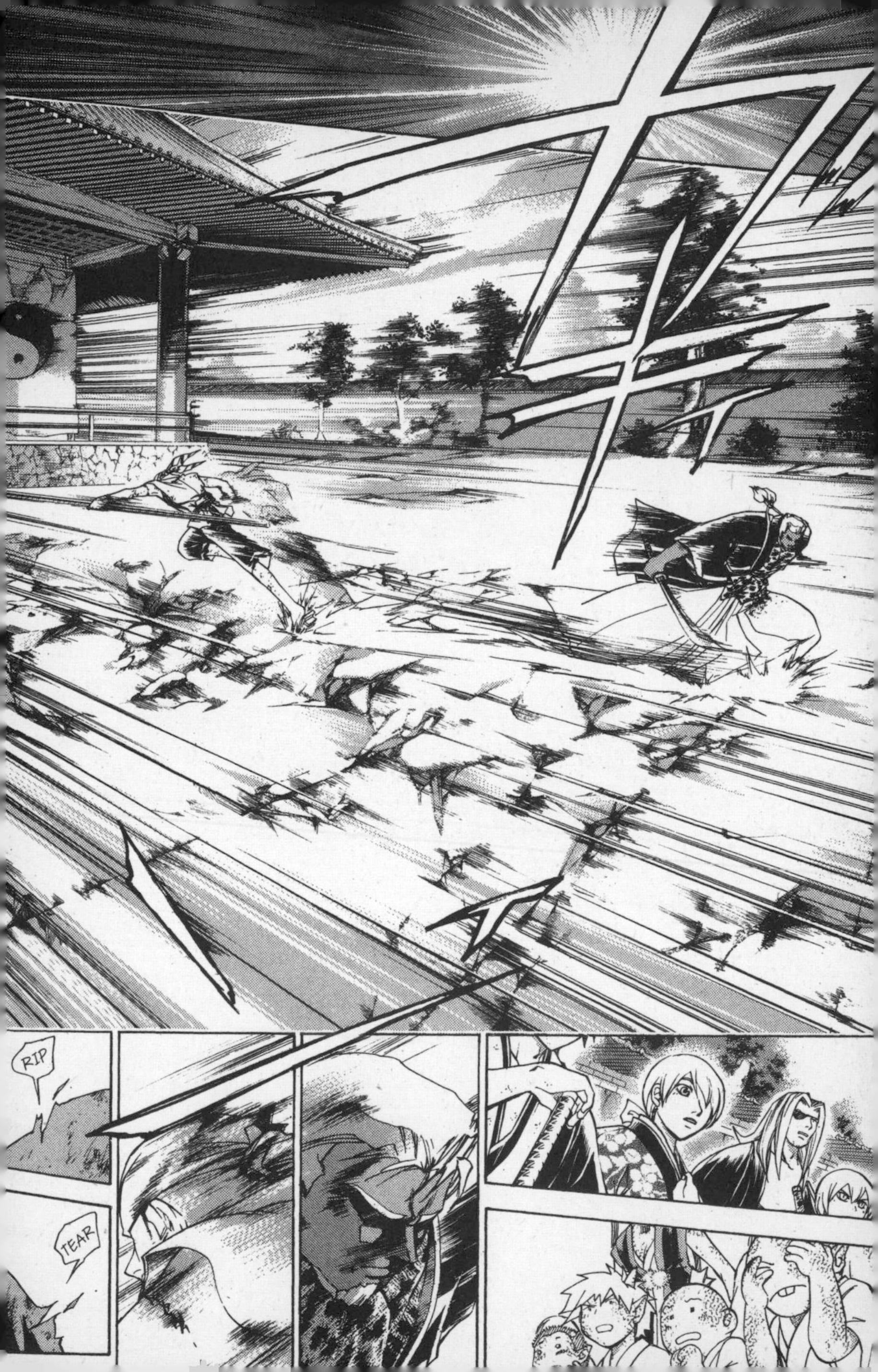
RIP
TEAR

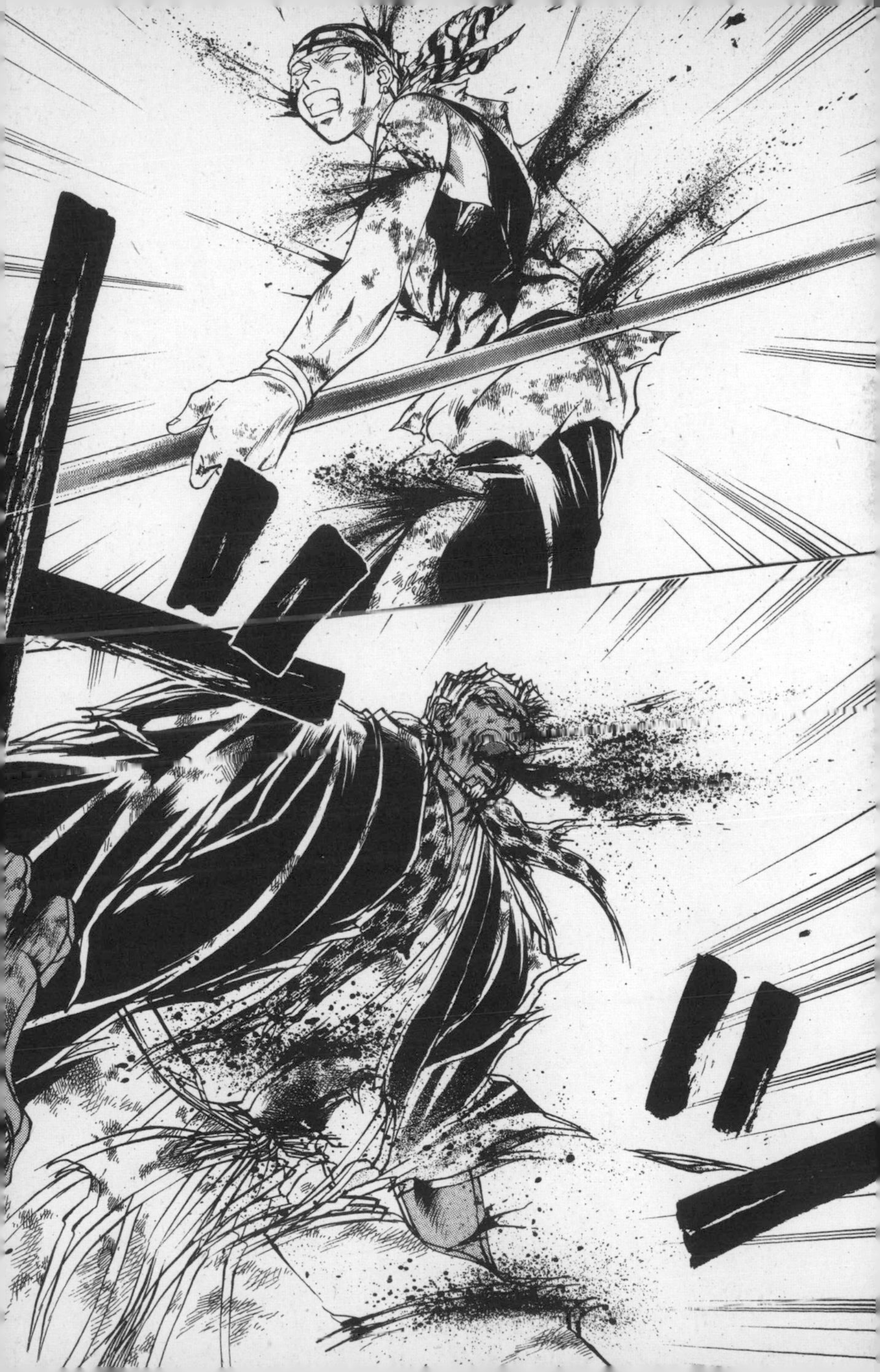

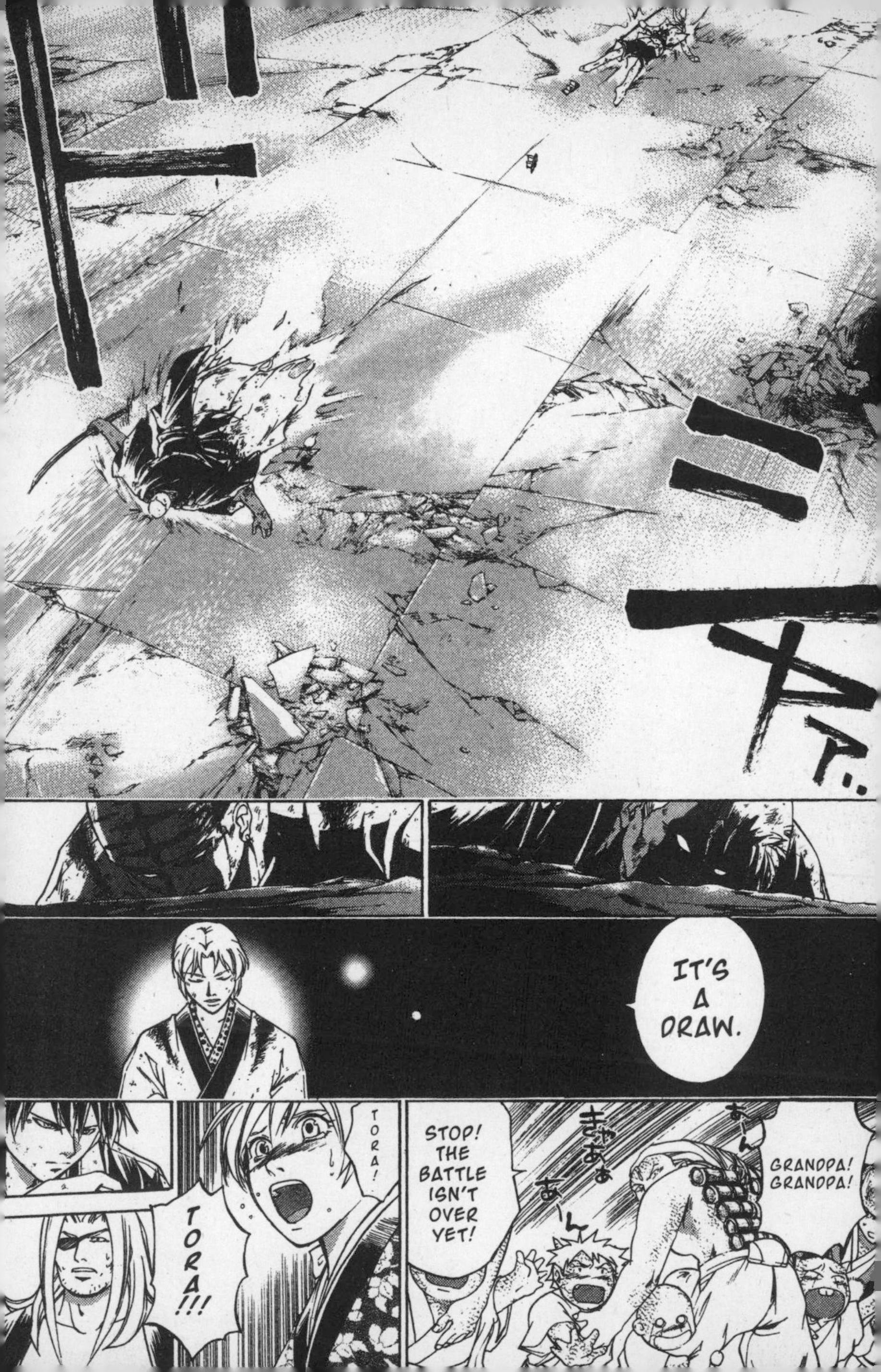
IT'S A DRAW.
GRANDPA! GRANDPA!
STOP! THE BATTLE ISN'T OVER YET!
TORA!
TORA!!!

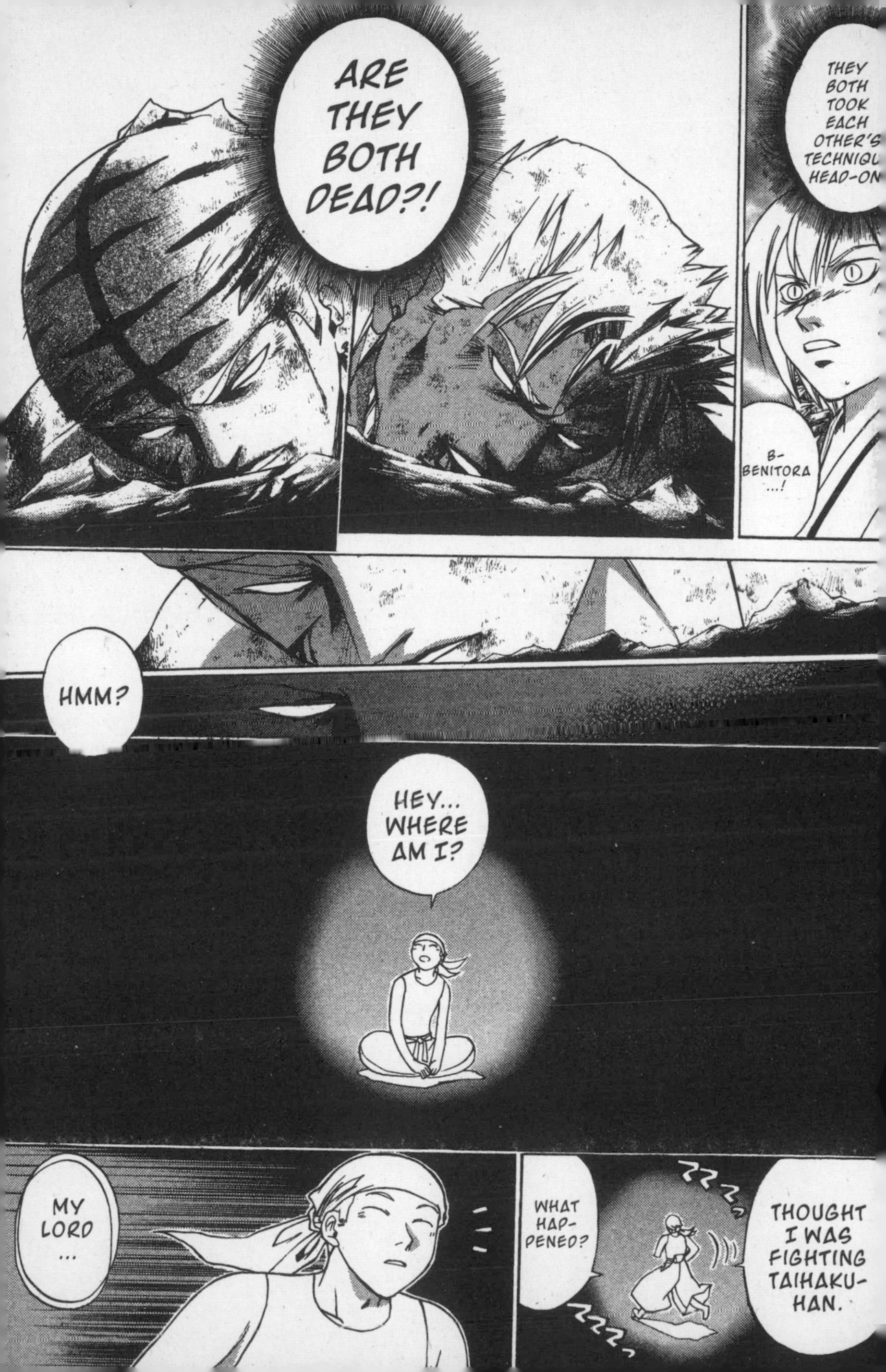
THEY BOTH TOOK EACH OTHER'S TECHNIQU HEAD-ON
B-BENITORA ...!
ARE THEY BOTH DEAD?!
HMM?
HEY... WHERE AM I?
THOUGHT I WAS FIGHTING TAIHAKU-HAN.
WHAT HAP-PENED?
MY LORD ...

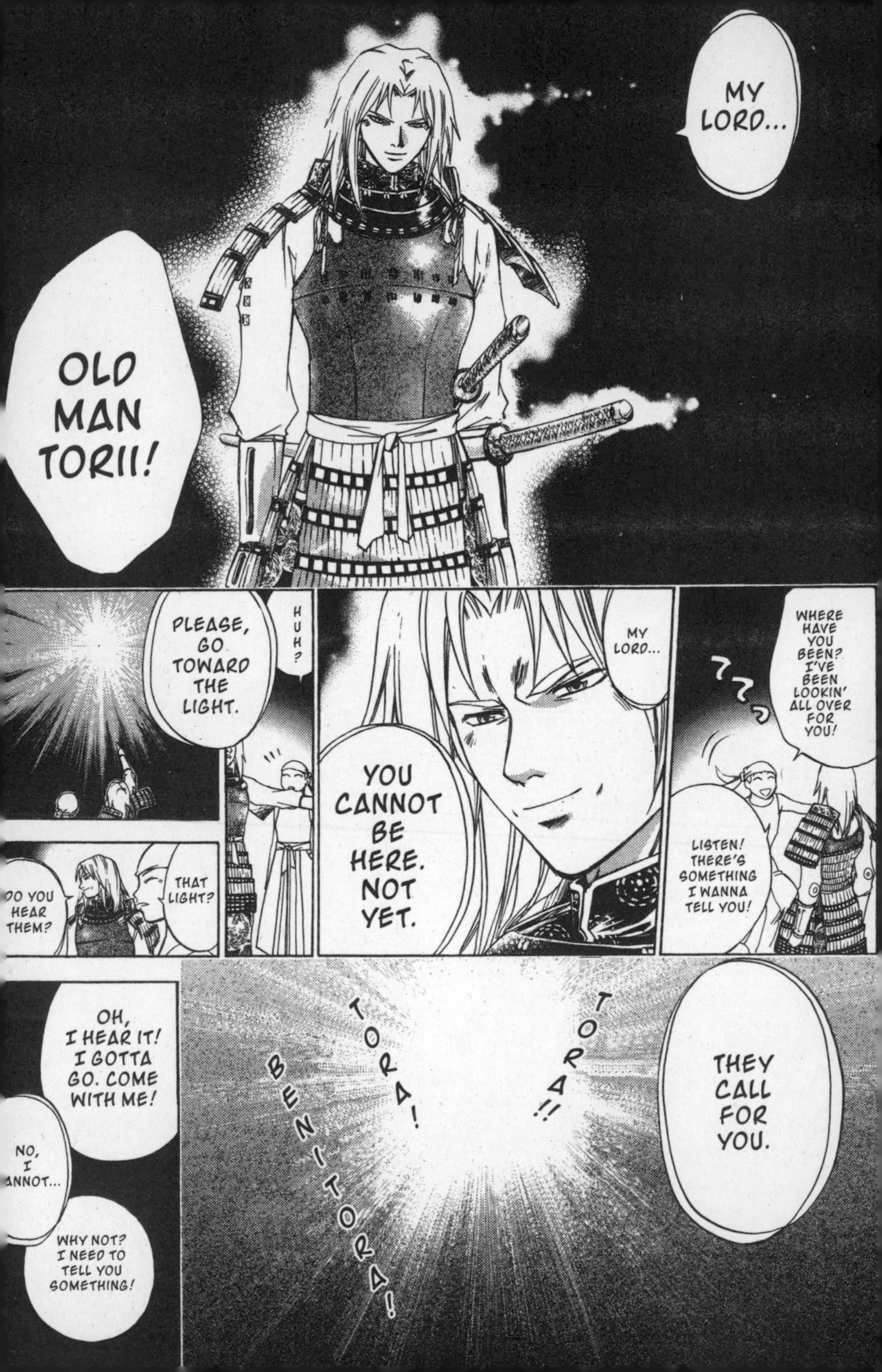
MY LORD...
OLD MAN TORII!
WHERE HAVE YOU BEEN? I'VE BEEN LOOKIN' ALL OVER FOR YOU!
LISTEN! THERE'S SOMETHING I WANNA TELL YOU!
MY LORD...
YOU CANNOT BE HERE. NOT YET.
HUH?
PLEASE, GO TOWARD THE LIGHT.
THAT LIGHT?
DO YOU HEAR THEM?
THEY CALL FOR YOU.
TORA!!
TORA!
BENITORA!
OH, I HEAR IT! I GOTTA GO. COME WITH ME!
NO, I ANNOT...
WHY NOT? I NEED TO TELL YOU SOMETHING!

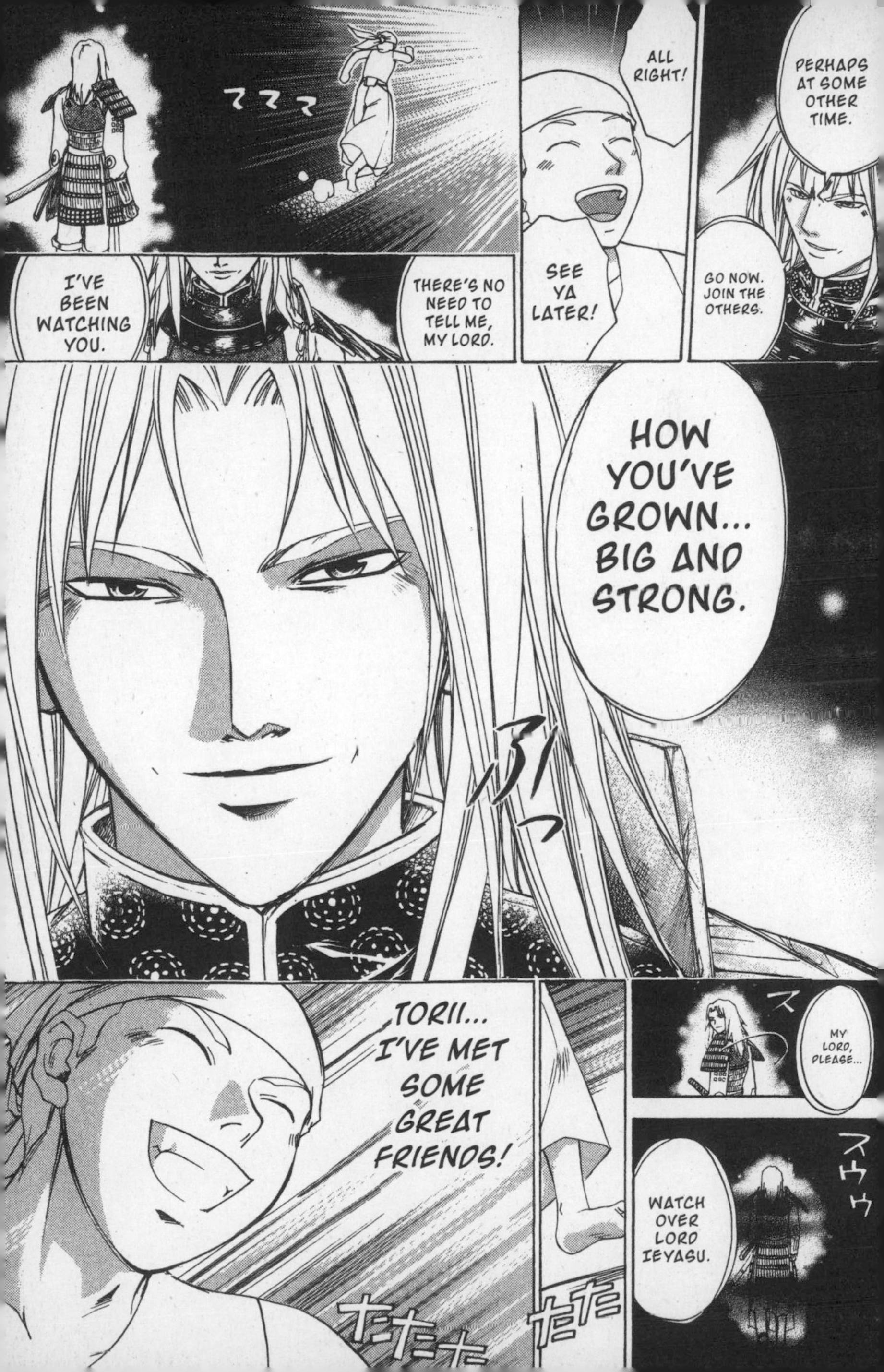
PERHAPS AT SOME OTHER TIME.
GO NOW. JOIN THE OTHERS.
ALL RIGHT!
SEE YA LATER!
THERE'S NO NEED TO TELL ME, MY LORD.
I'VE BEEN WATCHING YOU.
HOW YOU'VE GROWN... BIG AND STRONG.
MY LORD, PLEASE...
WATCH OVER LORD IEYASU.
TORII... I'VE MET SOME GREAT FRIENDS!

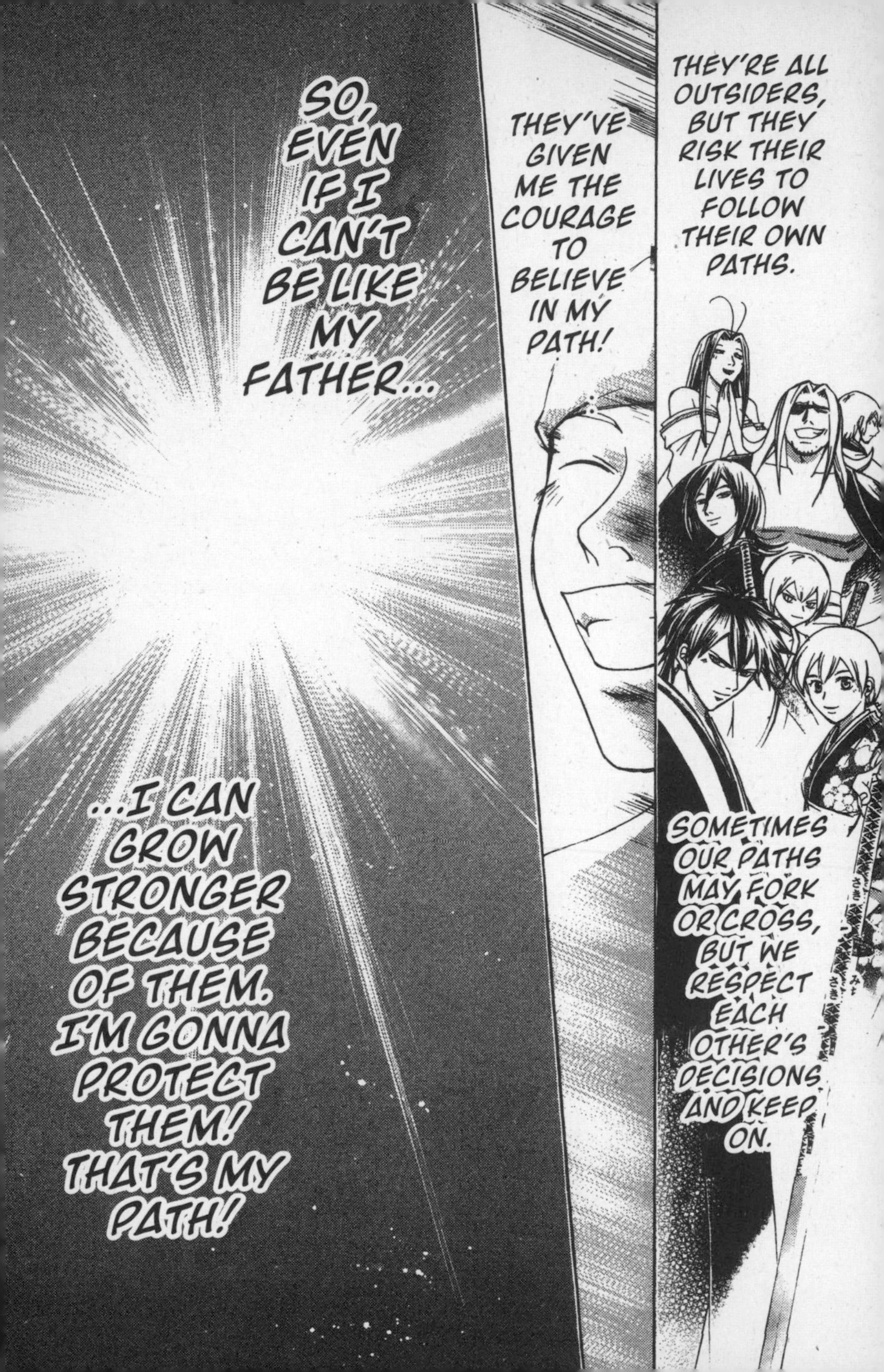
THEY'RE ALL OUTSIDERS, BUT THEY RISK THEIR LIVES TO FOLLOW THEIR OWN PATHS.
SOMETIMES OUR PATHS MAY FORK OR CROSS, BUT WE RESPECT EACH OTHER'S DECISIONS AND KEEP ON.
THEY'VE GIVEN ME THE COURAGE TO BELIEVE IN MY PATH!
SO, EVEN IF I CAN'T BE LIKE MY FATHER...
...I CAN GROW STRONGER BECAUSE OF THEM. I'M GONNA PROTECT THEM! THAT'S MY PATH!

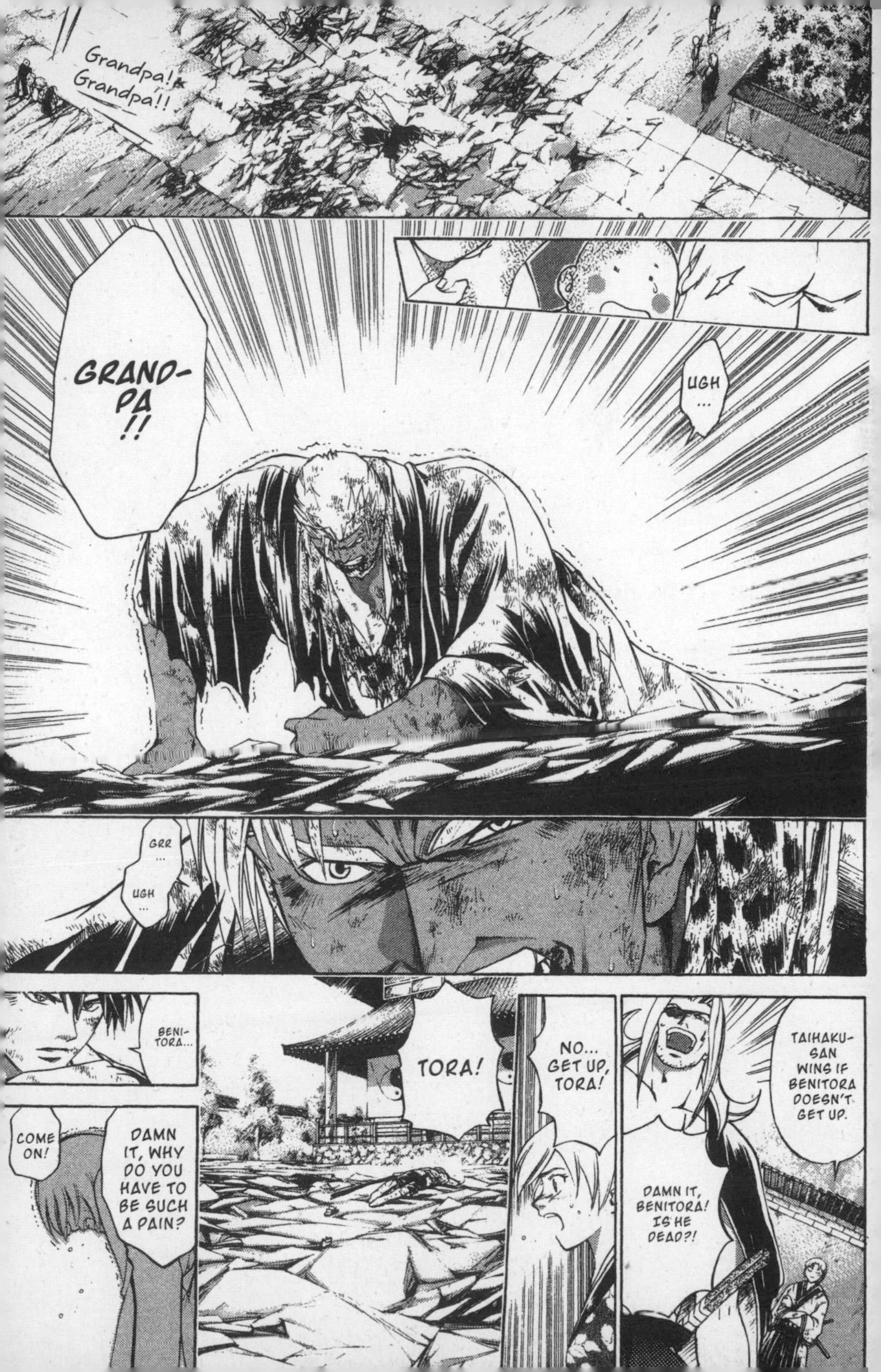
Grandpa! Grandpa!!
UGH ...
GRAND-PA!!
GRR ...
UGH ...
TAIHAKU-SAN WINS IF BENITORA DOESN'T GET UP.
DAMN IT, BENITORA! IS HE DEAD?!
NO... GET UP, TORA!
TORA!
BENI-TORA...
DAMN IT, WHY DO YOU HAVE TO BE SUCH A PAIN?
COME ON!

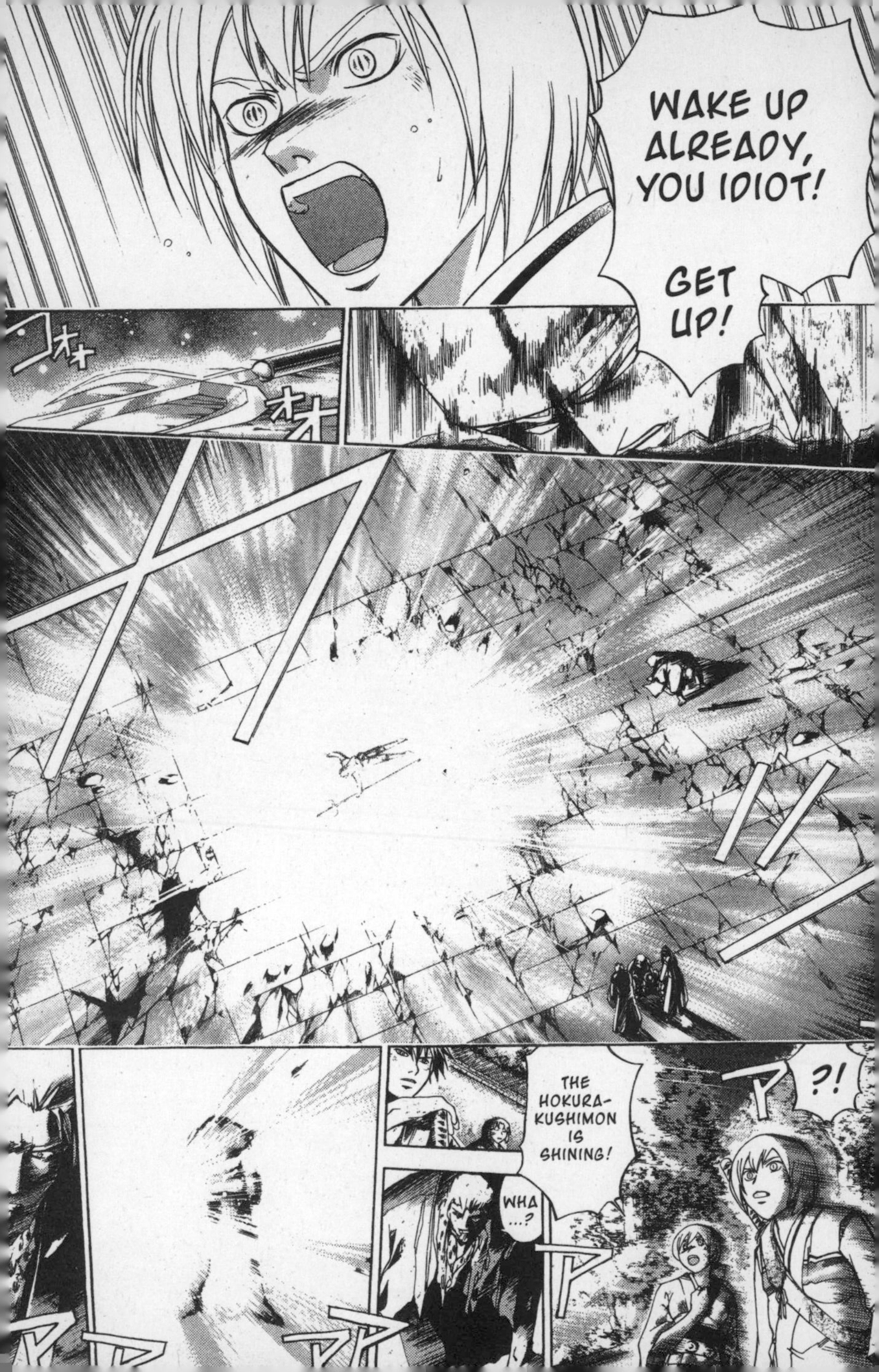
WAKE UP ALREADY, YOU IDIOT!
GET UP!
?!
THE HOKURA-KUSHIMON IS SHINING!
WHA ...?

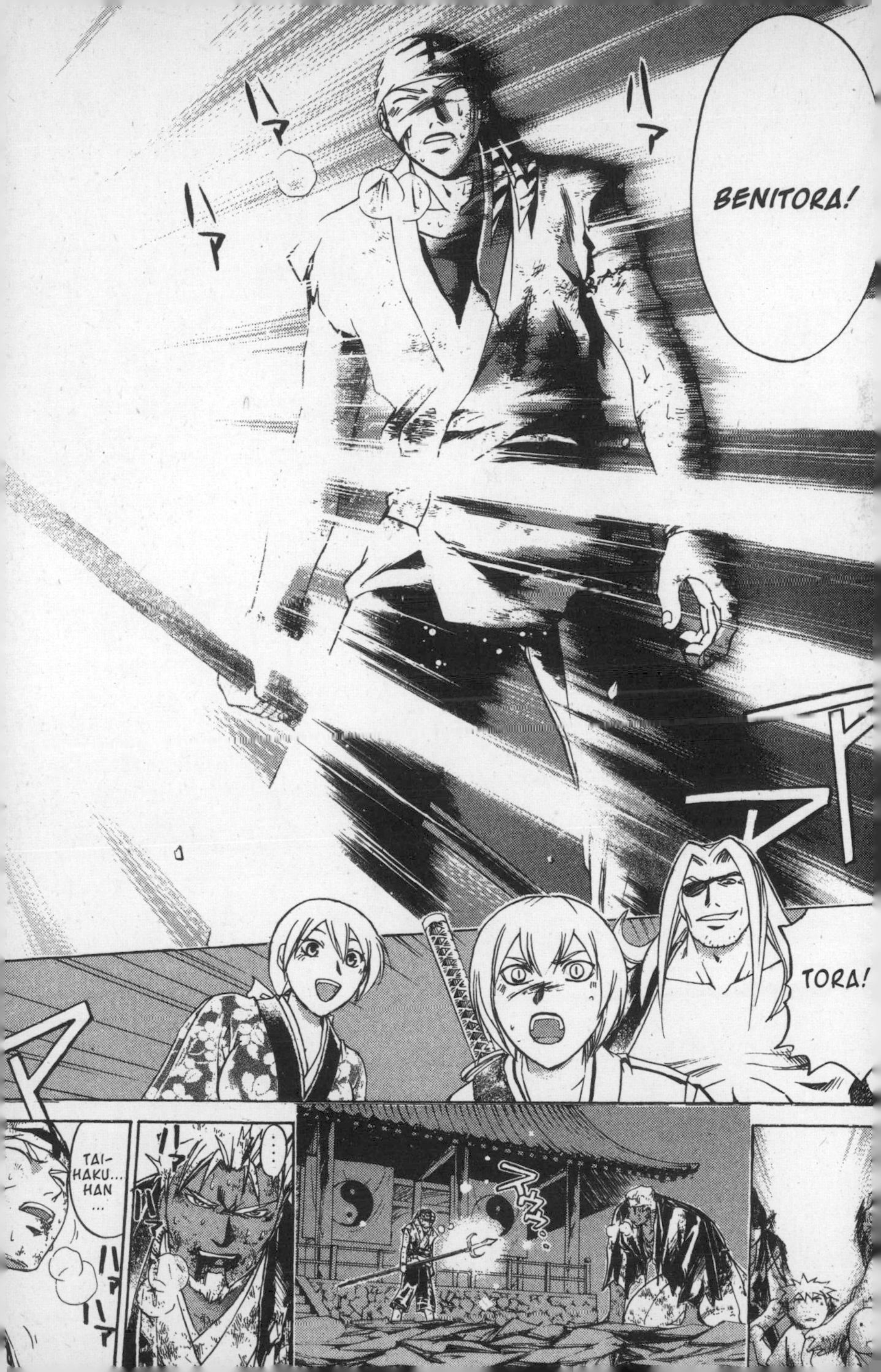
BENITORA!
TORA!
.....
TAI-HAKU... HAN ...

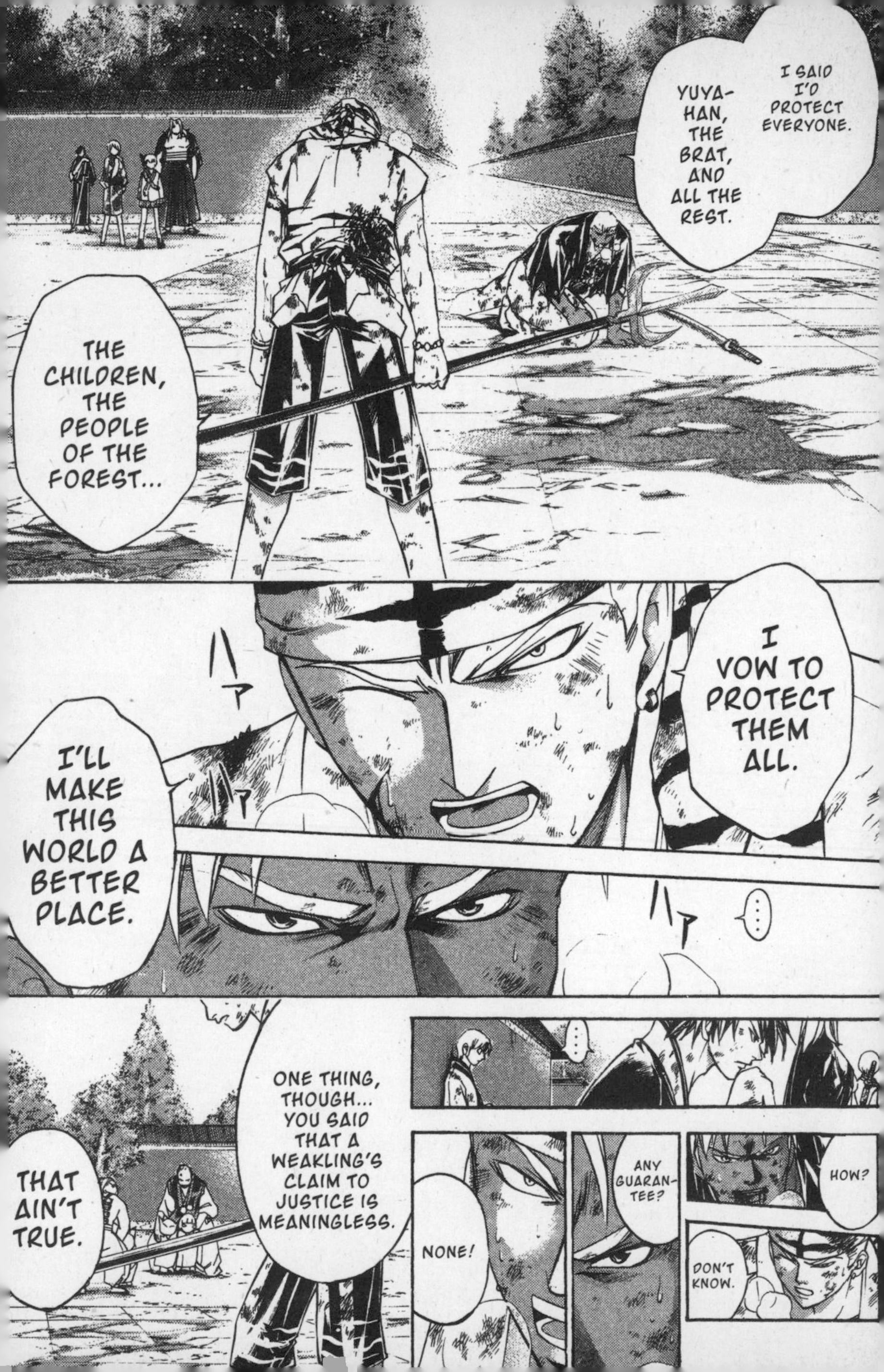
I SAID I'D PROTECT EVERYONE.
YUYA-HAN, THE BRAT, AND ALL THE REST.
THE CHILDREN, THE PEOPLE OF THE FOREST...
I VOW TO PROTECT THEM ALL.
ハァ
I'LL MAKE THIS WORLD A BETTER PLACE.
ハァ
...
...
HOW?
DON'T KNOW.
ANY GUARAN-TEE?
NONE!
ONE THING, THOUGH... YOU SAID THAT A WEAKLING'S CLAIM TO JUSTICE IS MEANINGLESS.
THAT AIN'T TRUE.

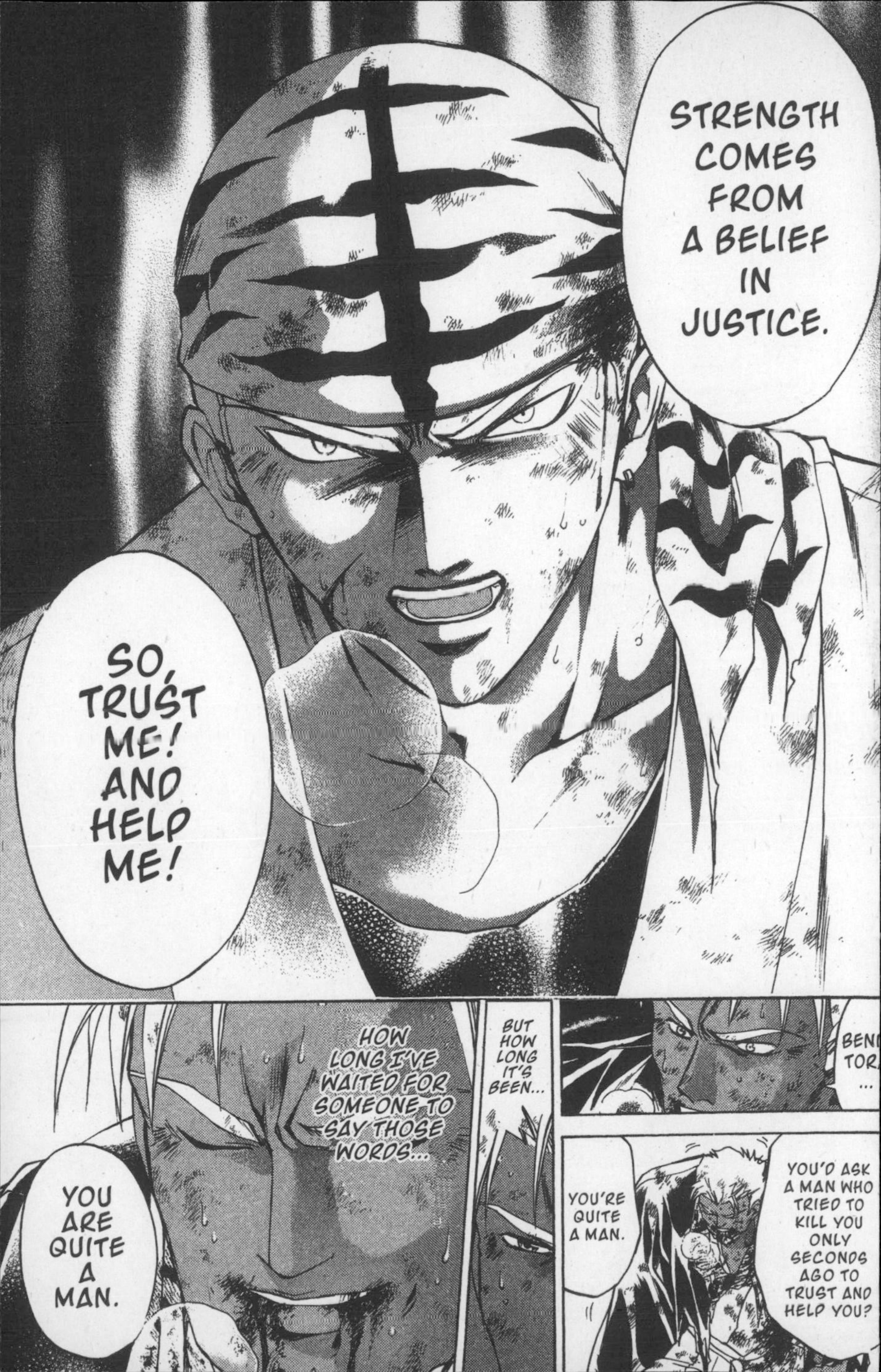
STRENGTH COMES FROM A BELIEF IN JUSTICE.
SO, TRUST ME! AND HELP ME!
BEN TOR ...
YOU'D ASK A MAN WHO TRIED TO KILL YOU ONLY SECONDS AGO TO TRUST AND HELP YOU?
YOU'RE QUITE A MAN.
BUT HOW LONG IT'S BEEN...
HOW LONG I'VE WAITED FOR SOMEONE TO SAY THOSE WORDS...
YOU ARE QUITE A MAN.

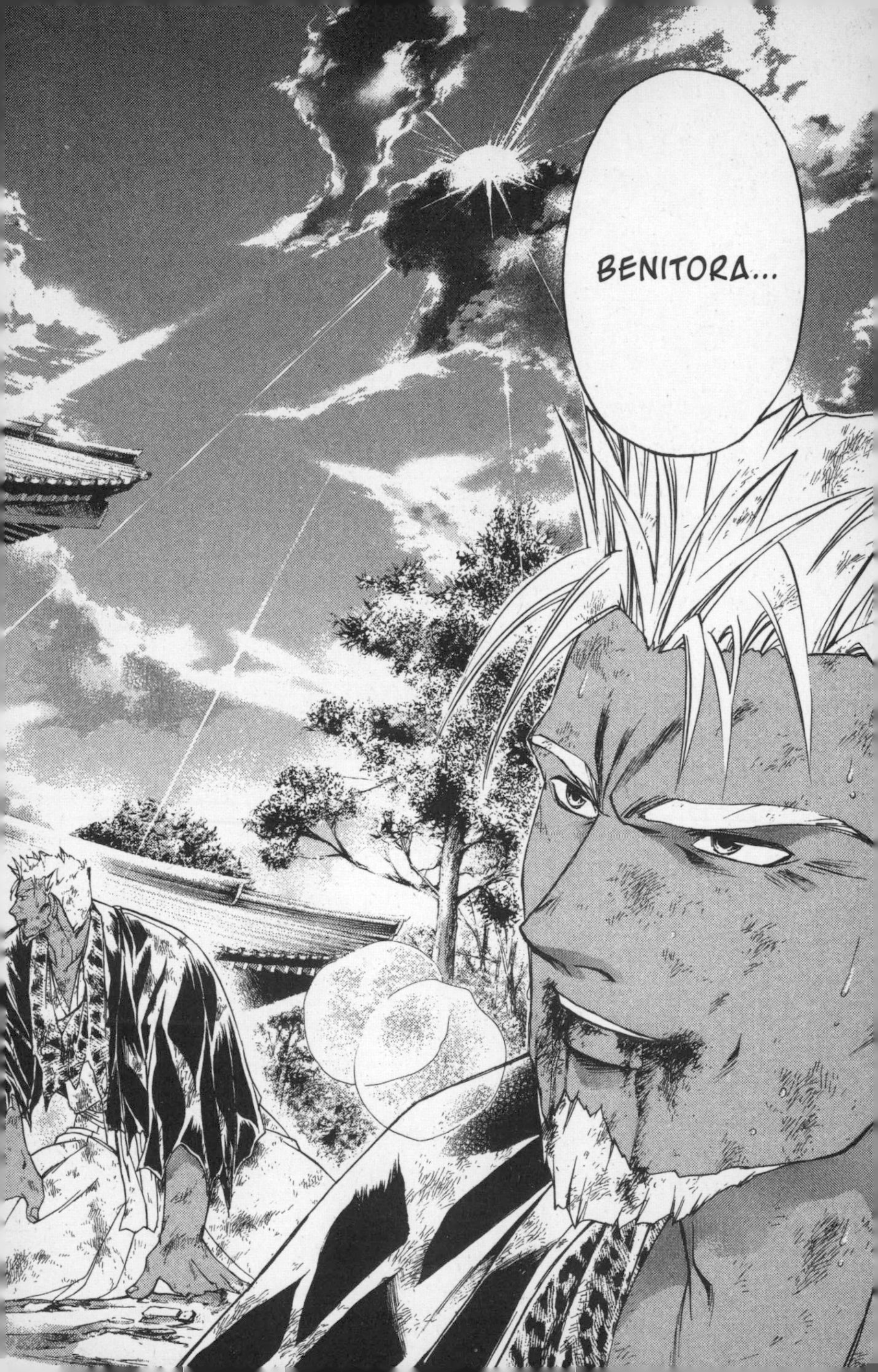
BENITORA...

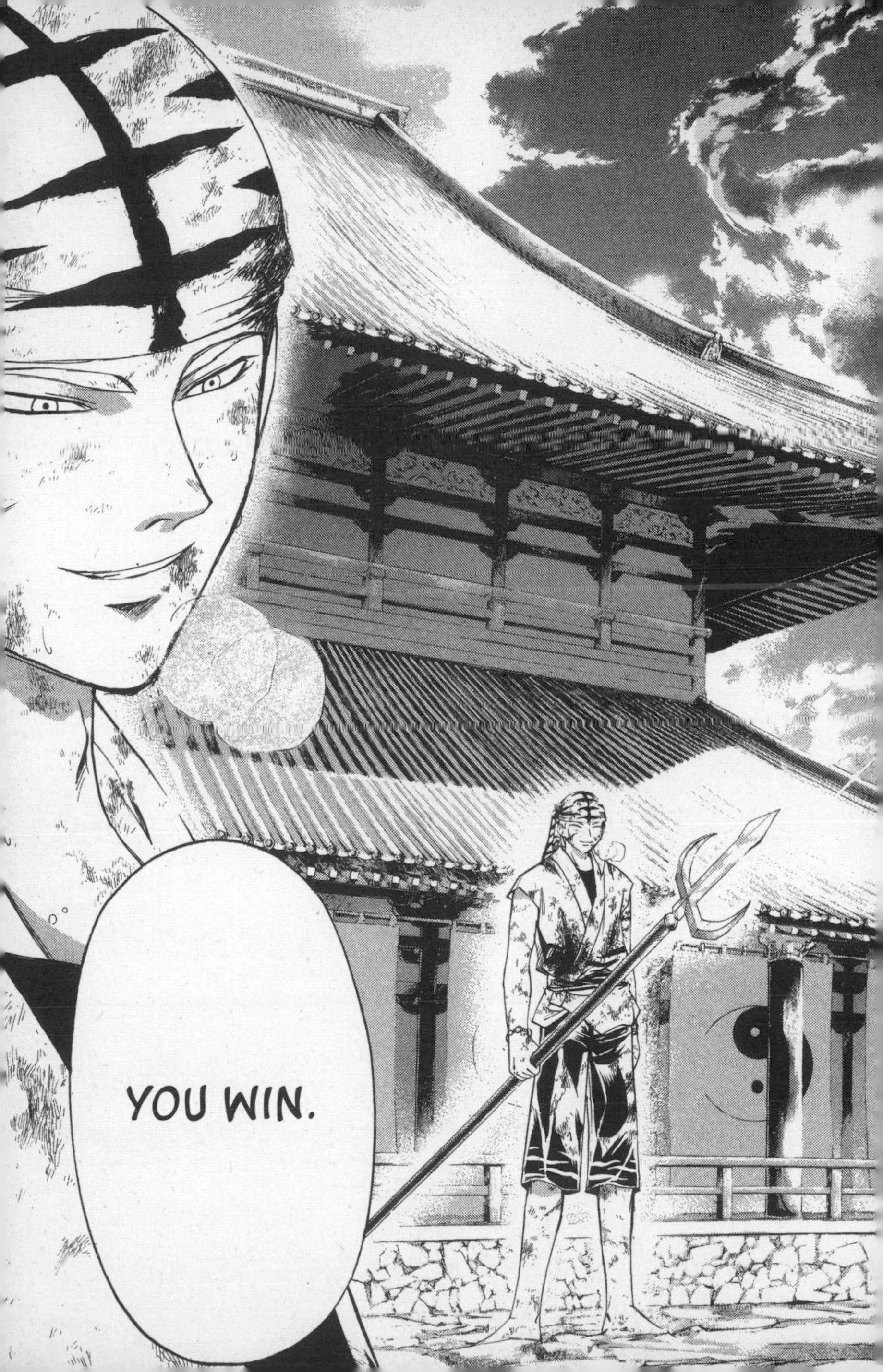
YOU WIN.

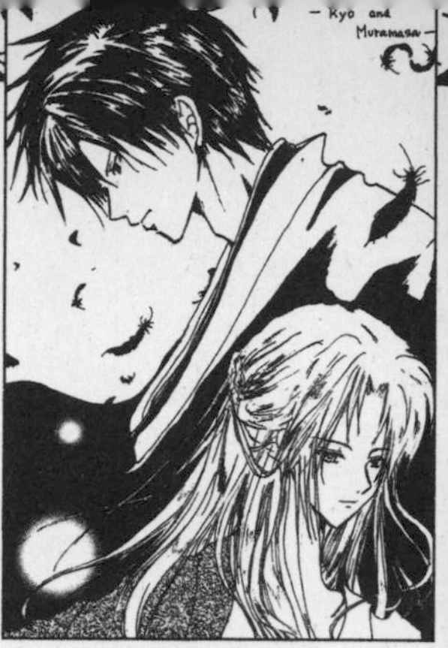
Kyo and Muramasa

Wowza! Clearly the work of a fine artist! [Ryuu / Hokkaido]

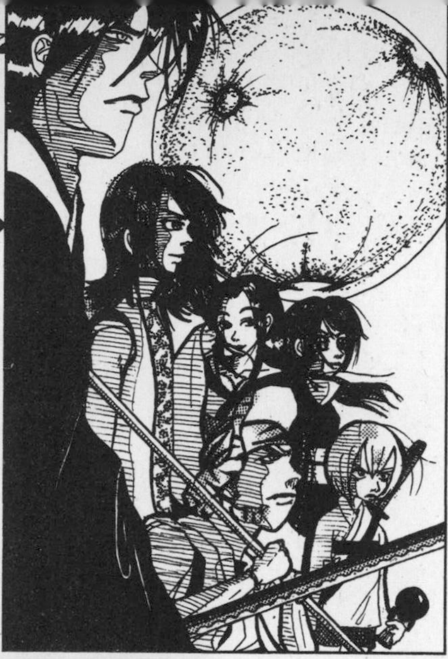

veryone, aiming or their goals! Kiyomi / Gunma]

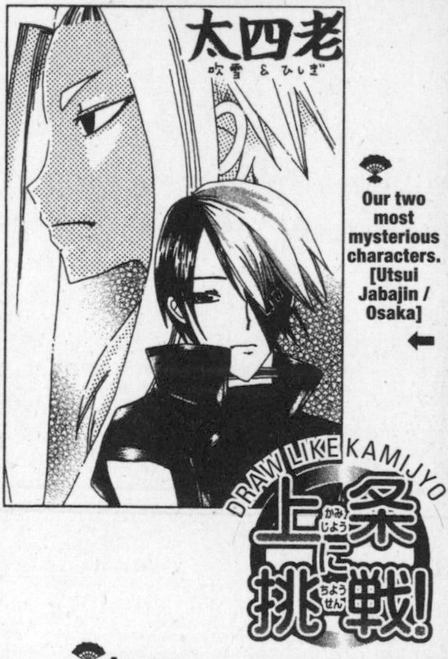
太四老
吹雪 & ひしぎ

Our two most mysterious characters. [Utsui Jabajin / Osaka]

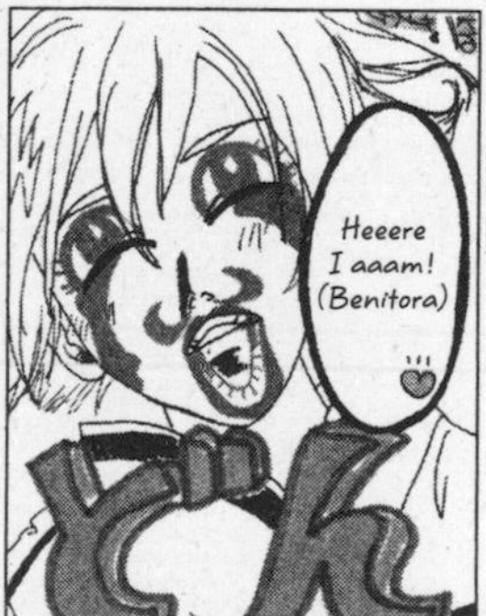
Heeere I aaam! (Benitora)
どん

Aw, man. Now that's just mean. (Ha ha) [Ringokko / Kyoto]

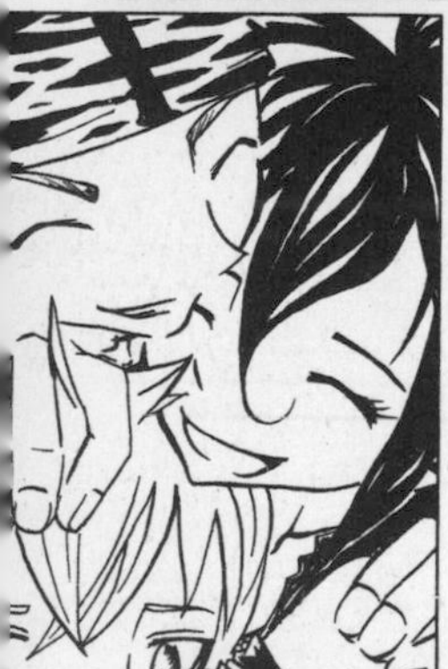

hat great pressions! [Satou Satoma / Niigata]

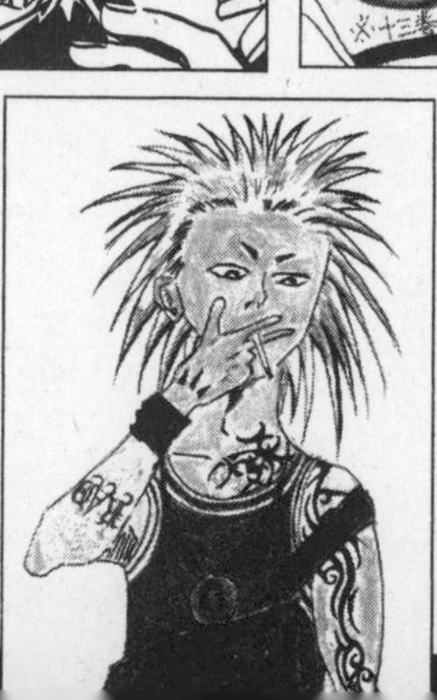

Awesome, White Crow goes modern! [Little Pudding / Aichi]

DRAW LIKE KAMIJYO

上条（かみじょう）に挑戦（ちょうせん）！

FAN ART INFO

SUBMISSION INFO

HOW TO SUBMIT:

1.) SEND YOUR WORK VIA REGULAR MAIL (NOT E-MAIL) TO:

SAMURAI DEEPER KYO FAN MAIL C/O TOKYOPOP
5900 WILSHIRE BLVD, SUITE 2000
LOS ANGELES, CA 90036

2.) ALL WORK SHOULD BE BLACK-AND-WHITE AND NO LARGER THAN 8.5"X11". (AND TRY NOT TO FOLD IT TOO MANY TIMES!) 3.) ANYTHING YOU SEND WILL NOT BE RETURNED. IF YOU WANT TO KEEP YOUR ORIGINAL, IT'S FINE TO SEND US A COPY. 4.) PLEASE INCLUDE YOUR FULL NAME, AGE, CITY, AND STATE FOR US TO PRINT WITH YOUR WORK. IF YOU'D RATHER US USE A PEN NAME, PLEASE INCLUDE THAT, TOO. 5.) IMPORTANT: IF YOU'RE UNDER THE AGE OF 18, YOU MUST HAVE YOUR PARENT'S PERMISSION IN ORDER FOR US TO PRINT YOUR WORK. ANY SUBMISSIONS WITHOUT A SIGNED NOTE OF PARENTAL CONSENT WILL NOT BE USED. 6.) FOR FULL DETAILS, PLEASE CHECK OUT HTTP://WWW.TOKYOPOP.COM/ABOUTUS/FANART.PHP

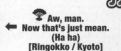

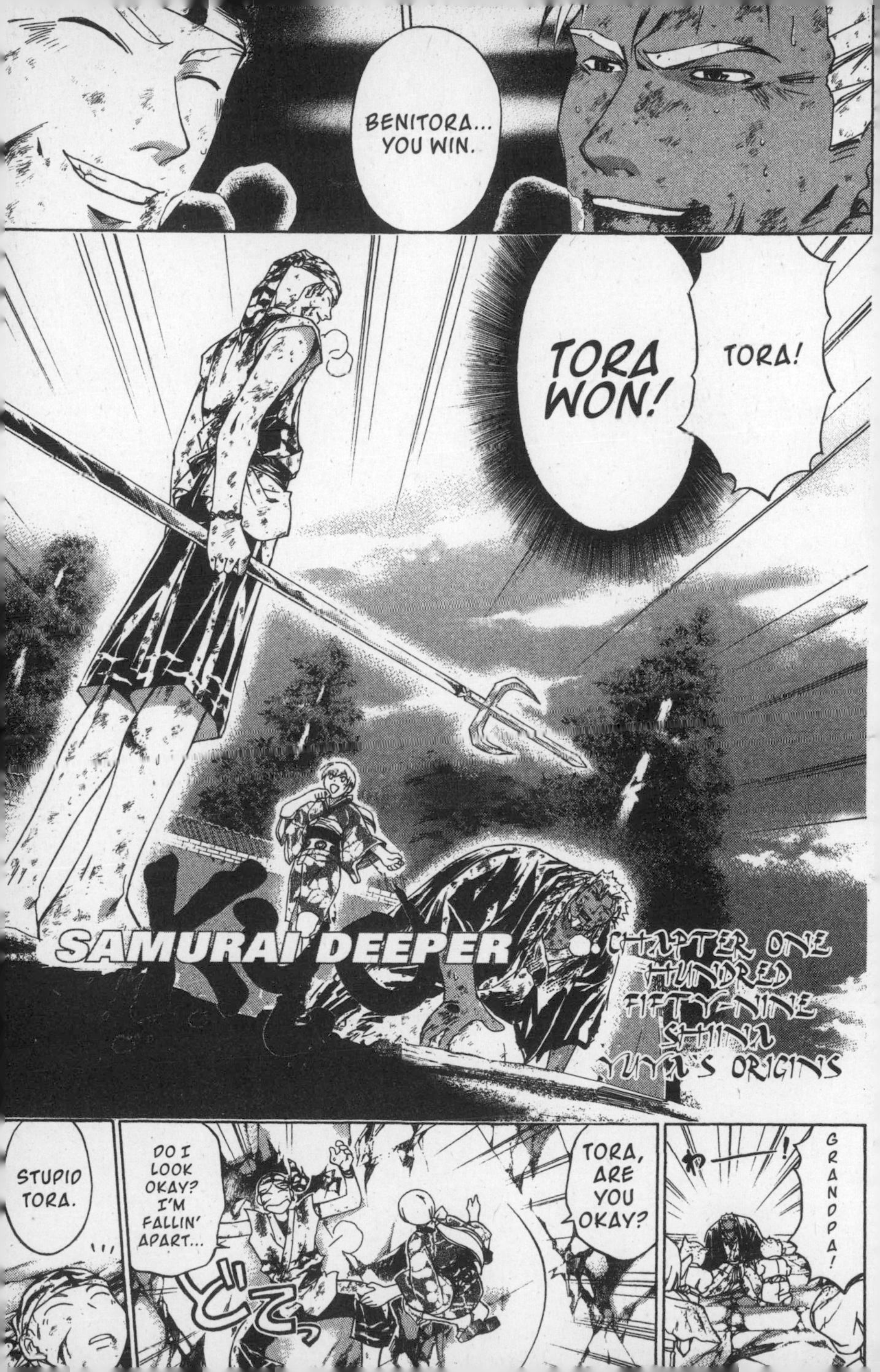
BENITORA... YOU WIN.
TORA!
TORA WON!
SAMURAI DEEPER
CHAPTER ONE HUNDRED FIFTY-NINE SHIINA YUYA'S ORIGINS
GRANDPA!
TORA, ARE YOU OKAY?
DO I LOOK OKAY? I'M FALLIN' APART...
STUPID TORA.

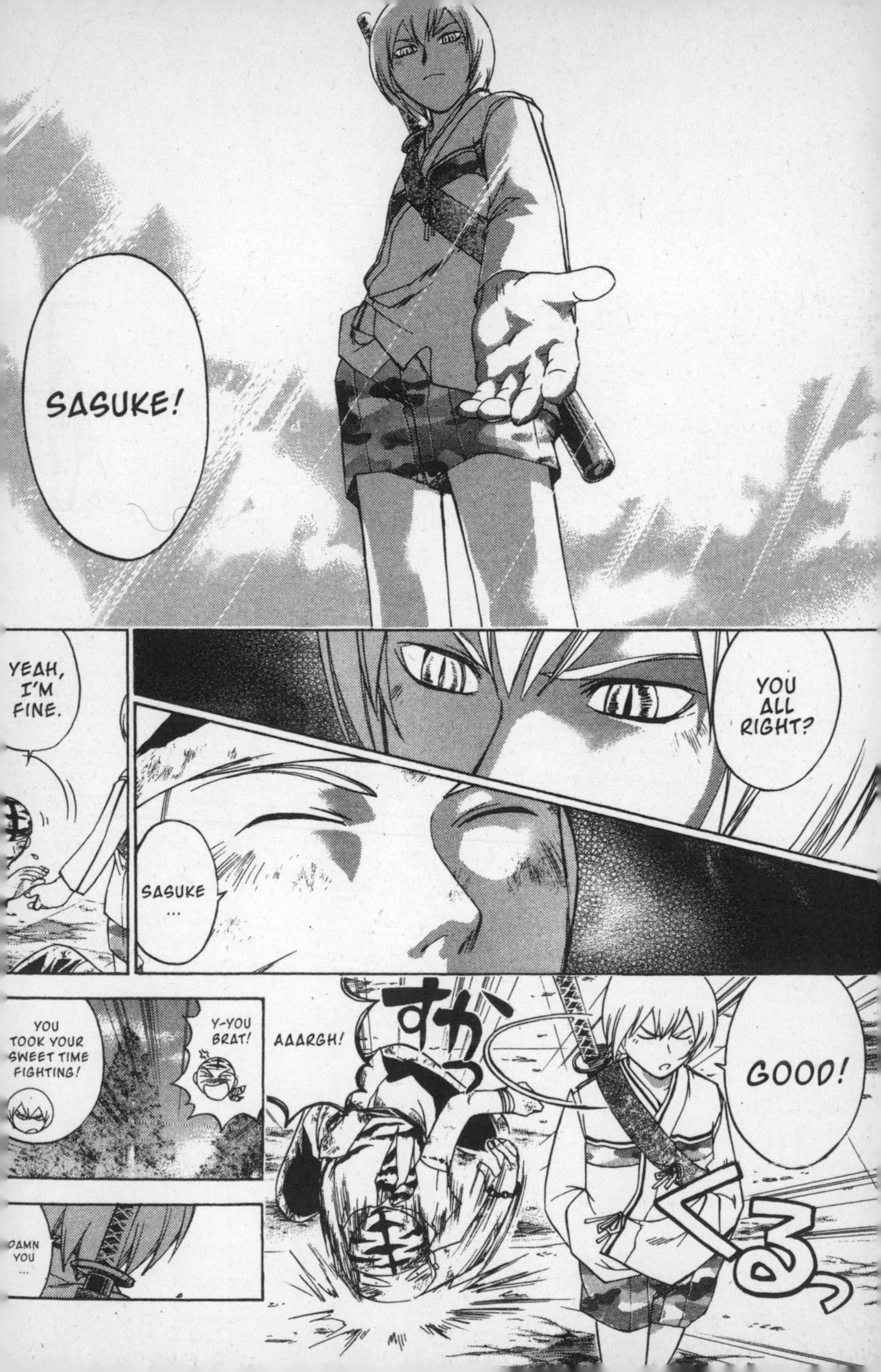
SASUKE!
YOU ALL RIGHT?
SASUKE ...
YEAH, I'M FINE.
GOOD!
すかっ
AAARGH!
くるっ
Y-YOU BRAT!
YOU TOOK YOUR SWEET TIME FIGHTING!
DAMN YOU ...

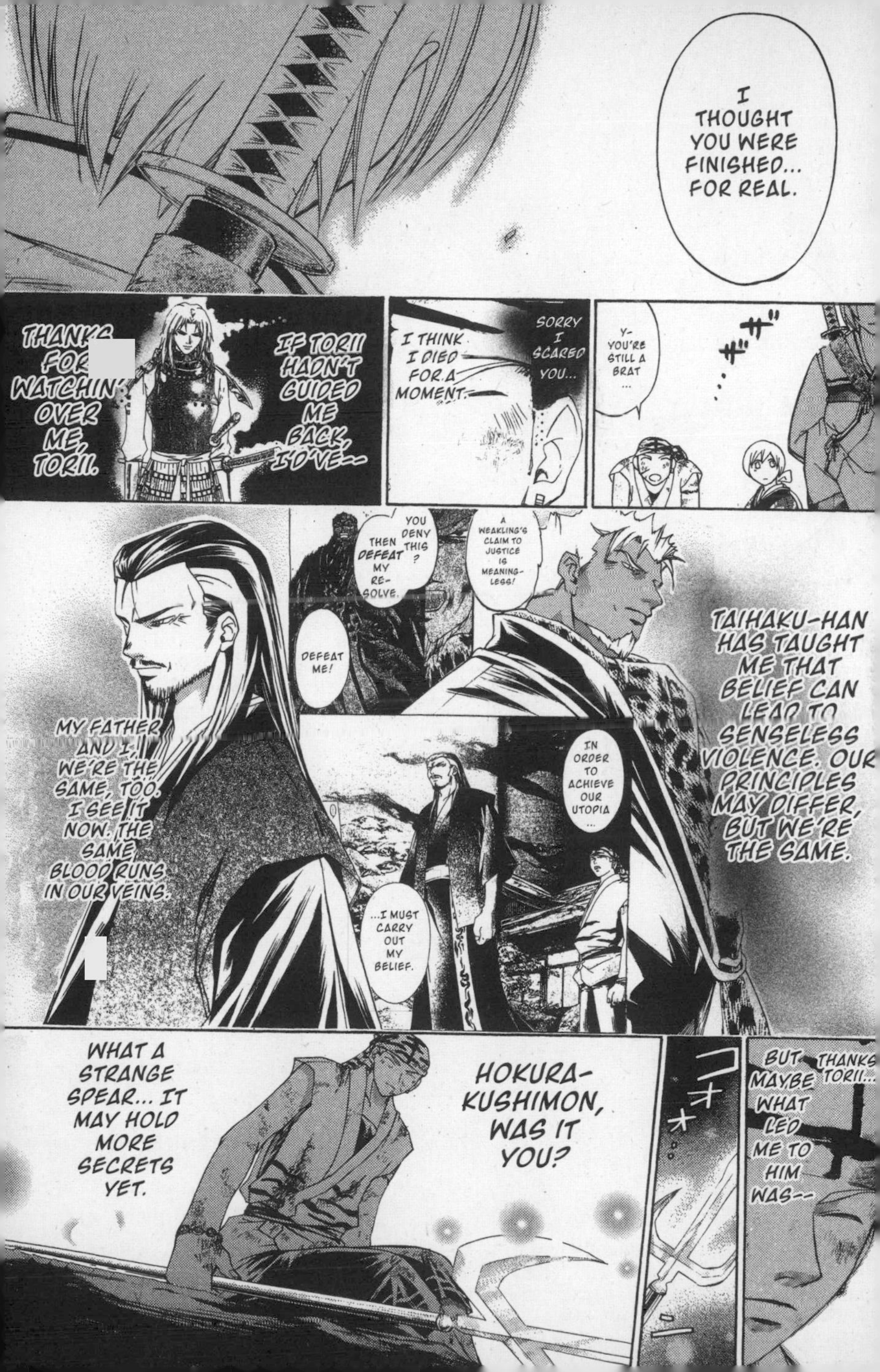

I THOUGHT YOU WERE FINISHED... FOR REAL.
Y- YOU'RE STILL A BRAT ...
SORRY I SCARED YOU...
I THINK I DIED FOR A MOMENT.
IF TORII HADN'T GUIDED ME BACK, I'D'VE--
THANKS FOR WATCHIN' OVER ME, TORII.
TAIHAKU-HAN HAS TAUGHT ME THAT BELIEF CAN LEAD TO SENSELESS VIOLENCE. OUR PRINCIPLES MAY DIFFER, BUT WE'RE THE SAME.
A WEAKLING'S CLAIM TO JUSTICE IS MEANING-LESS!
YOU DENY THIS?
THEN DEFEAT MY RE-SOLVE.
DEFEAT ME!
IN ORDER TO ACHIEVE OUR UTOPIA ...
...I MUST CARRY OUT MY BELIEF.
MY FATHER AND I, WE'RE THE SAME, TOO. I SEE IT NOW. THE SAME BLOOD RUNS IN OUR VEINS.
THANKS TORII...
BUT MAYBE WHAT LED ME TO HIM WAS--
HOKURA-KUSHIMON, WAS IT YOU?
WHAT A STRANGE SPEAR... IT MAY HOLD MORE SECRETS YET.

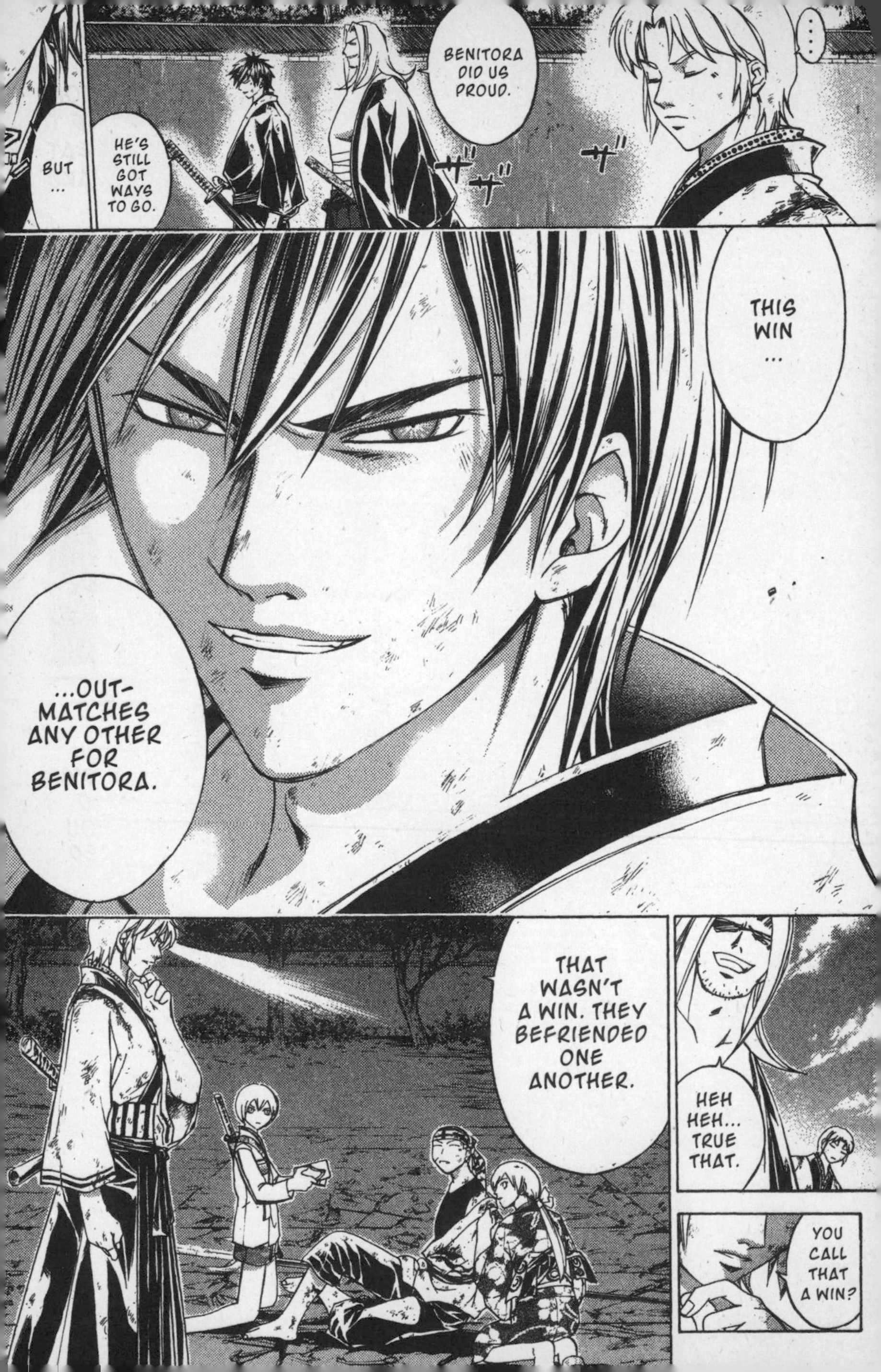

...
BENITORA DID US PROUD.
ザ ザ ザ
HE'S STILL GOT WAYS TO GO.
BUT ...
THIS WIN ...
...OUT-MATCHES ANY OTHER FOR BENITORA.
HEH HEH... TRUE THAT.
YOU CALL THAT A WIN?
THAT WASN'T A WIN. THEY BEFRIENDED ONE ANOTHER.

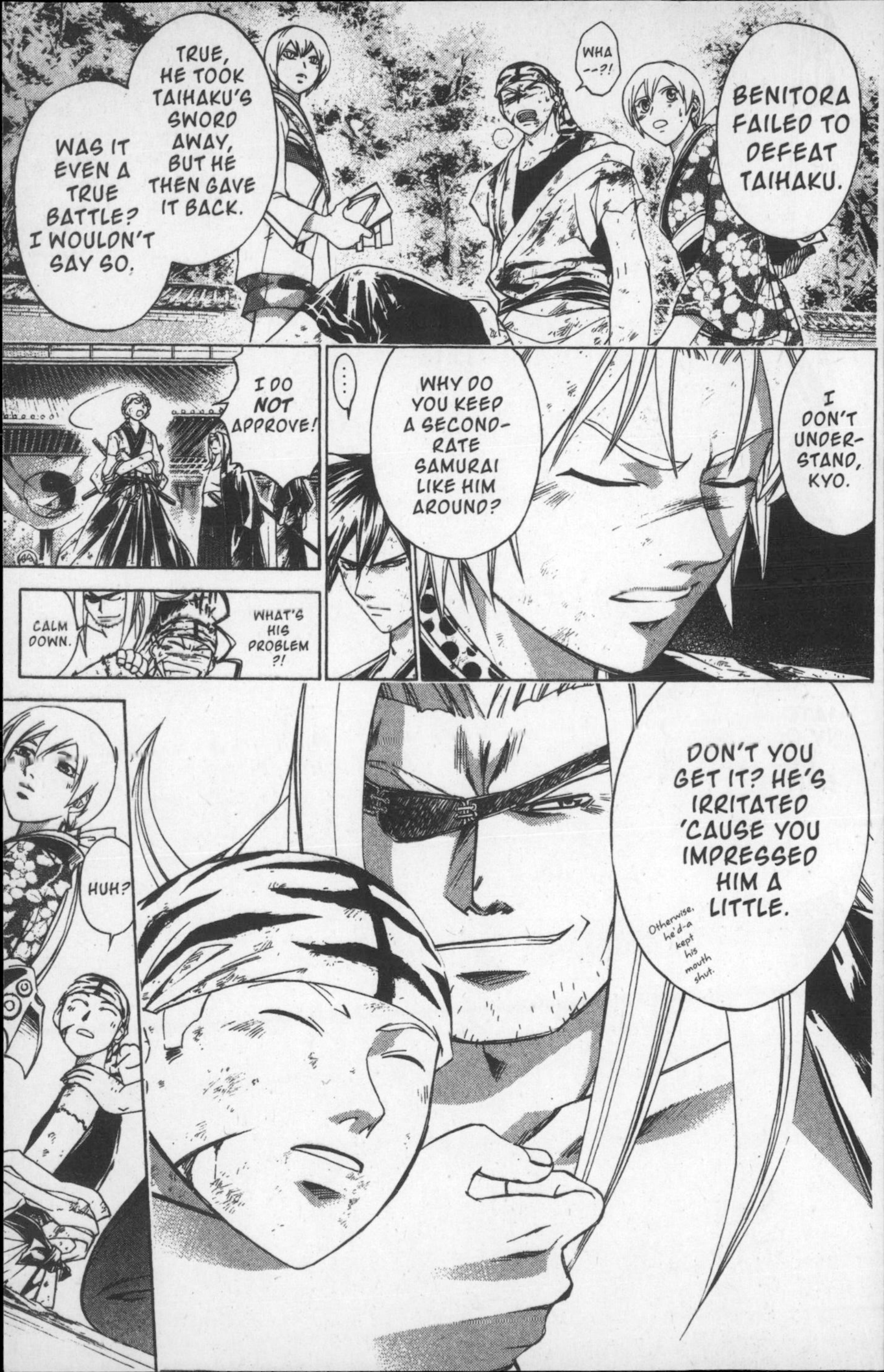
BENITORA FAILED TO DEFEAT TAIHAKU.
WHA--?!
TRUE, HE TOOK TAIHAKU'S SWORD AWAY, BUT HE THEN GAVE IT BACK.
WAS IT EVEN A TRUE BATTLE? I WOULDN'T SAY SO.
I DON'T UNDERSTAND, KYO.
WHY DO YOU KEEP A SECOND-RATE SAMURAI LIKE HIM AROUND?
...
I DO **NOT** APPROVE!
WHAT'S HIS PROBLEM?!
CALM DOWN.
DON'T YOU GET IT? HE'S IRRITATED 'CAUSE YOU IMPRESSED HIM A LITTLE.
Otherwise, he'd-a kept his mouth shut.
HUH?

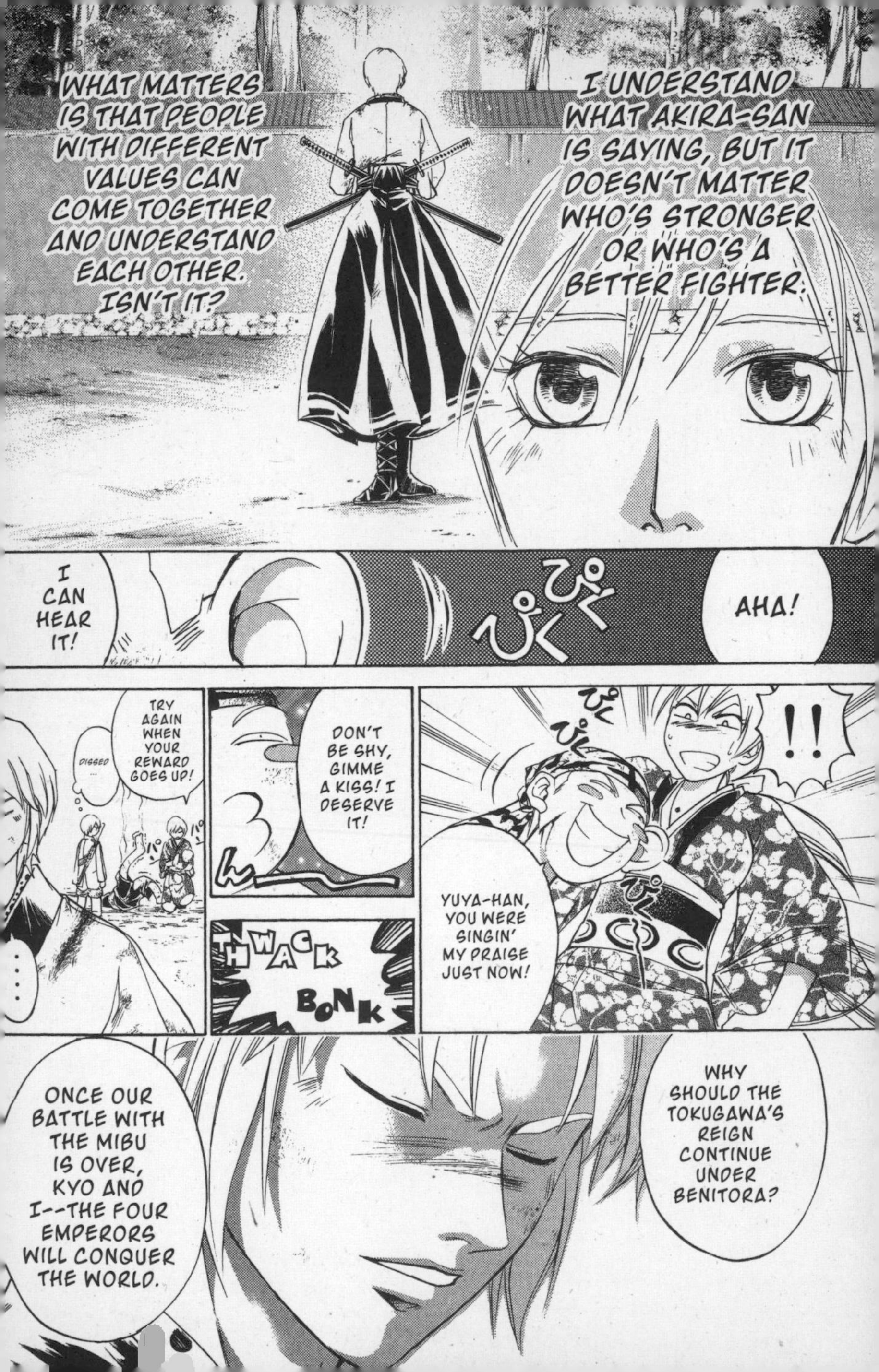
I UNDERSTAND WHAT AKIRA-SAN IS SAYING, BUT IT DOESN'T MATTER WHO'S STRONGER OR WHO'S A BETTER FIGHTER.
WHAT MATTERS IS THAT PEOPLE WITH DIFFERENT VALUES CAN COME TOGETHER AND UNDERSTAND EACH OTHER. ISN'T IT?
AHA!
ぴく ぴく
I CAN HEAR IT!
!!
ぴく
YUYA-HAN, YOU WERE SINGIN' MY PRAISE JUST NOW!
ぴく
DON'T BE SHY, GIMME A KISS! I DESERVE IT!
THWACK
BONK
TRY AGAIN WHEN YOUR REWARD GOES UP!
DISSED...
.....
WHY SHOULD THE TOKUGAWA'S REIGN CONTINUE UNDER BENITORA?
ONCE OUR BATTLE WITH THE MIBU IS OVER, KYO AND I--THE FOUR EMPERORS WILL CONQUER THE WORLD.

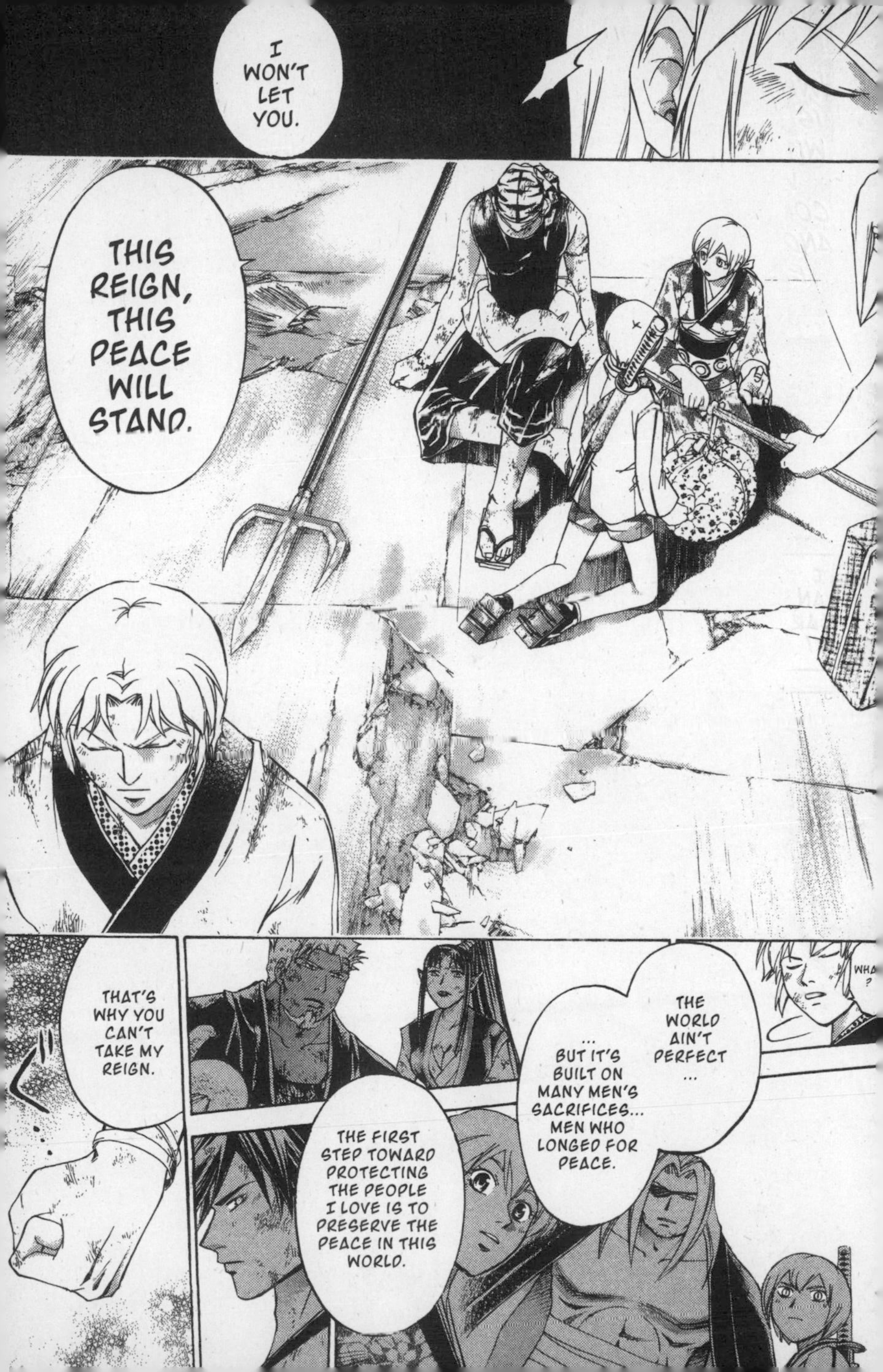
I WON'T LET YOU.
THIS REIGN, THIS PEACE WILL STAND.
THE WORLD AIN'T PERFECT ...
... BUT IT'S BUILT ON MANY MEN'S SACRIFICES... MEN WHO LONGED FOR PEACE.
THE FIRST STEP TOWARD PROTECTING THE PEOPLE I LOVE IS TO PRESERVE THE PEACE IN THIS WORLD.
THAT'S WHY YOU CAN'T TAKE MY REIGN.

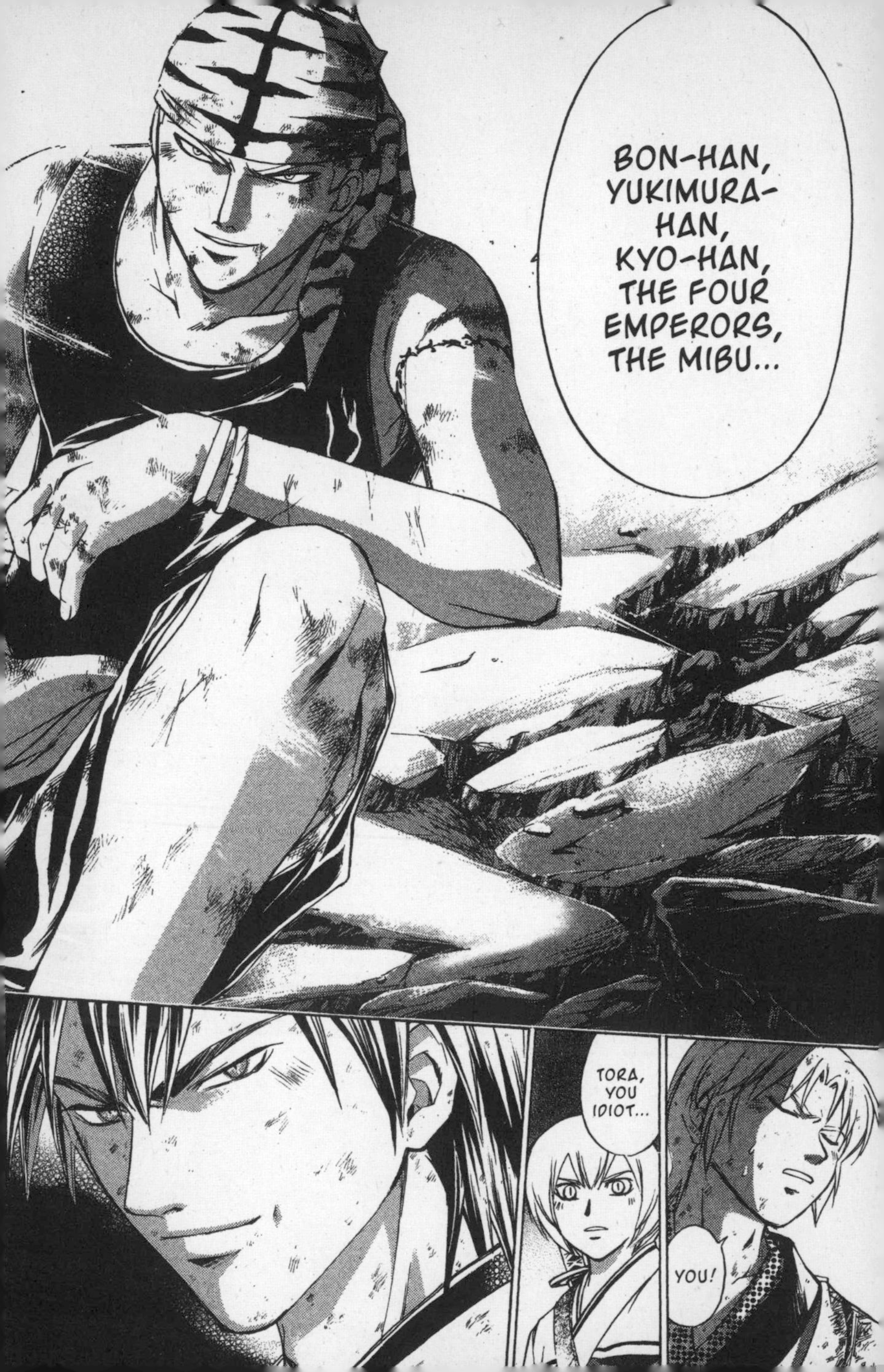
BON-HAN, YUKIMURA-HAN, KYO-HAN, THE FOUR EMPERORS, THE MIBU...
YOU!
TORA, YOU IDIOT...

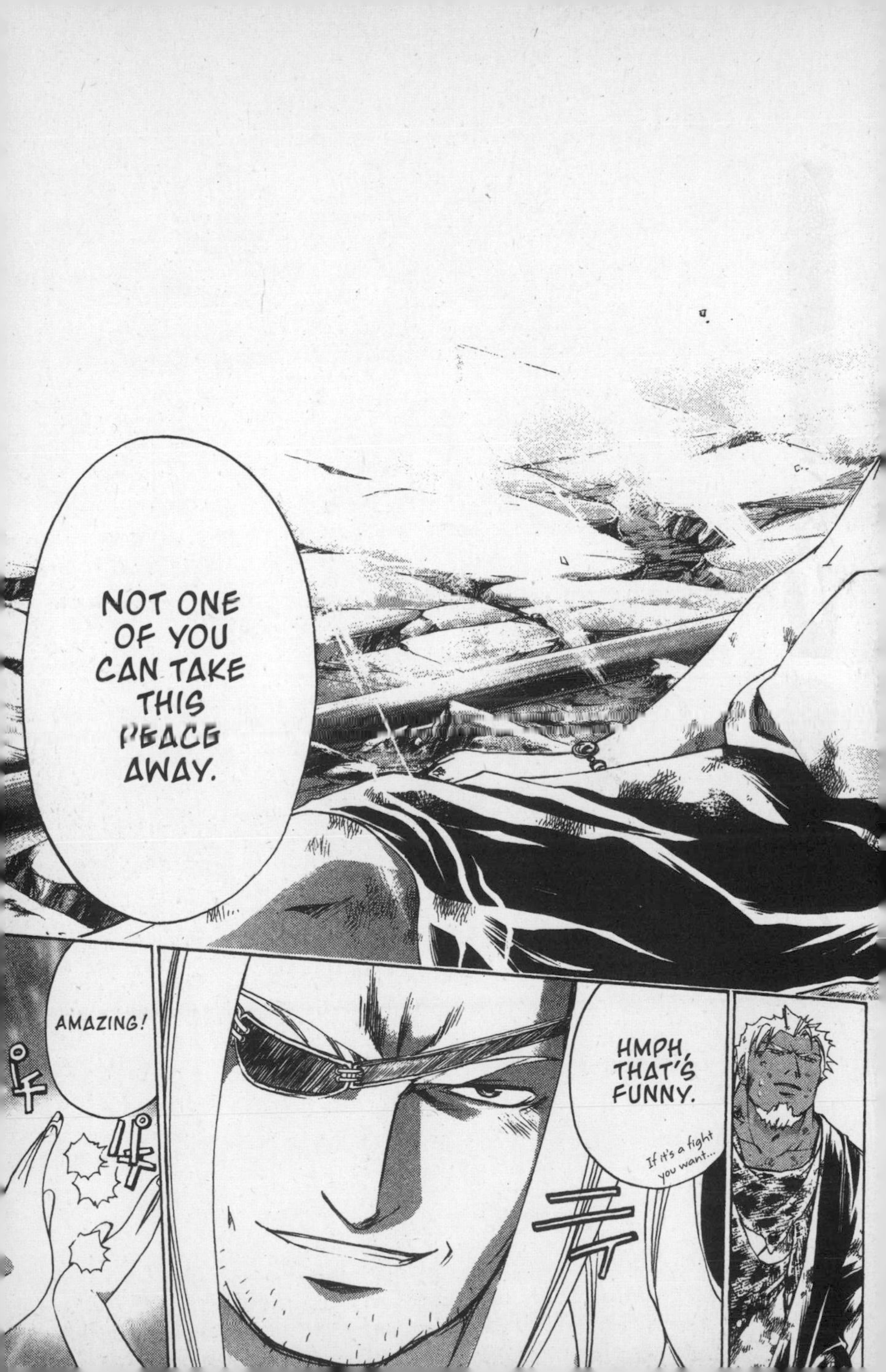
NOT ONE OF YOU CAN TAKE THIS PEACE AWAY.
HMPH, THAT'S FUNNY.
If it's a fight you want...
AMAZING!

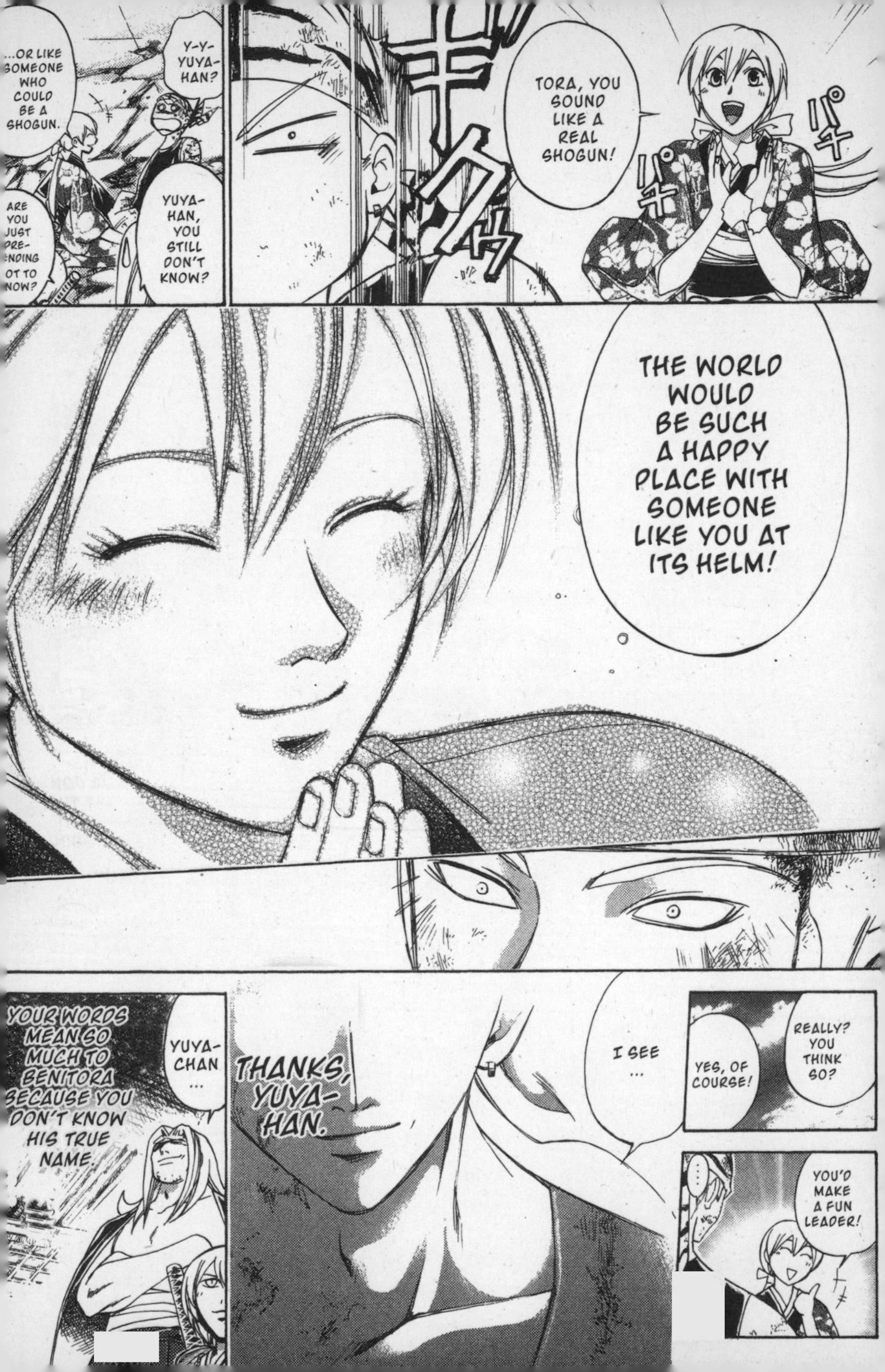

TORA, YOU SOUND LIKE A REAL SHOGUN!
Y-Y-YUYA-HAN?
...OR LIKE SOMEONE WHO COULD BE A SHOGUN.
YUYA-HAN, YOU STILL DON'T KNOW?
ARE YOU JUST PRE-ENDING OT TO NOW?
THE WORLD WOULD BE SUCH A HAPPY PLACE WITH SOMEONE LIKE YOU AT ITS HELM!
REALLY? YOU THINK SO?
YES, OF COURSE!
YOU'D MAKE A FUN LEADER!
...
I SEE ...
THANKS, YUYA-HAN.
YUYA-CHAN ...
YOUR WORDS MEAN SO MUCH TO BENITORA BECAUSE YOU DON'T KNOW HIS TRUE NAME.

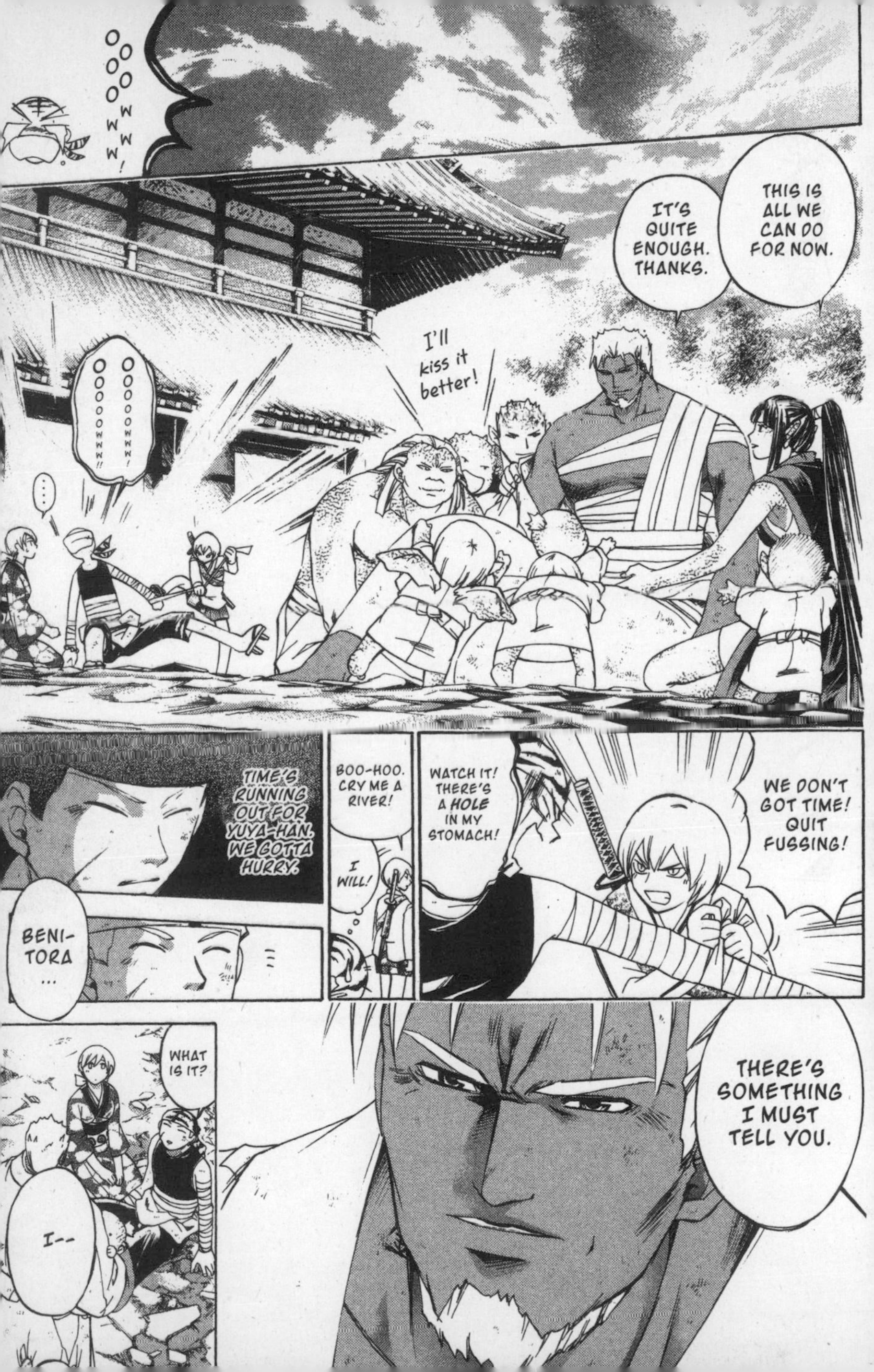
OOOOWWWW!
THIS IS ALL WE CAN DO FOR NOW.
IT'S QUITE ENOUGH. THANKS.
I'll kiss it better!
OOOOOOWWW!
OOOOOOWWW!!
...
WE DON'T GOT TIME! QUIT FUSSING!
WATCH IT! THERE'S A HOLE IN MY STOMACH!
BOO-HOO. CRY ME A RIVER!
I WILL!
TIME'S RUNNING OUT FOR YUYA-HAN. WE GOTTA HURRY.
BENI-TORA ...
THERE'S SOMETHING I MUST TELL YOU.
WHAT IS IT?
I--

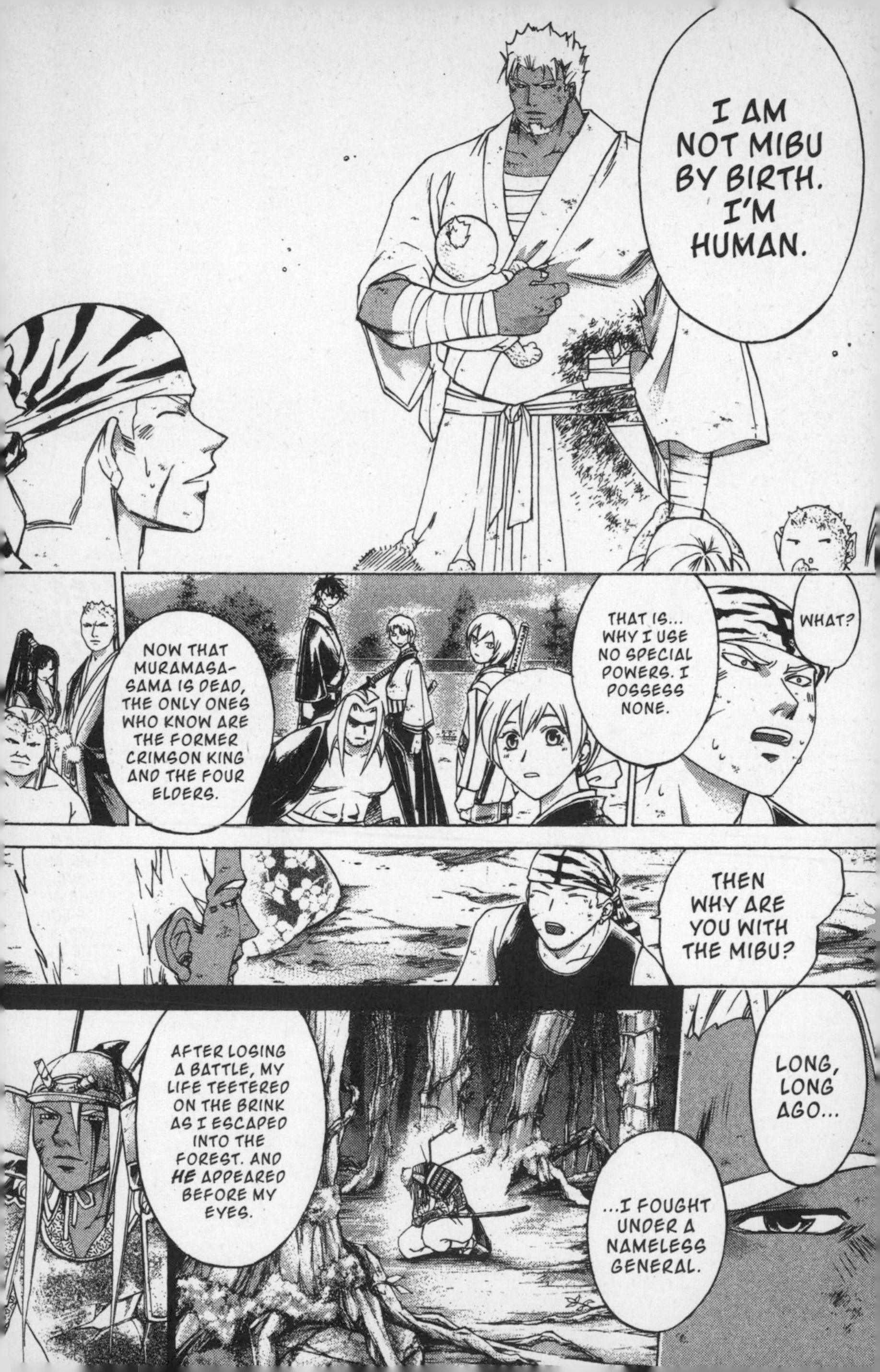
I AM NOT MIBU BY BIRTH. I'M HUMAN.
WHAT?
THAT IS... WHY I USE NO SPECIAL POWERS. I POSSESS NONE.
NOW THAT MURAMASA-SAMA IS DEAD, THE ONLY ONES WHO KNOW ARE THE FORMER CRIMSON KING AND THE FOUR ELDERS.
THEN WHY ARE YOU WITH THE MIBU?
LONG, LONG AGO...
...I FOUGHT UNDER A NAMELESS GENERAL.
AFTER LOSING A BATTLE, MY LIFE TEETERED ON THE BRINK AS I ESCAPED INTO THE FOREST. AND *HE* APPEARED BEFORE MY EYES.

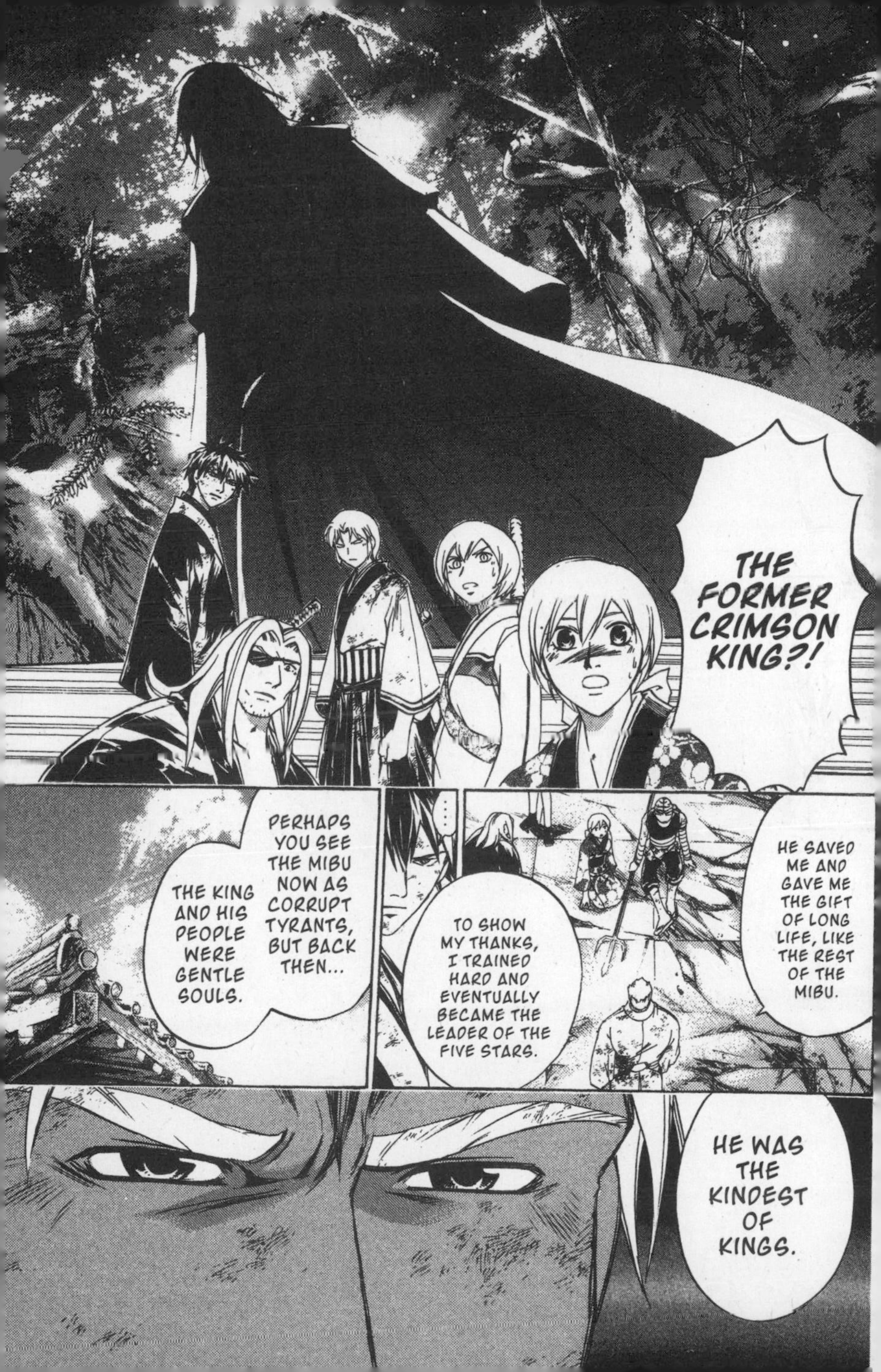
THE FORMER CRIMSON KING?!
HE SAVED ME AND GAVE ME THE GIFT OF LONG LIFE, LIKE THE REST OF THE MIBU.
...
TO SHOW MY THANKS, I TRAINED HARD AND EVENTUALLY BECAME THE LEADER OF THE FIVE STARS.
PERHAPS YOU SEE THE MIBU NOW AS CORRUPT TYRANTS, BUT BACK THEN...
THE KING AND HIS PEOPLE WERE GENTLE SOULS.
HE WAS THE KINDEST OF KINGS.

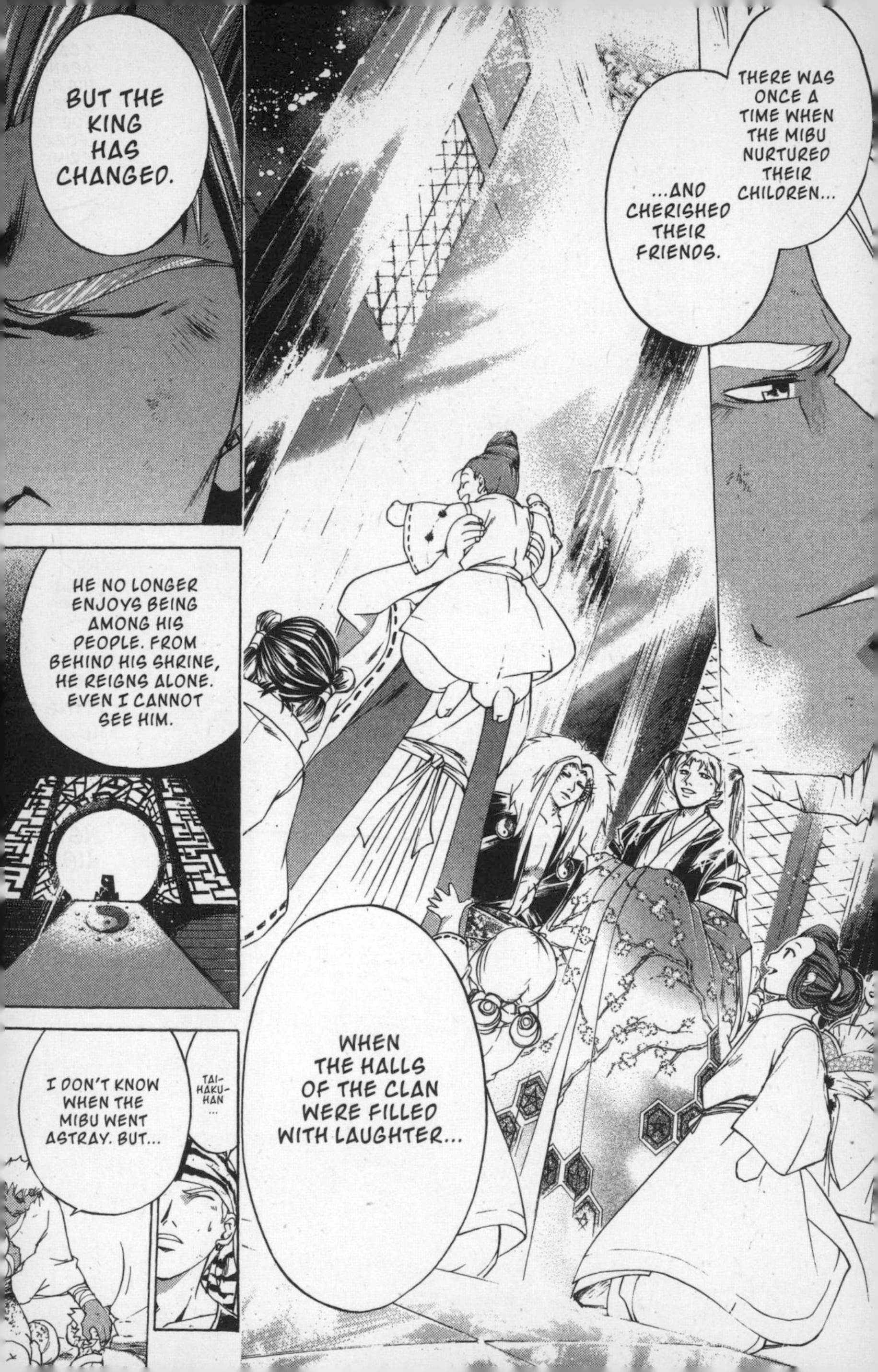
THERE WAS ONCE A TIME WHEN THE MIBU NURTURED THEIR CHILDREN...
...AND CHERISHED THEIR FRIENDS.
WHEN THE HALLS OF THE CLAN WERE FILLED WITH LAUGHTER...
BUT THE KING HAS CHANGED.
HE NO LONGER ENJOYS BEING AMONG HIS PEOPLE. FROM BEHIND HIS SHRINE, HE REIGNS ALONE. EVEN I CANNOT SEE HIM.
TAI-HAKU-HAN...
I DON'T KNOW WHEN THE MIBU WENT ASTRAY. BUT...

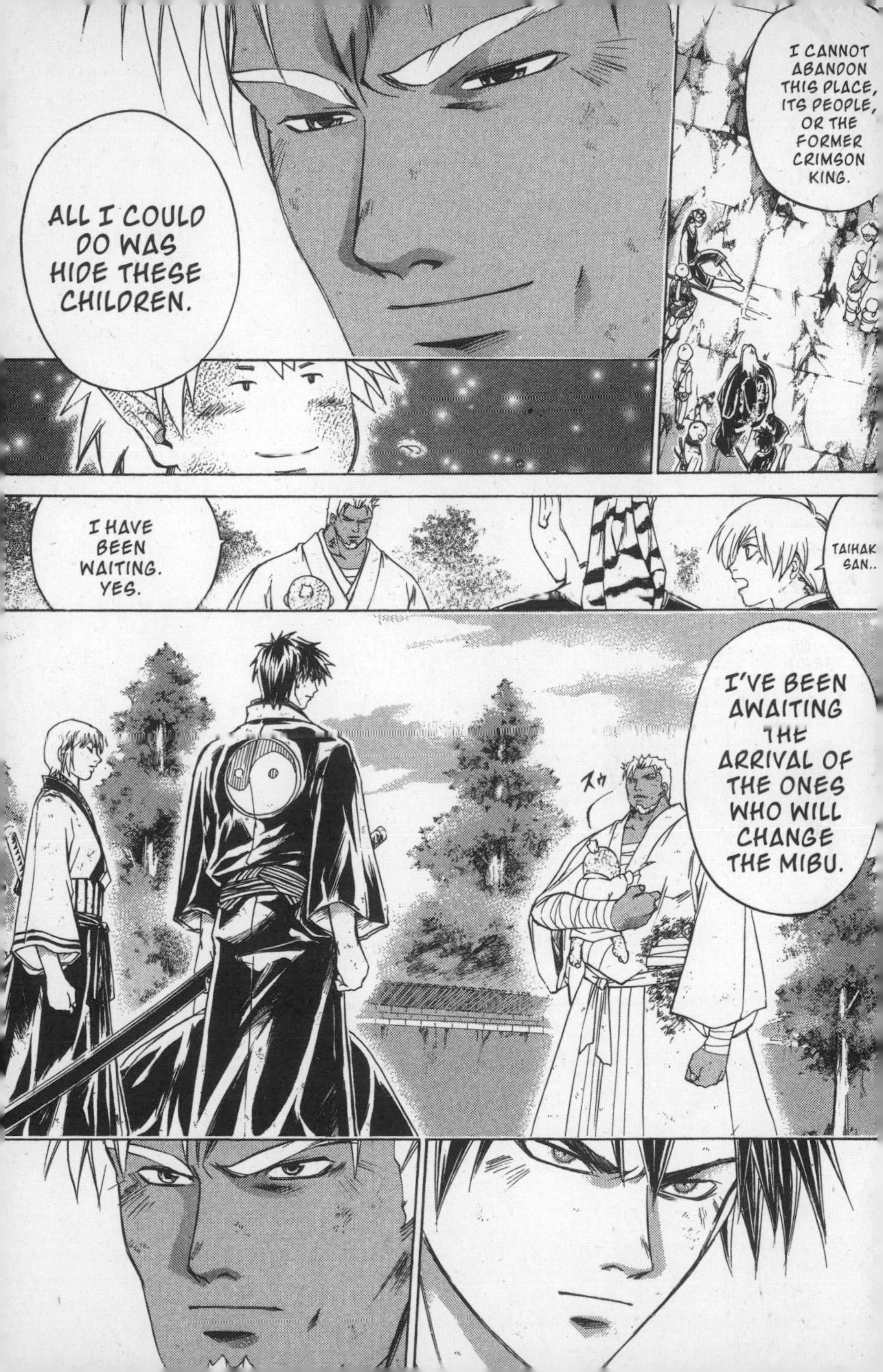
I CANNOT ABANDON THIS PLACE, ITS PEOPLE, OR THE FORMER CRIMSON KING.
ALL I COULD DO WAS HIDE THESE CHILDREN.
TAIHAK SAN..
I HAVE BEEN WAITING. YES.
I'VE BEEN AWAITING THE ARRIVAL OF THE ONES WHO WILL CHANGE THE MIBU.
スゥ

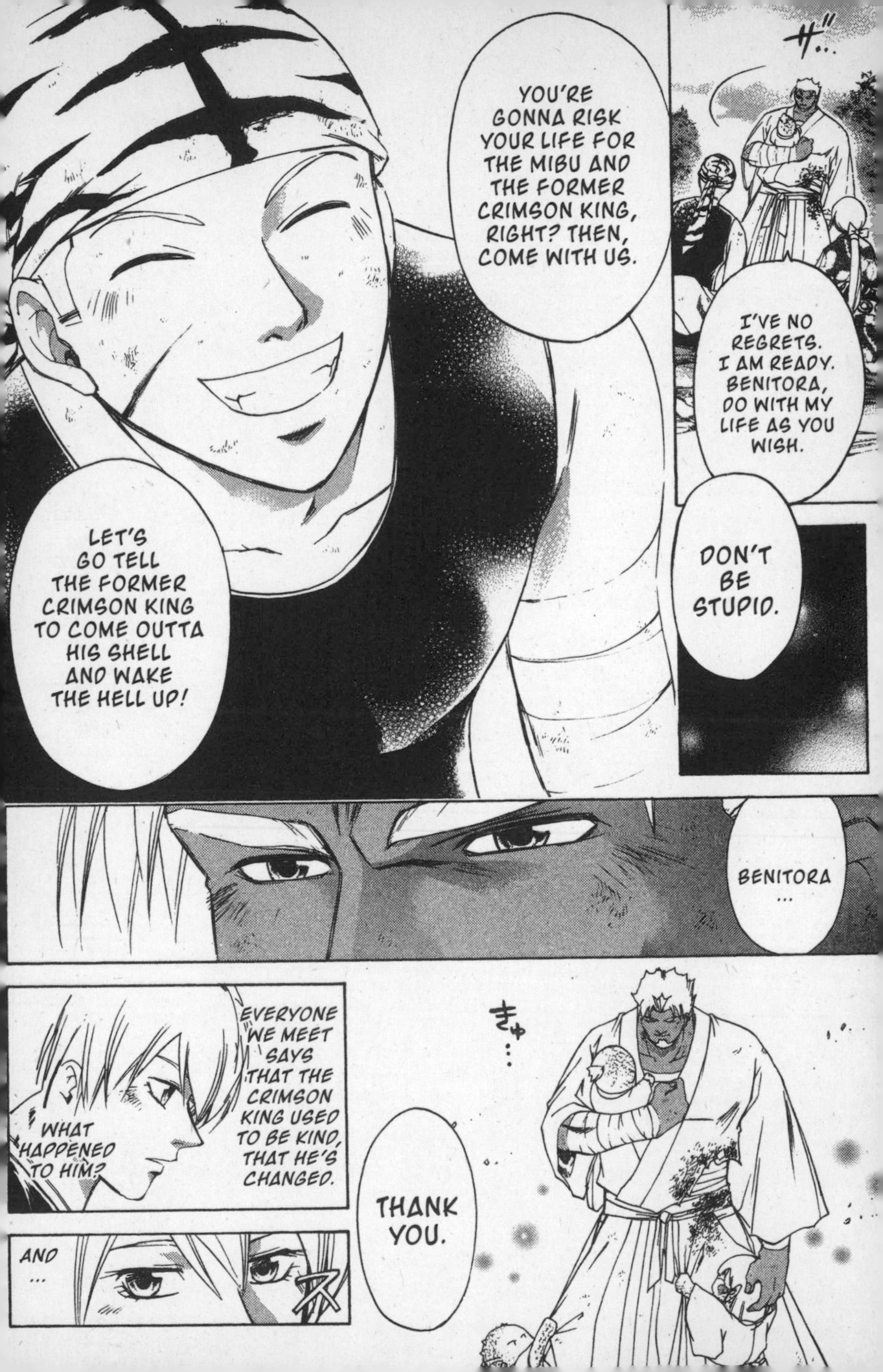
ザ..
I'VE NO REGRETS. I AM READY. BENITORA, DO WITH MY LIFE AS YOU WISH.
DON'T BE STUPID.
YOU'RE GONNA RISK YOUR LIFE FOR THE MIBU AND THE FORMER CRIMSON KING, RIGHT? THEN, COME WITH US.
LET'S GO TELL THE FORMER CRIMSON KING TO COME OUTTA HIS SHELL AND WAKE THE HELL UP!
BENITORA ...
きゅ...
THANK YOU.
EVERYONE WE MEET SAYS THAT THE CRIMSON KING USED TO BE KIND, THAT HE'S CHANGED.
WHAT HAPPENED TO HIM?
AND ...
ス

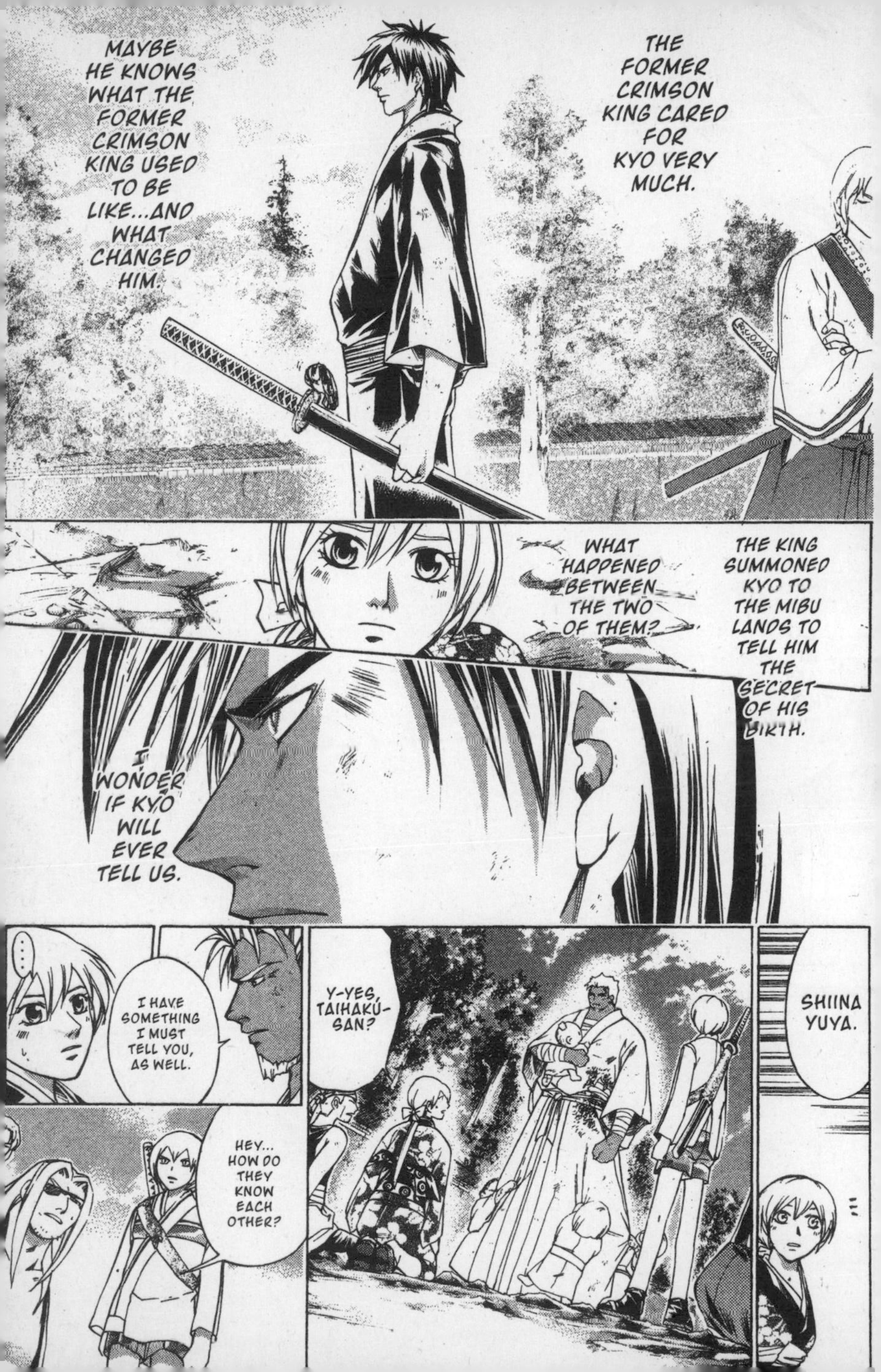
THE FORMER CRIMSON KING CARED FOR KYO VERY MUCH.
MAYBE HE KNOWS WHAT THE FORMER CRIMSON KING USED TO BE LIKE...AND WHAT CHANGED HIM.
THE KING SUMMONED KYO TO THE MIBU LANDS TO TELL HIM THE SECRET OF HIS BIRTH.
WHAT HAPPENED BETWEEN THE TWO OF THEM?
I WONDER IF KYO WILL EVER TELL US.
SHIINA YUYA.
Y-YES, TAIHAKU-SAN?
I HAVE SOMETHING I MUST TELL YOU, AS WELL.
...
HEY... HOW DO THEY KNOW EACH OTHER?

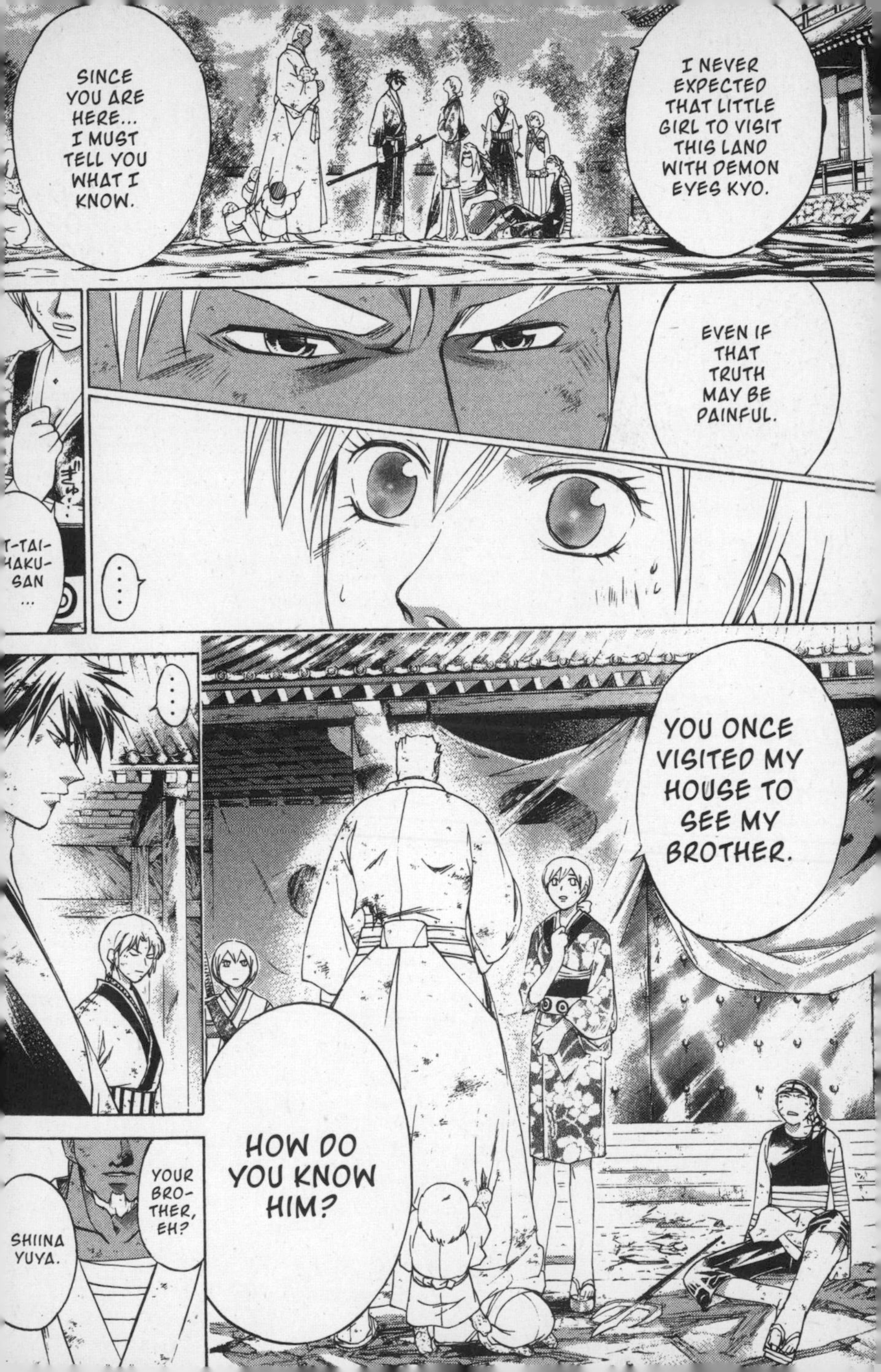
I NEVER EXPECTED THAT LITTLE GIRL TO VISIT THIS LAND WITH DEMON EYES KYO.
SINCE YOU ARE HERE... I MUST TELL YOU WHAT I KNOW.
EVEN IF THAT TRUTH MAY BE PAINFUL.
...
ぎゅ…
T-TAI-HAKU-SAN...
YOU ONCE VISITED MY HOUSE TO SEE MY BROTHER.
HOW DO YOU KNOW HIM?
...
YOUR BROTHER, EH?
SHIINA YUYA.

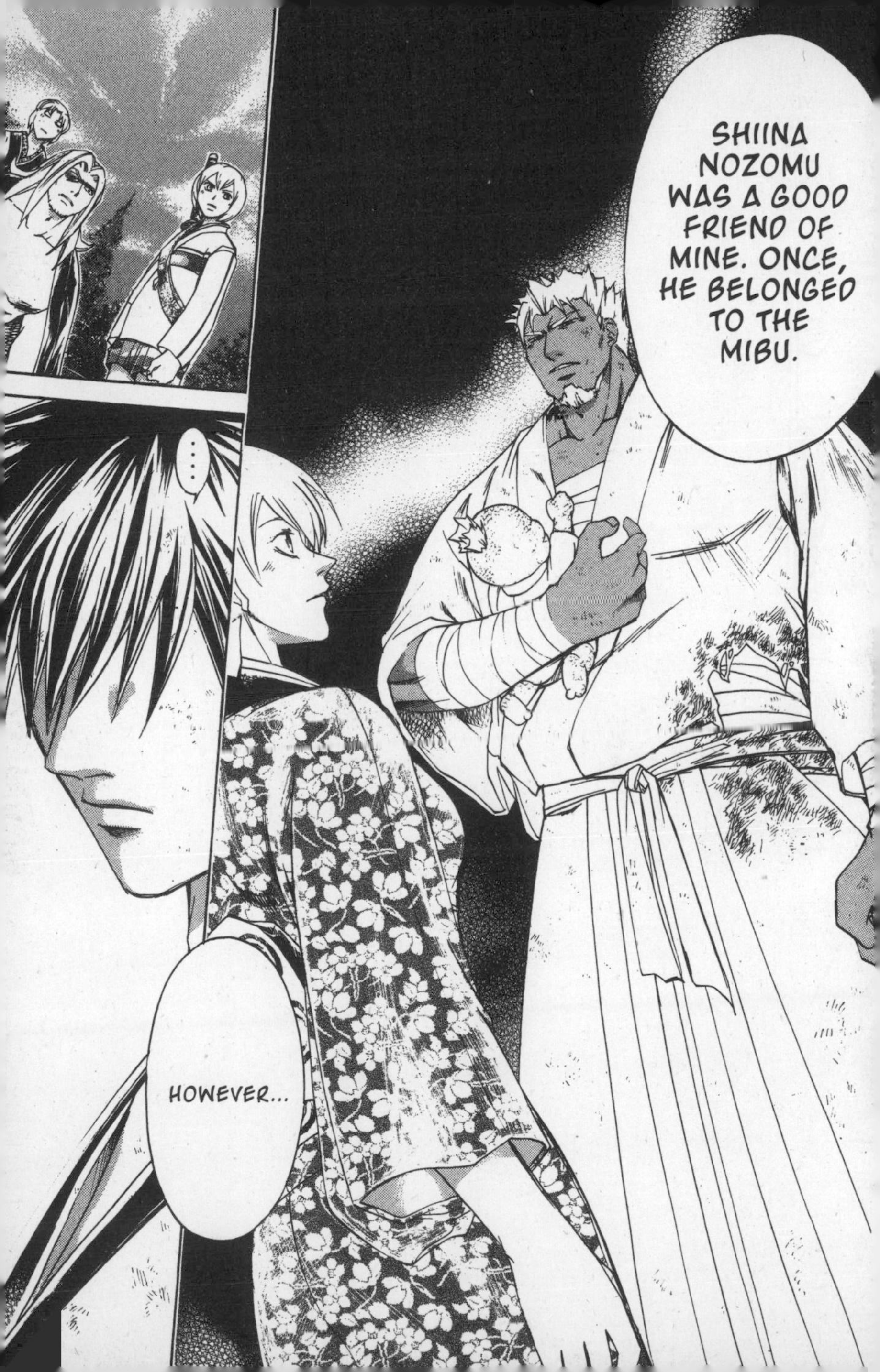
SHIINA NOZOMU WAS A GOOD FRIEND OF MINE. ONCE, HE BELONGED TO THE MIBU.
....
HOWEVER...

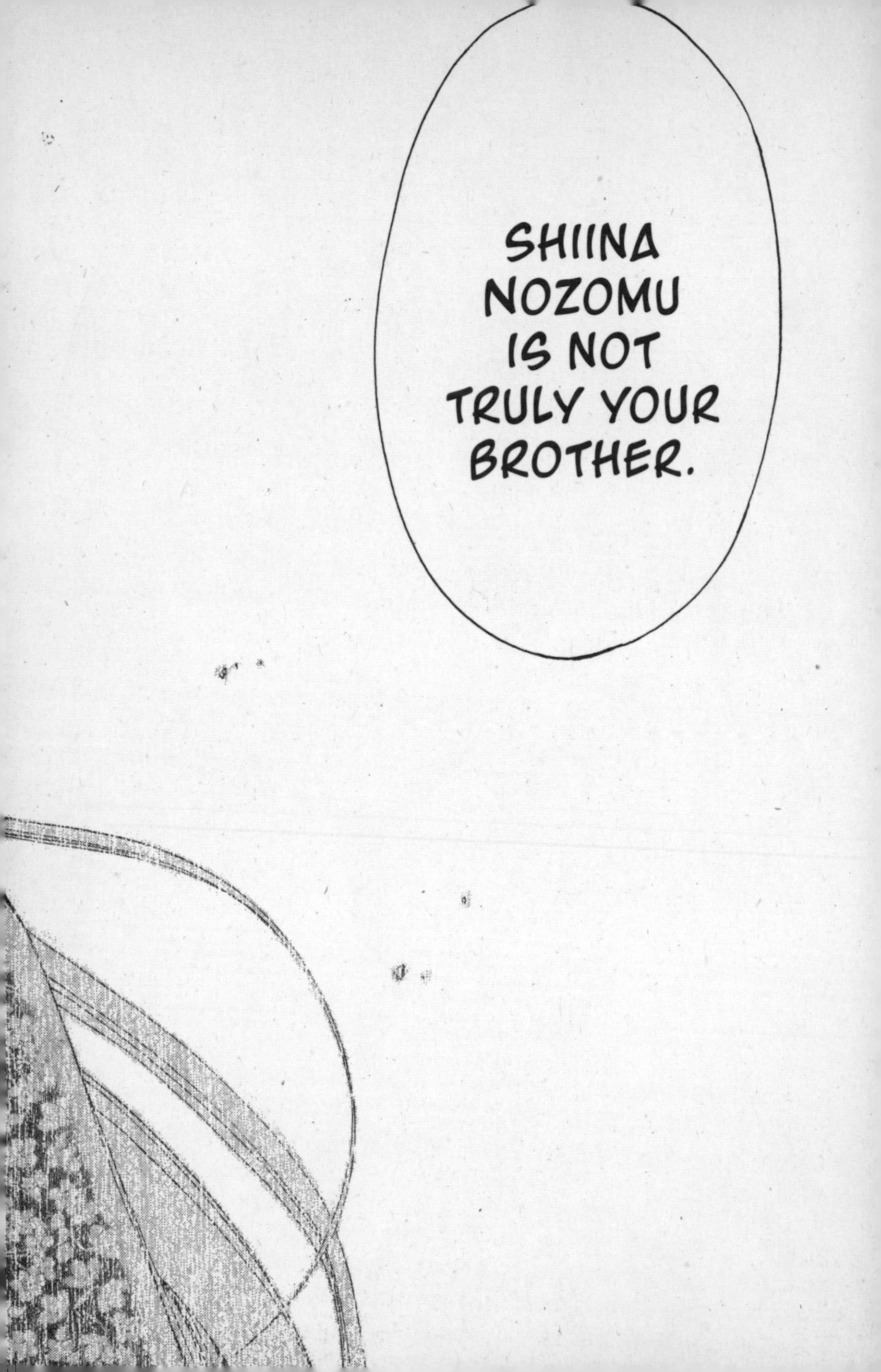
SHIINA NOZOMU IS NOT TRULY YOUR BROTHER.

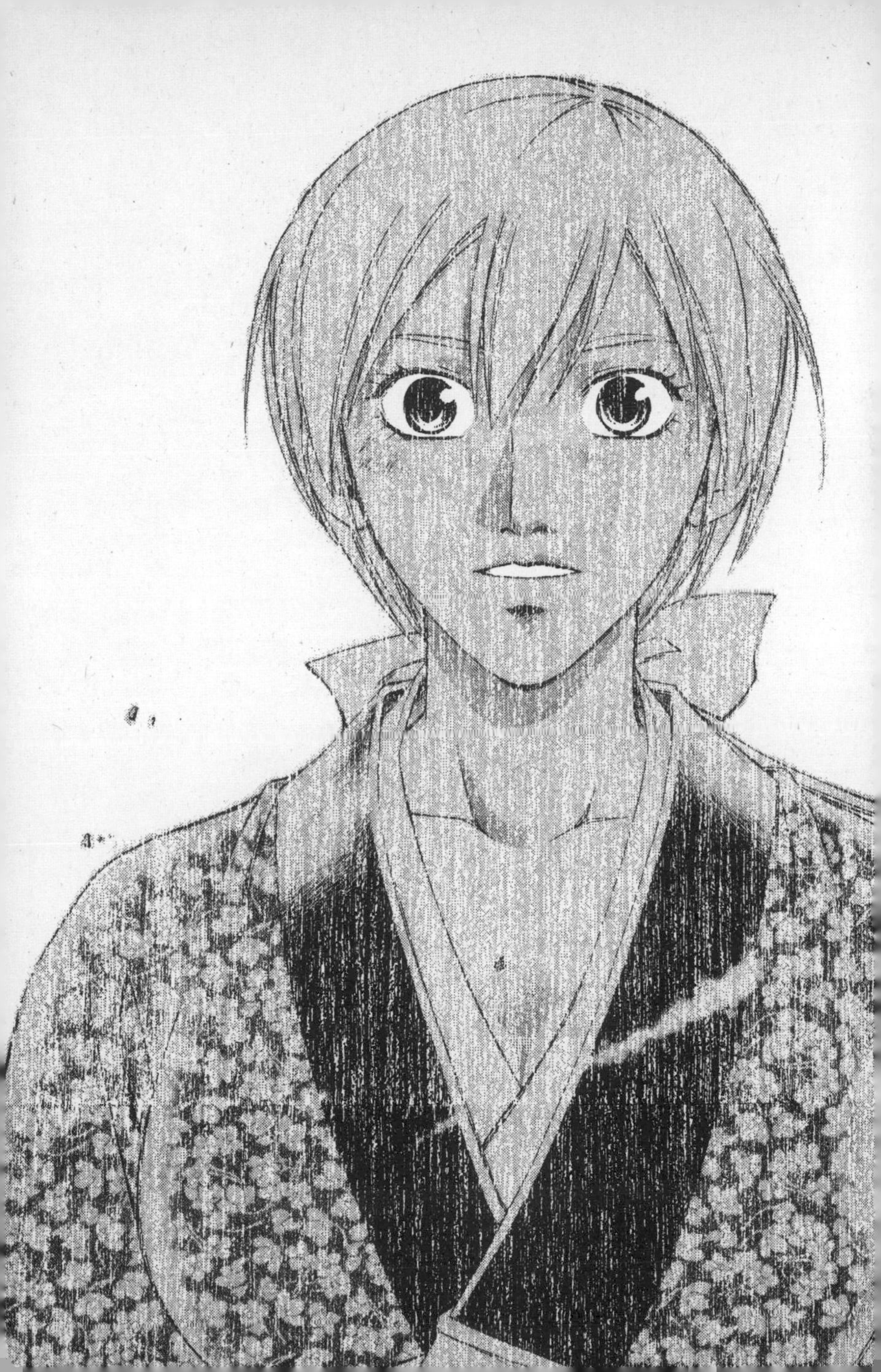

DRAW LIKE KAMIJYO

上条に挑戦!

Character Special "Four Emperors (-1) Then and Now"

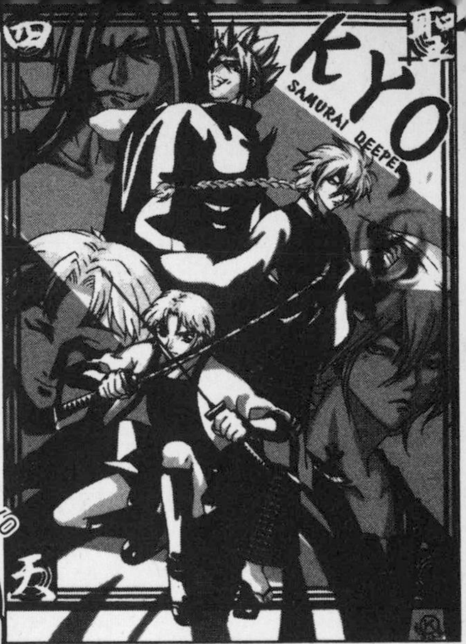

SAMURAI DEEPER KYO
四

Old really meets new with this picture. [Kanaru / Aichi]

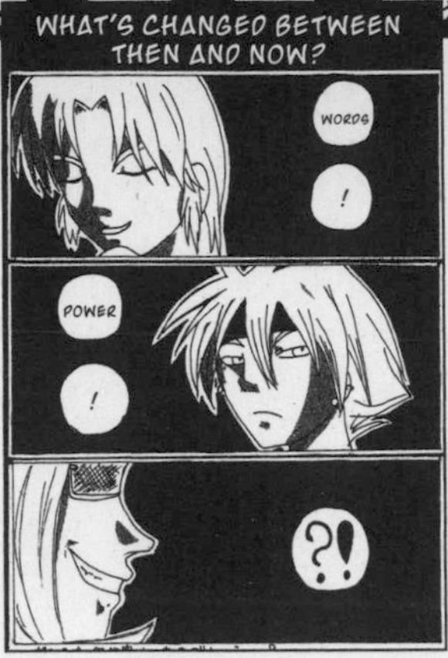

WHAT'S CHANGED BETWEEN THEN AND NOW?
WORDS
!
POWER
!
?!

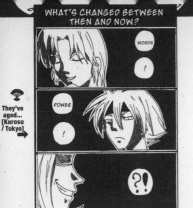

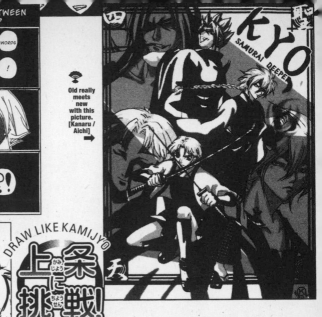

They've aged... [Kurosu / Tokyo]

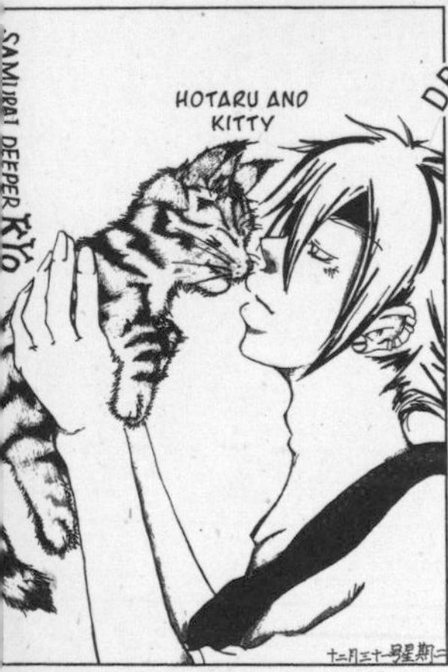

SAMURAI DEEPER KYO
HOTARU AND KITTY

Seems he's more of an animal-lover. (Ha ha) [Hiro / Kanagawa]

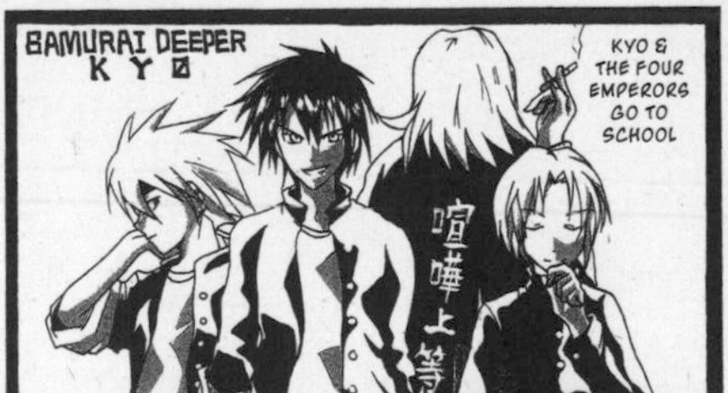

SAMURAI DEEPER KYO
KYO & THE FOUR EMPERORS GO TO SCHOOL
喧嘩上等

Watch our for these ruffians! [Furuguchi Ayumi / Tochigi]

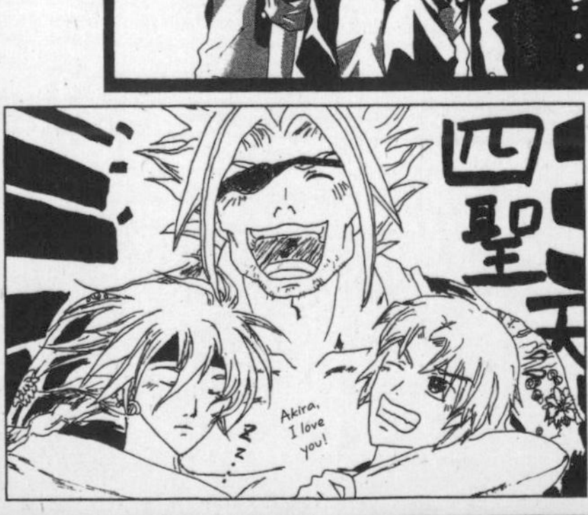

四聖天
Akira, I love you!

Oh, Bon-chan, how we love thee. [Kojima Kibou / Tokyo]

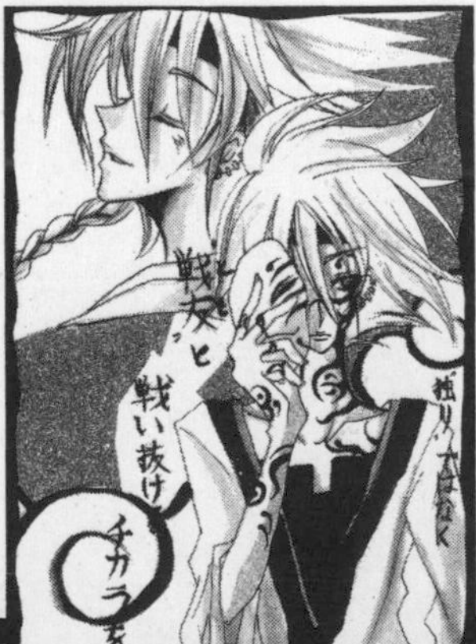

チカラを

So, he finally took off his iron mask, huh? [Neji / Gifu]

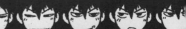

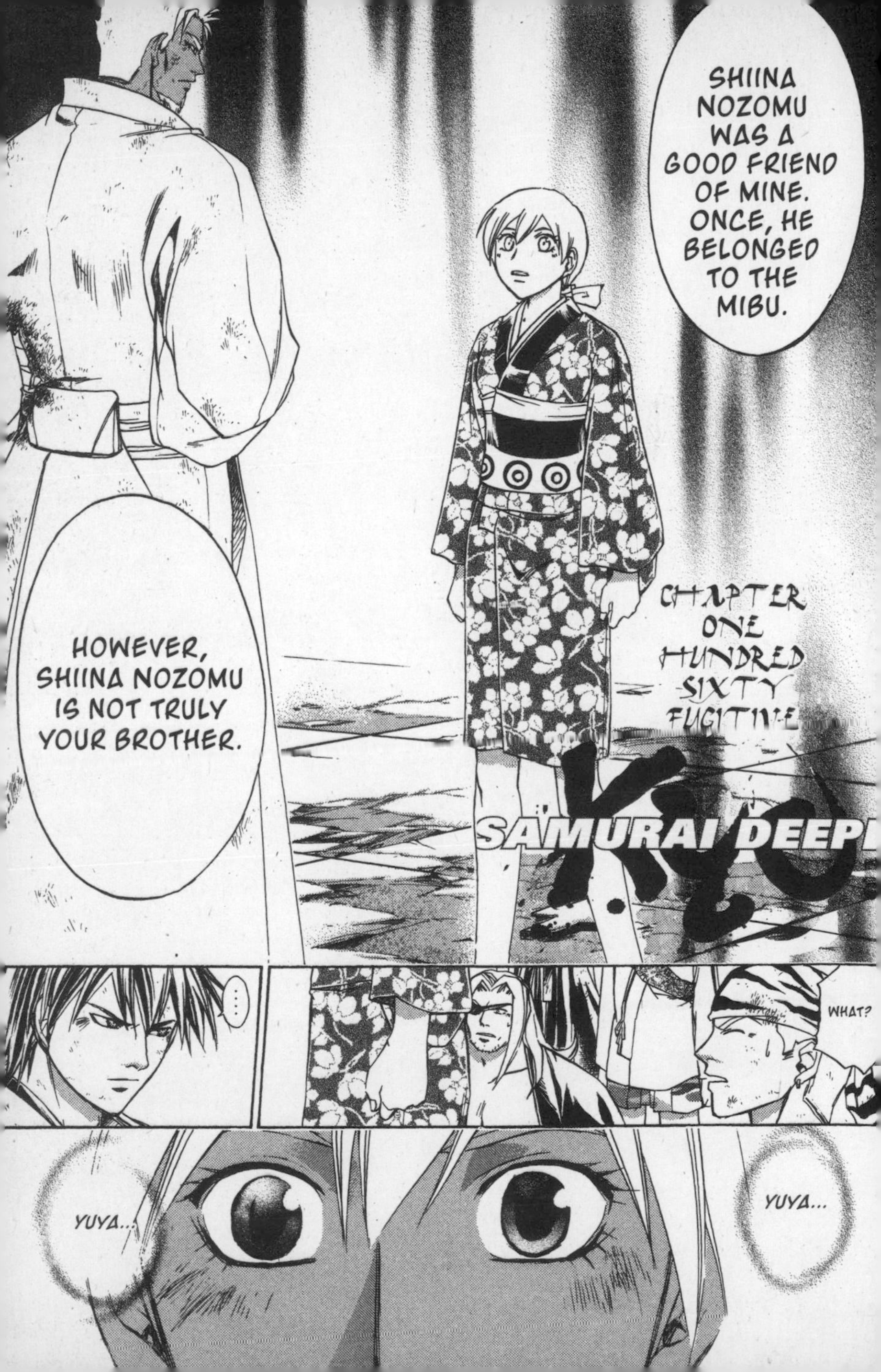
SHIINA NOZOMU WAS A GOOD FRIEND OF MINE. ONCE, HE BELONGED TO THE MIBU.
HOWEVER, SHIINA NOZOMU IS NOT TRULY YOUR BROTHER.
CHAPTER ONE HUNDRED SIXTY
FUGITIVE
SAMURAI DEEP
WHAT?
....
YUYA...
YUYA...

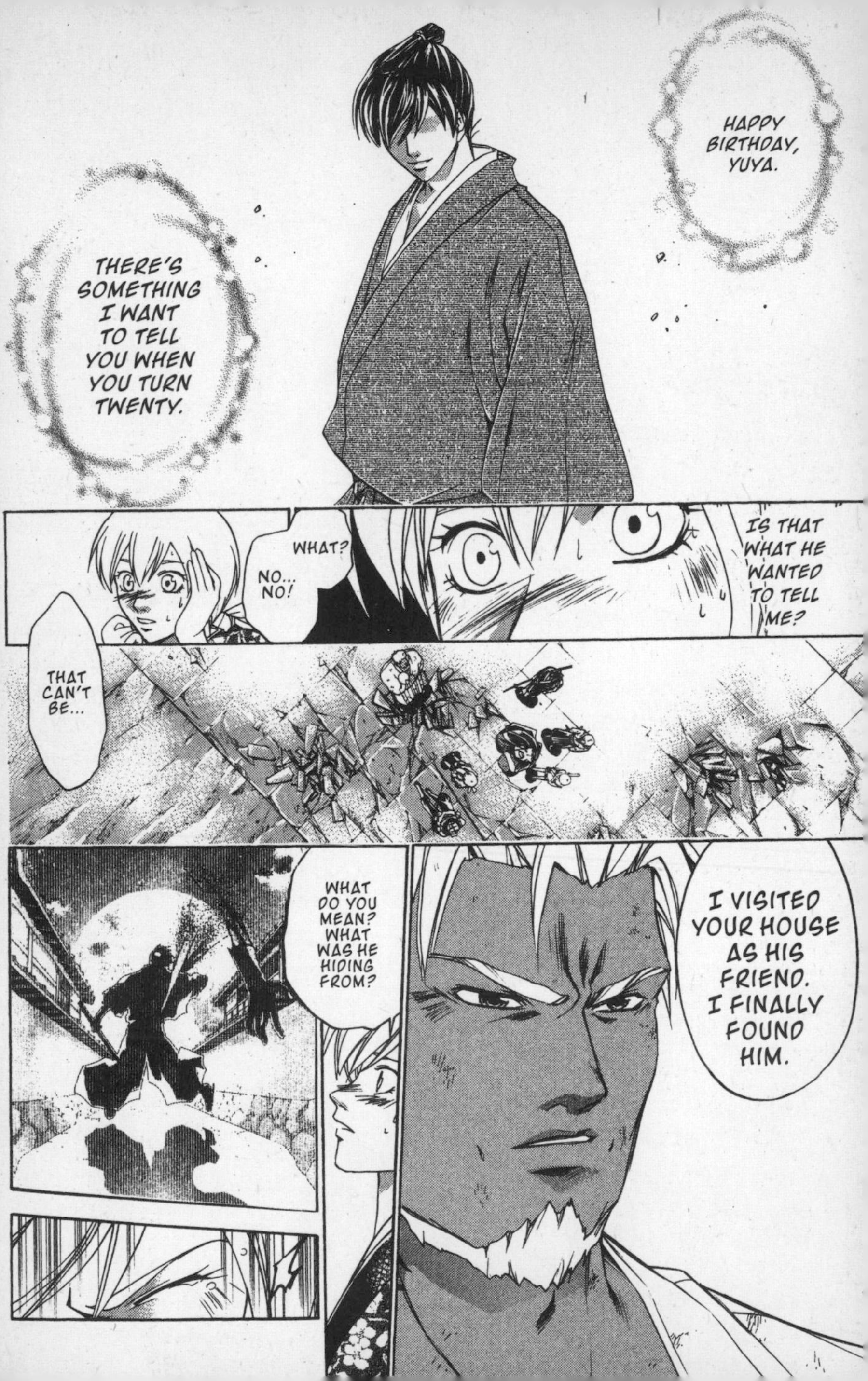
HAPPY BIRTHDAY, YUYA.
THERE'S SOMETHING I WANT TO TELL YOU WHEN YOU TURN TWENTY.
IS THAT WHAT HE WANTED TO TELL ME?
WHAT?
NO... NO!
THAT CAN'T BE...
I VISITED YOUR HOUSE AS HIS FRIEND. I FINALLY FOUND HIM.
WHAT DO YOU MEAN? WHAT WAS HE HIDING FROM?

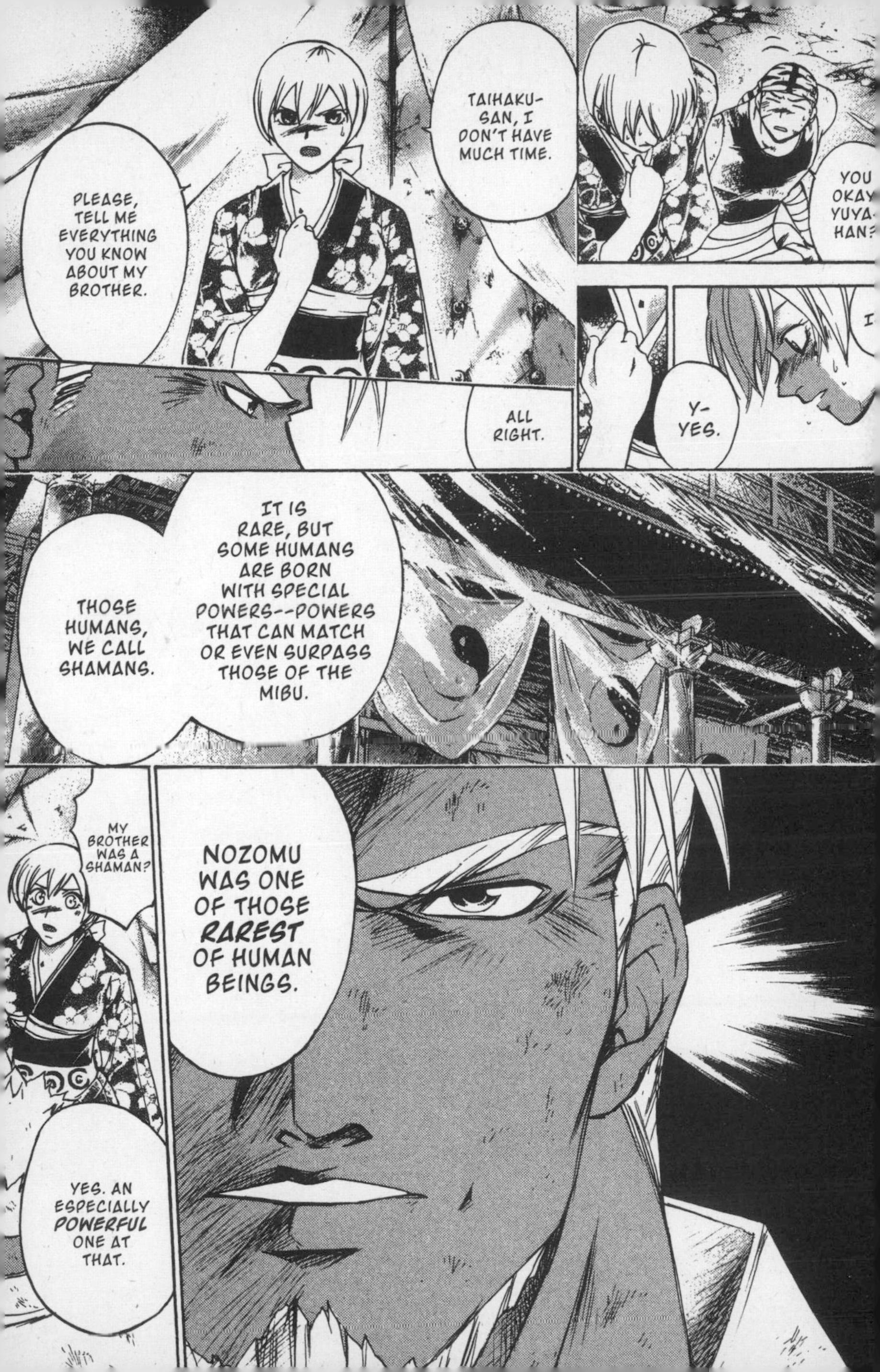
YOU OKAY YUYA-HAN?
I
Y- YES.
TAIHAKU-SAN, I DON'T HAVE MUCH TIME.
PLEASE, TELL ME EVERYTHING YOU KNOW ABOUT MY BROTHER.
ALL RIGHT.
IT IS RARE, BUT SOME HUMANS ARE BORN WITH SPECIAL POWERS--POWERS THAT CAN MATCH OR EVEN SURPASS THOSE OF THE MIBU.
THOSE HUMANS, WE CALL SHAMANS.
NOZOMU WAS ONE OF THOSE ***RAREST*** OF HUMAN BEINGS.
MY BROTHER WAS A SHAMAN?
YES. AN ESPECIALLY ***POWERFUL*** ONE AT THAT.

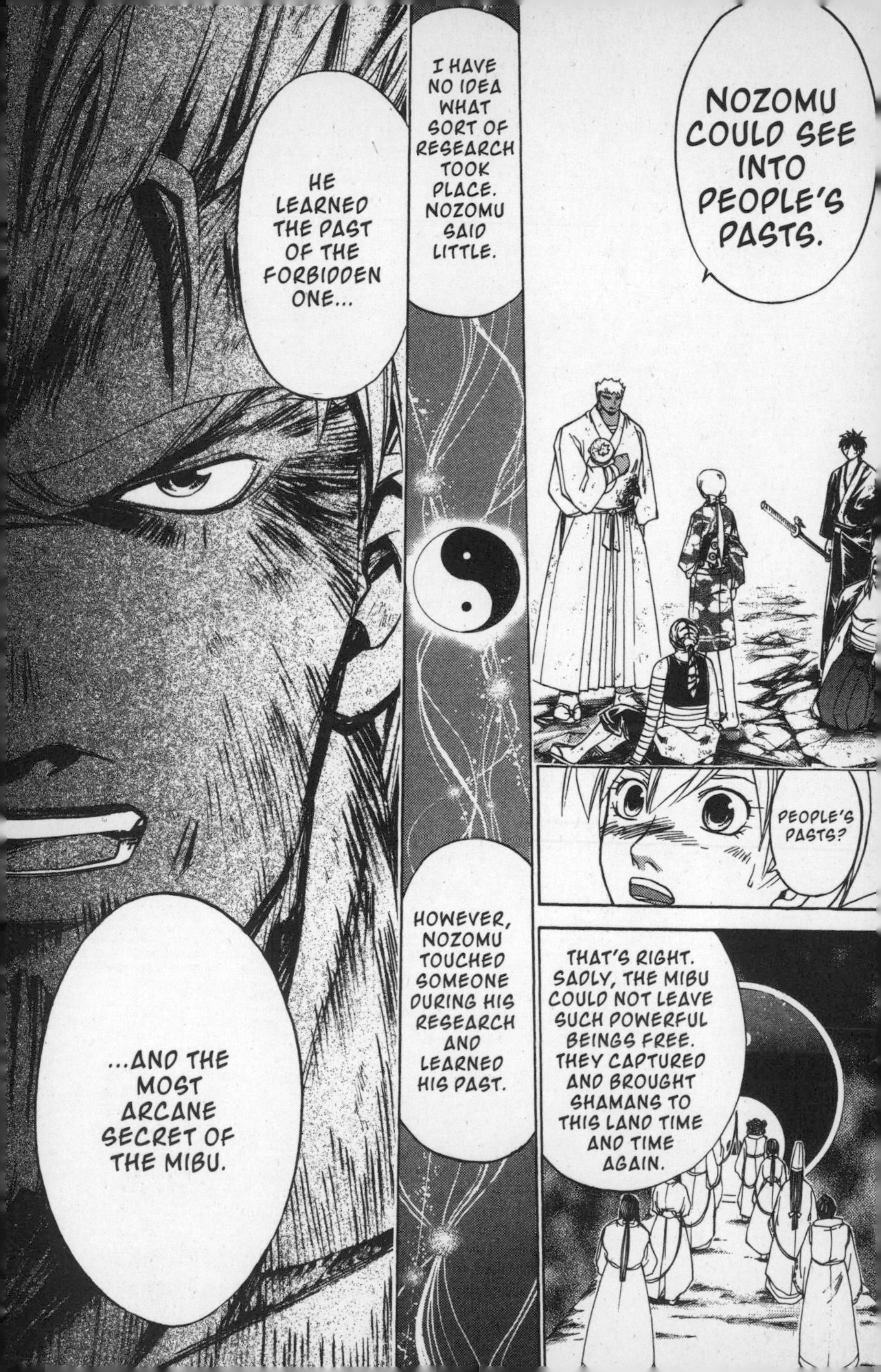
NOZOMU COULD SEE INTO PEOPLE'S PASTS.
PEOPLE'S PASTS?
THAT'S RIGHT. SADLY, THE MIBU COULD NOT LEAVE SUCH POWERFUL BEINGS FREE. THEY CAPTURED AND BROUGHT SHAMANS TO THIS LAND TIME AND TIME AGAIN.
I HAVE NO IDEA WHAT SORT OF RESEARCH TOOK PLACE. NOZOMU SAID LITTLE.
HOWEVER, NOZOMU TOUCHED SOMEONE DURING HIS RESEARCH AND LEARNED HIS PAST.
HE LEARNED THE PAST OF THE FORBIDDEN ONE...
...AND THE MOST ARCANE SECRET OF THE MIBU.

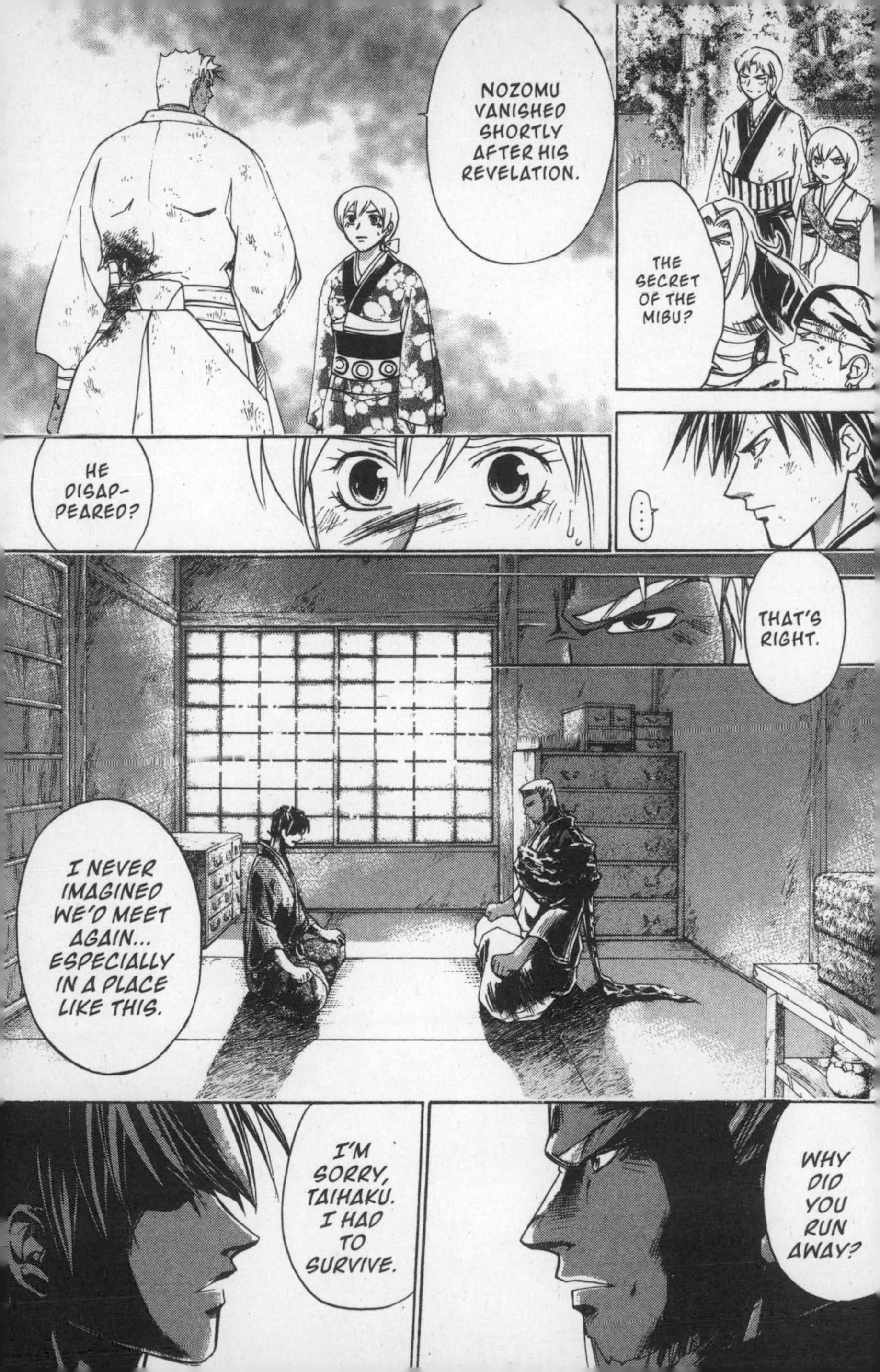
THE SECRET OF THE MIBU?
NOZOMU VANISHED SHORTLY AFTER HIS REVELATION.
...
HE DISAP-PEARED?
THAT'S RIGHT.
I NEVER IMAGINED WE'D MEET AGAIN... ESPECIALLY IN A PLACE LIKE THIS.
WHY DID YOU RUN AWAY?
I'M SORRY, TAIHAKU. I HAD TO SURVIVE.

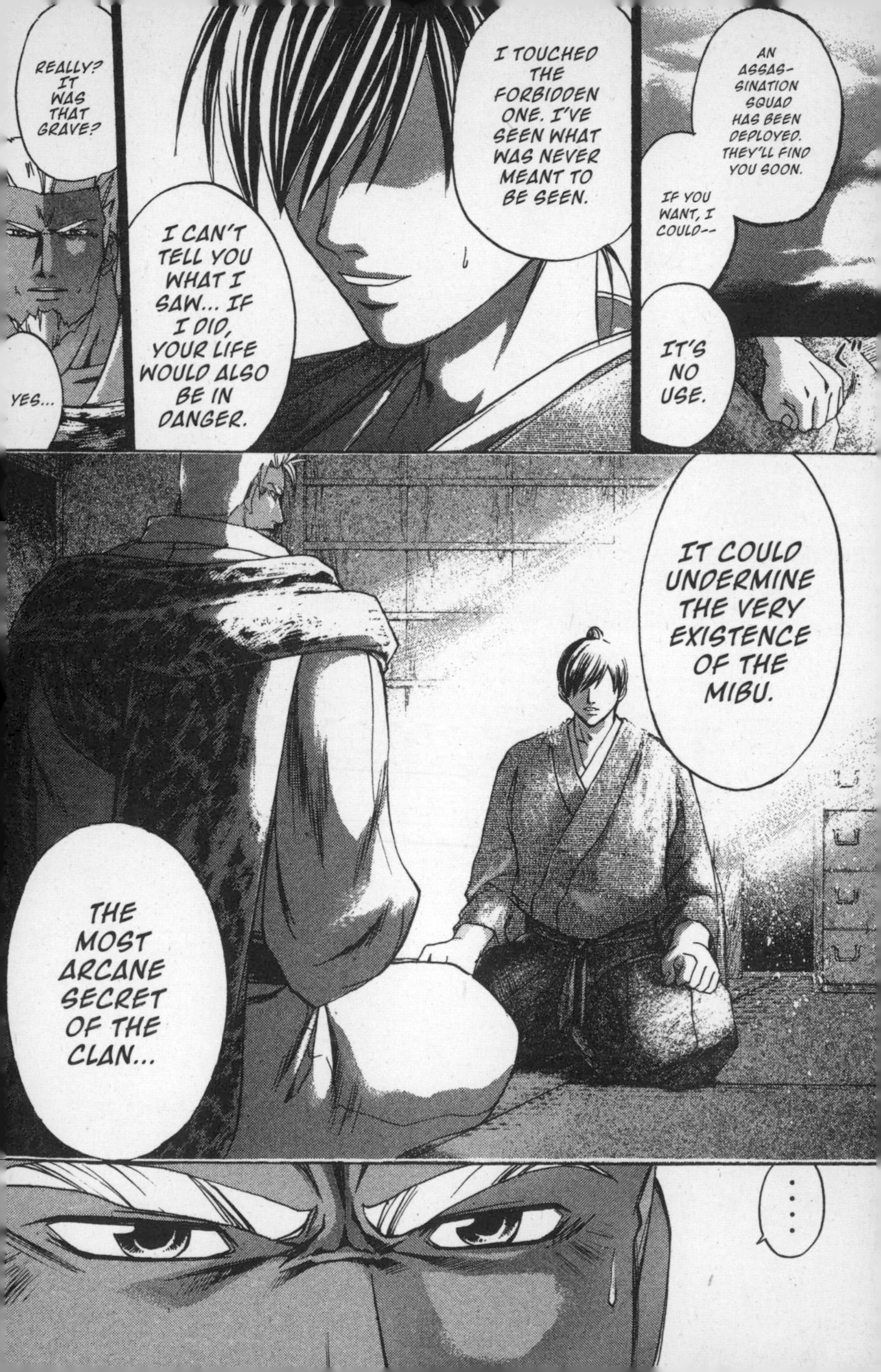
AN ASSAS-SINATION SQUAD HAS BEEN DEPLOYED. THEY'LL FIND YOU SOON.
IF YOU WANT, I COULD--
IT'S NO USE.
I TOUCHED THE FORBIDDEN ONE. I'VE SEEN WHAT WAS NEVER MEANT TO BE SEEN.
I CAN'T TELL YOU WHAT I SAW... IF I DID, YOUR LIFE WOULD ALSO BE IN DANGER.
REALLY? IT WAS THAT GRAVE?
YES...
IT COULD UNDERMINE THE VERY EXISTENCE OF THE MIBU.
THE MOST ARCANE SECRET OF THE CLAN...
....

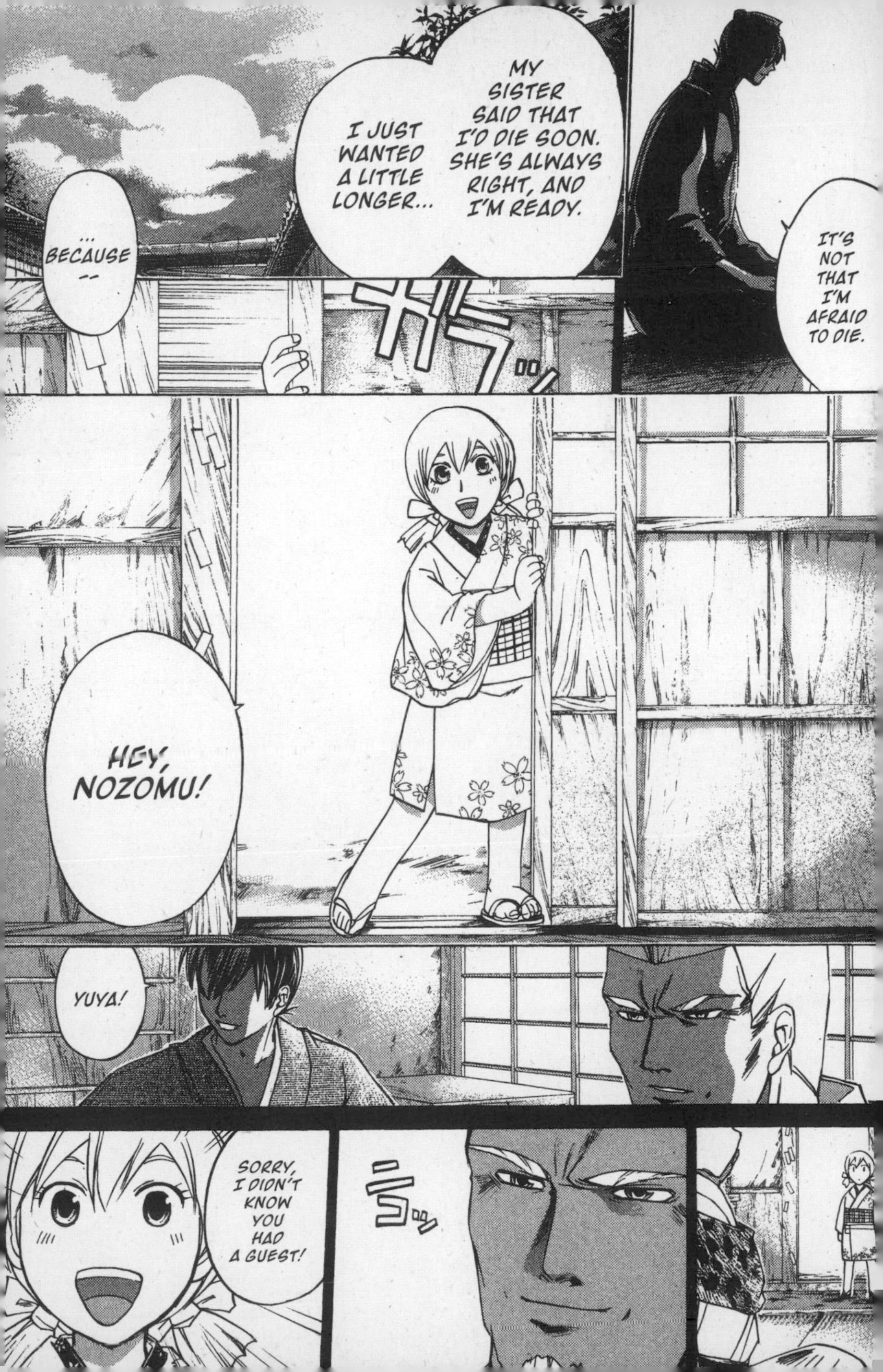
IT'S NOT THAT I'M AFRAID TO DIE.
MY SISTER SAID THAT I'D DIE SOON. SHE'S ALWAYS RIGHT, AND I'M READY.
I JUST WANTED A LITTLE LONGER...
...BECAUSE --
ガラッ
HEY, NOZOMU!
YUYA!
SORRY, I DIDN'T KNOW YOU HAD A GUEST!

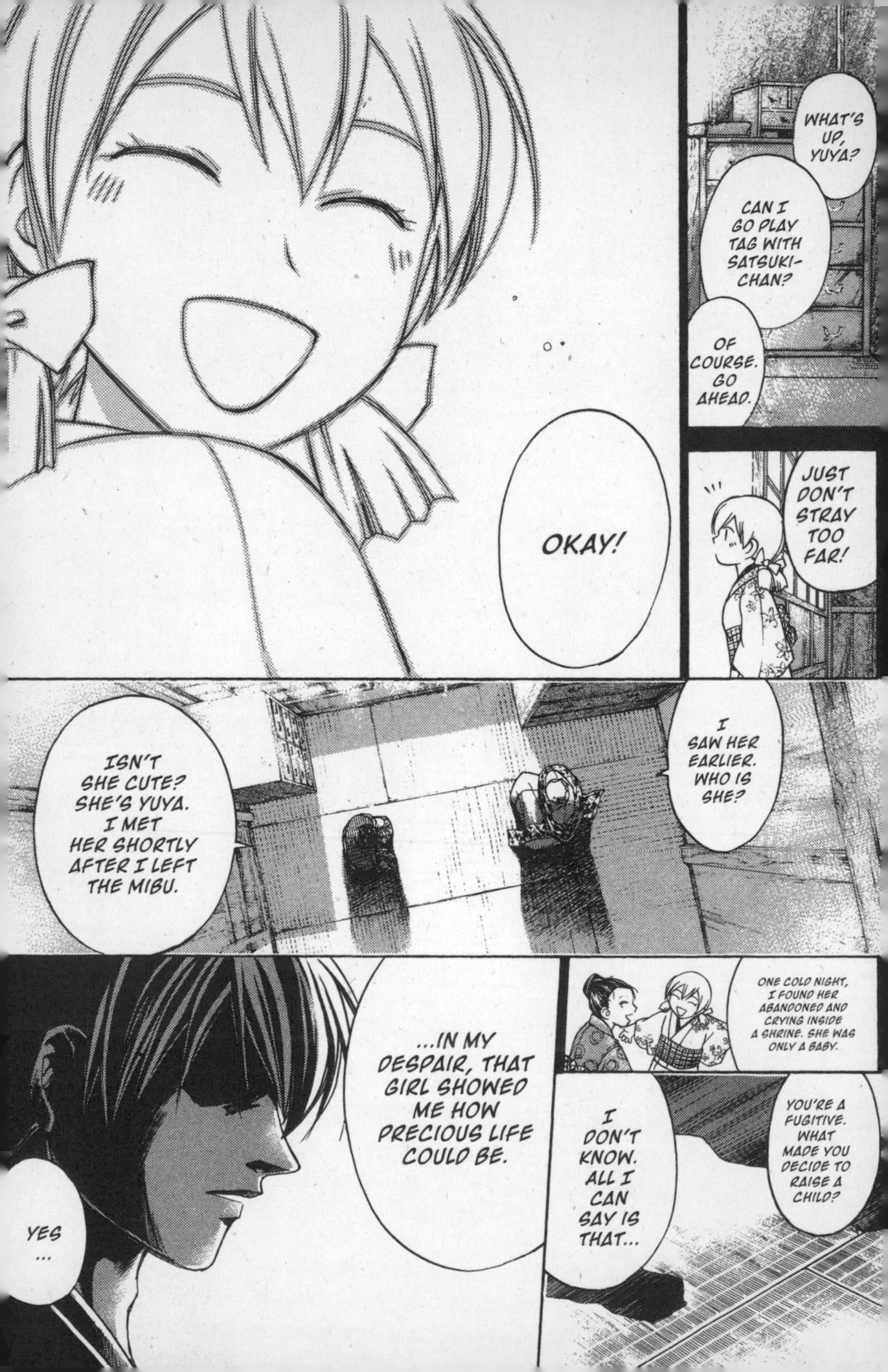
WHAT'S UP, YUYA?
CAN I GO PLAY TAG WITH SATSUKI-CHAN?
OF COURSE. GO AHEAD.
JUST DON'T STRAY TOO FAR!
OKAY!
I SAW HER EARLIER. WHO IS SHE?
ISN'T SHE CUTE? SHE'S YUYA. I MET HER SHORTLY AFTER I LEFT THE MIBU.
ONE COLD NIGHT, I FOUND HER ABANDONED AND CRYING INSIDE A SHRINE. SHE WAS ONLY A BABY.
YOU'RE A FUGITIVE. WHAT MADE YOU DECIDE TO RAISE A CHILD?
I DON'T KNOW. ALL I CAN SAY IS THAT...
...IN MY DESPAIR, THAT GIRL SHOWED ME HOW PRECIOUS LIFE COULD BE.
YES ...

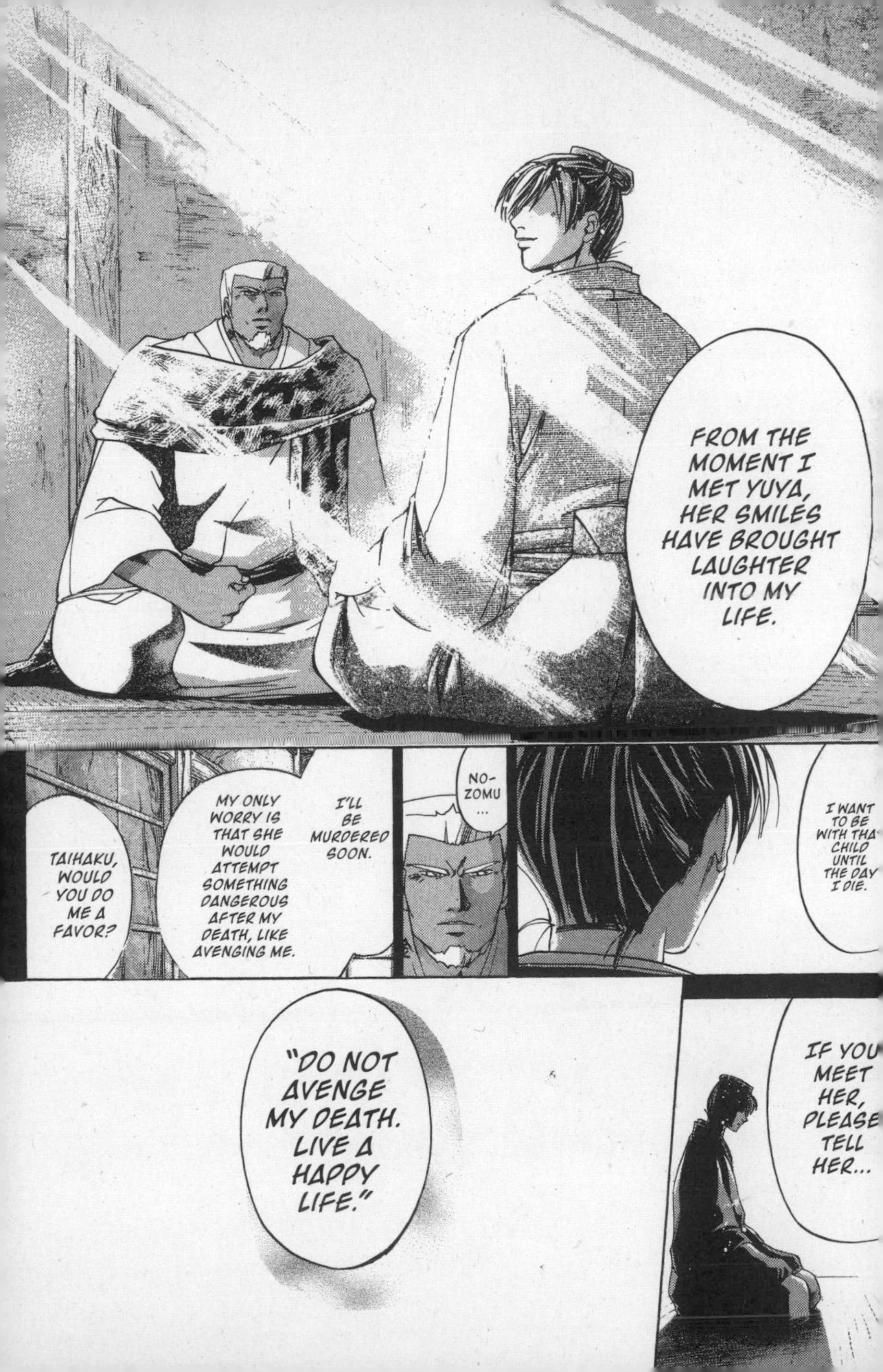
FROM THE MOMENT I MET YUYA, HER SMILES HAVE BROUGHT LAUGHTER INTO MY LIFE.
I WANT TO BE WITH THA CHILD UNTIL THE DAY I DIE.
NO-ZOMU ...
I'LL BE MURDERED SOON.
MY ONLY WORRY IS THAT SHE WOULD ATTEMPT SOMETHING DANGEROUS AFTER MY DEATH, LIKE AVENGING ME.
TAIHAKU, WOULD YOU DO ME A FAVOR?
IF YOU MEET HER, PLEASE TELL HER...
"DO NOT AVENGE MY DEATH. LIVE A HAPPY LIFE."

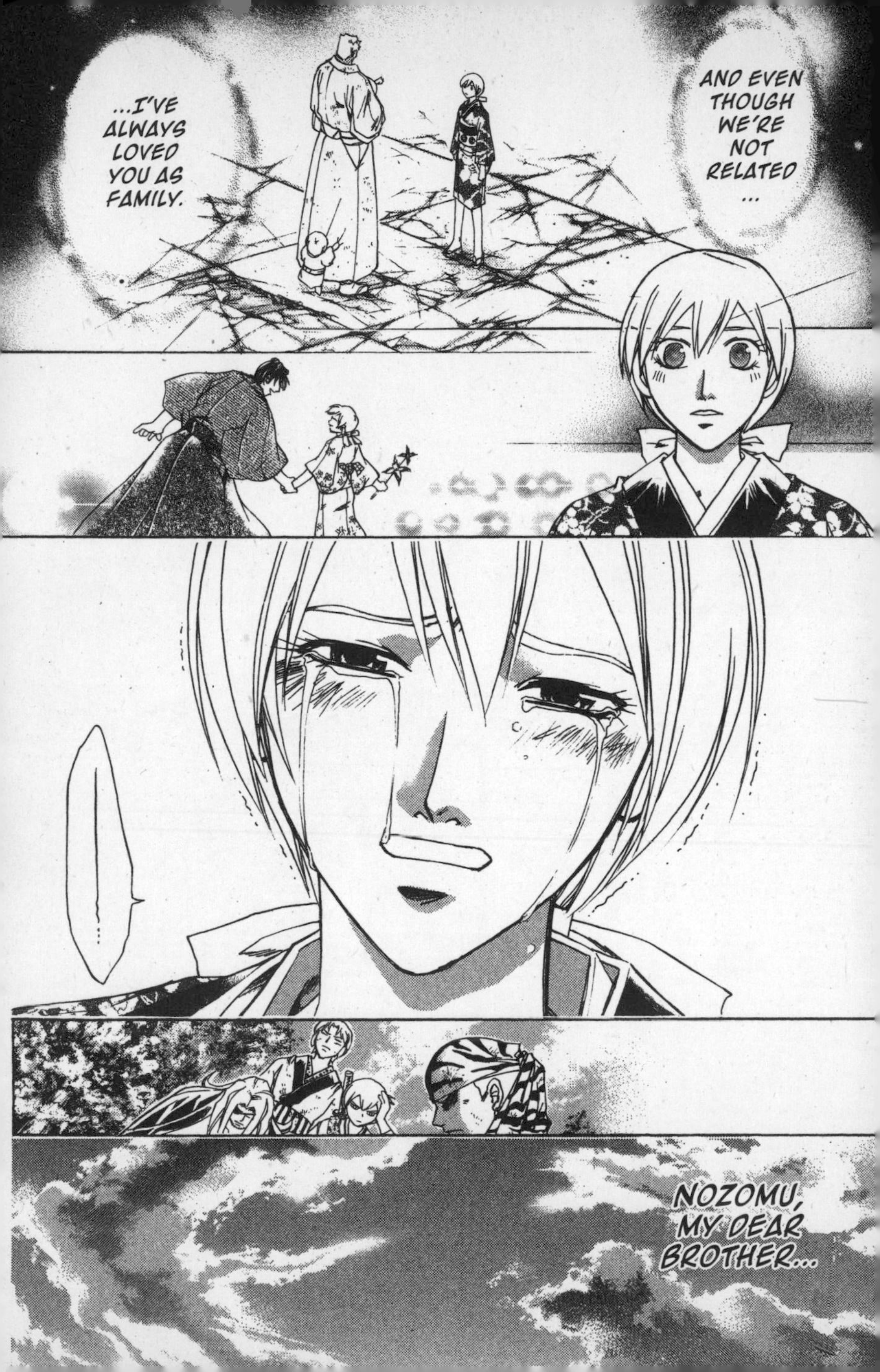
AND EVEN THOUGH WE'RE NOT RELATED ...
...I'VE ALWAYS LOVED YOU AS FAMILY.
NOZOMU, MY DEAR BROTHER...

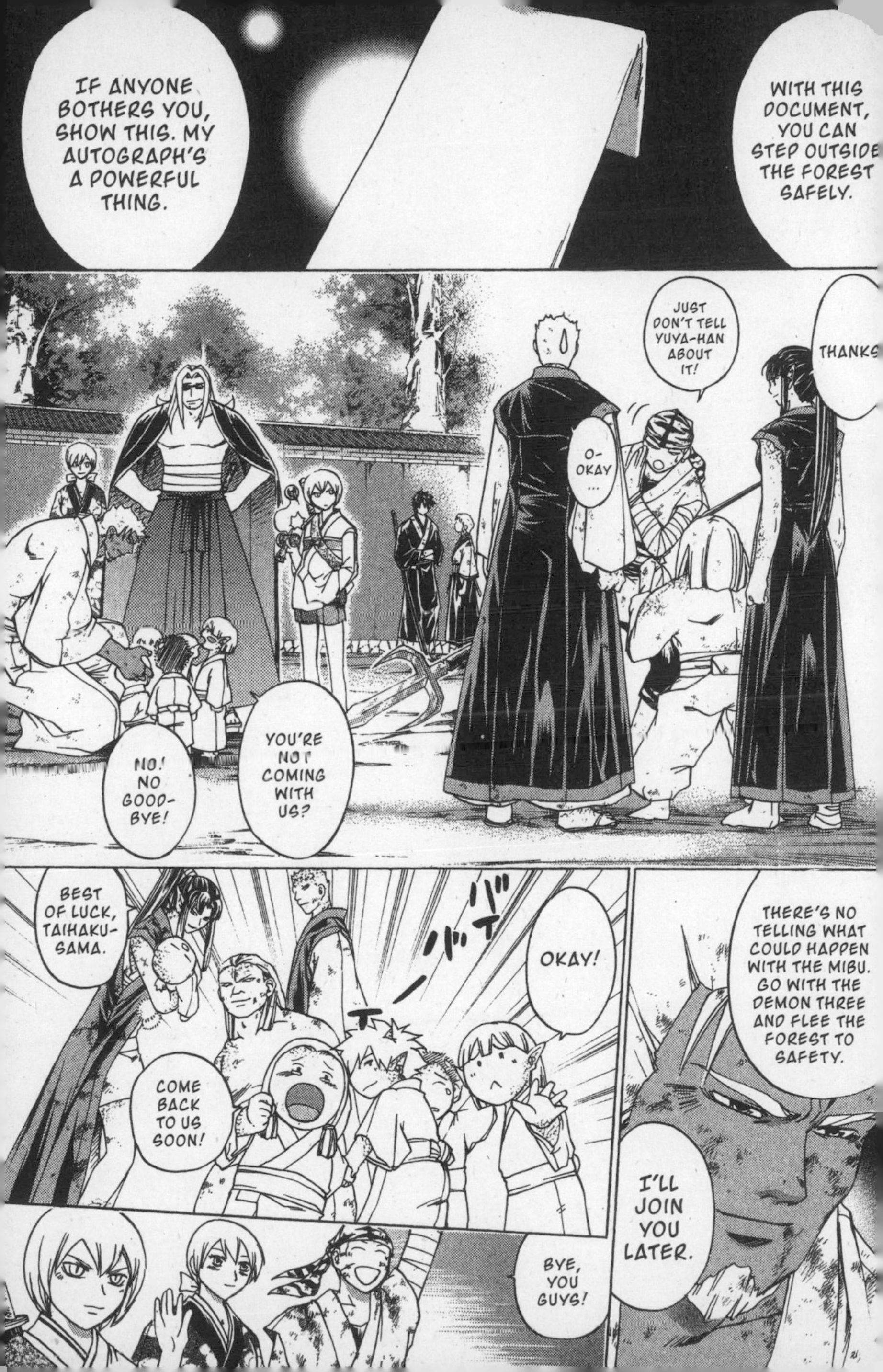
WITH THIS DOCUMENT, YOU CAN STEP OUTSIDE THE FOREST SAFELY.
IF ANYONE BOTHERS YOU, SHOW THIS. MY AUTOGRAPH'S A POWERFUL THING.
THANKS
JUST DON'T TELL YUYA-HAN ABOUT IT!
O-OKAY...
YOU'RE NOT COMING WITH US?
NO! NO GOOD-BYE!
THERE'S NO TELLING WHAT COULD HAPPEN WITH THE MIBU. GO WITH THE DEMON THREE AND FLEE THE FOREST TO SAFETY.
I'LL JOIN YOU LATER.
OKAY!
BEST OF LUCK, TAIHAKU-SAMA.
COME BACK TO US SOON!
BYE, YOU GUYS!

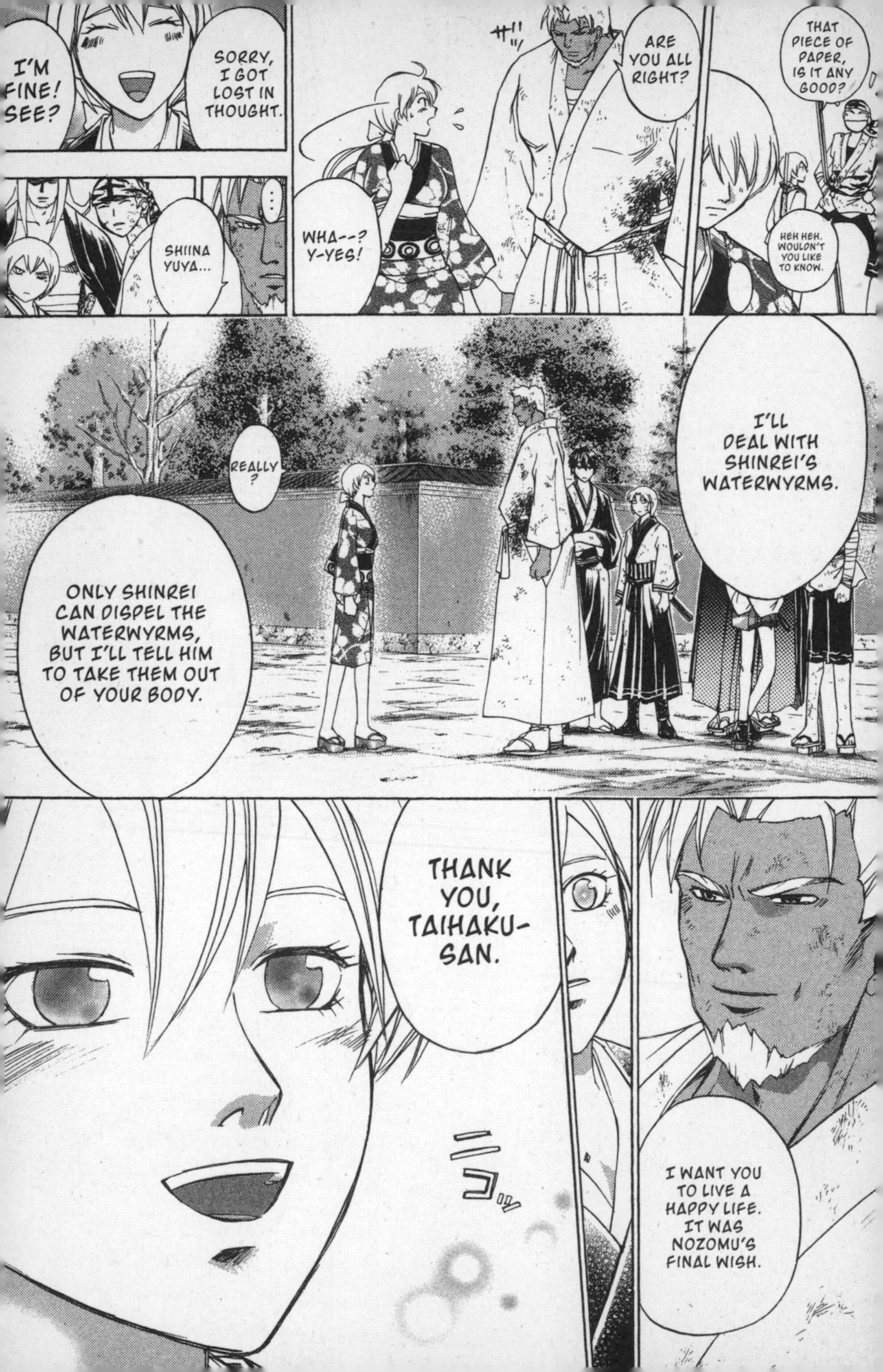
THAT PIECE OF PAPER, IS IT ANY GOOD?
HEH HEH. WOULDN'T YOU LIKE TO KNOW.
ARE YOU ALL RIGHT?
WHA--? Y-YES!
SORRY, I GOT LOST IN THOUGHT.
I'M FINE! SEE?
...
SHIINA YUYA...
I'LL DEAL WITH SHINREI'S WATERWYRMS.
REALLY?
ONLY SHINREI CAN DISPEL THE WATERWYRMS, BUT I'LL TELL HIM TO TAKE THEM OUT OF YOUR BODY.
I WANT YOU TO LIVE A HAPPY LIFE. IT WAS NOZOMU'S FINAL WISH.
THANK YOU, TAIHAKU-SAN.
ニコッ

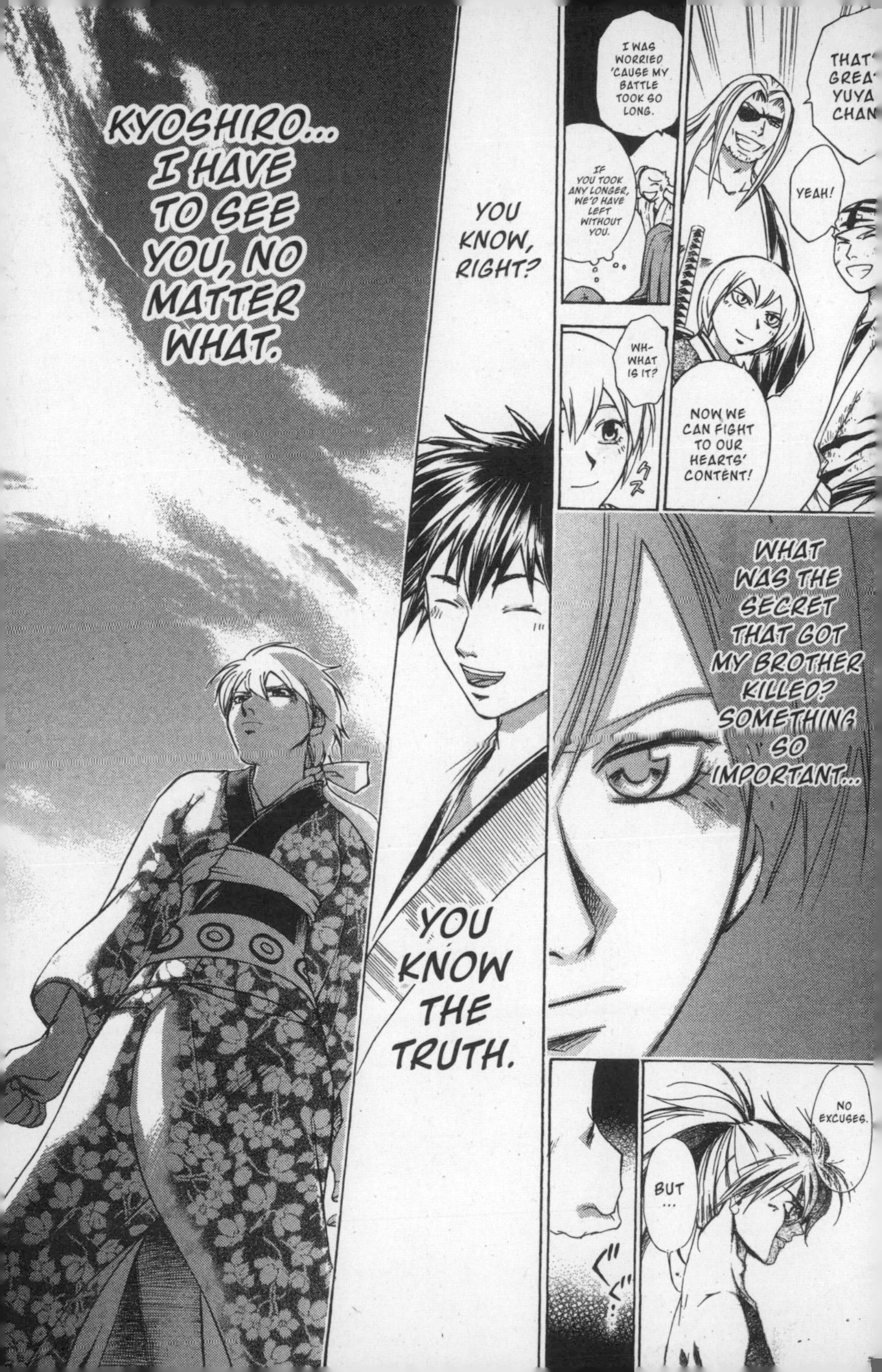
THAT' GREA YUYA CHAN
YEAH!
NOW WE CAN FIGHT TO OUR HEARTS' CONTENT!
I WAS WORRIED 'CAUSE MY BATTLE TOOK SO LONG.
IF YOU TOOK ANY LONGER, WE'D HAVE LEFT WITHOUT YOU.
WH- WHAT IS IT?
クス
WHAT WAS THE SECRET THAT GOT MY BROTHER KILLED? SOMETHING SO IMPORTANT...
NO EXCUSES.
BUT ...
YOU KNOW, RIGHT?
YOU KNOW THE TRUTH.
KYOSHIRO... I HAVE TO SEE YOU, NO MATTER WHAT.

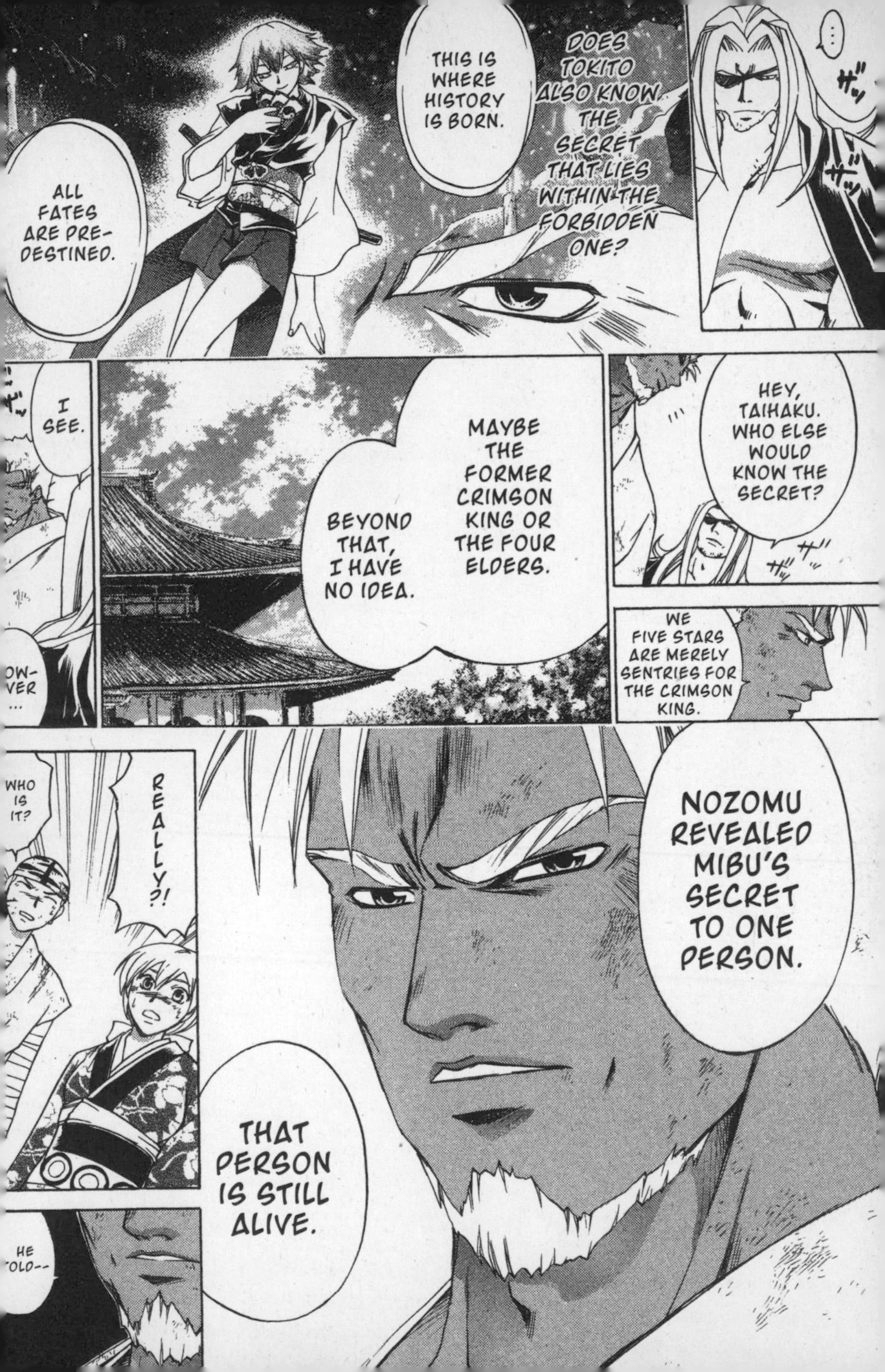
...
DOES TOKITO ALSO KNOW THE SECRET THAT LIES WITHIN THE FORBIDDEN ONE?
THIS IS WHERE HISTORY IS BORN.
ALL FATES ARE PRE-DESTINED.
HEY, TAIHAKU. WHO ELSE WOULD KNOW THE SECRET?
WE FIVE STARS ARE MERELY SENTRIES FOR THE CRIMSON KING.
MAYBE THE FORMER CRIMSON KING OR THE FOUR ELDERS.
BEYOND THAT, I HAVE NO IDEA.
I SEE.
OW-VER ...
NOZOMU REVEALED MIBU'S SECRET TO ONE PERSON.
THAT PERSON IS STILL ALIVE.
REALLY?!
WHO IS IT?
HE TOLD--

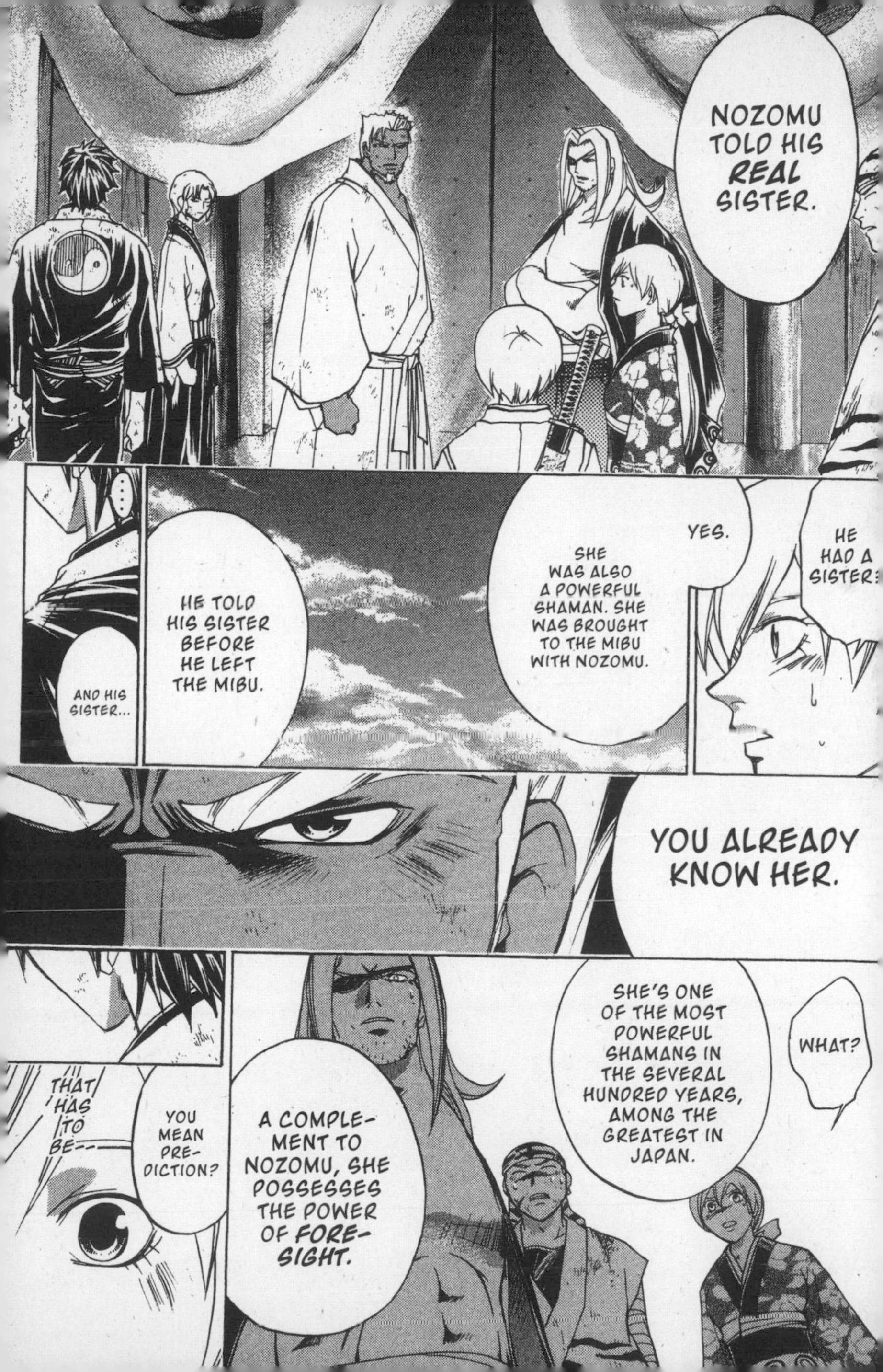
NOZOMU TOLD HIS REAL SISTER.
HE HAD A SISTER?
YES.
SHE WAS ALSO A POWERFUL SHAMAN. SHE WAS BROUGHT TO THE MIBU WITH NOZOMU.
HE TOLD HIS SISTER BEFORE HE LEFT THE MIBU.
...
AND HIS SISTER...
YOU ALREADY KNOW HER.
WHAT?
SHE'S ONE OF THE MOST POWERFUL SHAMANS IN THE SEVERAL HUNDRED YEARS, AMONG THE GREATEST IN JAPAN.
A COMPLEMENT TO NOZOMU, SHE POSSESSES THE POWER OF FORESIGHT.
YOU MEAN PREDICTION?
THAT HAS TO BE--

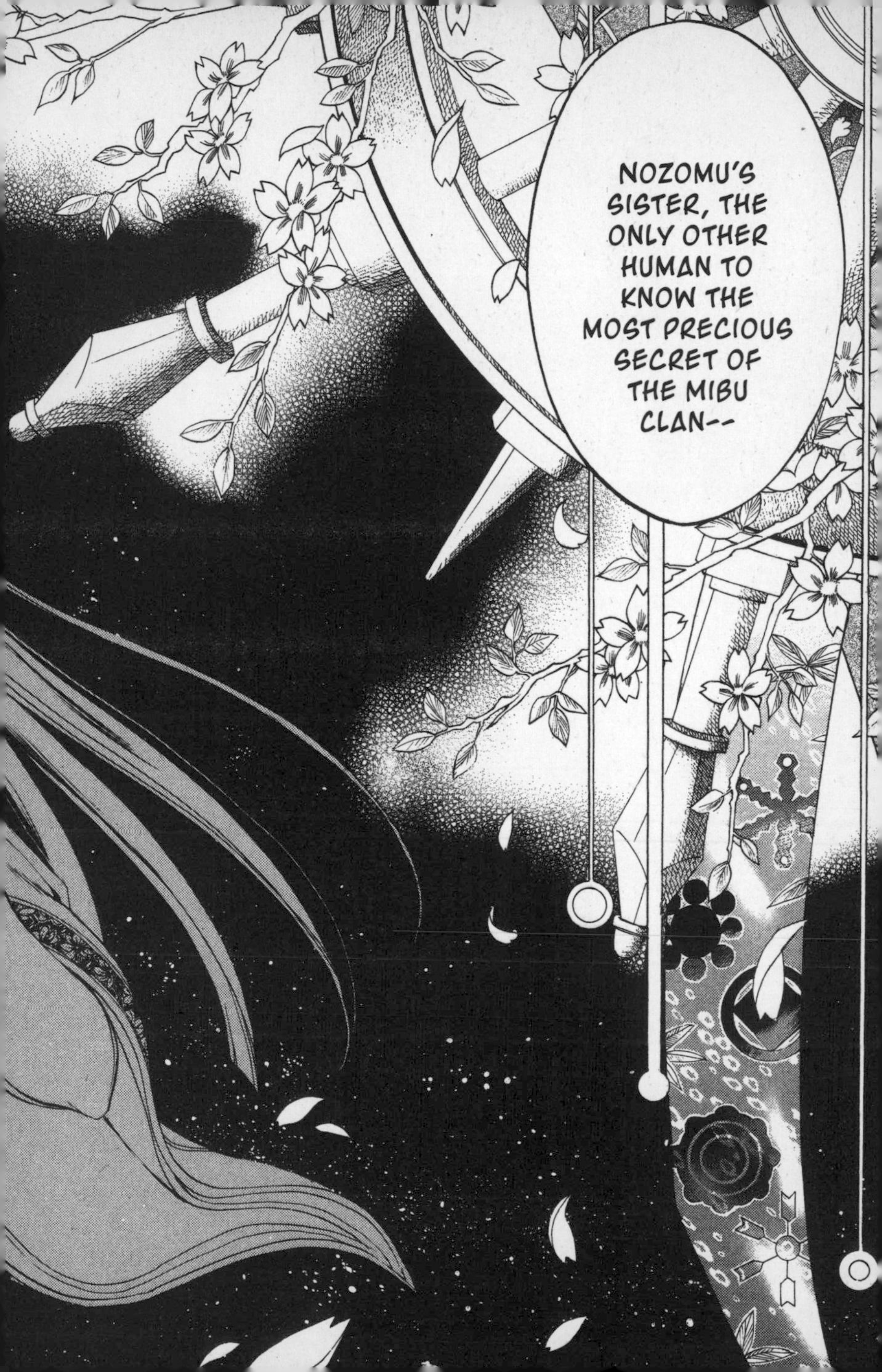
NOZOMU'S SISTER, THE ONLY OTHER HUMAN TO KNOW THE MOST PRECIOUS SECRET OF THE MIBU CLAN--

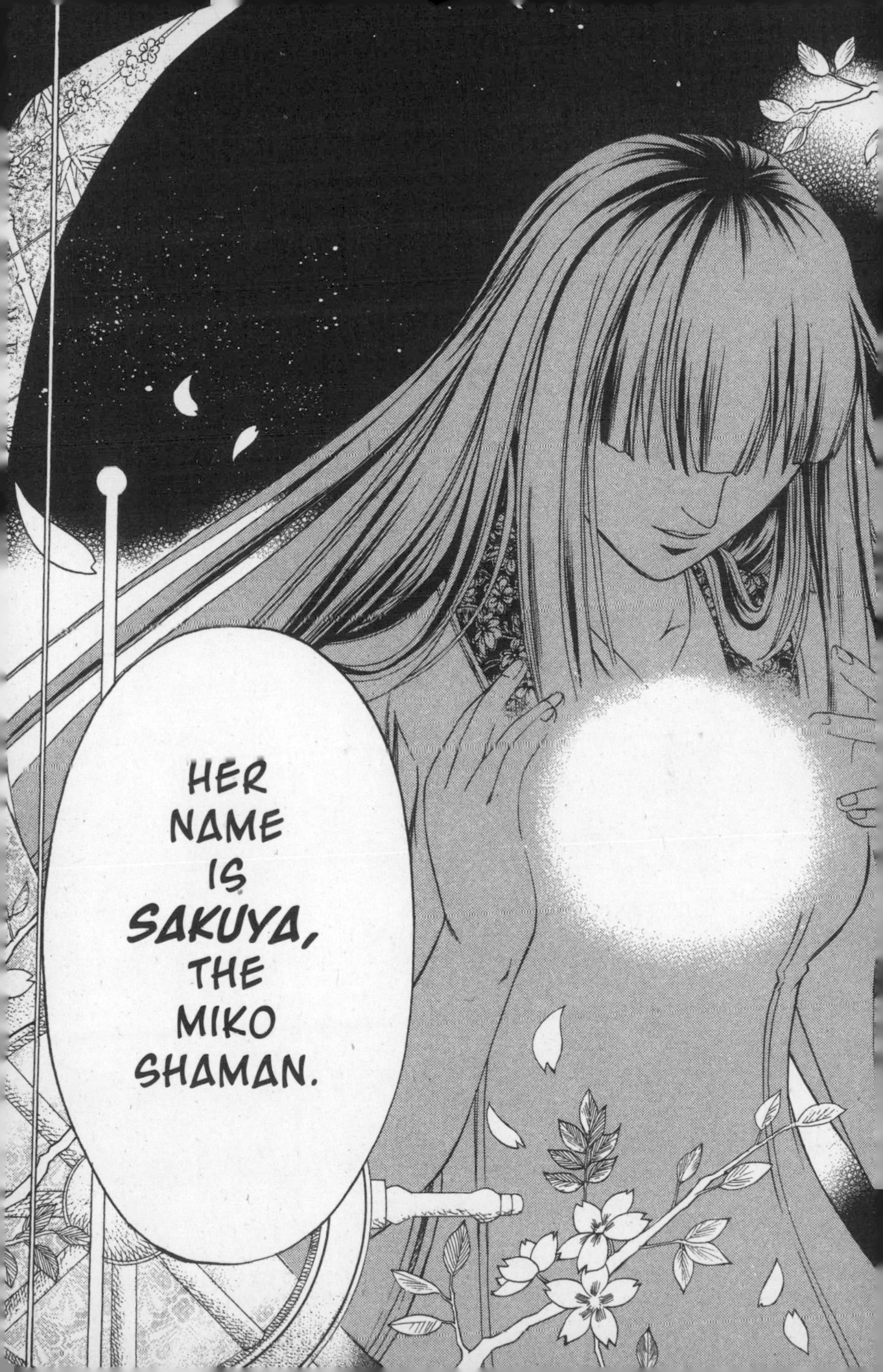
HER NAME IS SAKUYA, THE MIKO SHAMAN.

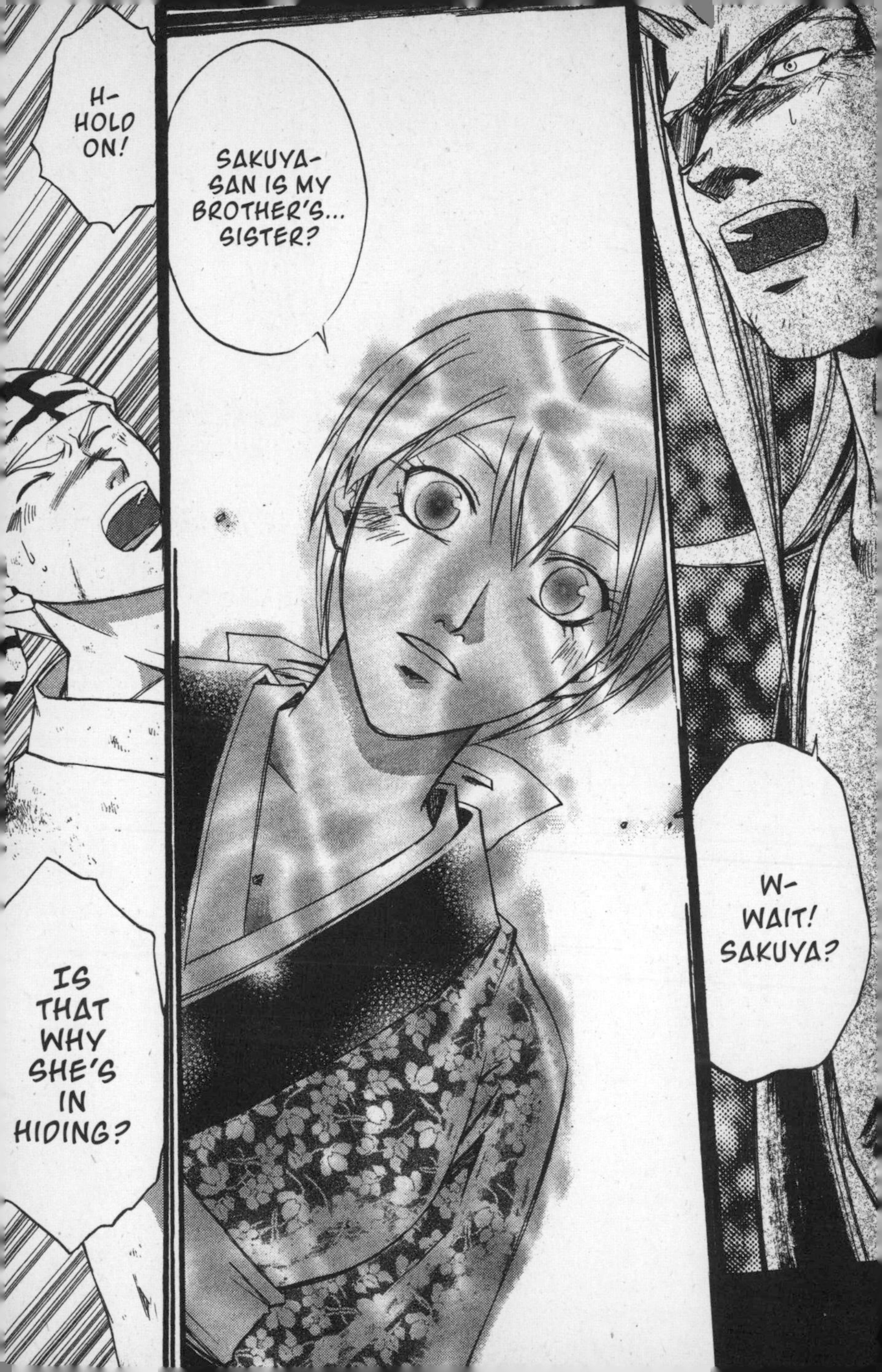
W-WAIT! SAKUYA?
SAKUYA-SAN IS MY BROTHER'S... SISTER?
H-HOLD ON!
IS THAT WHY SHE'S IN HIDING?

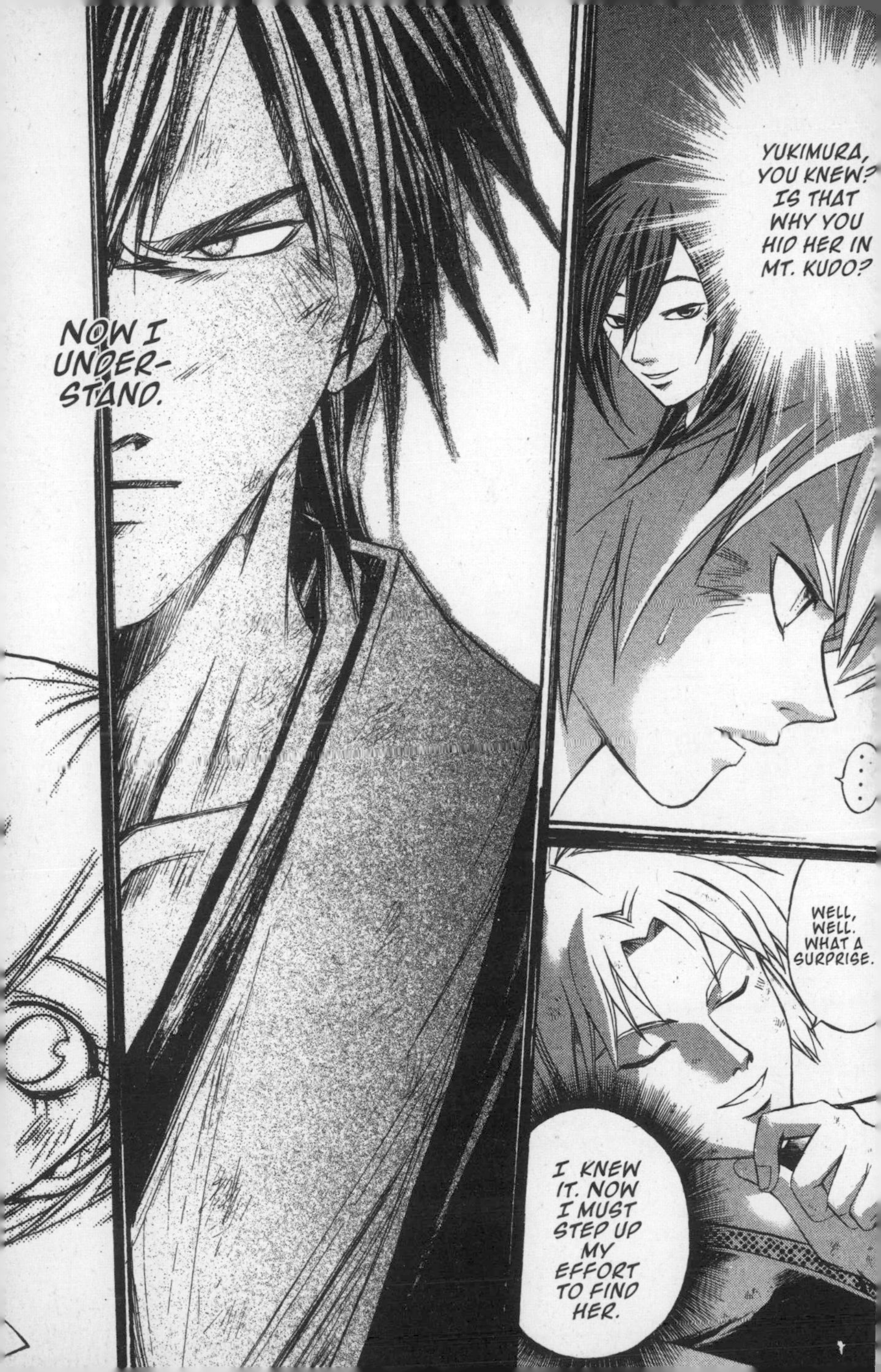
YUKIMURA, YOU KNEW? IS THAT WHY YOU HID HER IN MT. KUDO?
...
WELL, WELL. WHAT A SURPRISE.
I KNEW IT. NOW I MUST STEP UP MY EFFORT TO FIND HER.
NOW I UNDER-STAND.

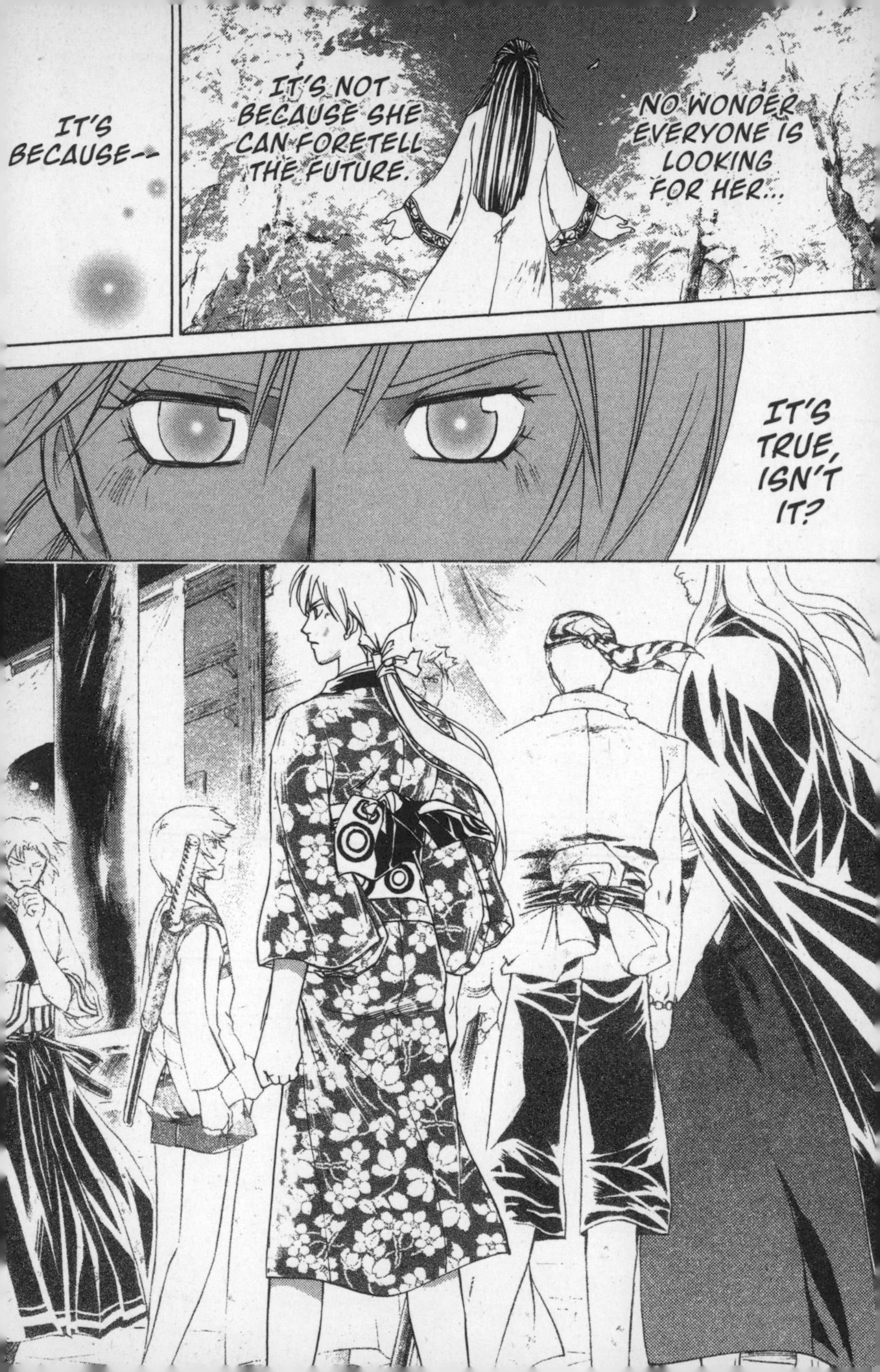
NO WONDER EVERYONE IS LOOKING FOR HER...
IT'S NOT BECAUSE SHE CAN FORETELL THE FUTURE.
IT'S BECAUSE--
IT'S TRUE, ISN'T IT?

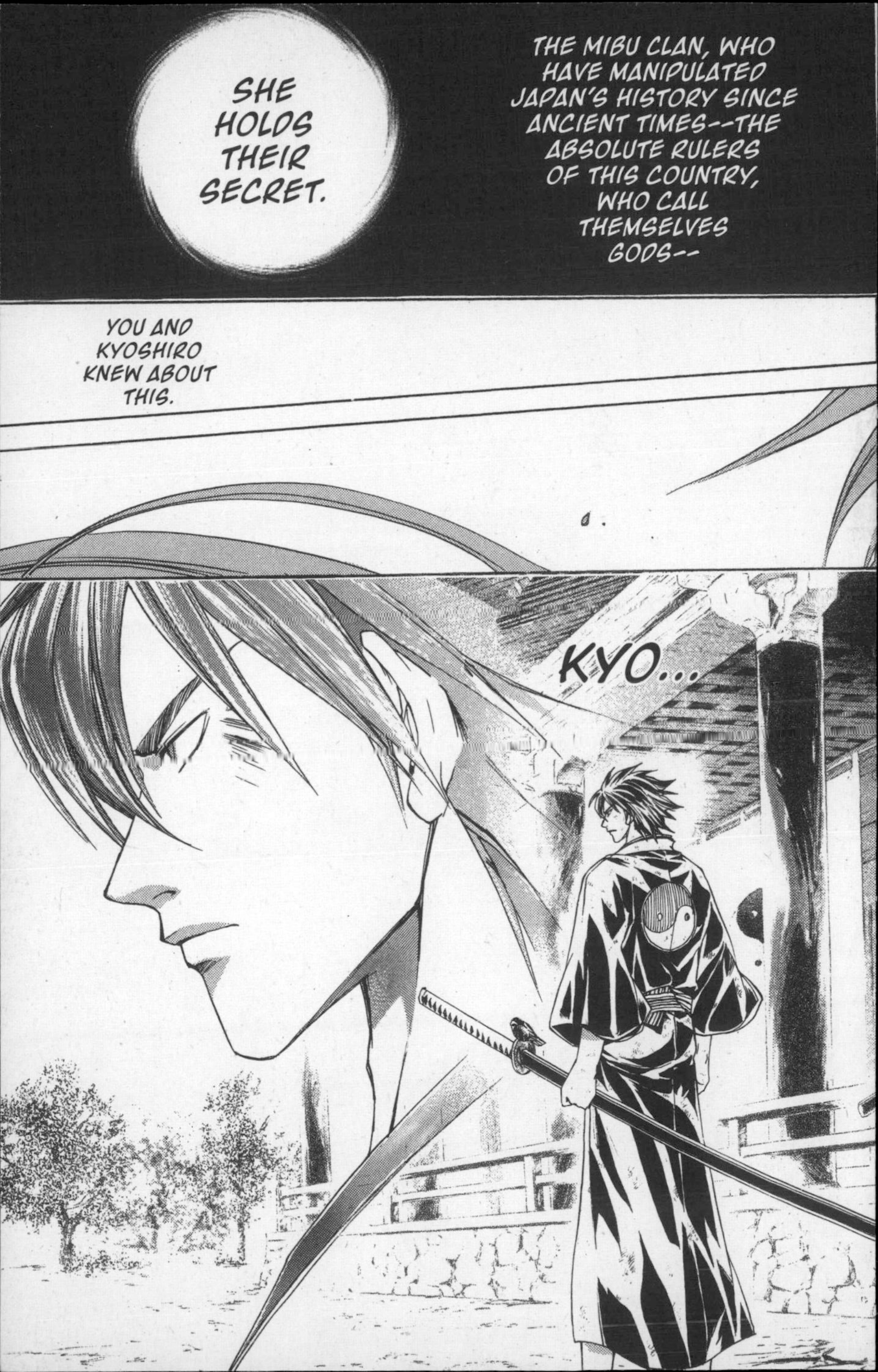
THE MIBU CLAN, WHO HAVE MANIPULATED JAPAN'S HISTORY SINCE ANCIENT TIMES--THE ABSOLUTE RULERS OF THIS COUNTRY, WHO CALL THEMSELVES GODS--
SHE HOLDS THEIR SECRET.
YOU AND KYOSHIRO KNEW ABOUT THIS.
KYO...

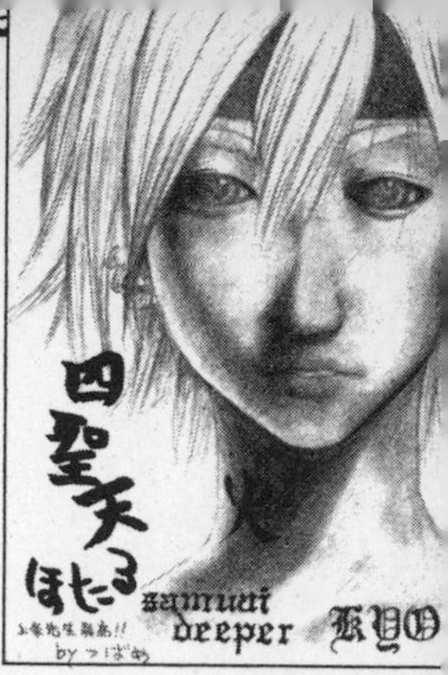
四聖天
ほたる
samurai deeper KYO
by つばめ

Wow! Talk about real!
[Tsubame / Okayama]

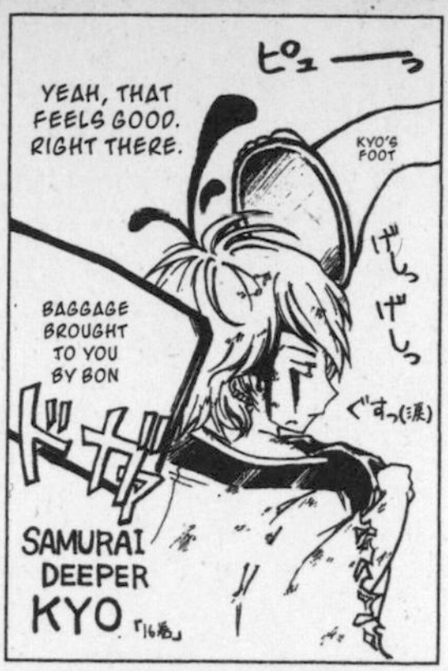
ピュ〜っ
YEAH, THAT FEELS GOOD. RIGHT THERE.
KYO'S FOOT
げしっ げしっ
BAGGAGE BROUGHT TO YOU BY BON
ドサ
ぐすっ(涙)
SAMURAI DEEPER KYO
「16巻」

His memories have been beautified! (Ha ha)
[Kuba / Hiyougo]

It's totally A-OKAY!
[Micchy / Mie]

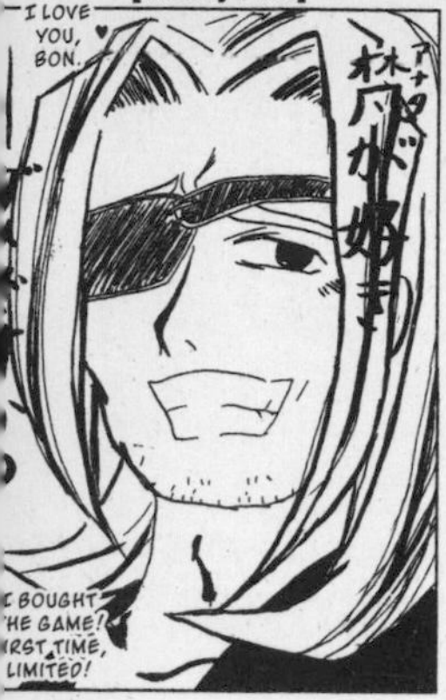
I LOVE YOU, BON.

Character Special "The Four Emperors (-1) Then and Now"

kamijyou ni chousen
上条に挑戦!

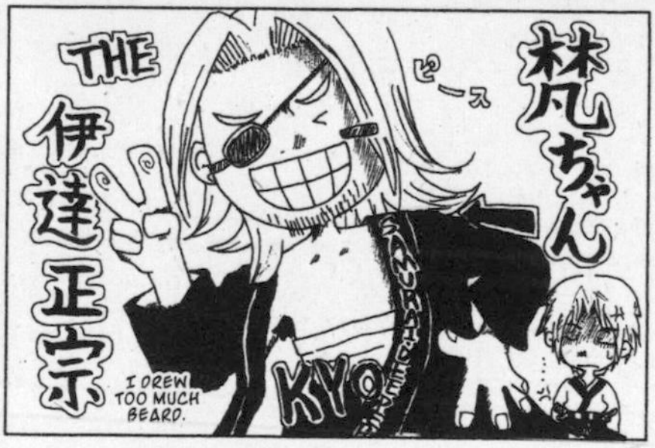
梵ちゃん
ピース
THE
伊達正宗
I DREW TOO MUCH BEARD.
KYO

The armpit hair... the armpit hair. (Ha ha!)
[Keishima Nozomi / Miyagi]

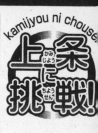

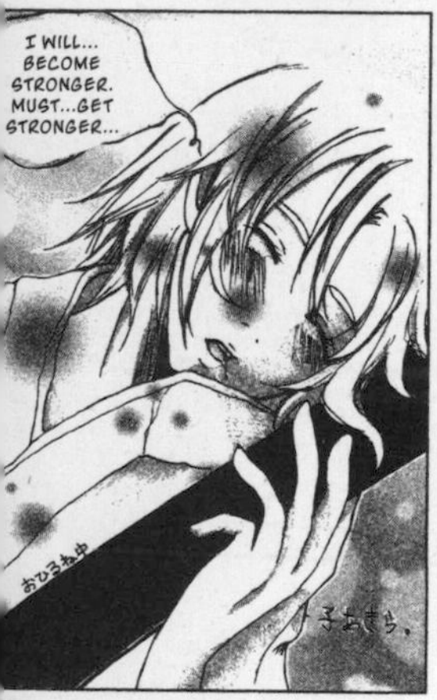
I WILL... BECOME STRONGER. MUST...GET STRONGER...

Is that Kyo's scabbard?! Ew, there's gonna be some drool stains on that thing.
[Kaneko Shiori / Chiba]

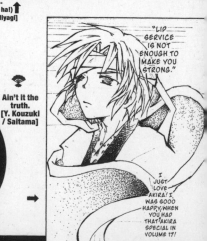

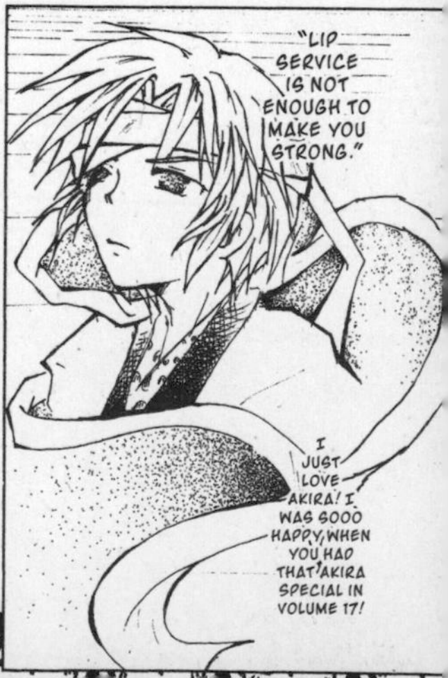
"LIP SERVICE IS NOT ENOUGH TO MAKE YOU STRONG."
I JUST LOVE AKIRA! I WAS SOOO HAPPY WHEN YOU HAD THAT AKIRA SPECIAL IN VOLUME 17!

Ain't it the truth.
[Y. Kouzuki / Saitama]

A message from Akimine Kamijyo!

SORRY FOR STUFFING IN THREE CHARACTERS IN ONE PAGE...I'LL BE DOING ANOTHER "FOUR EMPERORS (-1) THEN AND NOW" THEME NEXT VOLUME, TOO, SO UNTIL THEN!

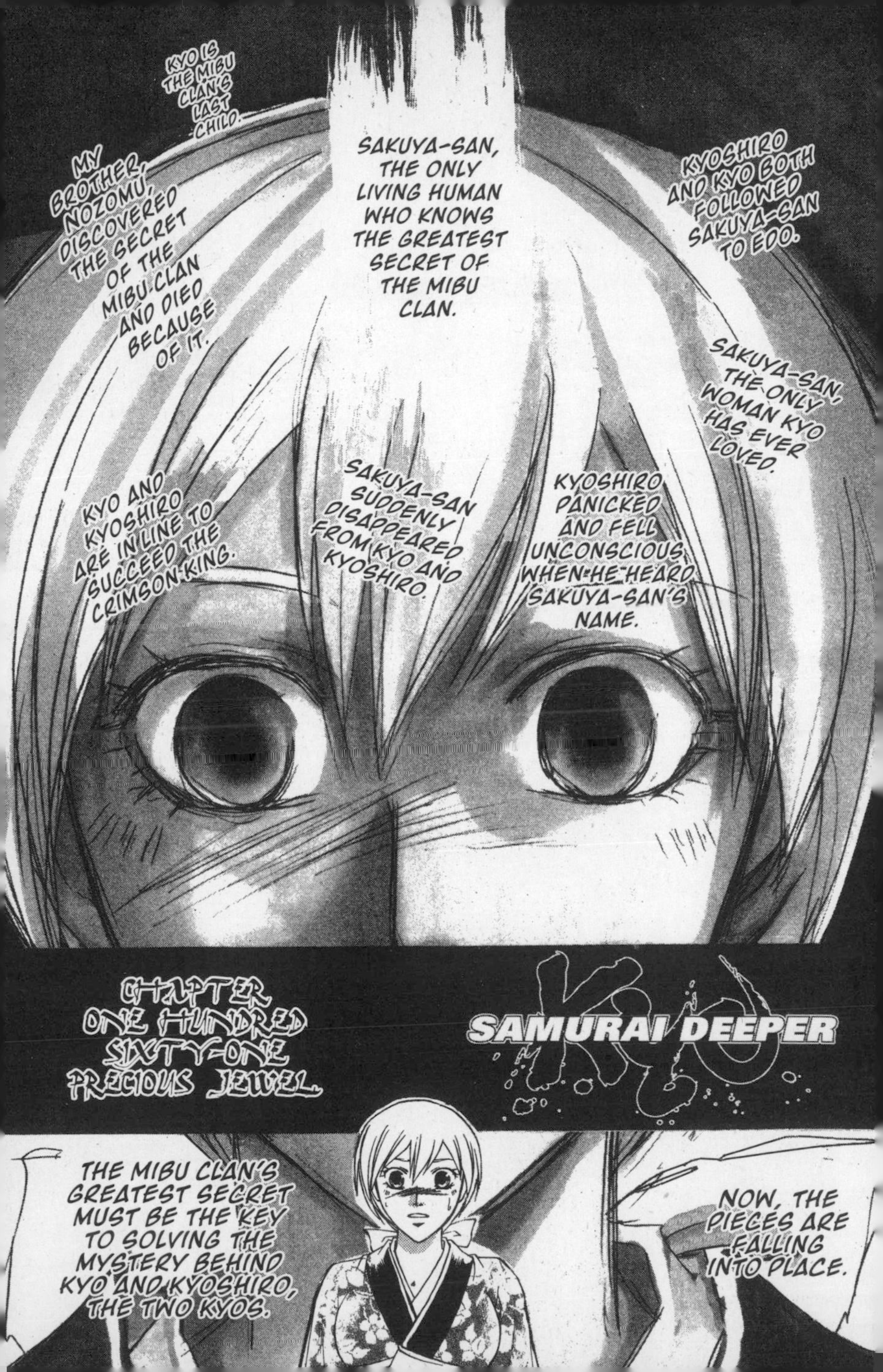
KYOSHIRO AND KYO BOTH FOLLOWED SAKUYA-SAN TO EDO.
SAKUYA-SAN, THE ONLY LIVING HUMAN WHO KNOWS THE GREATEST SECRET OF THE MIBU CLAN.
KYO IS THE MIBU CLAN'S LAST CHILD.
MY BROTHER, NOZOMU, DISCOVERED THE SECRET OF THE MIBU CLAN AND DIED BECAUSE OF IT.
SAKUYA-SAN, THE ONLY WOMAN KYO HAS EVER LOVED.
KYOSHIRO PANICKED AND FELL UNCONSCIOUS WHEN HE HEARD SAKUYA-SAN'S NAME.
SAKUYA-SAN SUDDENLY DISAPPEARED FROM KYO AND KYOSHIRO.
KYO AND KYOSHIRO ARE IN LINE TO SUCCEED THE CRIMSON KING.
SAMURAI DEEPER KYO
CHAPTER ONE HUNDRED SIXTY-ONE PRECIOUS JEWEL
NOW, THE PIECES ARE FALLING INTO PLACE.
THE MIBU CLAN'S GREATEST SECRET MUST BE THE KEY TO SOLVING THE MYSTERY BEHIND KYO AND KYOSHIRO, THE TWO KYOS.

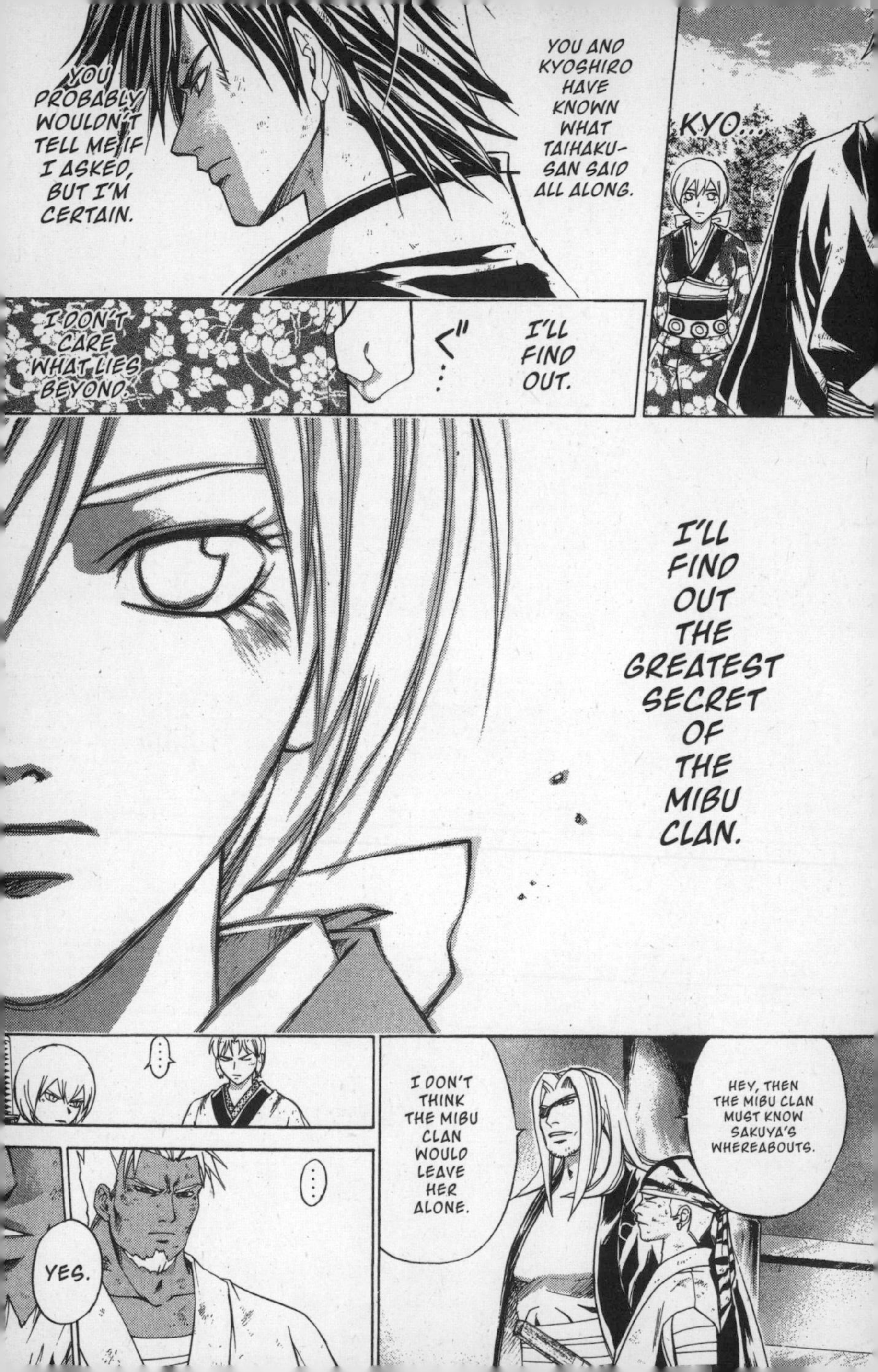
KYO...
YOU AND KYOSHIRO HAVE KNOWN WHAT TAIHAKU-SAN SAID ALL ALONG.
YOU PROBABLY WOULDN'T TELL ME IF I ASKED, BUT I'M CERTAIN.
I'LL FIND OUT.
I DON'T CARE WHAT LIES BEYOND.
I'LL FIND OUT THE GREATEST SECRET OF THE MIBU CLAN.
HEY, THEN THE MIBU CLAN MUST KNOW SAKUYA'S WHEREABOUTS.
I DON'T THINK THE MIBU CLAN WOULD LEAVE HER ALONE.
...
...
YES.

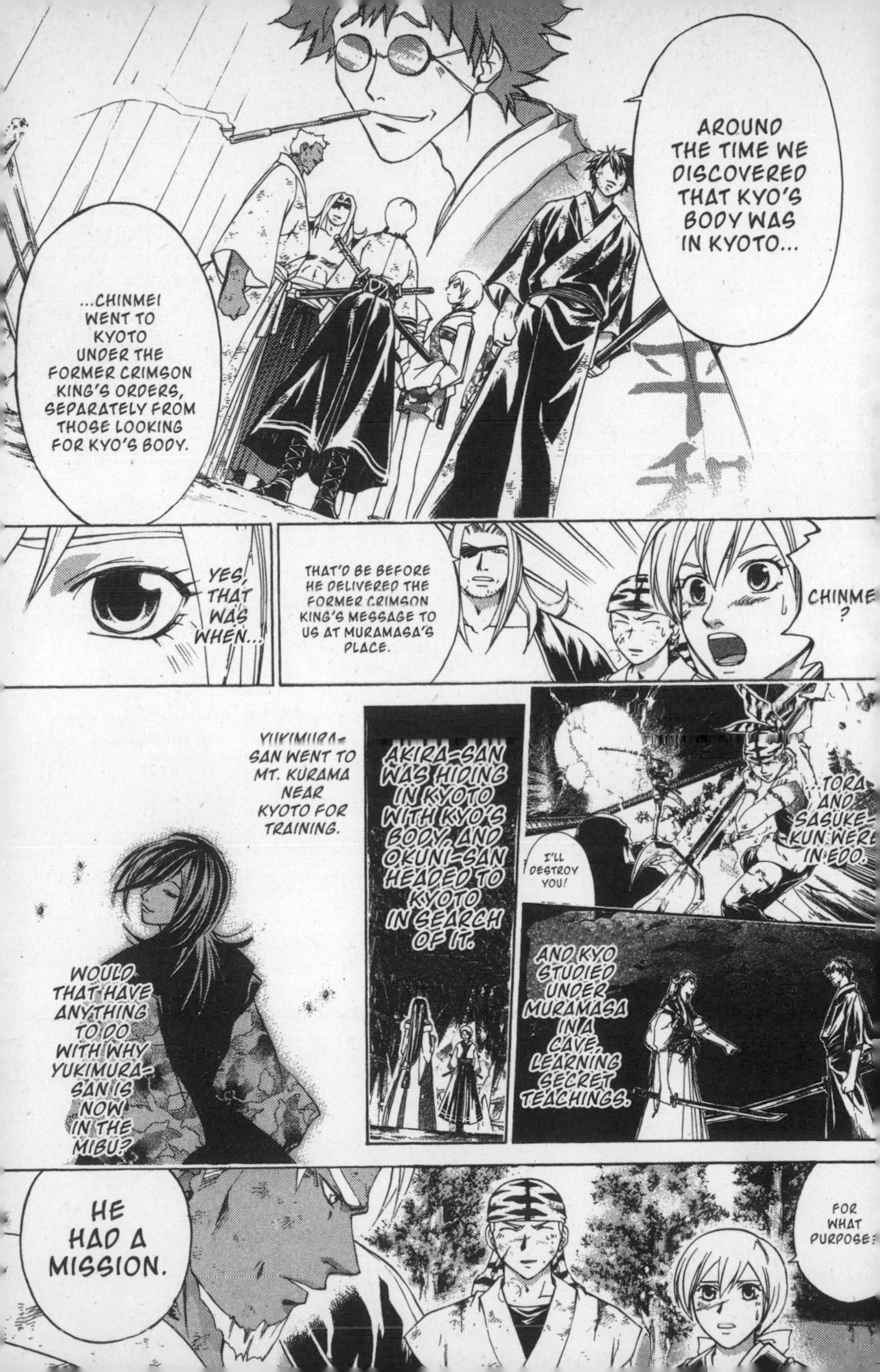
AROUND THE TIME WE DISCOVERED THAT KYO'S BODY WAS IN KYOTO...
...CHINMEI WENT TO KYOTO UNDER THE FORMER CRIMSON KING'S ORDERS, SEPARATELY FROM THOSE LOOKING FOR KYO'S BODY.
CHINME ?
THAT'D BE BEFORE HE DELIVERED THE FORMER CRIMSON KING'S MESSAGE TO US AT MURAMASA'S PLACE.
YES, THAT WAS WHEN...
...TORA AND SASUKE-KUN WERE IN EDO.
I'LL DESTROY YOU!
AND KYO STUDIED UNDER MURAMASA IN A CAVE, LEARNING SECRET TEACHINGS.
AKIRA-SAN WAS HIDING IN KYOTO WITH KYO'S BODY, AND OKUNI-SAN HEADED TO KYOTO IN SEARCH OF IT.
YUKIMURA-SAN WENT TO MT. KURAMA NEAR KYOTO FOR TRAINING.
WOULD THAT HAVE ANYTHING TO DO WITH WHY YUKIMURA-SAN IS NOW IN THE MIBU?
FOR WHAT PURPOSE?
HE HAD A MISSION.

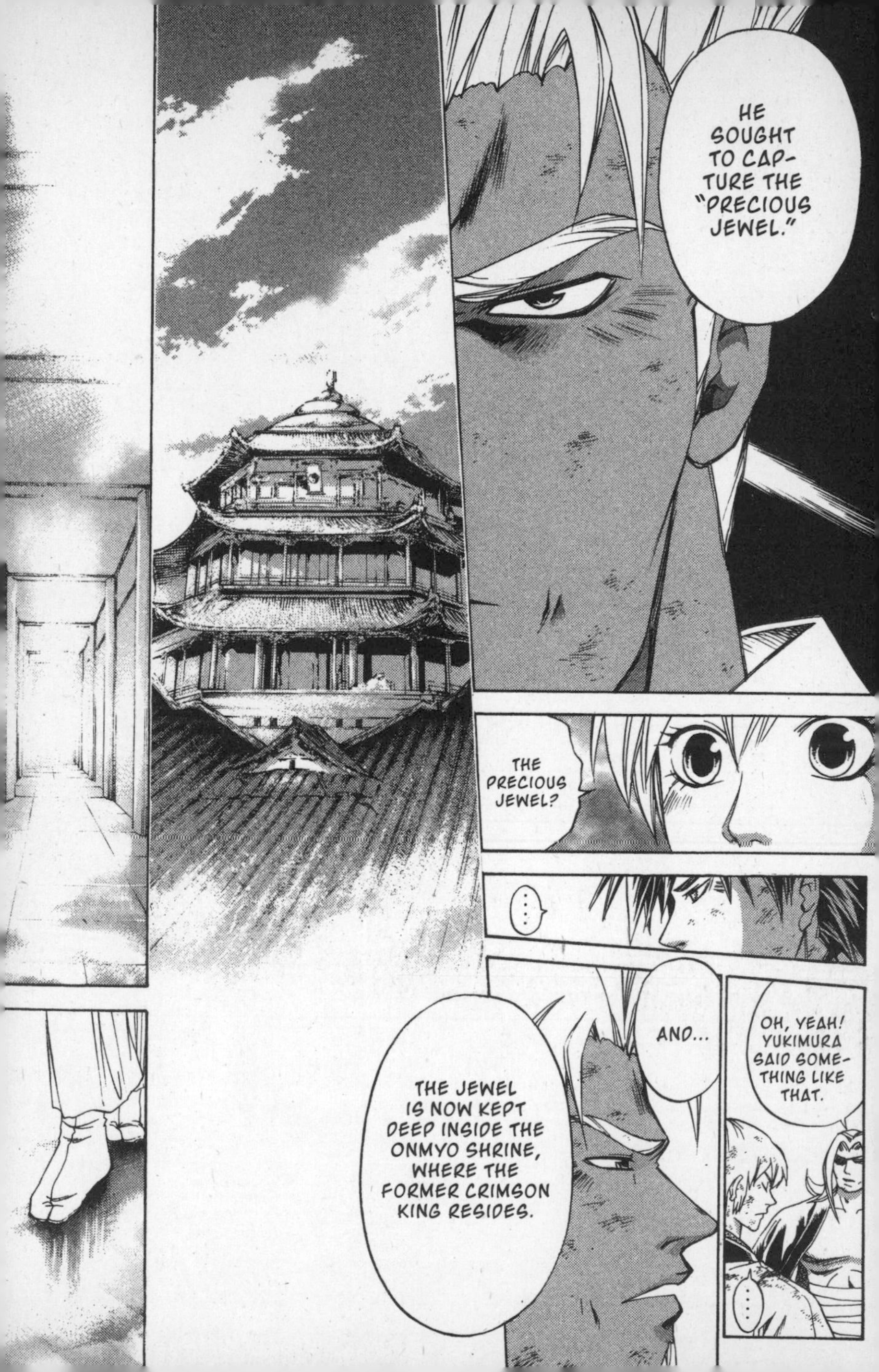
HE SOUGHT TO CAPTURE THE "PRECIOUS JEWEL."
THE PRECIOUS JEWEL?
...
OH, YEAH! YUKIMURA SAID SOMETHING LIKE THAT.
...
AND...
THE JEWEL IS NOW KEPT DEEP INSIDE THE ONMYO SHRINE, WHERE THE FORMER CRIMSON KING RESIDES.

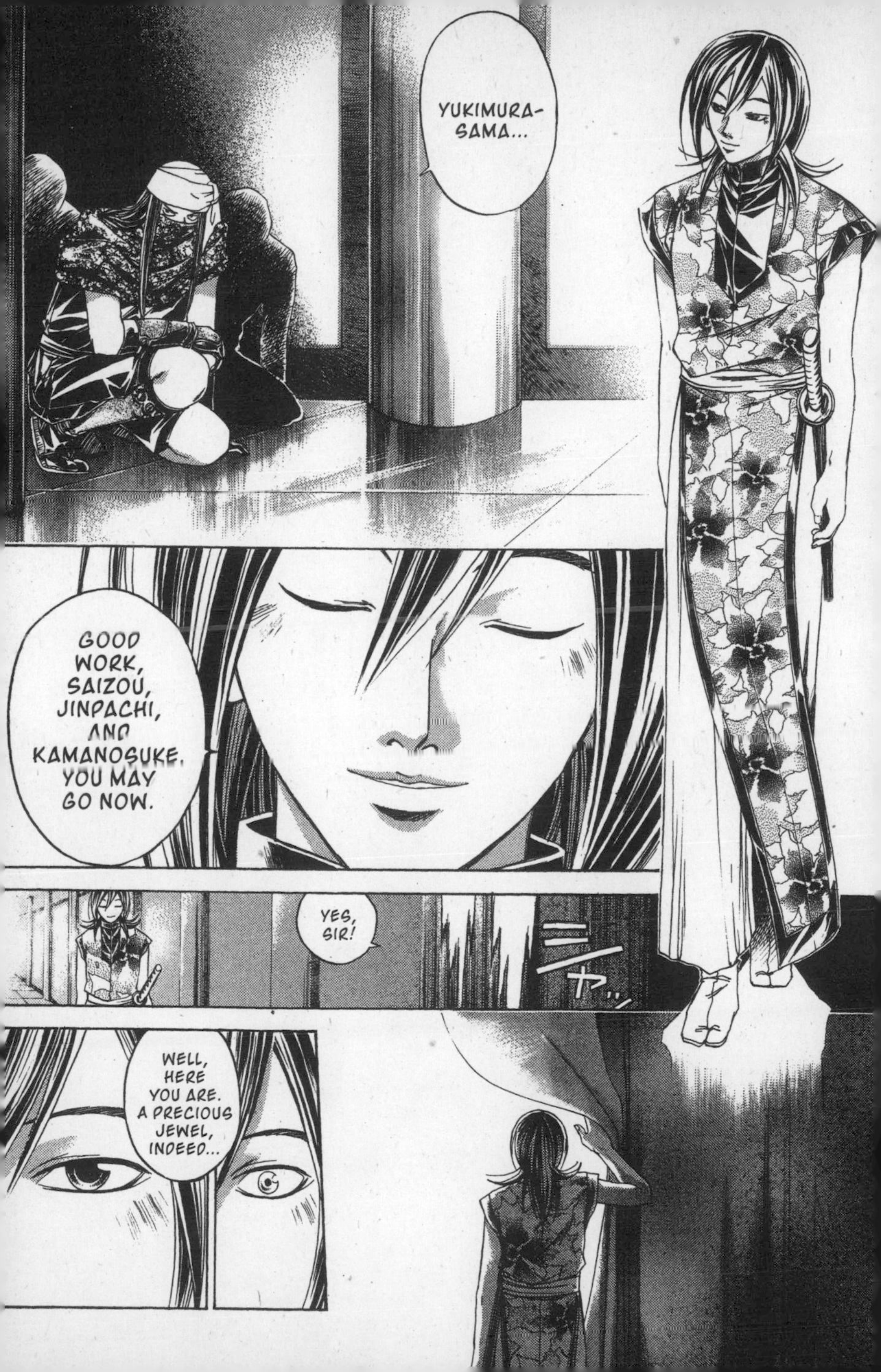
YUKIMURA-SAMA...
GOOD WORK, SAIZOU, JINPACHI, AND KAMANOSUKE. YOU MAY GO NOW.
YES, SIR!
シャッ
WELL, HERE YOU ARE. A PRECIOUS JEWEL, INDEED...

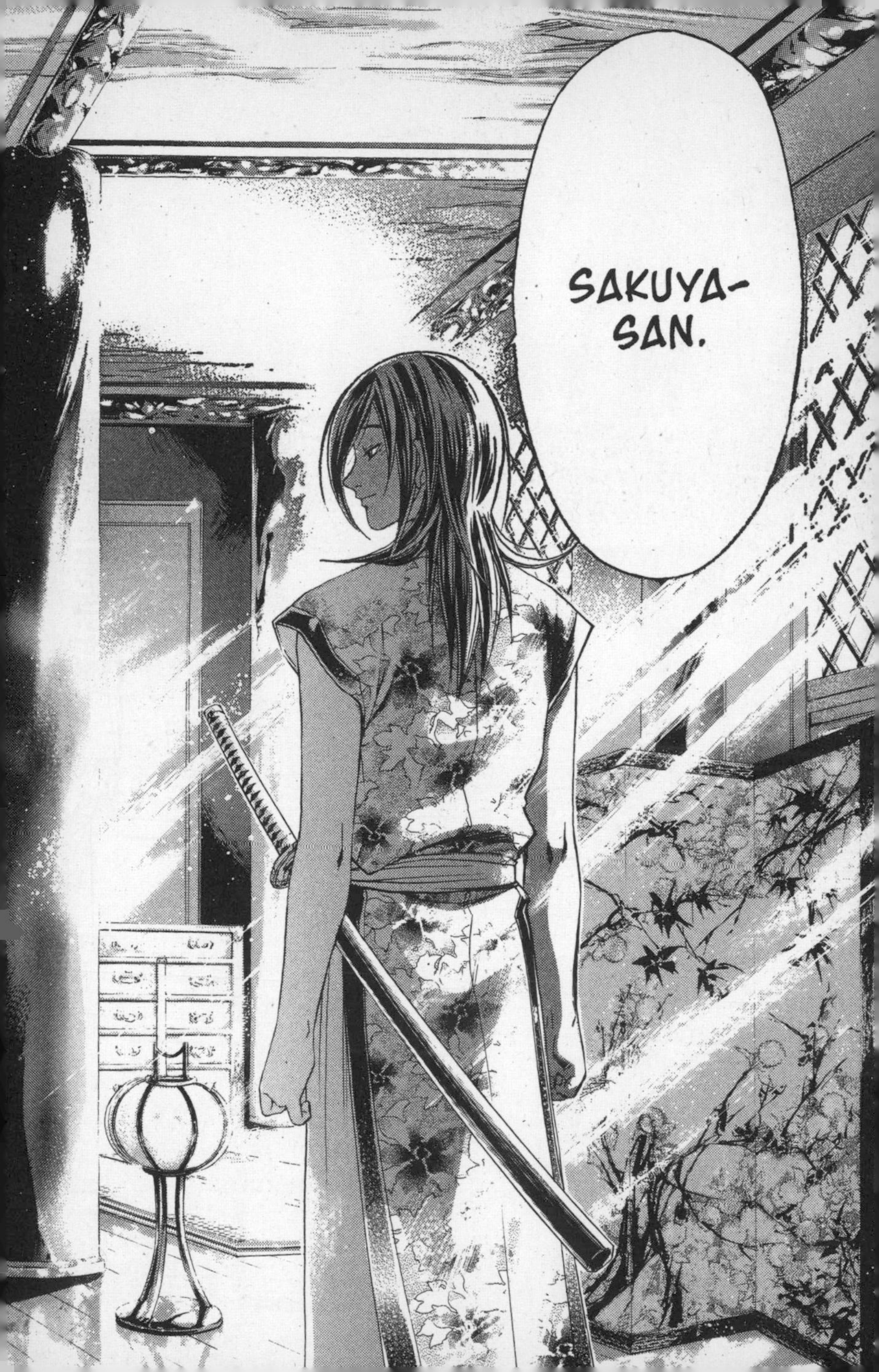
SAKUYA-SAN.

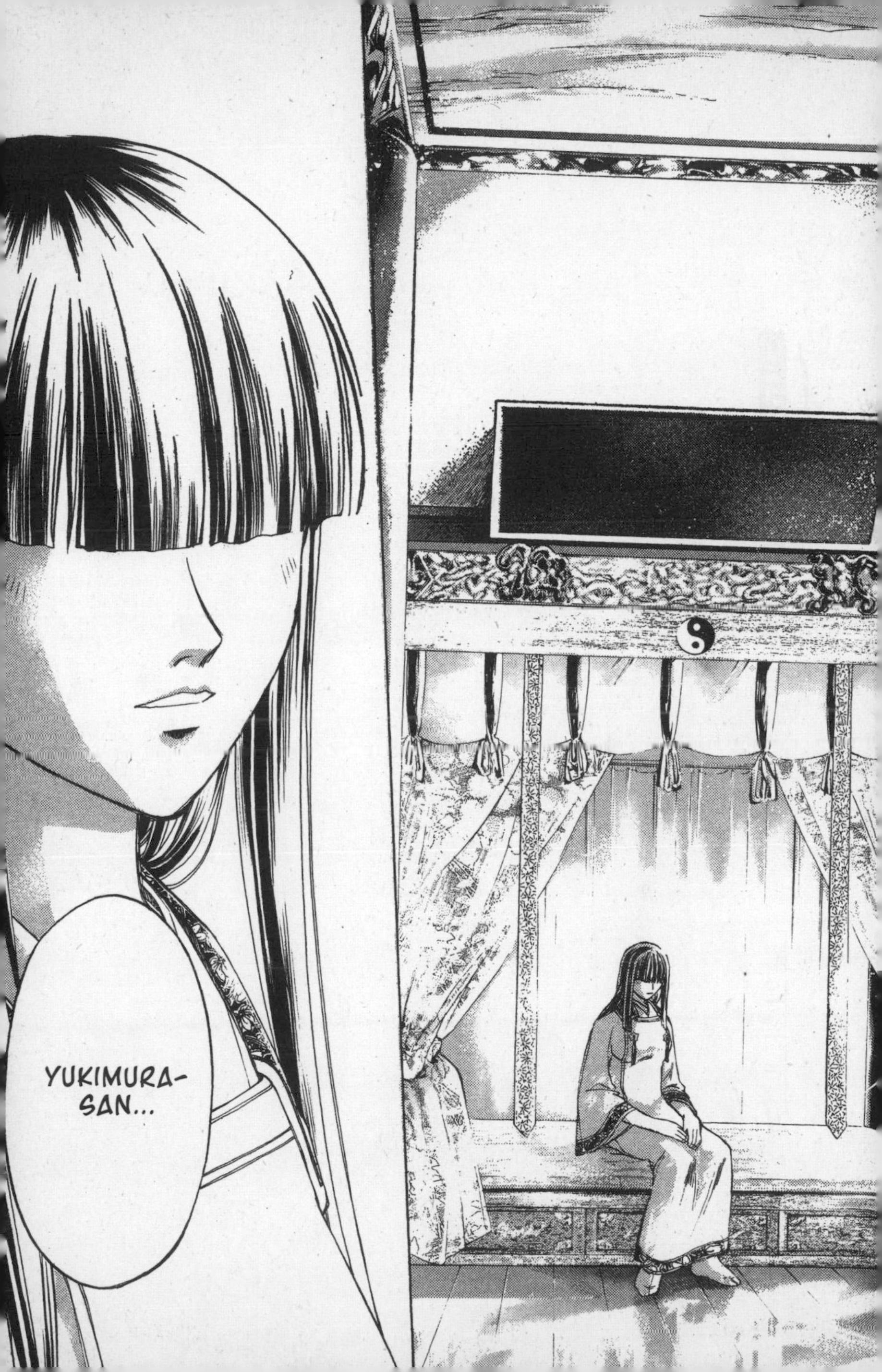
YUKIMURA-SAN...

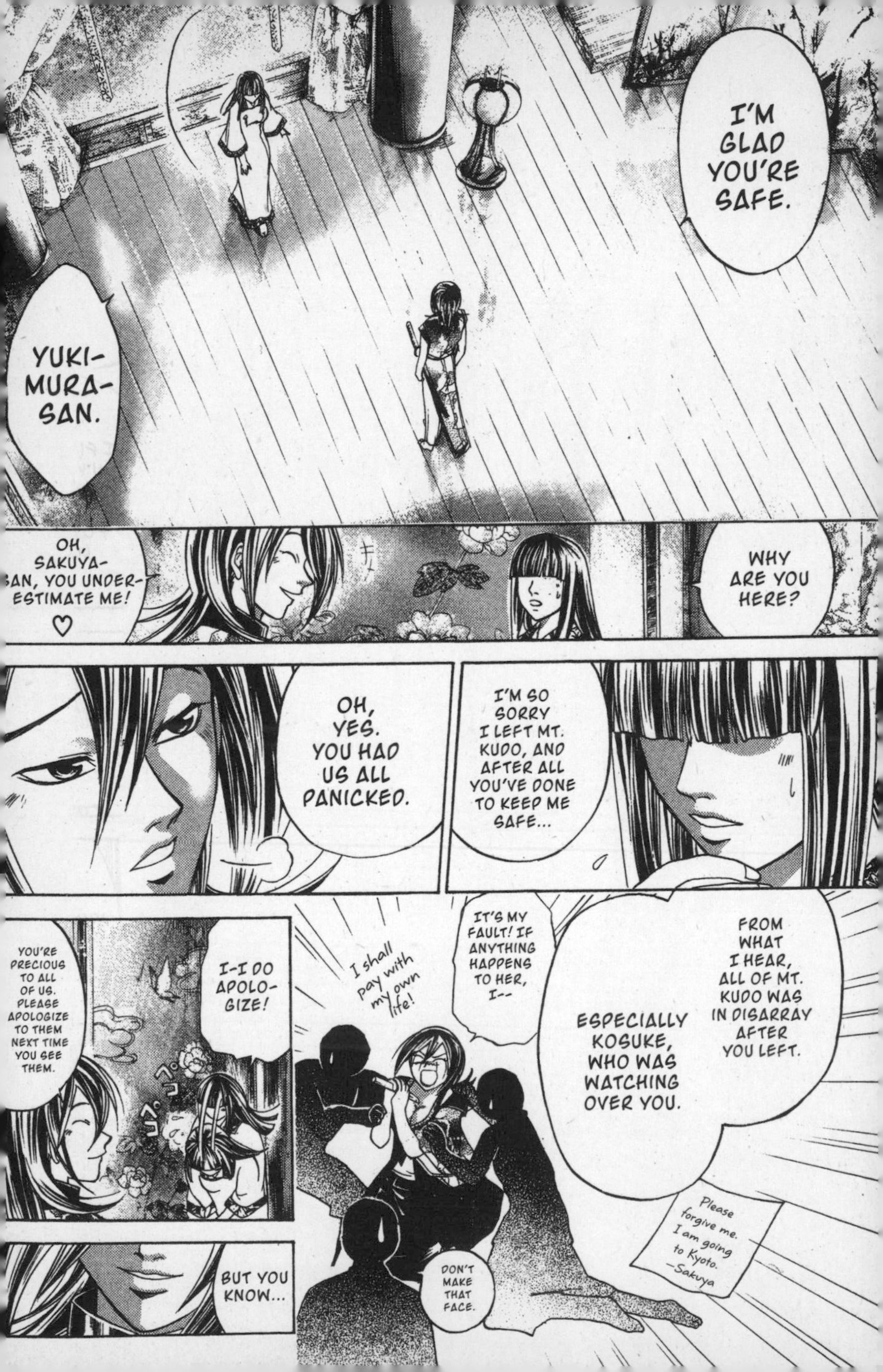
I'M GLAD YOU'RE SAFE.
YUKI-MURA-SAN.
WHY ARE YOU HERE?
OH, SAKUYA-SAN, YOU UNDER-ESTIMATE ME! ♡
I'M SO SORRY I LEFT MT. KUDO, AND AFTER ALL YOU'VE DONE TO KEEP ME SAFE...
OH, YES. YOU HAD US ALL PANICKED.
FROM WHAT I HEAR, ALL OF MT. KUDO WAS IN DISARRAY AFTER YOU LEFT.
ESPECIALLY KOSUKE, WHO WAS WATCHING OVER YOU.
IT'S MY FAULT! IF ANYTHING HAPPENS TO HER, I--
I shall pay with my own life!
Please forgive me. I am going to Kyoto. —Sakuya
DON'T MAKE THAT FACE.
I-I DO APOLOGIZE!
YOU'RE PRECIOUS TO ALL OF US. PLEASE APOLOGIZE TO THEM NEXT TIME YOU SEE THEM.
BUT YOU KNOW...

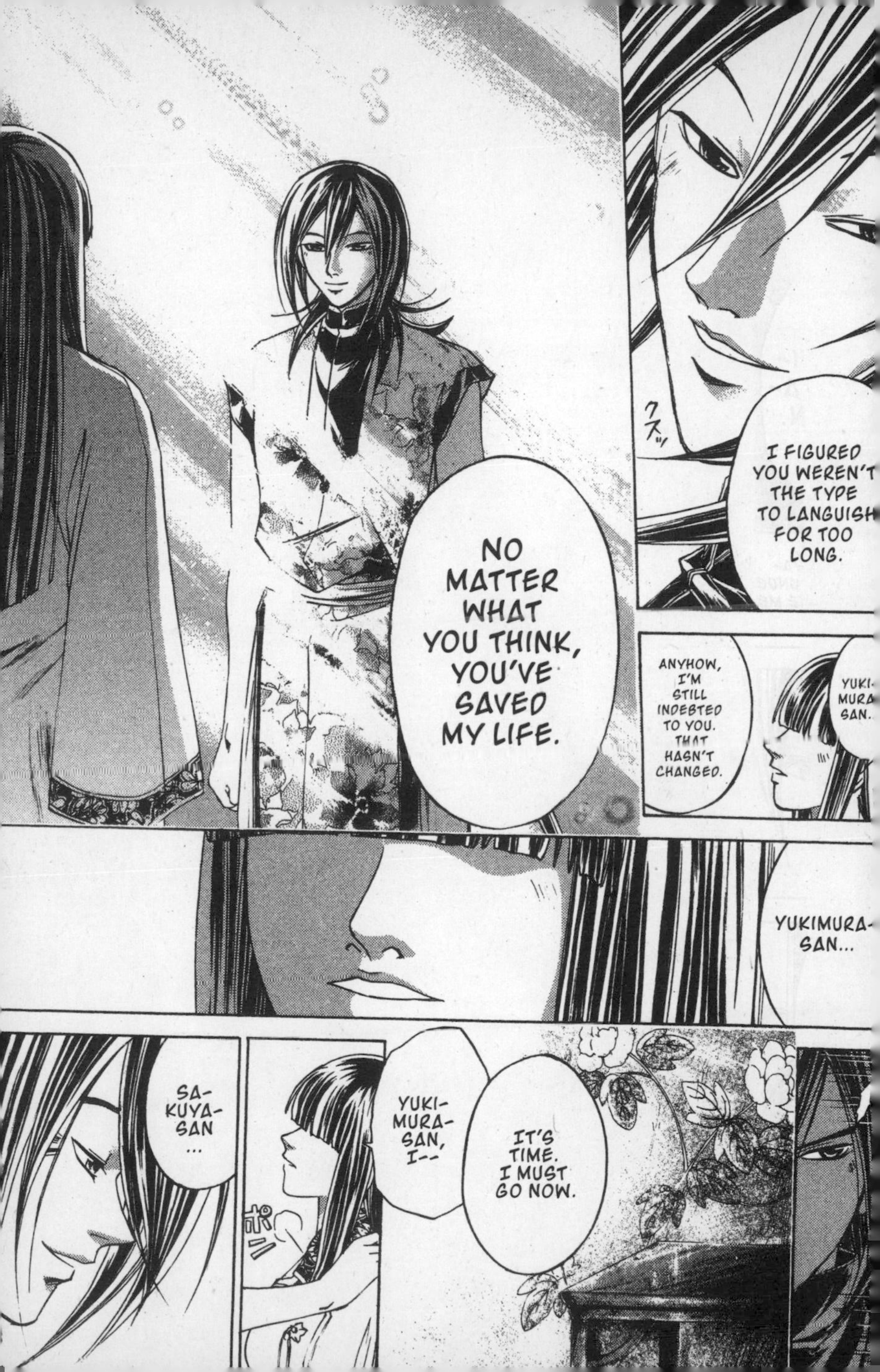

クスッ
I FIGURED YOU WEREN'T THE TYPE TO LANGUISH FOR TOO LONG.
YUKI-MURA-SAN...
ANYHOW, I'M STILL INDEBTED TO YOU. THAT HASN'T CHANGED.
NO MATTER WHAT YOU THINK, YOU'VE SAVED MY LIFE.
YUKIMURA-SAN...
YUKI-MURA-SAN, I--
IT'S TIME. I MUST GO NOW.
SA-KUYA-SAN ...

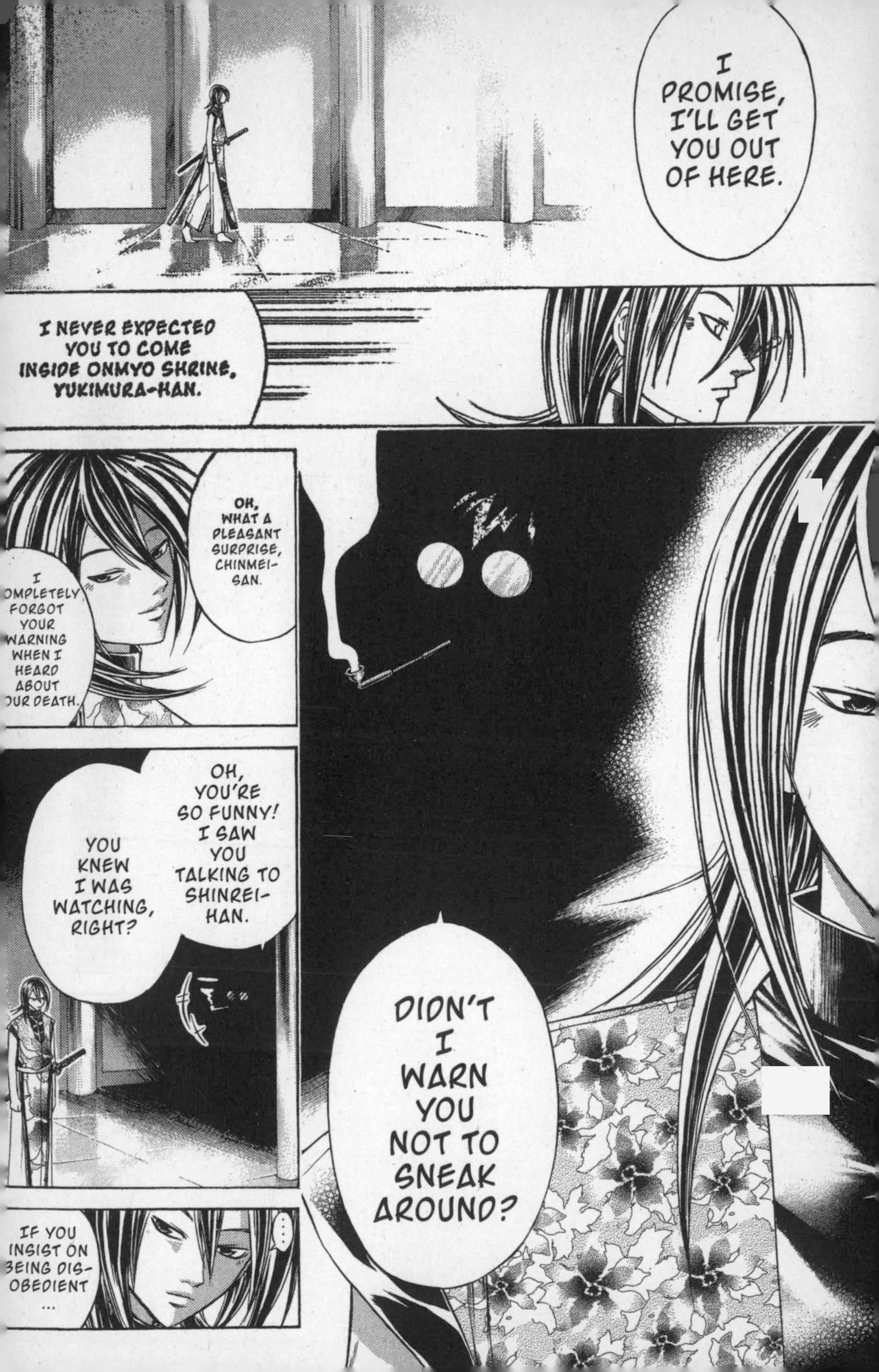
I PROMISE, I'LL GET YOU OUT OF HERE.
I NEVER EXPECTED YOU TO COME INSIDE ONMYO SHRINE, YUKIMURA-HAN.
DIDN'T I WARN YOU NOT TO SNEAK AROUND?
OH, WHAT A PLEASANT SURPRISE, CHINMEI-SAN.
I OMPLETELY FORGOT YOUR WARNING WHEN I HEARD ABOUT OUR DEATH.
OH, YOU'RE SO FUNNY! I SAW YOU TALKING TO SHINREI-HAN.
YOU KNEW I WAS WATCHING, RIGHT?
...
IF YOU INSIST ON BEING DIS-OBEDIENT ...

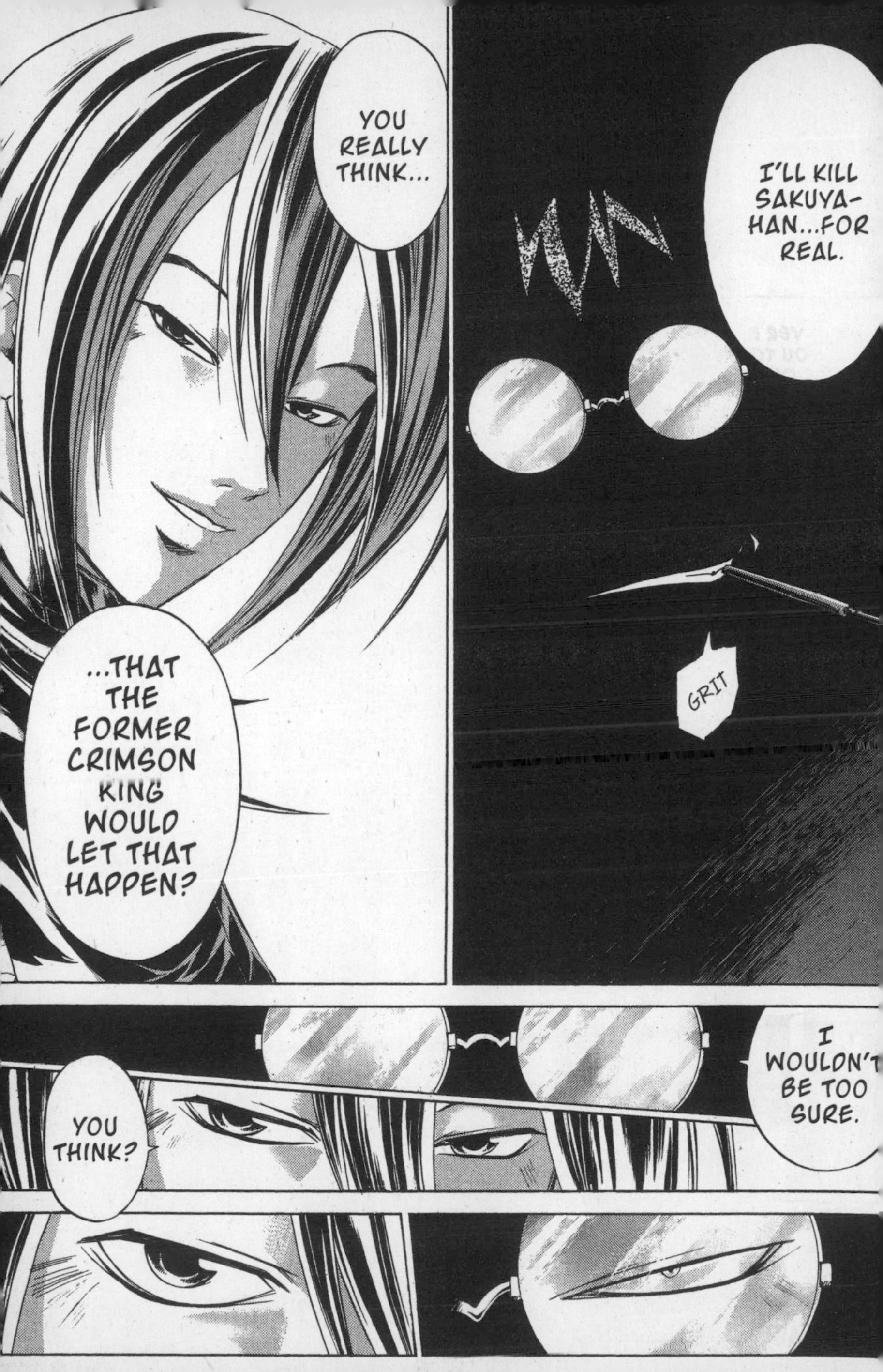
I'LL KILL SAKUYA-HAN...FOR REAL.
GRIT
YOU REALLY THINK...
...THAT THE FORMER CRIMSON KING WOULD LET THAT HAPPEN?
I WOULDN'T BE TOO SURE.
YOU THINK?

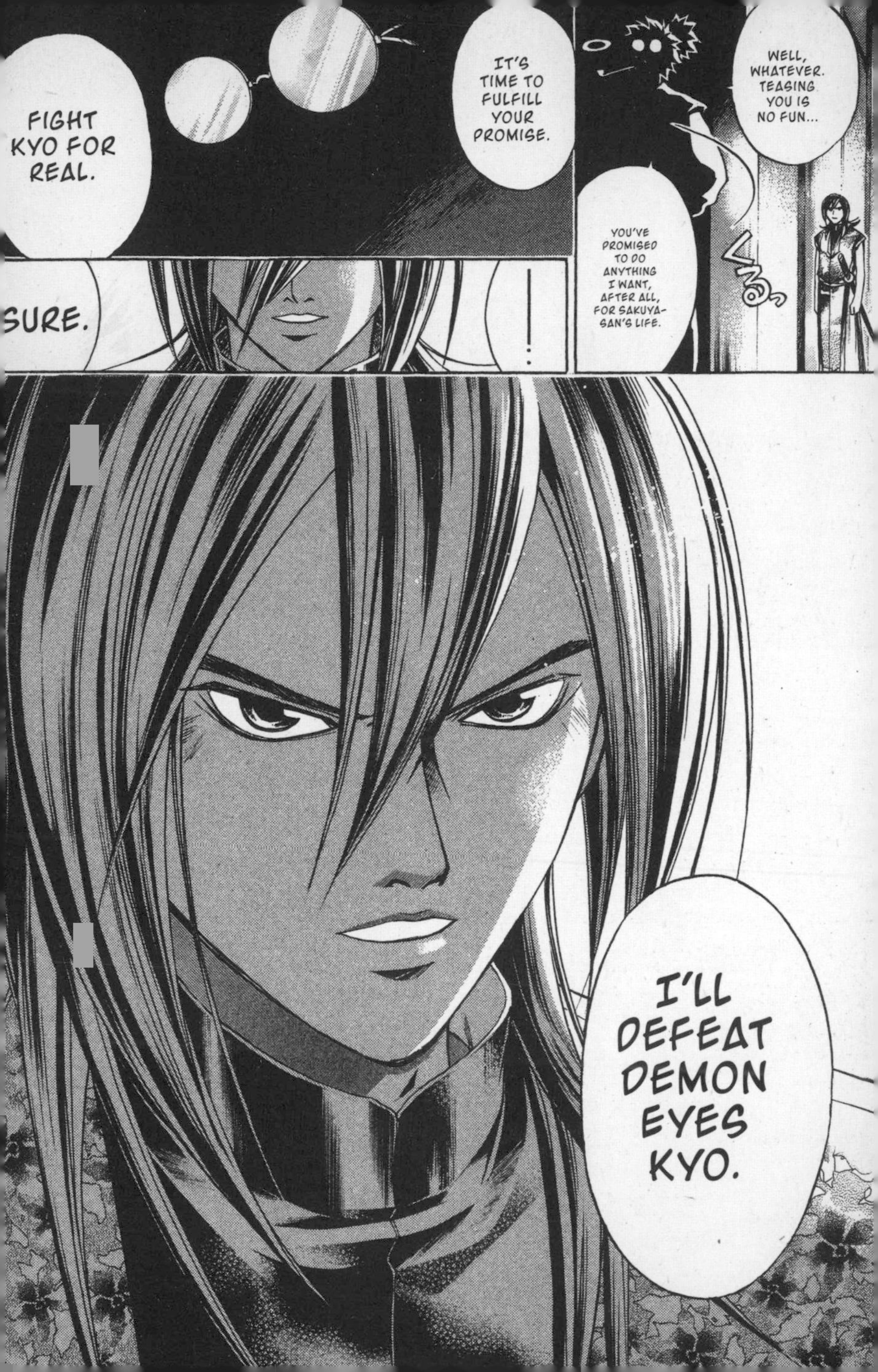
WELL, WHATEVER. TEASING YOU IS NO FUN...
くるっ
YOU'VE PROMISED TO DO ANYTHING I WANT, AFTER ALL, FOR SAKUYA-SAN'S LIFE.
IT'S TIME TO FULFILL YOUR PROMISE.
FIGHT KYO FOR REAL.
!
SURE.
I'LL DEFEAT DEMON EYES KYO.

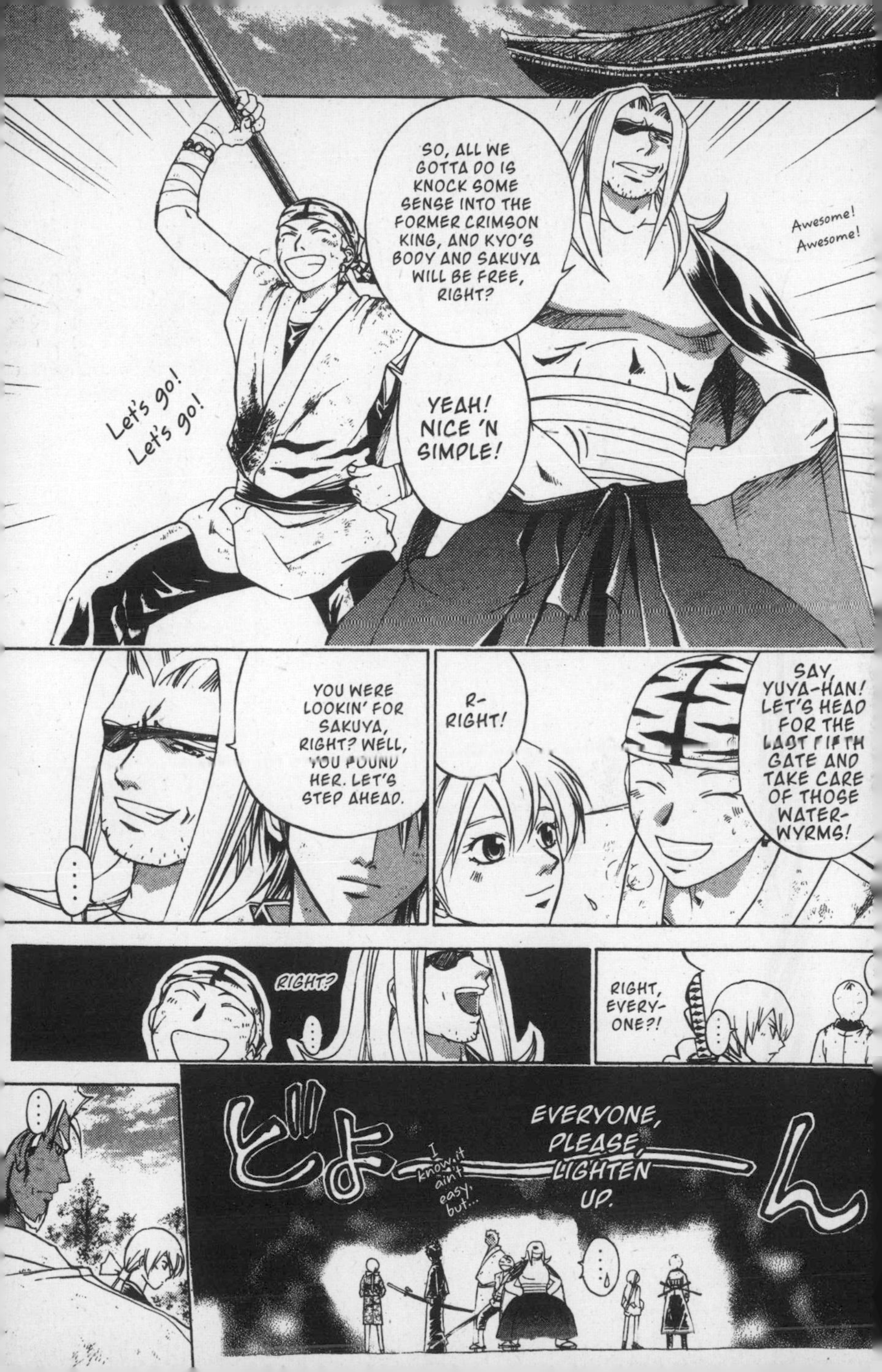
SO, ALL WE GOTTA DO IS KNOCK SOME SENSE INTO THE FORMER CRIMSON KING, AND KYO'S BODY AND SAKUYA WILL BE FREE, RIGHT?
Awesome! Awesome!
YEAH! NICE 'N SIMPLE!
Let's go! Let's go!
SAY, YUYA-HAN! LET'S HEAD FOR THE LAST FIFTH GATE AND TAKE CARE OF THOSE WATER-WYRMS!
R- RIGHT!
YOU WERE LOOKIN' FOR SAKUYA, RIGHT? WELL, YOU FOUND HER. LET'S STEP AHEAD.
...
RIGHT, EVERYONE?!
...
RIGHT?
...
どよ――ん
EVERYONE, PLEASE, LIGHTEN UP.
I know it ain't easy, but...
...
...

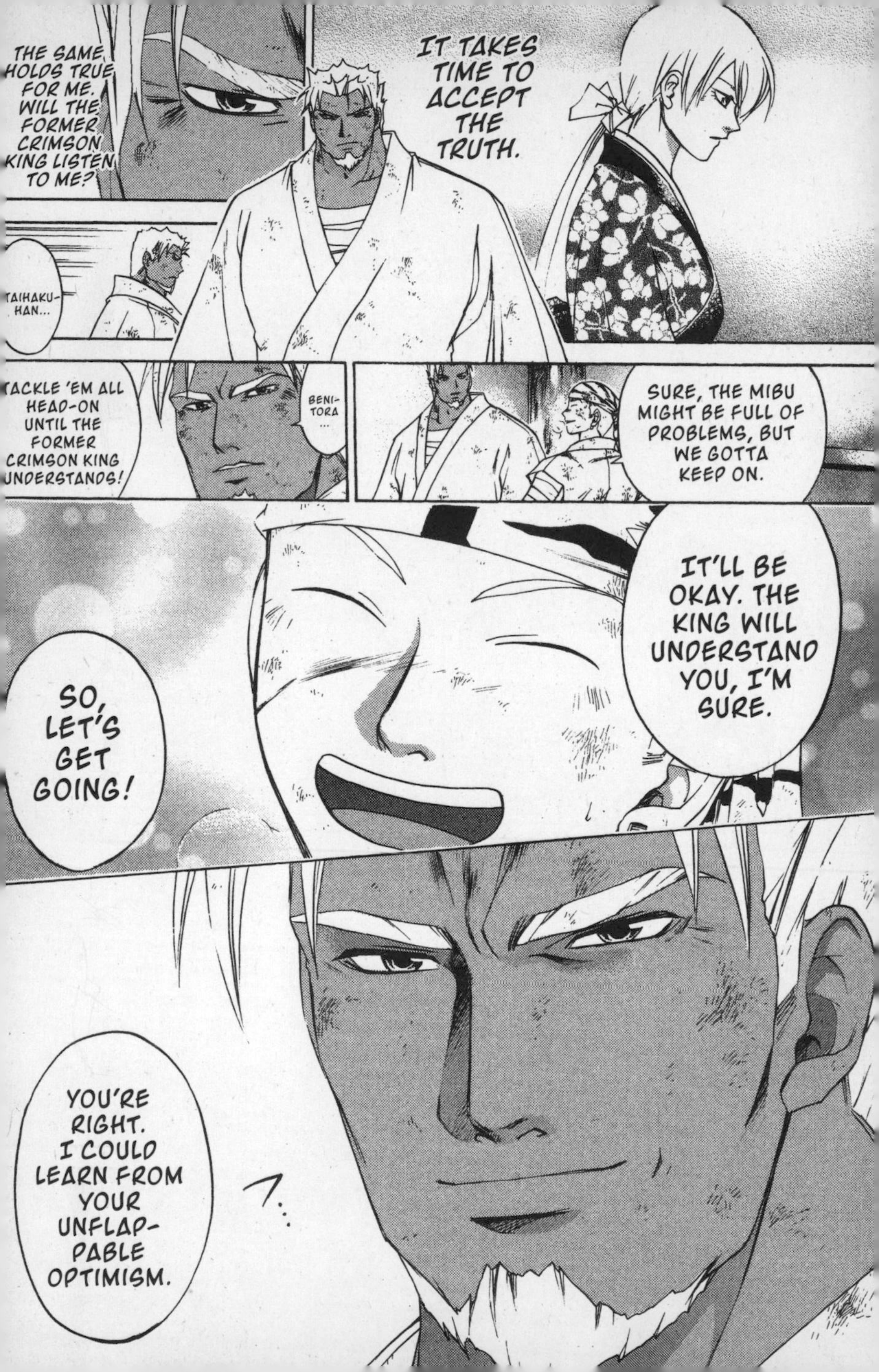
IT TAKES TIME TO ACCEPT THE TRUTH.
THE SAME HOLDS TRUE FOR ME. WILL THE FORMER CRIMSON KING LISTEN TO ME?
TAIHAKU-HAN...
SURE, THE MIBU MIGHT BE FULL OF PROBLEMS, BUT WE GOTTA KEEP ON.
BENI-TORA ...
TACKLE 'EM ALL HEAD-ON UNTIL THE FORMER CRIMSON KING UNDERSTANDS!
IT'LL BE OKAY. THE KING WILL UNDERSTAND YOU, I'M SURE.
SO, LET'S GET GOING!
YOU'RE RIGHT. I COULD LEARN FROM YOUR UNFLAP-PABLE OPTIMISM.

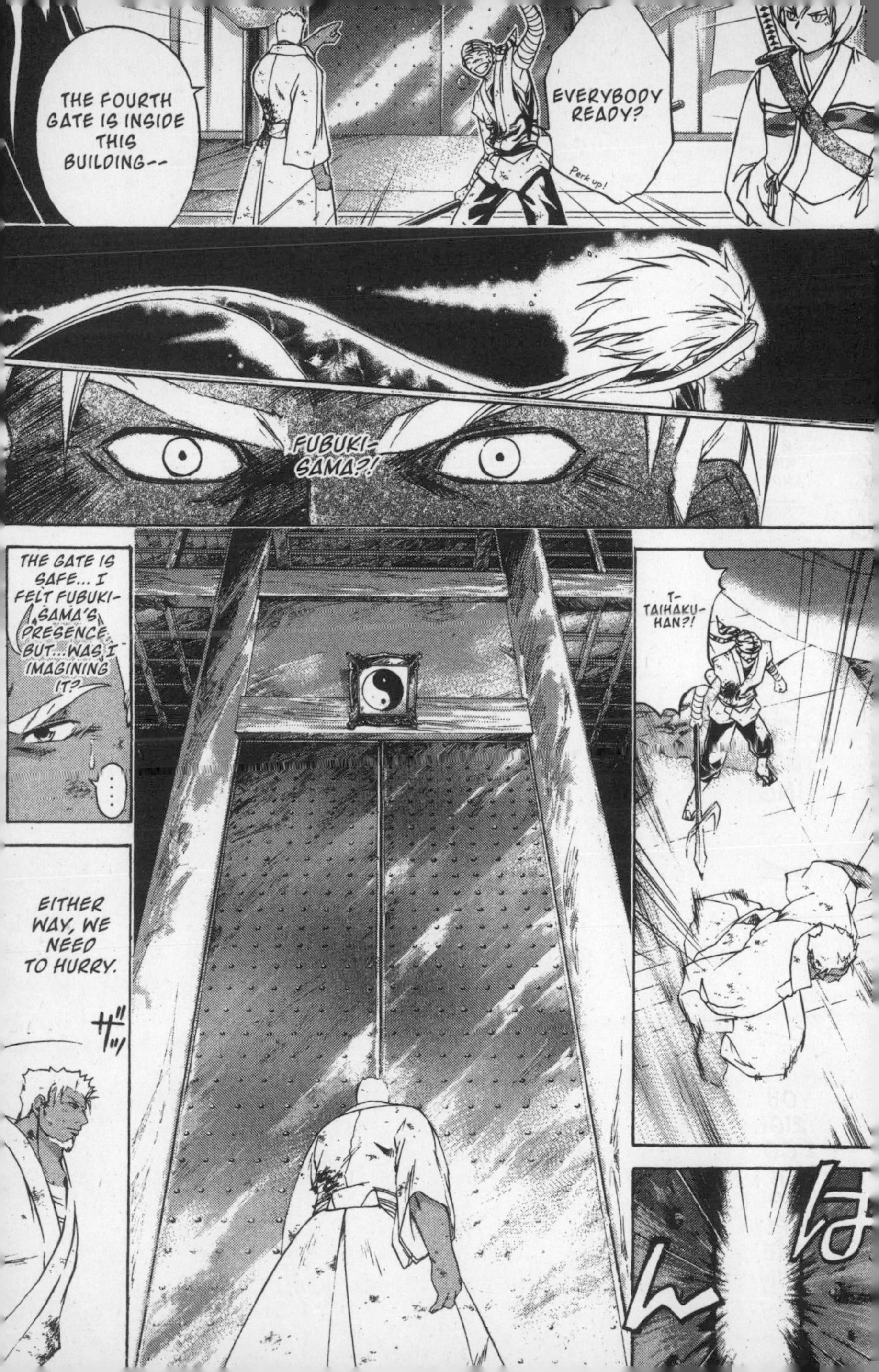
EVERYBODY READY?
Perk up!
THE FOURTH GATE IS INSIDE THIS BUILDING--
FUBUKI-SAMA?!
T-TAIHAKU-HAN?!
THE GATE IS SAFE... I FELT FUBUKI-SAMA'S PRESENCE BUT...WAS I IMAGINING IT?
....
EITHER WAY, WE NEED TO HURRY.
ザッ
はん

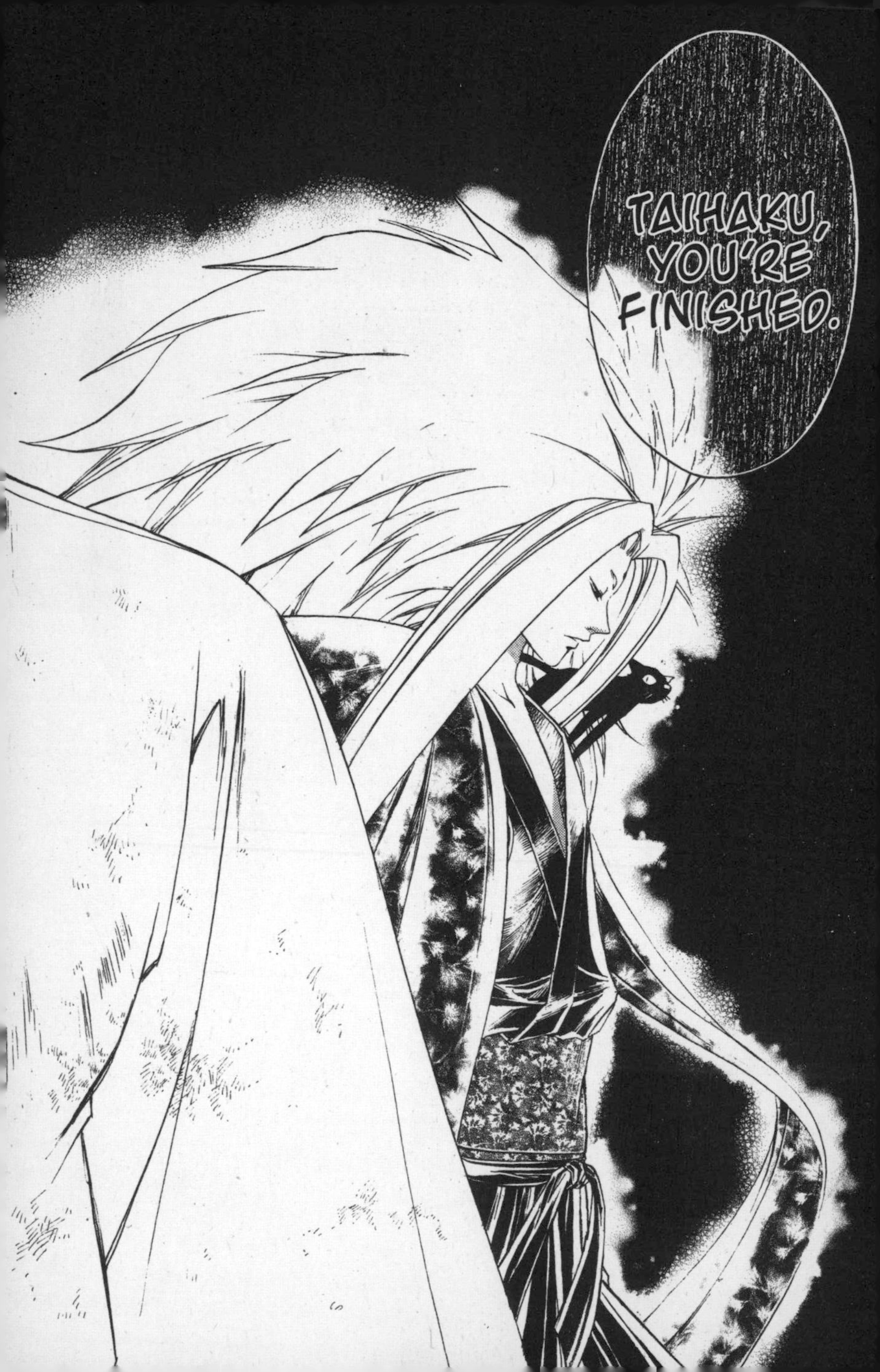
TAIHAKU, YOU'RE FINISHED.

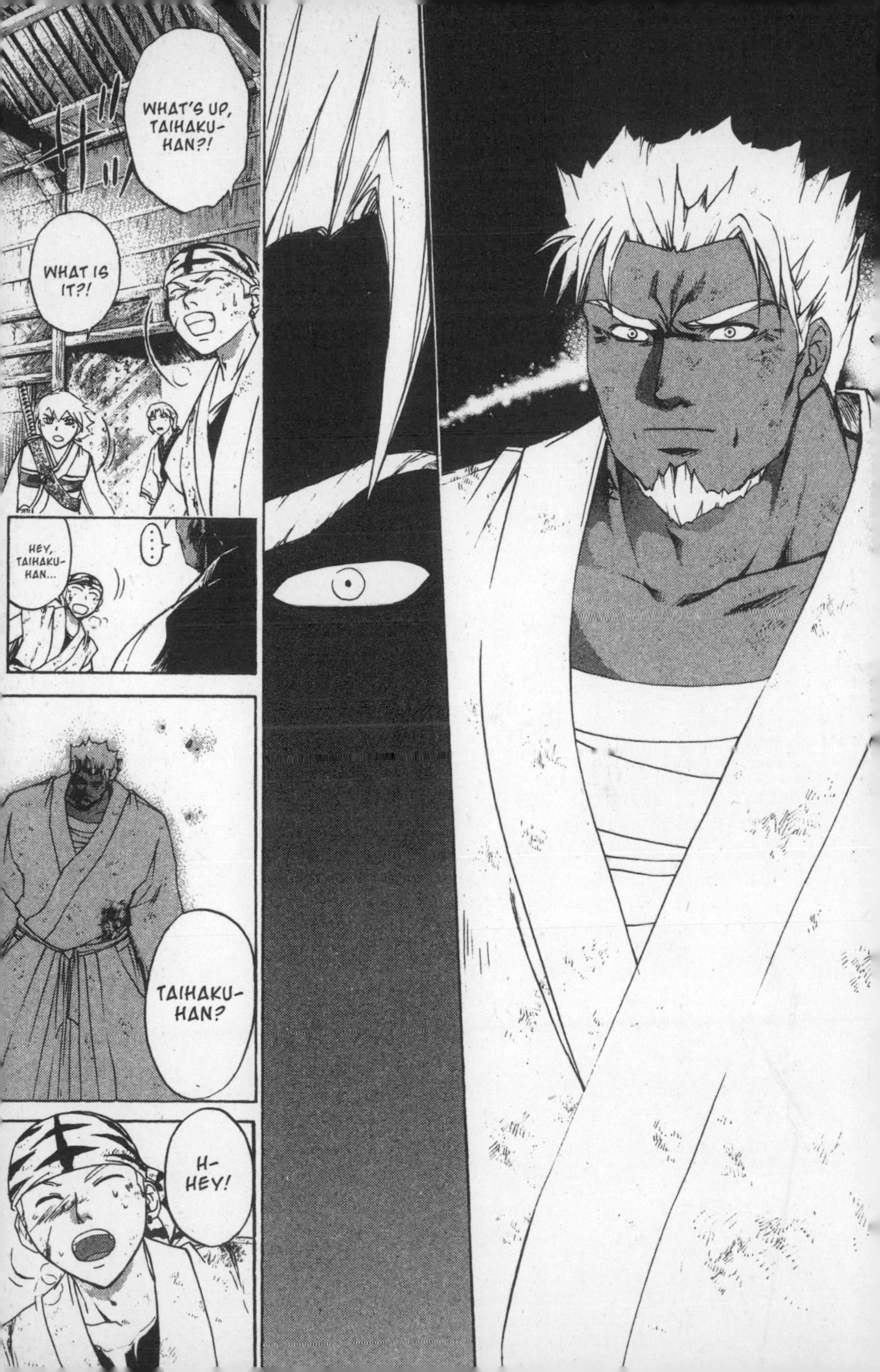
WHAT'S UP, TAIHAKU-HAN?!
WHAT IS IT?!
...
HEY, TAIHAKU-HAN...
TAIHAKU-HAN?
H-HEY!

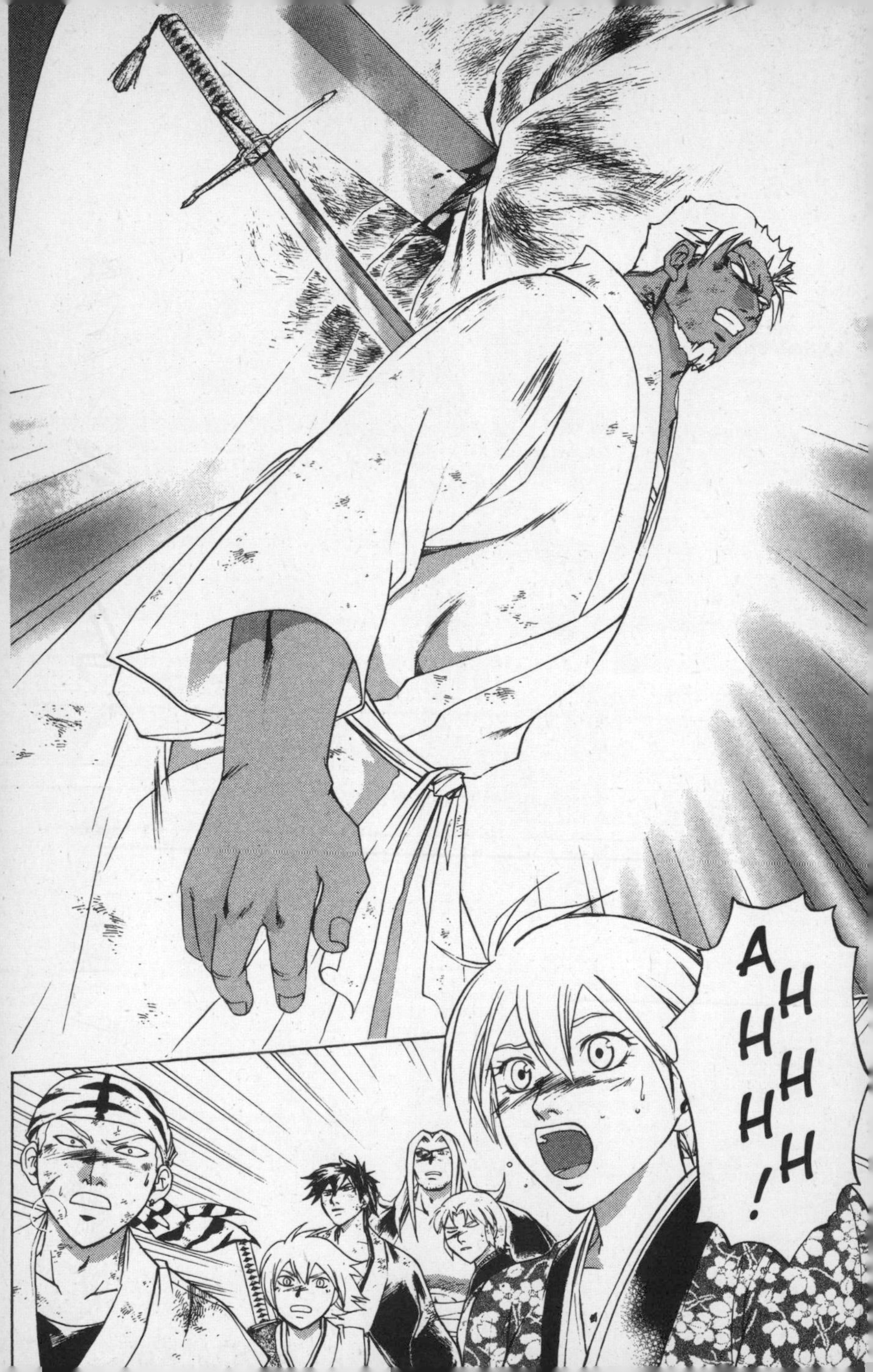
AHHHHHH!

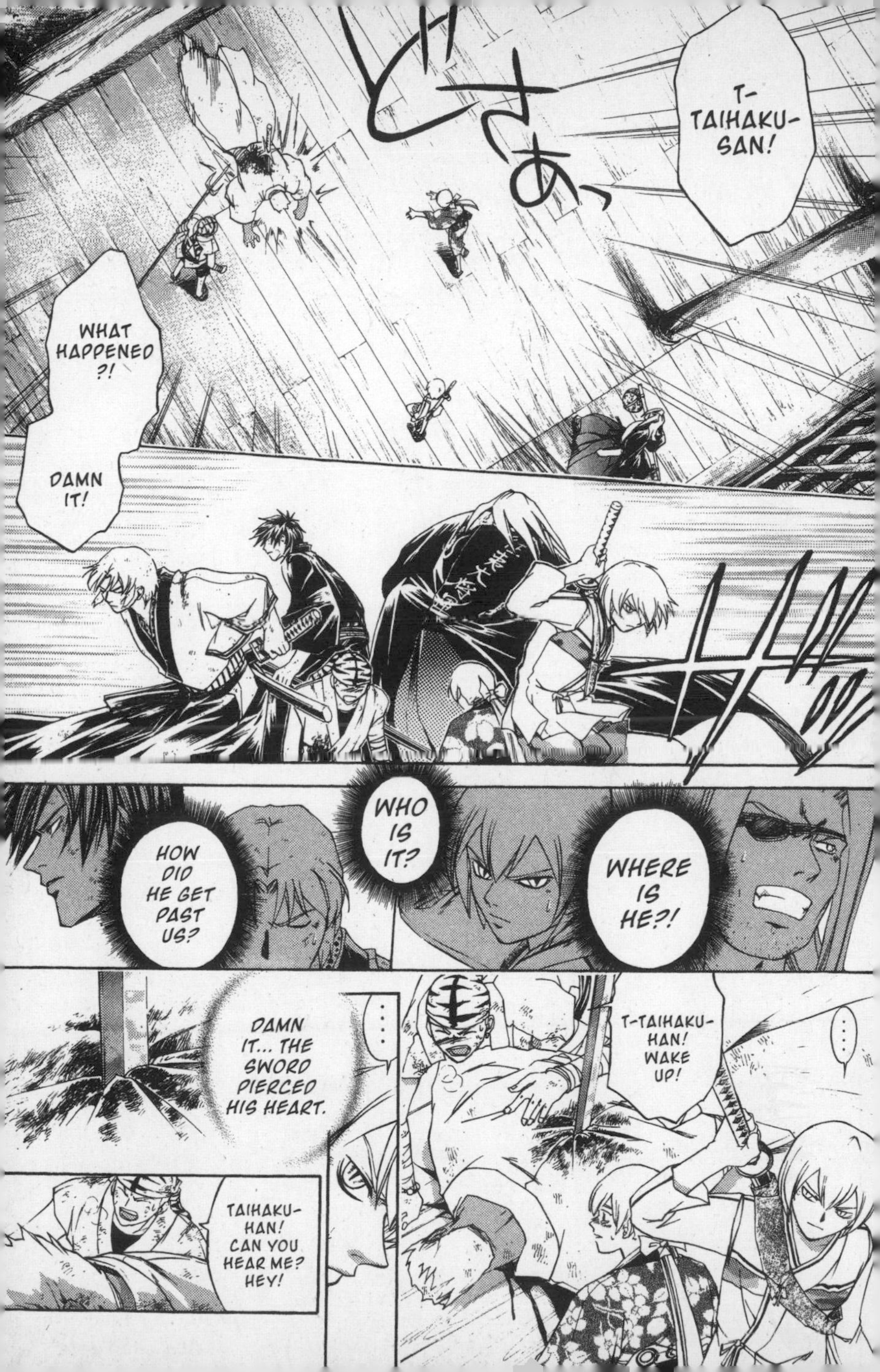

T-TAIHAKU-SAN!
どさあっ
WHAT HAPPENED?!
DAMN IT!
WHERE IS HE?!
WHO IS IT?
HOW DID HE GET PAST US?
...
T-TAIHAKU-HAN! WAKE UP!
...
DAMN IT... THE SWORD PIERCED HIS HEART.
TAIHAKU-HAN! CAN YOU HEAR ME? HEY!

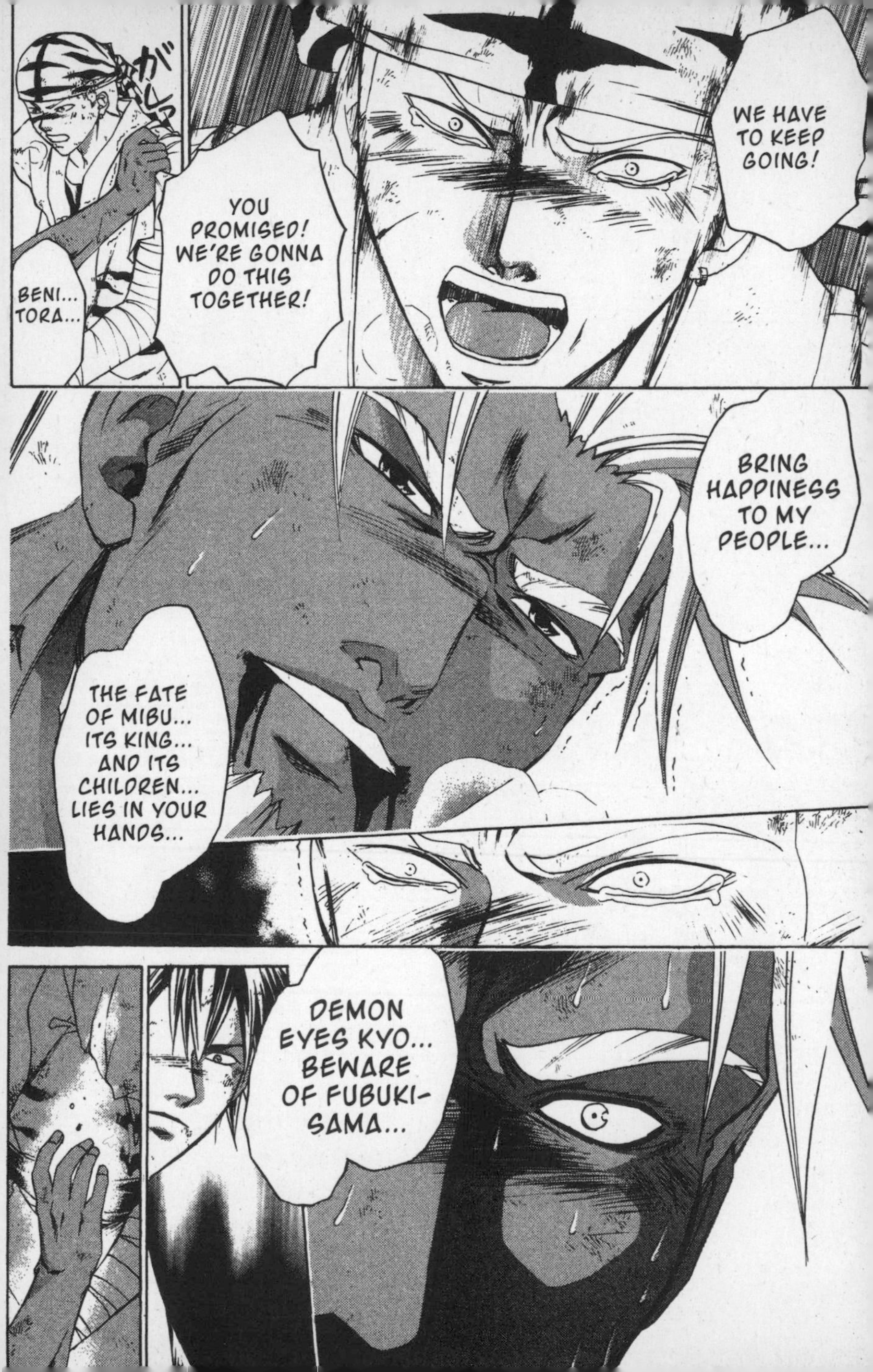
WE HAVE TO KEEP GOING!
YOU PROMISED! WE'RE GONNA DO THIS TOGETHER!
BENI... TORA...
BRING HAPPINESS TO MY PEOPLE...
THE FATE OF MIBU... ITS KING... AND ITS CHILDREN... LIES IN YOUR HANDS...
DEMON EYES KYO... BEWARE OF FUBUKI-SAMA...

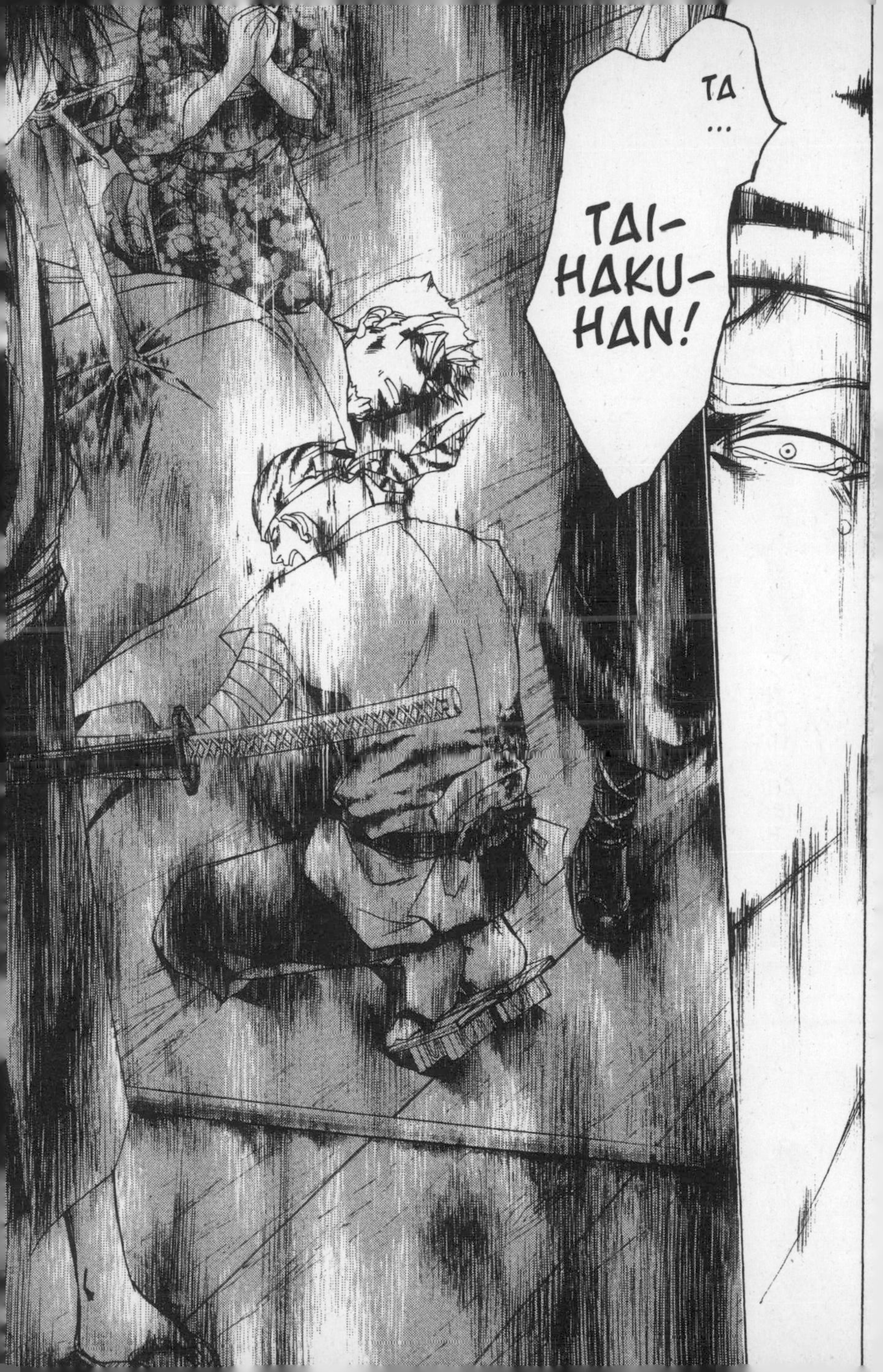
TA ... TAI-HAKU-HAN!

▮STAFFS▮

Hazuki Asami (The Chief)
Soma Akatsuki (The Sub-Chief)
The Gentleman Pumpkin
Shiba Tateoka
Seishi Kamimura
Takaya Nagao

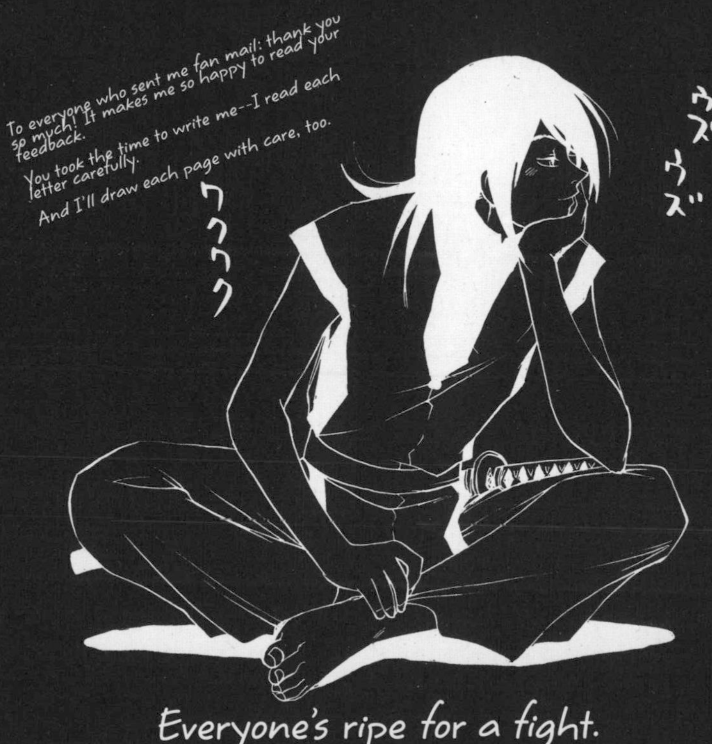
To everyone who sent me fan mail: thank you so much! It makes me so happy to read your feedback.
You took the time to write me--I read each letter carefully.
And I'll draw each page with care, too.
ウズウズ
ワククク
Everyone's ripe for a fight.

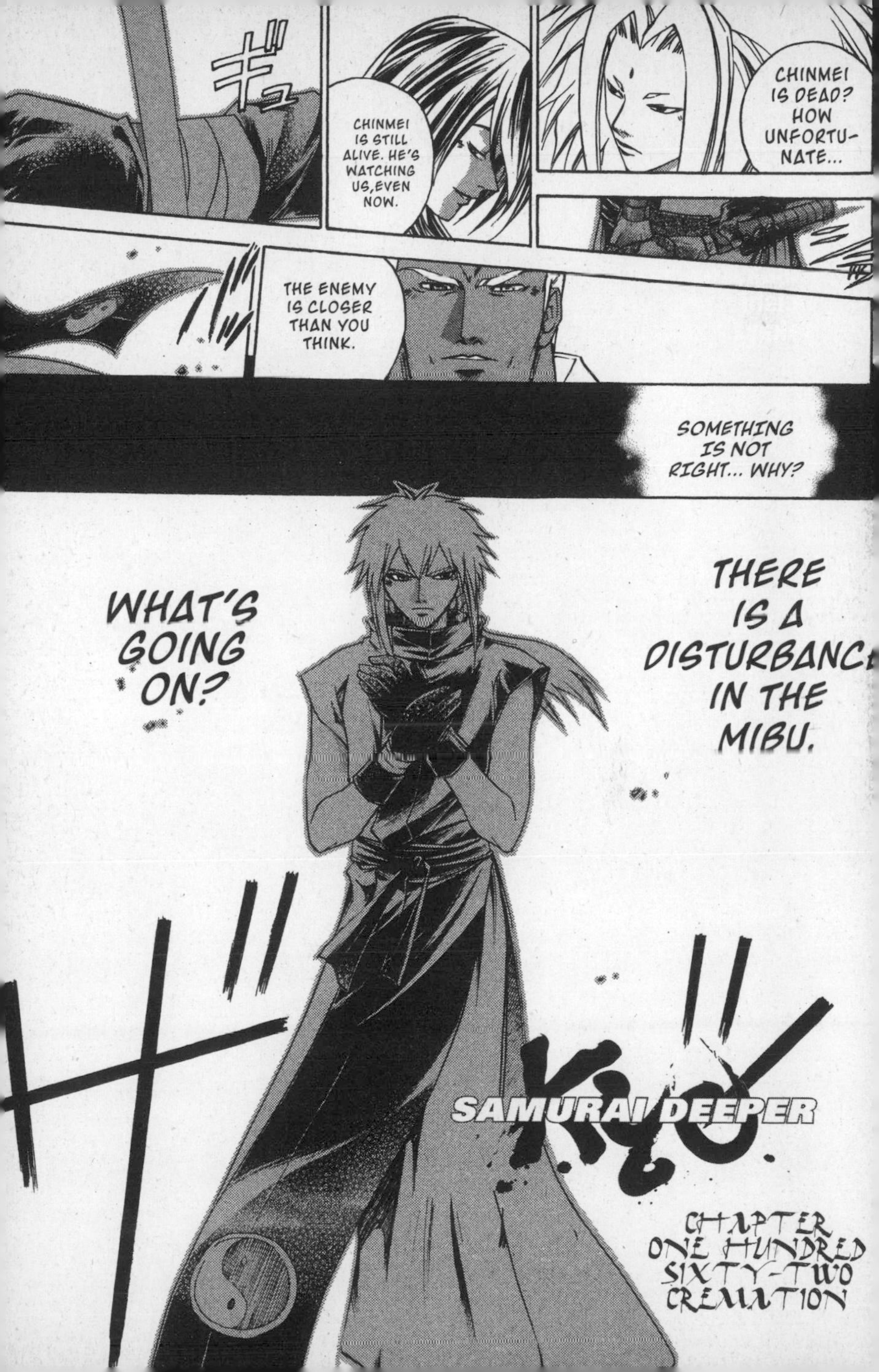

CHINMEI IS DEAD? HOW UNFORTUNATE...
CHINMEI IS STILL ALIVE. HE'S WATCHING US, EVEN NOW.
ギュ
THE ENEMY IS CLOSER THAN YOU THINK.
SOMETHING IS NOT RIGHT... WHY?
THERE IS A DISTURBANCE IN THE MIBU.
WHAT'S GOING ON?
SAMURAI DEEPER KYO
CHAPTER ONE HUNDRED SIXTY-TWO CREMATION

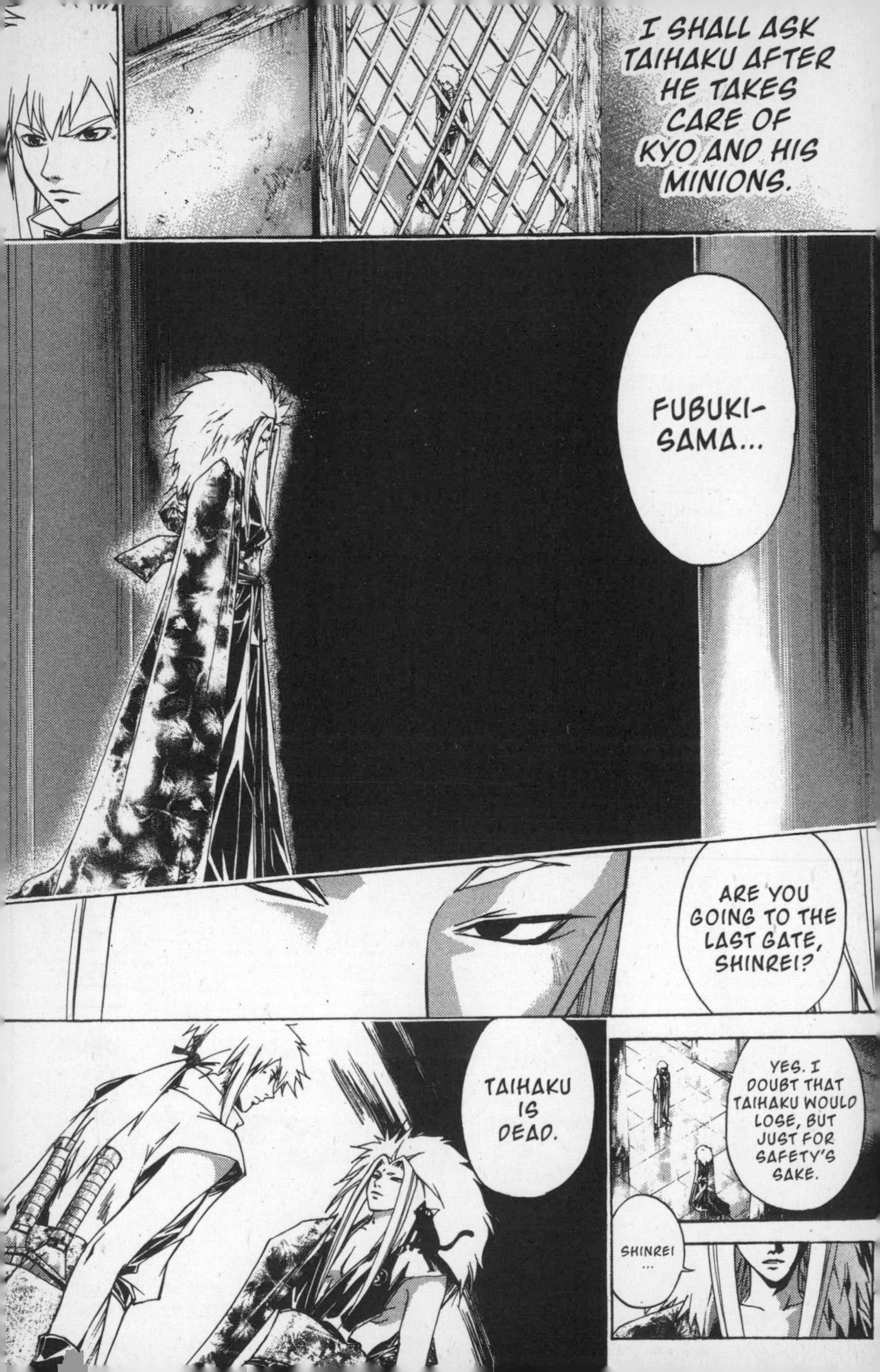
I SHALL ASK TAIHAKU AFTER HE TAKES CARE OF KYO AND HIS MINIONS.
FUBUKI-SAMA...
ARE YOU GOING TO THE LAST GATE, SHINREI?
YES. I DOUBT THAT TAIHAKU WOULD LOSE, BUT JUST FOR SAFETY'S SAKE.
SHINREI ...
TAIHAKU IS DEAD.

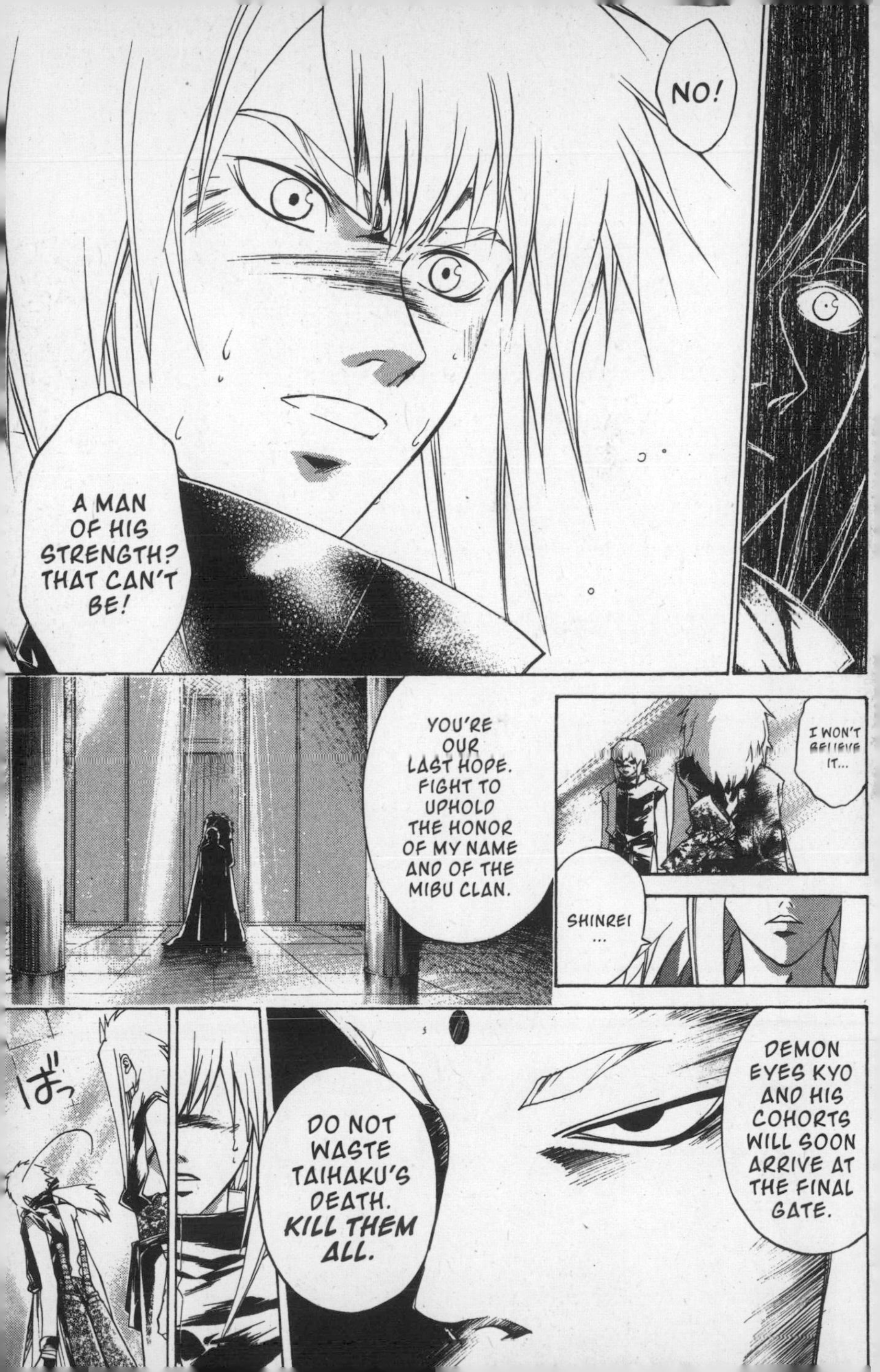
NO!
A MAN OF HIS STRENGTH? THAT CAN'T BE!
I WON'T BELIEVE IT...
SHINREI ...
YOU'RE OUR LAST HOPE. FIGHT TO UPHOLD THE HONOR OF MY NAME AND OF THE MIBU CLAN.
DEMON EYES KYO AND HIS COHORTS WILL SOON ARRIVE AT THE FINAL GATE.
DO NOT WASTE TAIHAKU'S DEATH. **KILL THEM ALL.**
ばっ

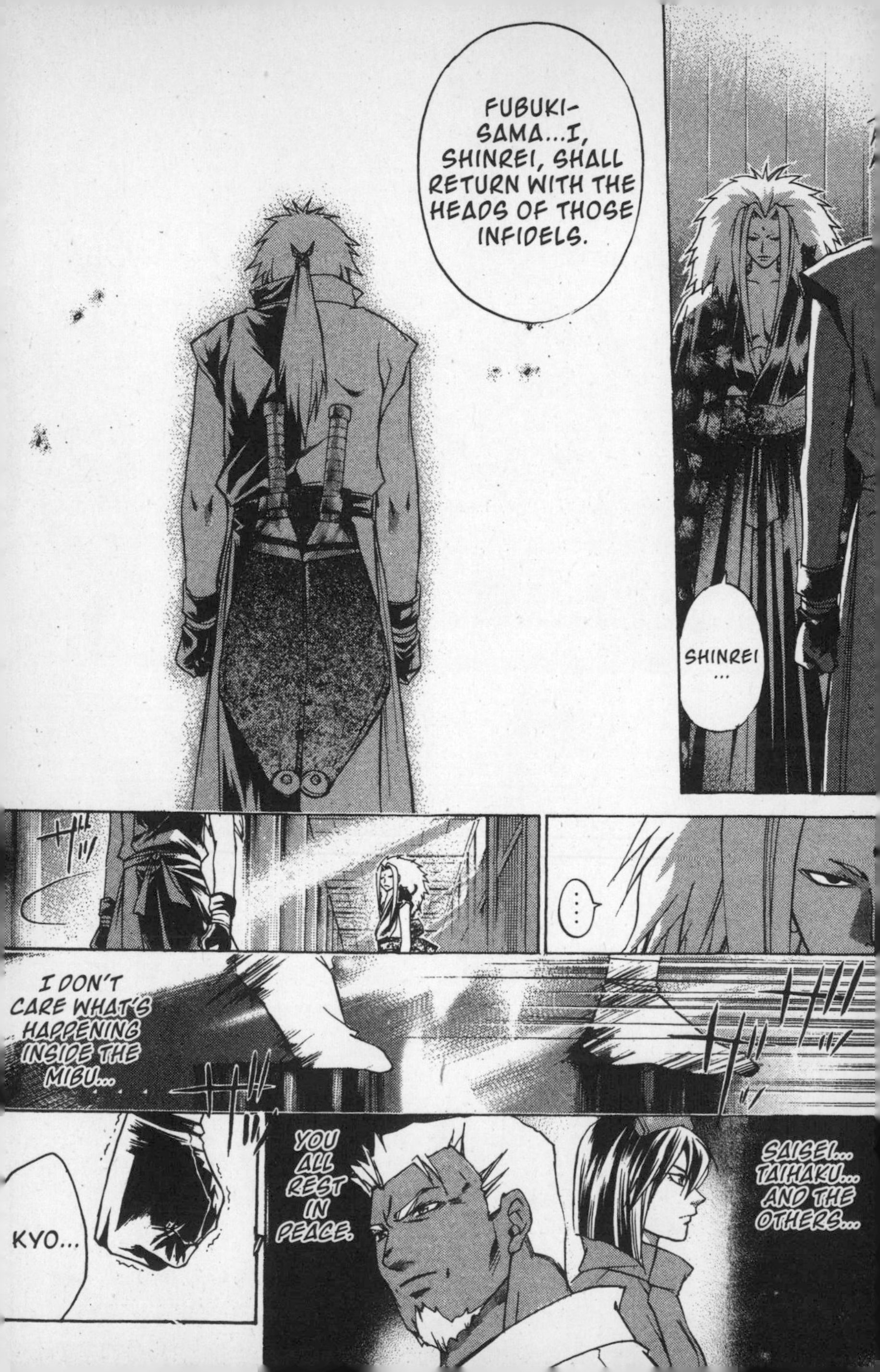
FUBUKI-SAMA...I, SHINREI, SHALL RETURN WITH THE HEADS OF THOSE INFIDELS.
SHINREI ...
. . . .
I DON'T CARE WHAT'S HAPPENING INSIDE THE MIBU...
SAISEI... TAIHAKU... AND THE OTHERS...
YOU ALL REST IN PEACE.
KYO...

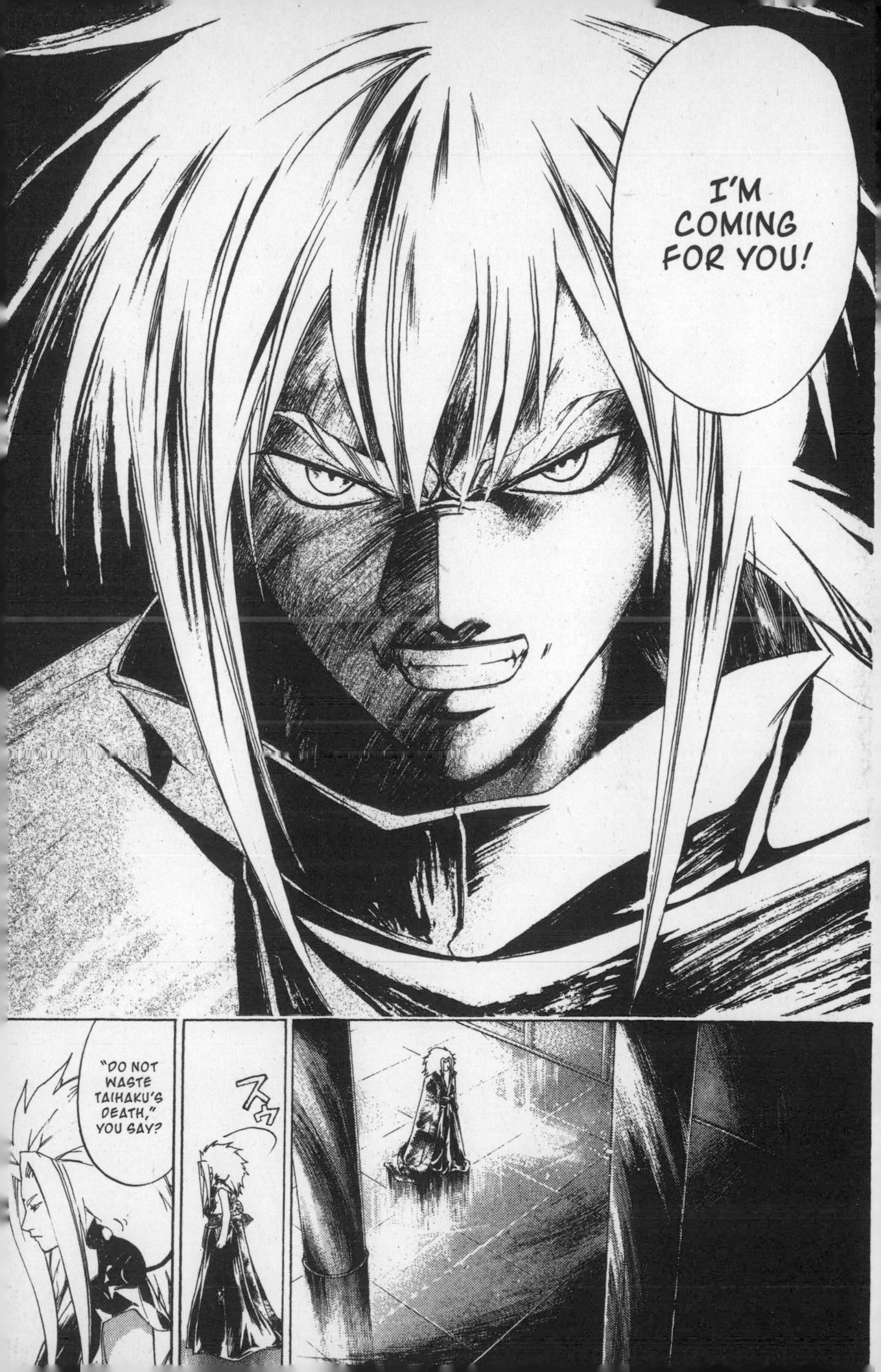
I'M COMING FOR YOU!
スッ
"DO NOT WASTE TAIHAKU'S DEATH," YOU SAY?

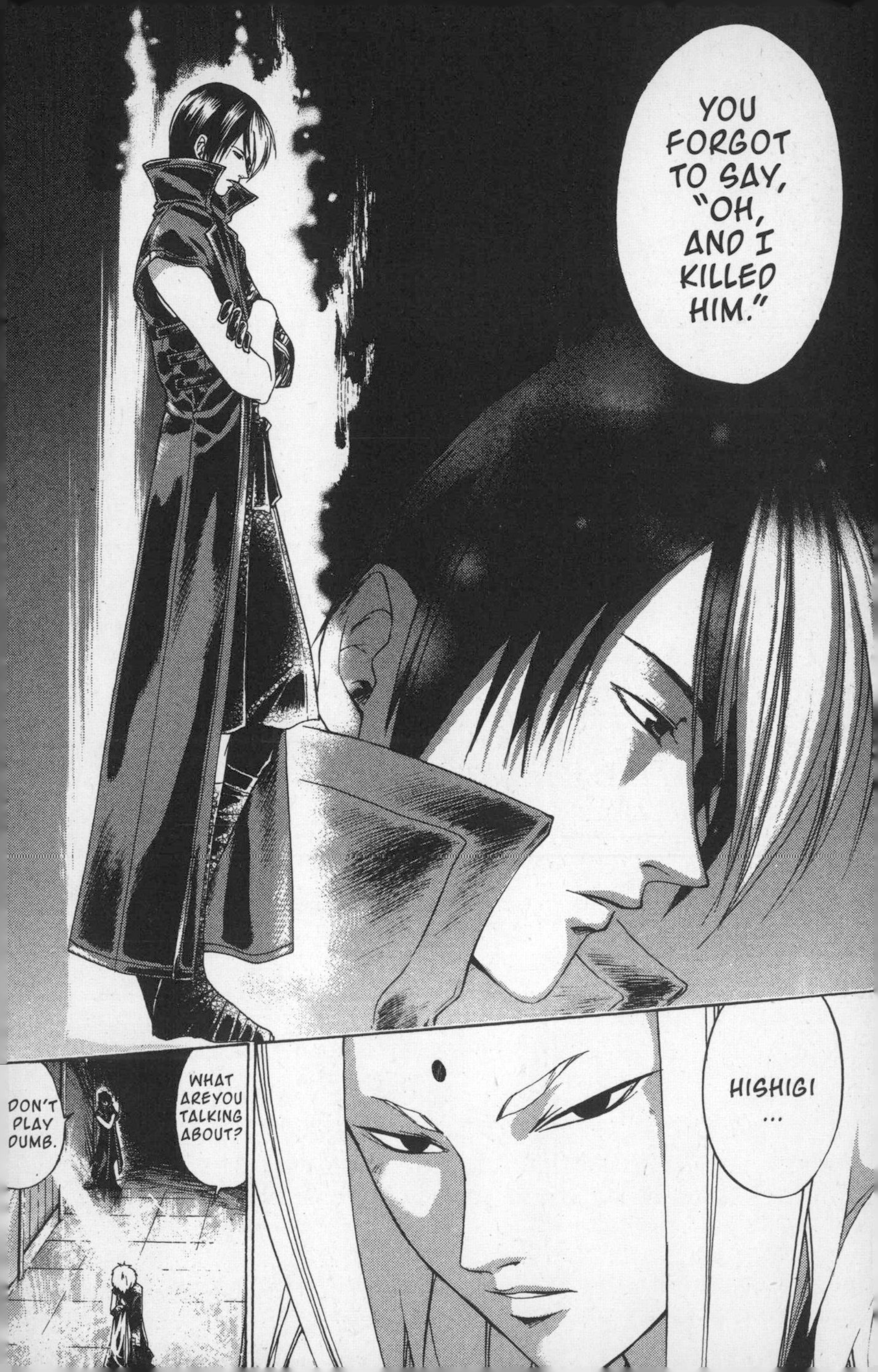
YOU FORGOT TO SAY, "OH, AND I KILLED HIM."
HISHIGI ...
WHAT ARE YOU TALKING ABOUT?
DON'T PLAY DUMB.

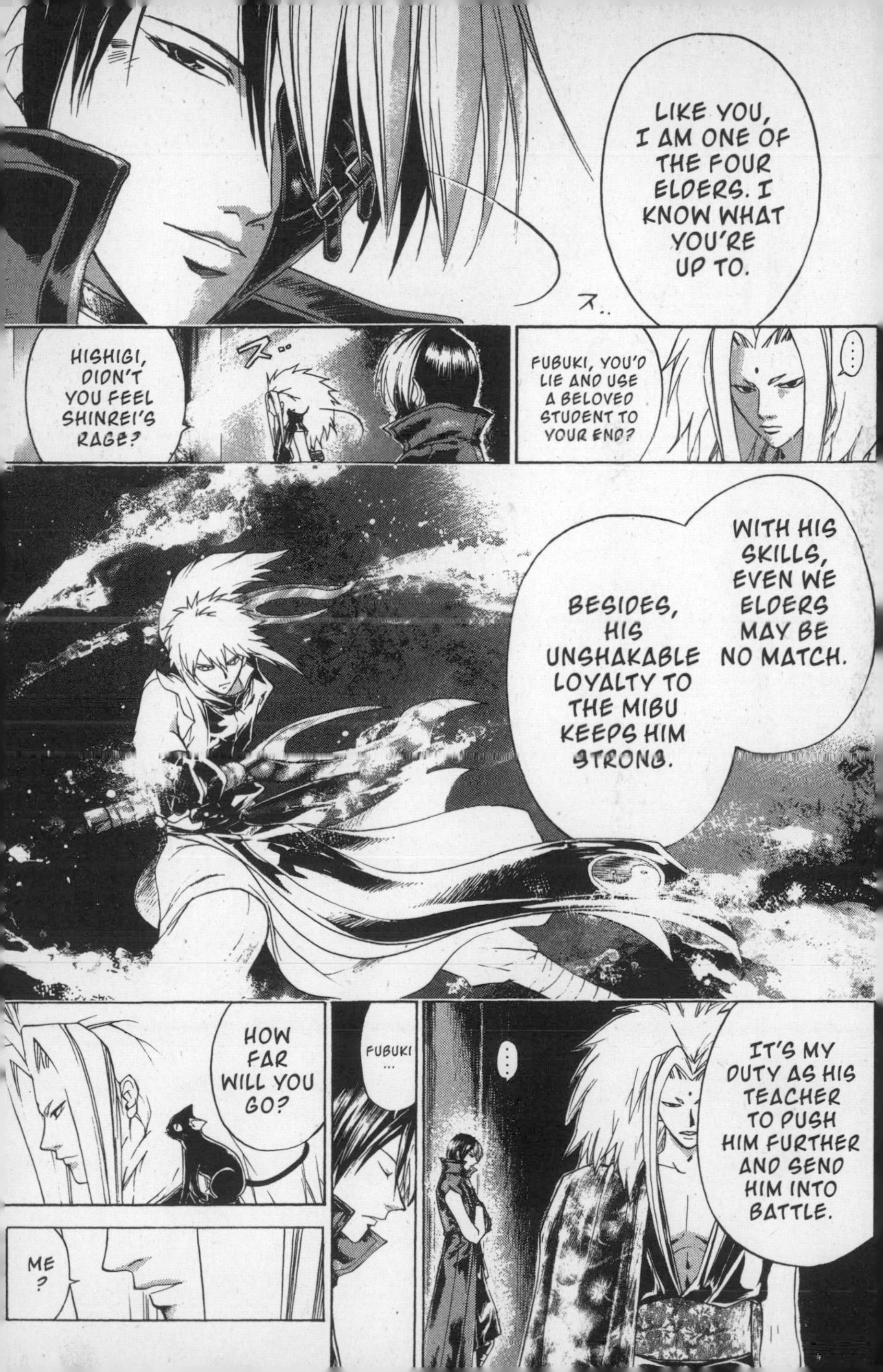
LIKE YOU, I AM ONE OF THE FOUR ELDERS. I KNOW WHAT YOU'RE UP TO.
ス..
...
FUBUKI, YOU'D LIE AND USE A BELOVED STUDENT TO YOUR END?
ス..
HISHIGI, DIDN'T YOU FEEL SHINREI'S RAGE?
WITH HIS SKILLS, EVEN WE ELDERS MAY BE NO MATCH.
BESIDES, HIS UNSHAKABLE LOYALTY TO THE MIBU KEEPS HIM STRONG.
IT'S MY DUTY AS HIS TEACHER TO PUSH HIM FURTHER AND SEND HIM INTO BATTLE.
...
FUBUKI ...
HOW FAR WILL YOU GO?
ME ?

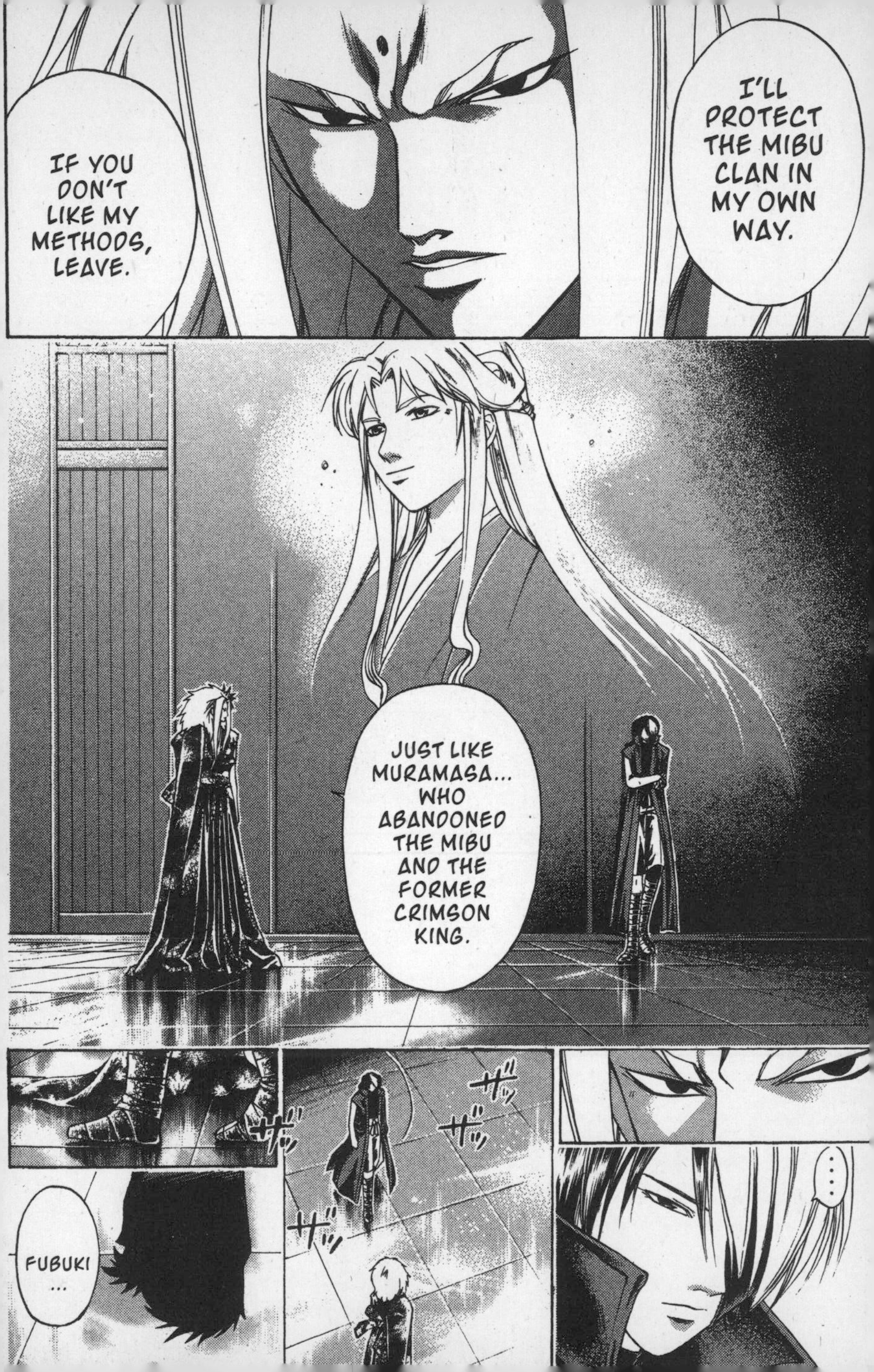
I'LL PROTECT THE MIBU CLAN IN MY OWN WAY.
IF YOU DON'T LIKE MY METHODS, LEAVE.
JUST LIKE MURAMASA... WHO ABANDONED THE MIBU AND THE FORMER CRIMSON KING.
....
ザッ
ザッ
ザッ
ザッ
FUBUKI ...

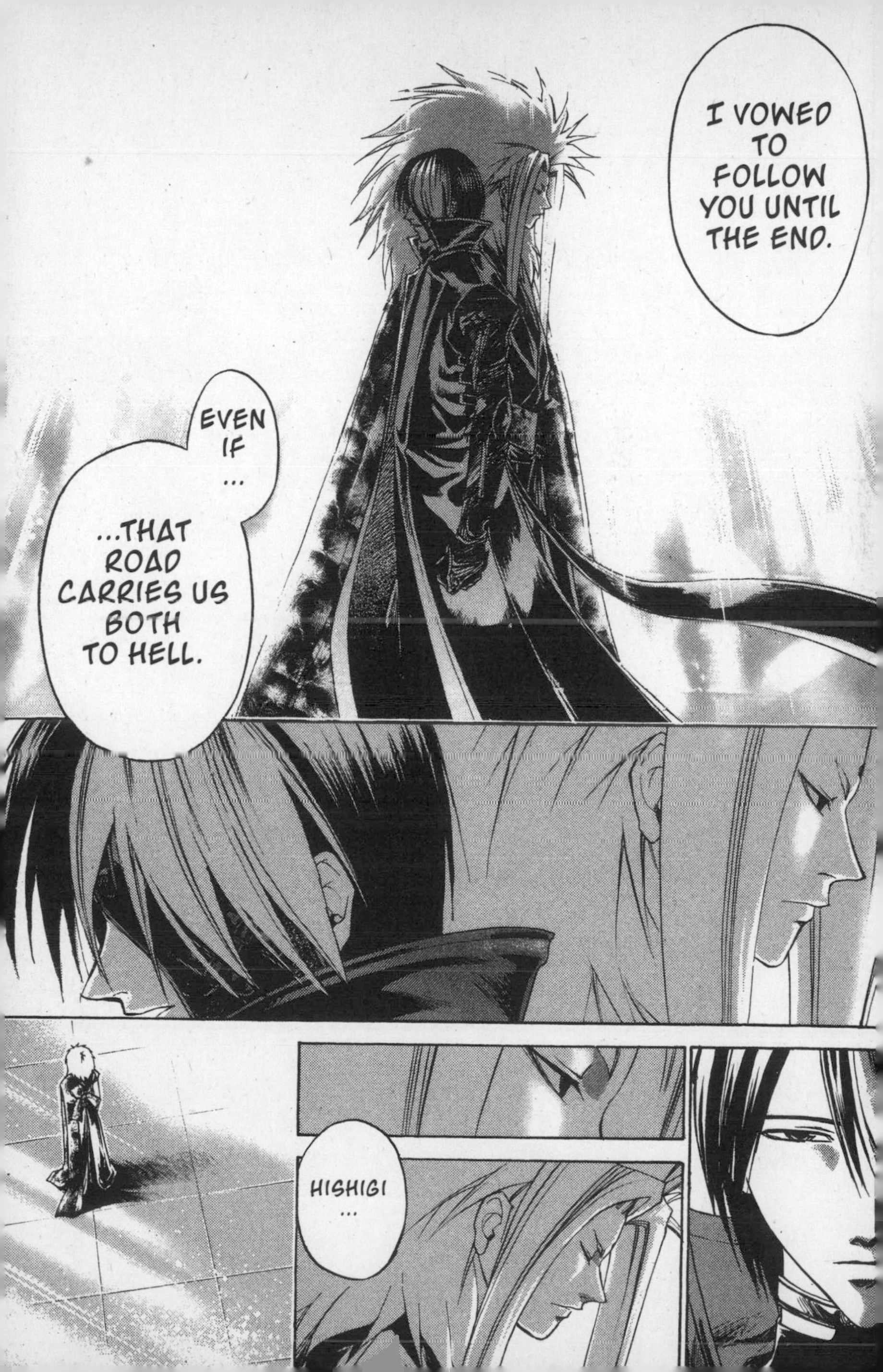
I VOWED TO FOLLOW YOU UNTIL THE END.
EVEN IF ...
...THAT ROAD CARRIES US BOTH TO HELL.
HISHIGI ...

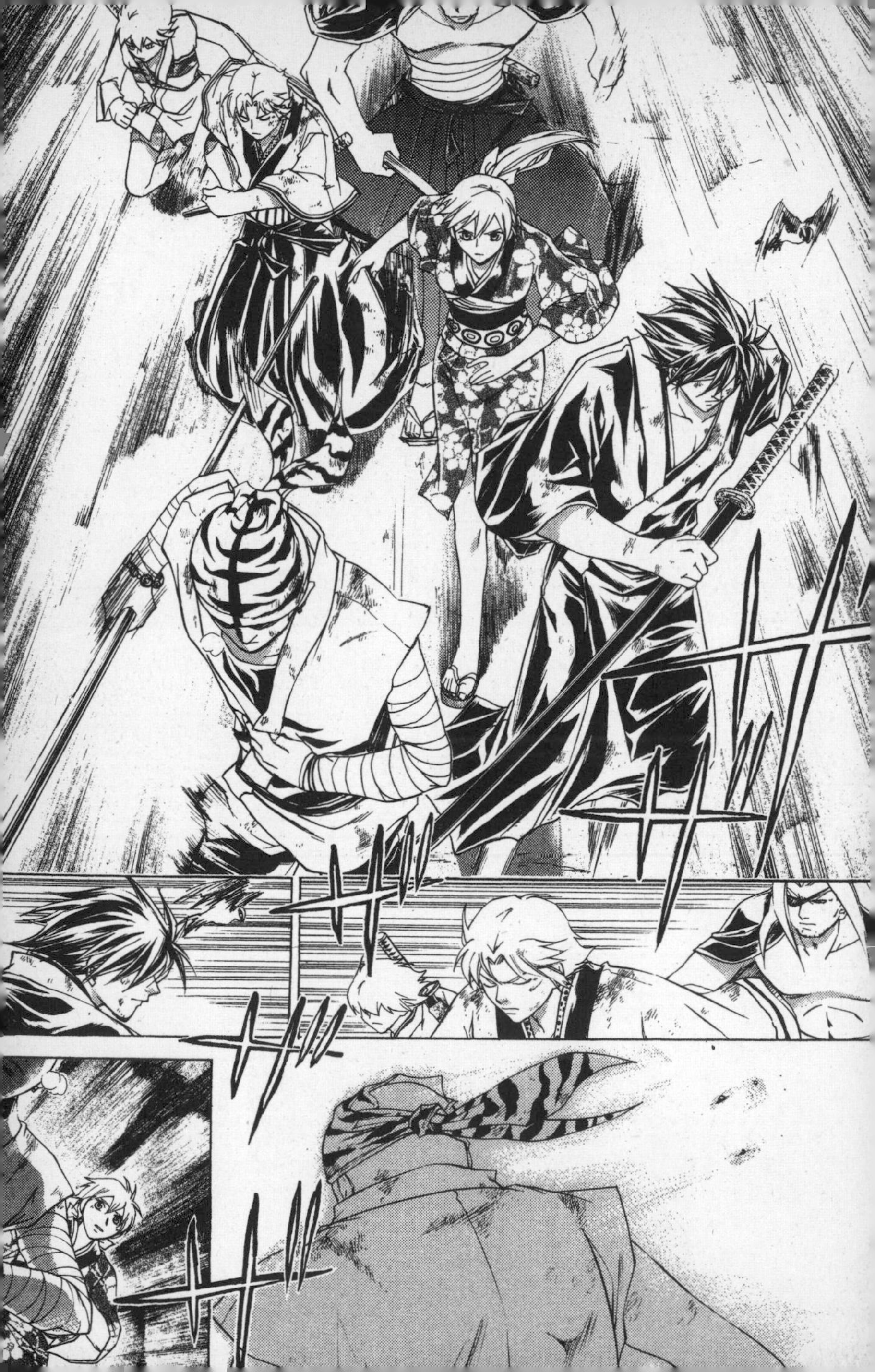

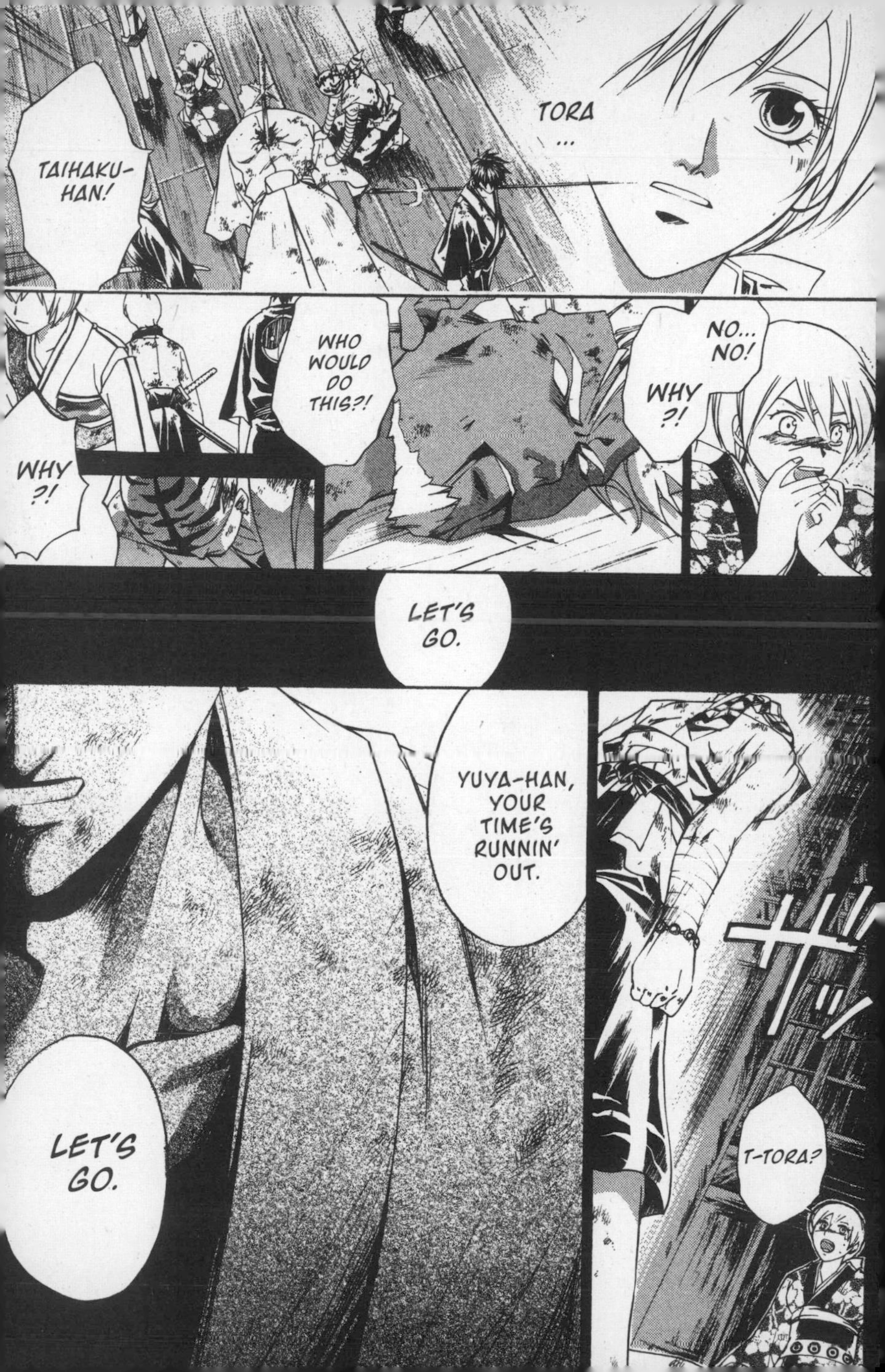
TORA ...
TAIHAKU-HAN!
NO... NO!
WHY?!
WHO WOULD DO THIS?!
WHY?!
LET'S GO.
ザッ
T-TORA?
YUYA-HAN, YOUR TIME'S RUNNIN' OUT.
LET'S GO.

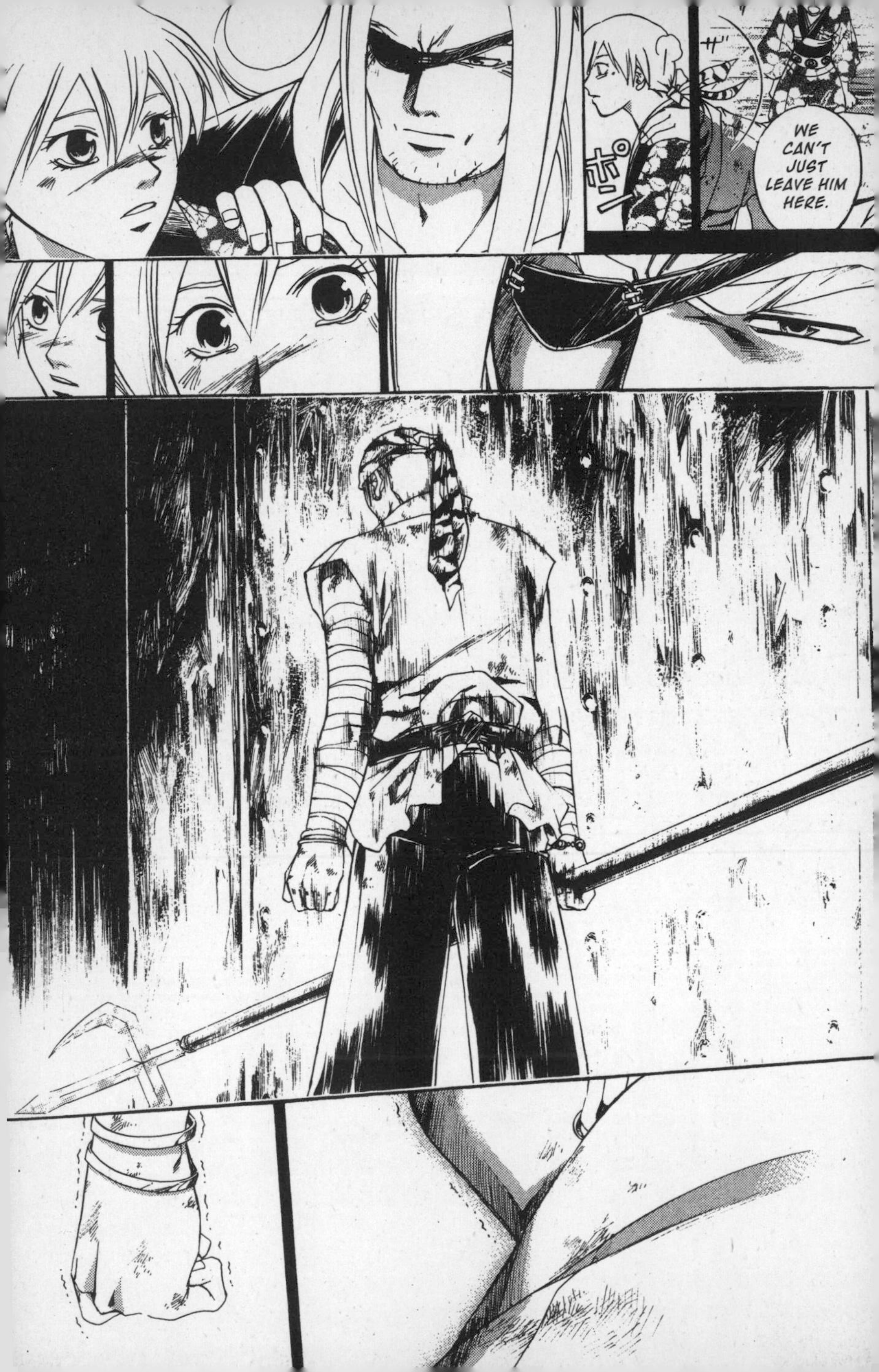
WE CAN'T JUST LEAVE HIM HERE.

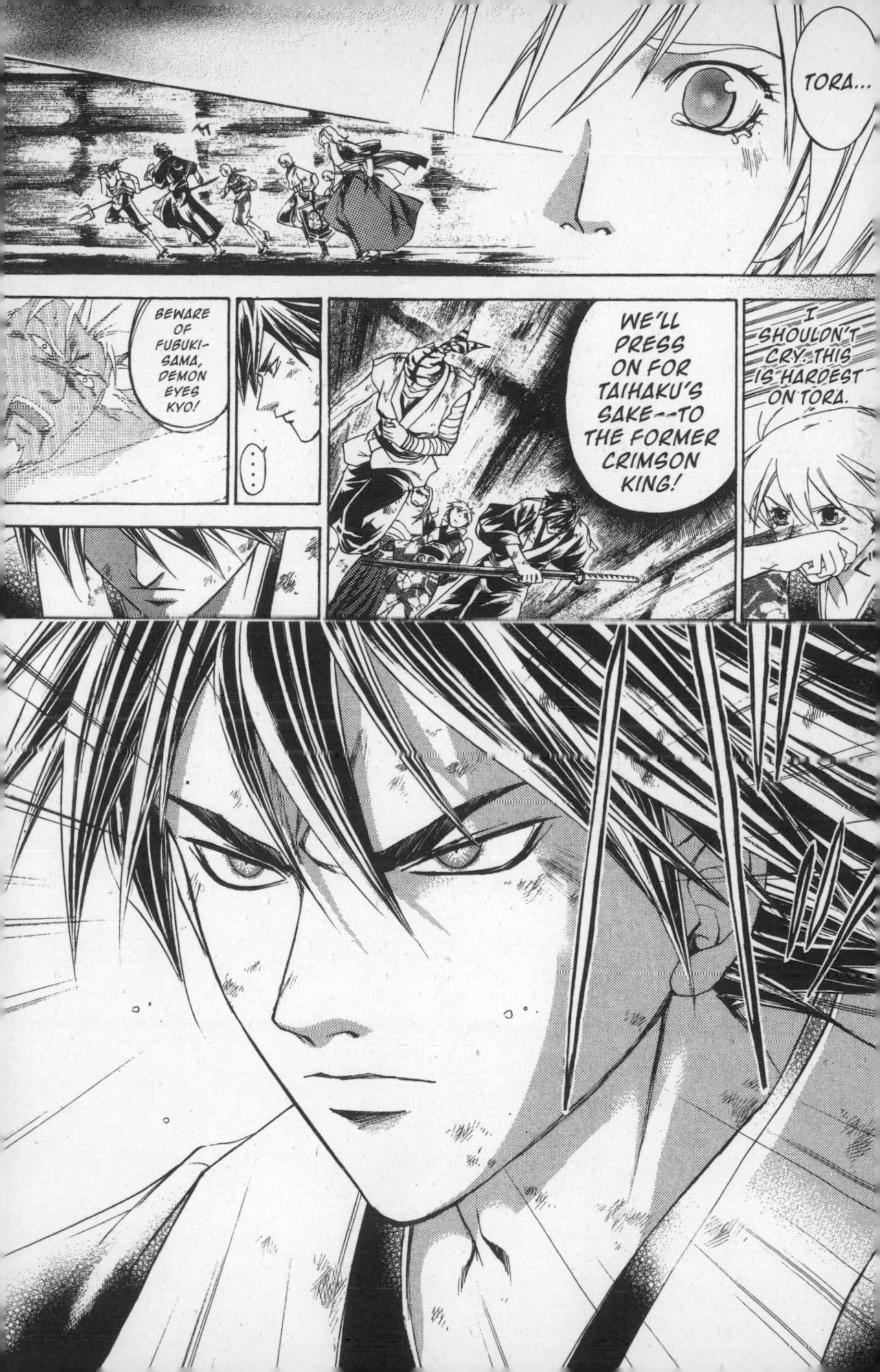
TORA...
I SHOULDN'T CRY. THIS IS HARDEST ON TORA.
WE'LL PRESS ON FOR TAIHAKU'S SAKE--TO THE FORMER CRIMSON KING!
...
BEWARE OF FUBUKI-SAMA, DEMON EYES KYO!

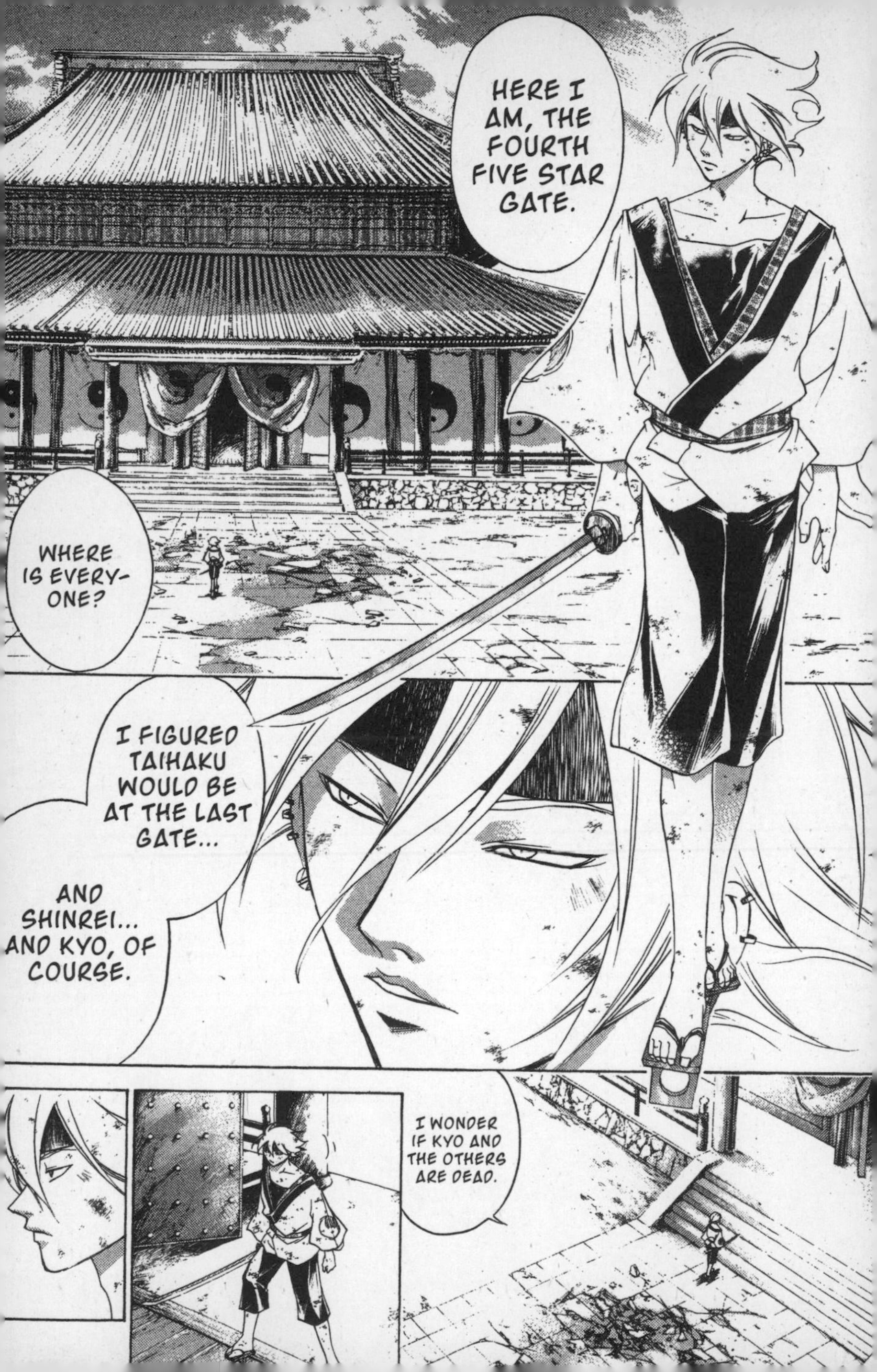
HERE I AM, THE FOURTH FIVE STAR GATE.
WHERE IS EVERY-ONE?
I FIGURED TAIHAKU WOULD BE AT THE LAST GATE...
AND SHINREI... AND KYO, OF COURSE.
I WONDER IF KYO AND THE OTHERS ARE DEAD.

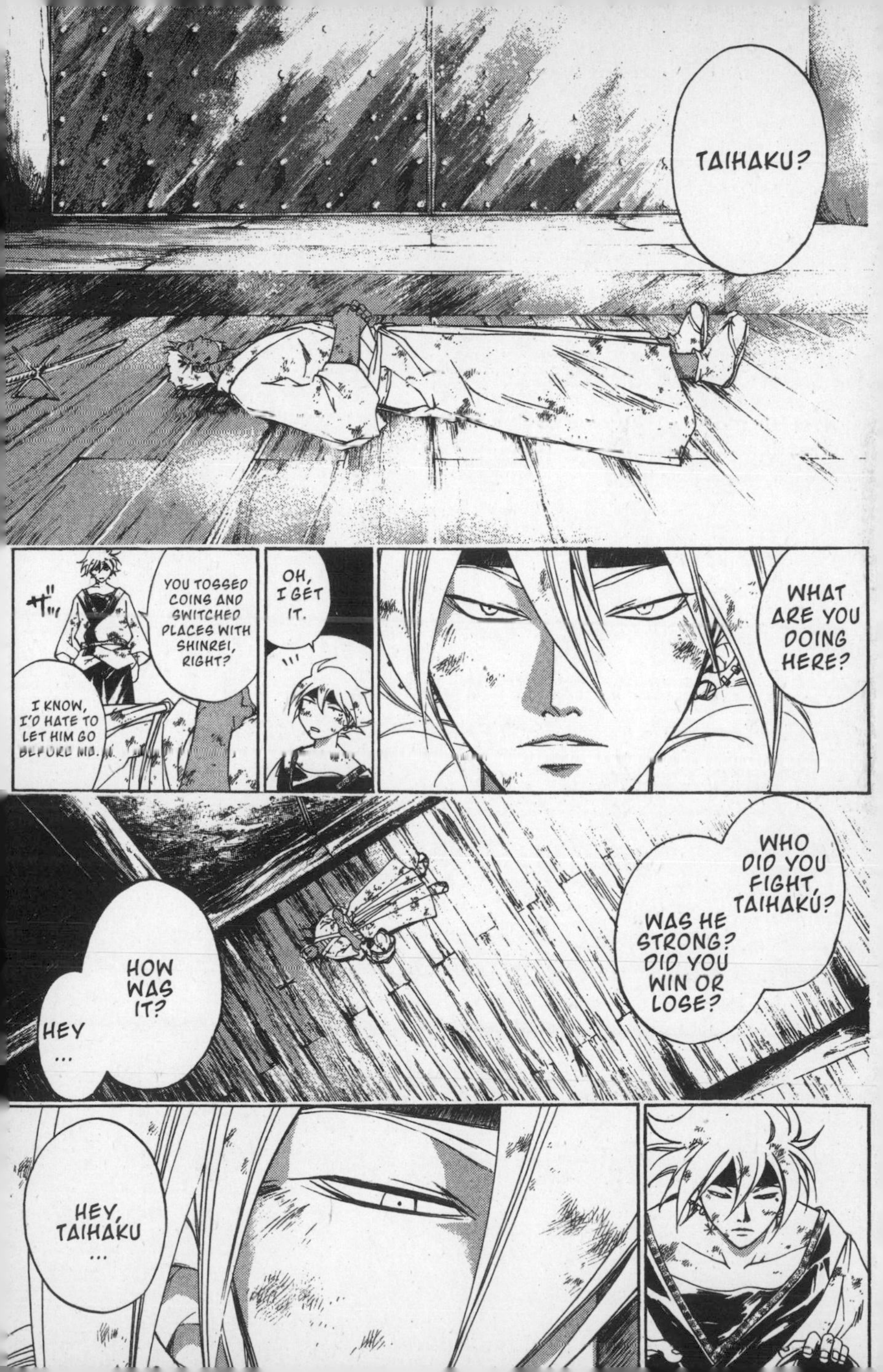
TAIHAKU?
WHAT ARE YOU DOING HERE?
OH, I GET IT.
YOU TOSSED COINS AND SWITCHED PLACES WITH SHINREI, RIGHT?
I KNOW, I'D HATE TO LET HIM GO BEFORE ME.
WHO DID YOU FIGHT, TAIHAKU?
WAS HE STRONG? DID YOU WIN OR LOSE?
HOW WAS IT?
HEY ...
HEY, TAIHAKU ...

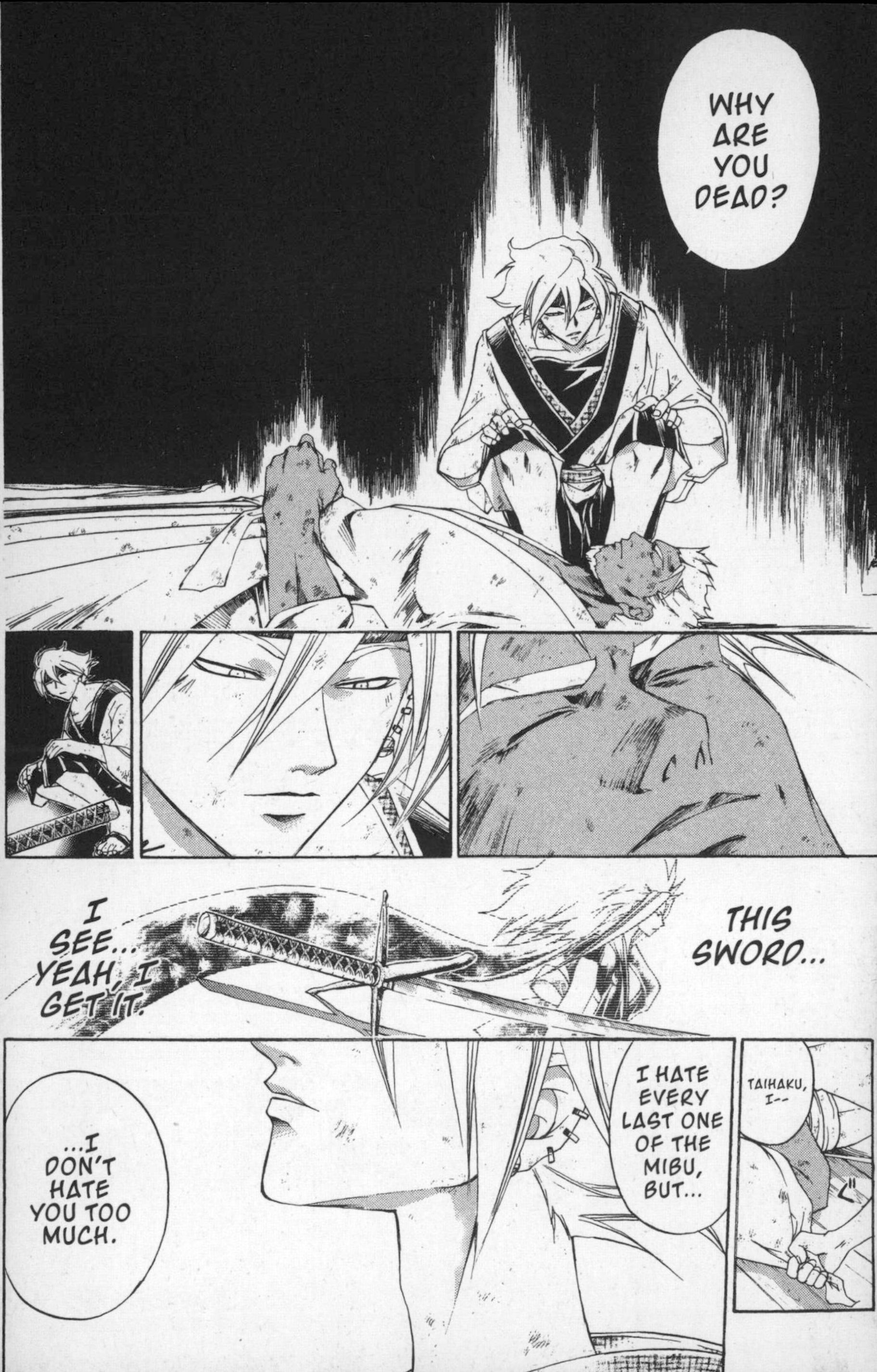
WHY ARE YOU DEAD?
THIS SWORD...
I SEE... YEAH, I GET IT.
TAIHAKU, I--
I HATE EVERY LAST ONE OF THE MIBU, BUT...
...I DON'T HATE YOU TOO MUCH.

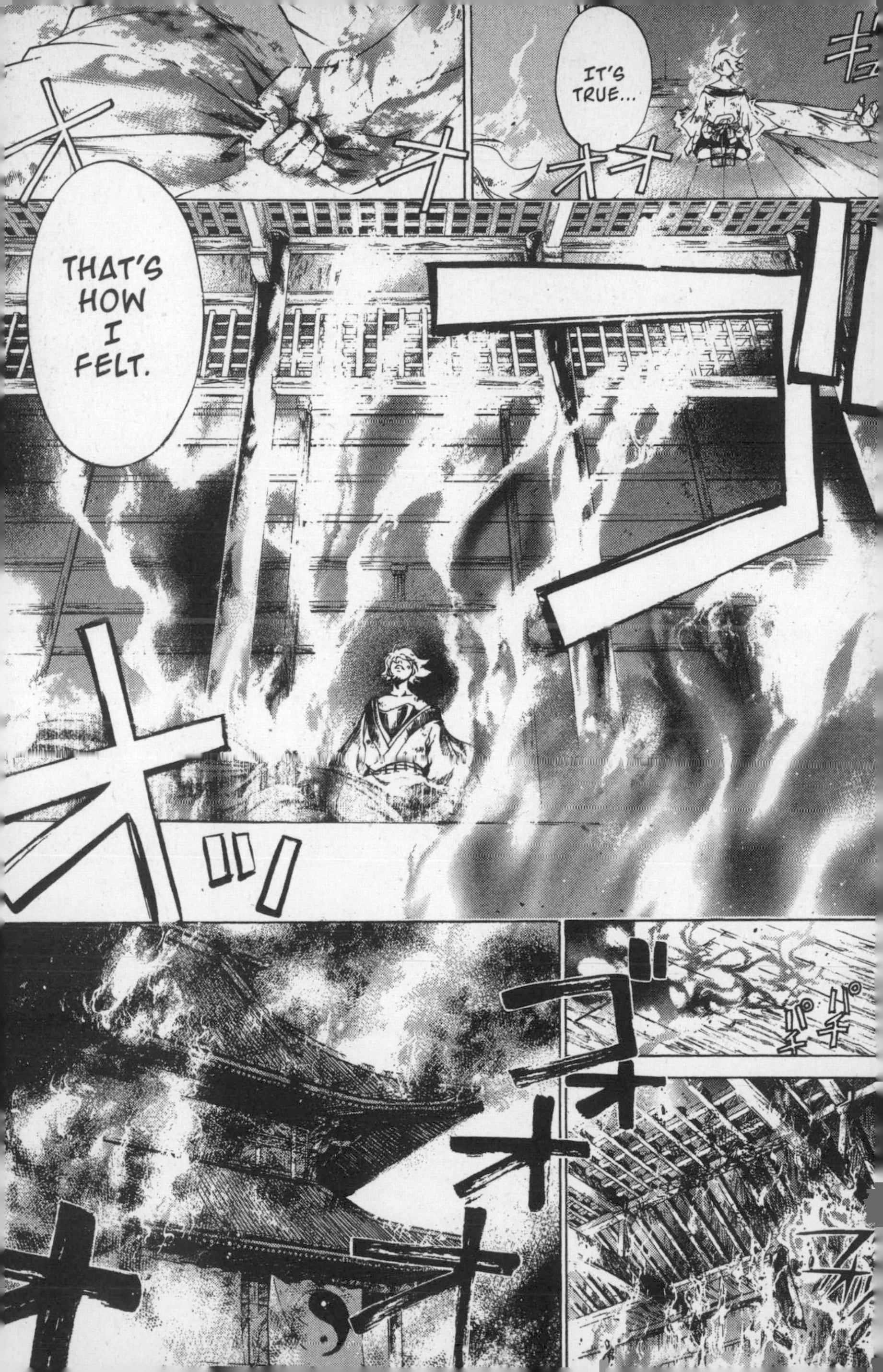
IT'S TRUE...
THAT'S HOW I FELT.

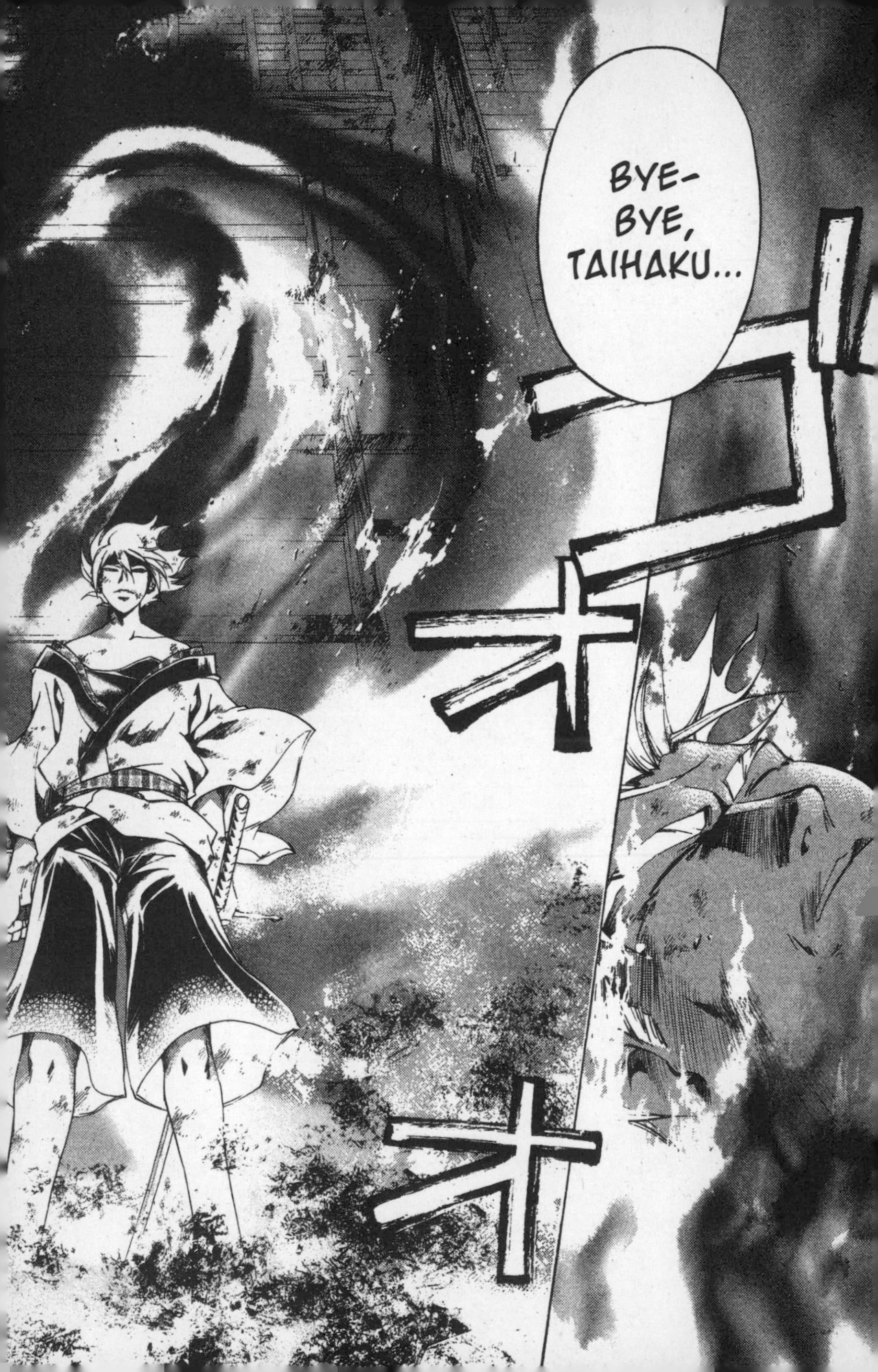
BYE-BYE, TAIHAKU...

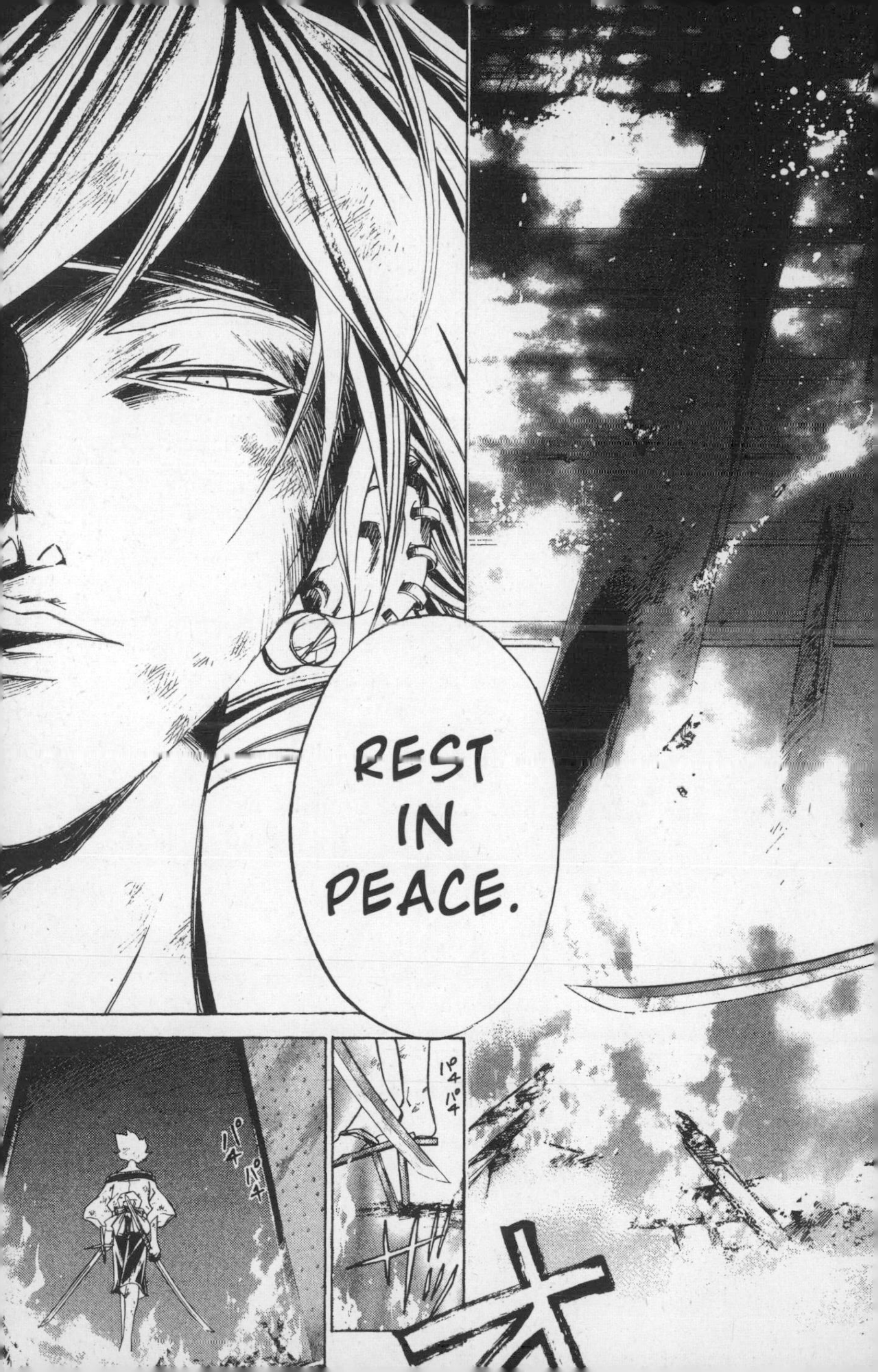
REST IN PEACE.
パチパチ
パチパチ

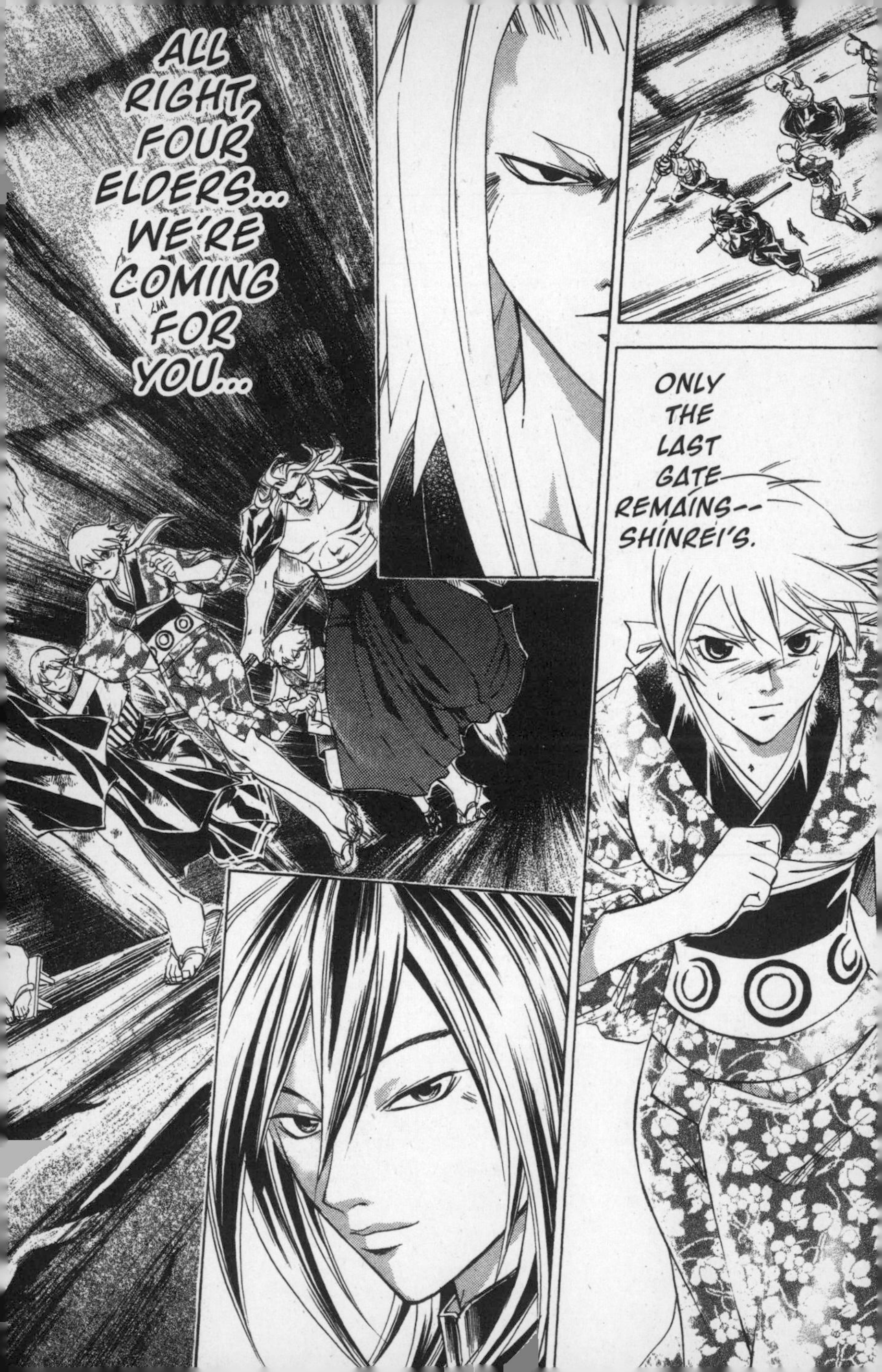
ONLY THE LAST GATE REMAINS--SHINREI'S.
ALL RIGHT, FOUR ELDERS... WE'RE COMING FOR YOU...

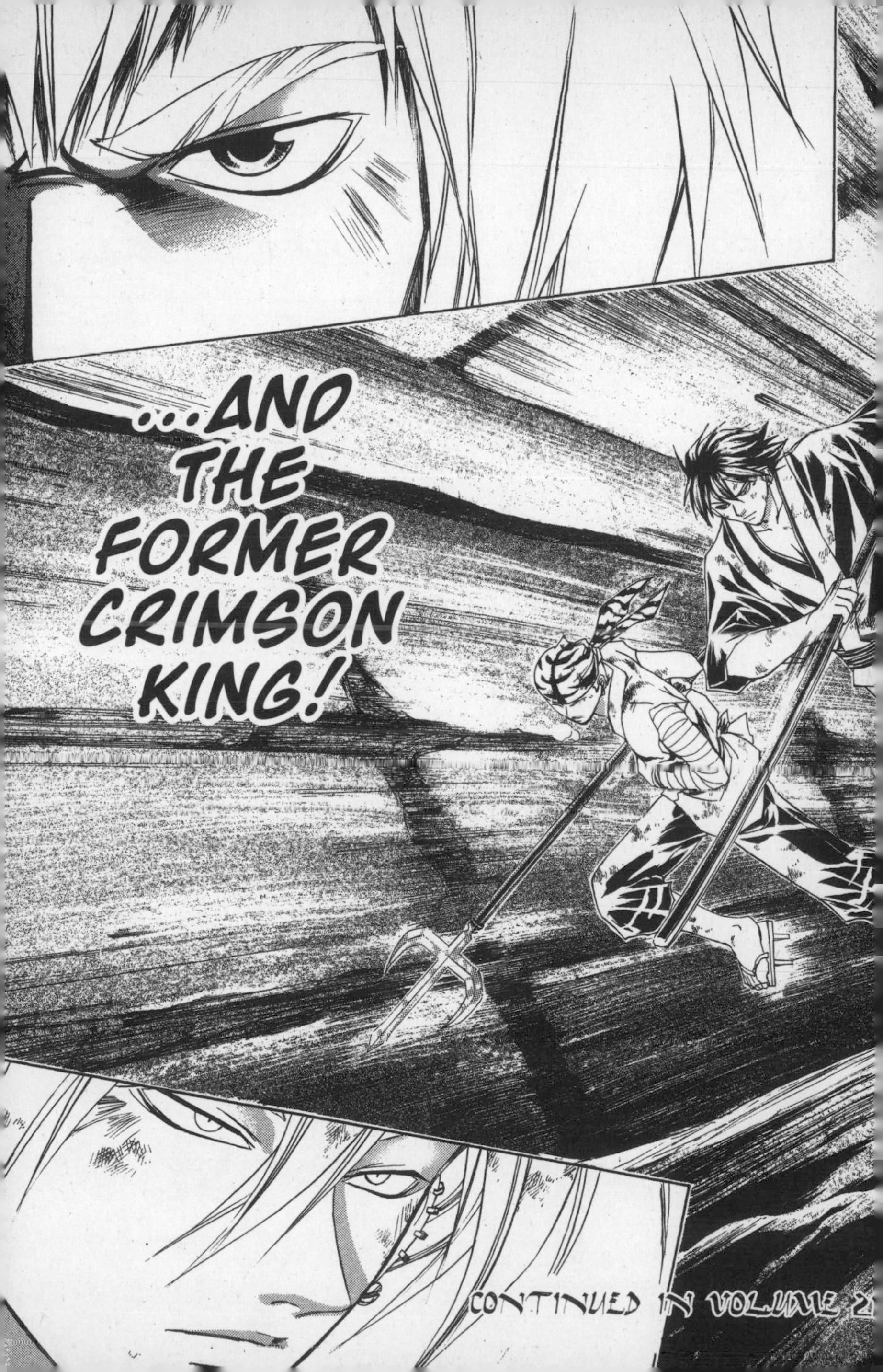
...AND THE FORMER CRIMSON KING!
CONTINUED IN VOLUME 2

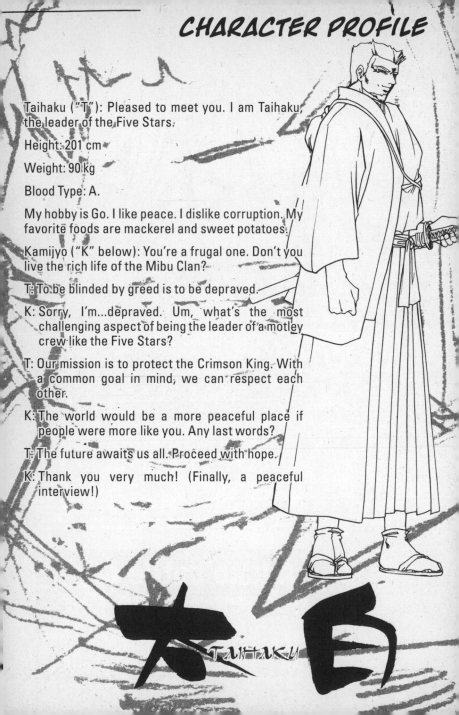

Taihaku ("T"): Pleased to meet you. I am Taihaku, the leader of the Five Stars.

Height: 201 cm

Weight: 90 kg

Blood Type: A.

My hobby is Go. I like peace. I dislike corruption. My favorite foods are mackerel and sweet potatoes.

Kamijyo ("K" below): You're a frugal one. Don't you live the rich life of the Mibu Clan?

T: To be blinded by greed is to be depraved.

K: Sorry, I'm...depraved. Um, what's the most challenging aspect of being the leader of a motley crew like the Five Stars?

T: Our mission is to protect the Crimson King. With a common goal in mind, we can respect each other.

K: The world would be a more peaceful place if people were more like you. Any last words?

T: The future awaits us all. Proceed with hope.

K: Thank you very much! (Finally, a peaceful interview!)

TAIHAKU

SAMURAI DEEPER KYO NEXT!

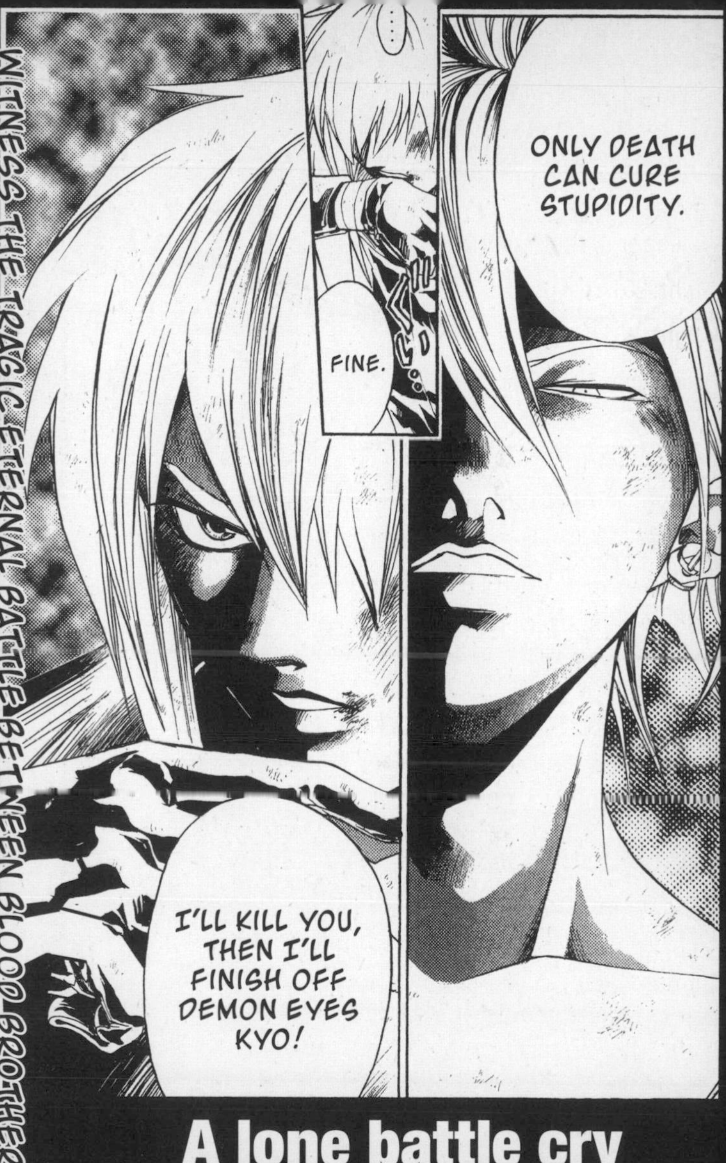
ONLY DEATH CAN CURE STUPIDITY.
FINE.
I'LL KILL YOU, THEN I'LL FINISH OFF DEMON EYES KYO!
WITNESS THE TRAGIC ETERNAL BATTLE BETWEEN BLOOD BROTHERS UNFOLD!

A lone battle cry echoes across the pages in Volume 21 of SDK!!

Akimine Kamijyo Challenge

Vicky Kimiko S.
Age 23
Phoenix, AZ

Wow! Look at those clean lines and brilliant contrast! Beautiful work, Vicky!

DEMON EYE'S
KYO

Tiffany B.
Age 14
Pocatello, ID

If only our readers could've seen the color on this one! The eyes bleed a brilliant red!

Rachel "Kiumi" B.
Age 15
Ridley Park, PA

Finally, Izumo gets her time in the spotlight after her long break.

Message from the Editor

Thank you for all the amazing art! Please keep sending it in!

四聖天のほたる・五曜星のけいこく

Patty "Kagami" Y.
Cerritos, CA

Kagami entered two pictures, and it was hard to choose between them...but I couldn't resist the bishounen face!

SAMURAI DEEPER KYO

Justin B.
Bradenton, FL

What a unique composition, Justin! Great job!

Raven A. Nightsky
Twickenham, England

Aw, a touching moment between Antera and Sasuke. Could Antera really warm Sasuke's heart? Woo-hoo, *SDK* fans livin' it up in England!

EYES
KYO

Kimberley "Zajavia" J.
Age 35
Houston, TX

Kyo looking oh-so slick thanks to Zajavia's mad drawing skillz!

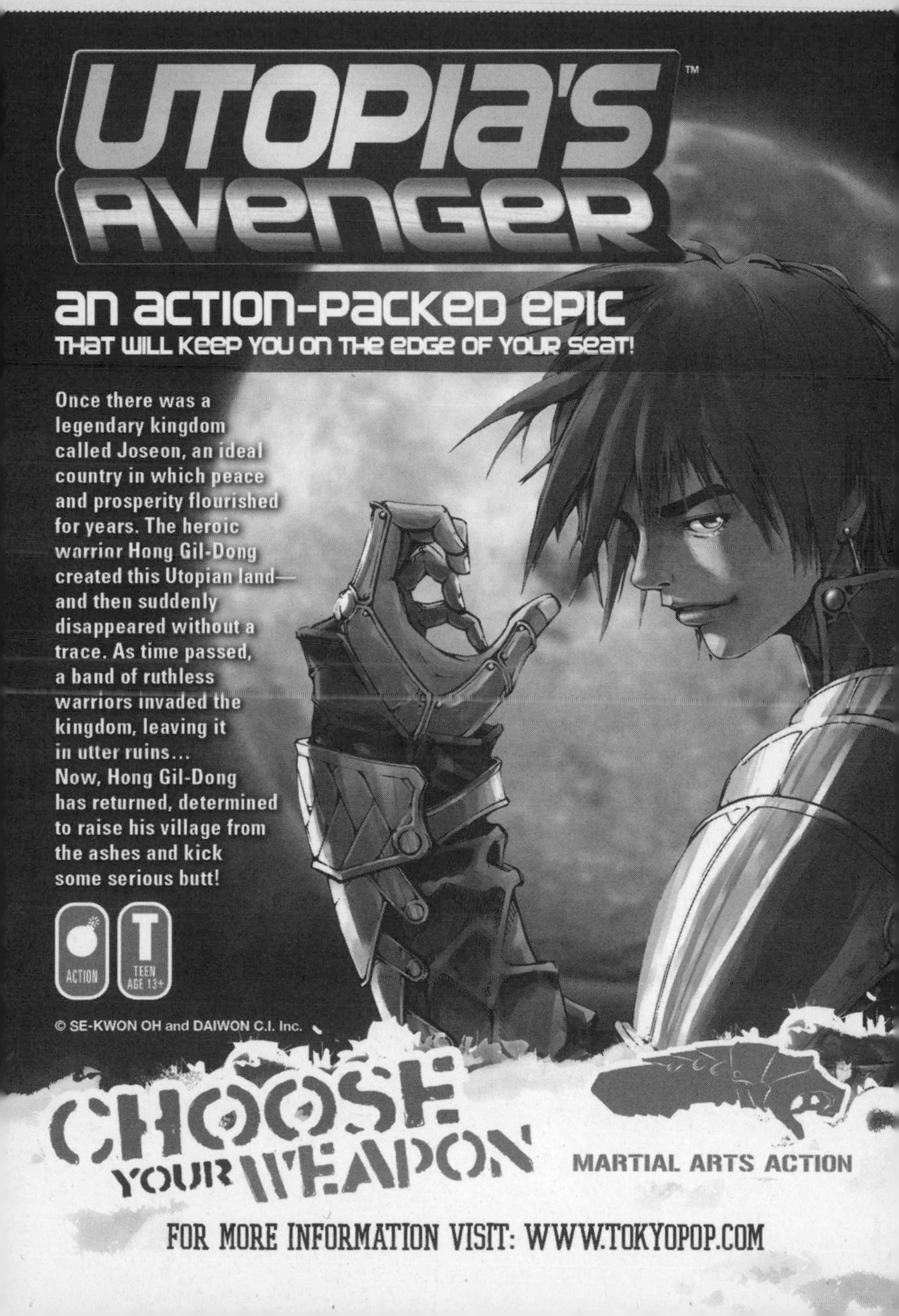
UTOPIA'S AVENGER™
AN ACTION-PACKED EPIC
THAT WILL KEEP YOU ON THE EDGE OF YOUR SEAT!
Once there was a legendary kingdom called Joseon, an ideal country in which peace and prosperity flourished for years. The heroic warrior Hong Gil-Dong created this Utopian land—and then suddenly disappeared without a trace. As time passed, a band of ruthless warriors invaded the kingdom, leaving it in utter ruins... Now, Hong Gil-Dong has returned, determined to raise his village from the ashes and kick some serious butt!
ACTION
T
TEEN AGE 13+
© SE-KWON OH and DAIWON C.I. Inc.
CHOOSE YOUR WEAPON
MARTIAL ARTS ACTION
FOR MORE INFORMATION VISIT: WWW.TOKYOPOP.COM

STOP!

This is the back of the book.
You wouldn't want to spoil a great ending!

This book is printed "manga-style," in the authentic Japanese right-to-left format. Since none of the artwork has been flipped or altered, readers get to experience the story just as the creator intended. You've been asking for it, so TOKYOPOP® delivered: authentic, hot-off-the-press, and far more fun!

DIRECTIONS

If this is your first time reading manga-style, here's a quick guide to help you understand how it works.

It's easy... just start in the top right panel and follow the numbers. Have fun, and look for more 100% authentic manga from TOKYOPOP®!